The Year Without
a World Series

The Year Without
a World Series

*Major League Baseball and the Road
to the 1994 Players' Strike*

ROBERT C. COTTRELL

McFarland & Company, Inc., Publishers
Jefferson, North Carolina

ISBN (print) 978-1-4766-9247-0
ISBN (ebook) 978-1-4766-5023-4

LIBRARY OF CONGRESS AND BRITISH LIBRARY
CATALOGUING DATA ARE AVAILABLE

Library of Congress Control Number 2023024574

Front cover: (foreground) Photograph of Olympic Stadium in Montreal
by Jim Dow (National Gallery of Canada);
background photograph by Franck Camhi (Shutterstock)

Printed in the United States of America

*McFarland & Company, Inc., Publishers
Box 611, Jefferson, North Carolina 28640
www.mcfarlandpub.com*

To Sue and Jordan

Table of Contents

Acknowledgments

A LOVE OF THE GAME AND MY PREVIOUS INVESTIGATIONS OF THE SPORT, along with teaching popular culture and the history of baseball over several decades, spurred a determination to explore in greater depth the 1994 major league season that began with such high hopes before fading into ashes. The bad feelings between players and management, of course, culminated in the cancellation of the final seven weeks of that year's baseball campaign. That in turn prevented the holding of the scheduled extended playoffs and, for only the second time since it began in 1903, the World Series pitting pennant winners from the National and American leagues.

I have written three other baseball books, one focusing on 1920, the year Babe Ruth joined the New York Yankees, Rube Foster established the Negro National League, Buck Weaver became one of eight Chicago White Sox players charged with having dumped the recent World Series, and Judge Kenesaw Mountain Landis was named the first commissioner of Organized Baseball. Those were the protagonists in *Blackball, the Black Sox and the Babe: Baseball's Crucial 1920 Season* (McFarland, 2002), the writing of which also induced me to craft *The Best Pitcher in Baseball: The Life of Rube Foster, Negro League Giant* (New York University Press, 2001). The harsh realities of race and anti–Semitism, along with two players' brilliance on the baseball diamond, induced me to produce a dual biography, *Two Pioneers: How Hank Greenberg and Jackie Robinson Transformed Baseball—and America* (Potomac, 2012).

So it was only natural, as I conducted research for this latest baseball monograph, that my reach became greater still, leading me back in time to some of the earliest clashes pitting players against team owners and league officials. It also ensured that, yet again, my dissection of the National Pastime would include an examination of figures, both well-known and little remembered, but also the myth-making that has made baseball a favorite for fans across the globe, including intellectuals determined to wax eloquent about it. And yes, for me, as in the case of my previous undertakings, heroes and villains abound. Ruth, Foster, and the banished Weaver came across as larger-than-life figures. So did Judge Landis, but his celebrity failed to shield his selective enforcement of the rules he devised to ban the Black Sox, as well as his reprehensible upholding of Organized Baseball's racial barriers. Both Greenberg and Robinson battled against terrible prejudices while retaining the utmost dignity, a stalwart stance that proved particularly costly to the great African American star as it had to Foster earlier.

This volume presents baseball labor pioneers John Montgomery Ward, Dave Fultz, Robert Murphy, Danny Gardella, Ralph Kiner, and Allie Reynolds before undergoing a deeper dive into the Major League Baseball Players Association, which became a force to be reckoned with under Marvin Miller and Donald Fehr. For over a century, many baseball moguls proved intransigent, determined to crush resistance from the players, let alone the determination of some to organize. That remained the case throughout the labor wars that culminated in the 1994 clashes that ended so disastrously for lovers of the game and left blank spots in the historical record.

◆ ◆ ◆

My previous baseball studies, undertaken before the terribly disruptive pandemic, involved a great amount of archival work as well as usage of microfilm and microfiche. Such investigations took me around the country to the National Baseball Hall of Fame Library in Cooperstown, the Library of Congress in Washington, D.C., the Sporting News Archives in St. Louis, the Chicago Historical Society, and a series of academic institutions, including my home campus, California State University, Chico, in Northern California. This study resulted from research in the age of Covid-19, which included electronic and telephonic exchanges, in addition to a considerable amount of reading and digging online. John Horne sent me photographs from the Hall of Fame Collection, and the Library of Congress collection contains several fitting images of baseball players, managers, owners, and executives, particularly from the 1870s into the 1950s. Digitized newspapers, magazines, and materials proved enormously helpful, including those appearing courtesy of *Baseball Digest*, the California Digital Newspaper Collection, Global Newsstream, the Los Angeles Times Digital Archive, the National Baseball Hall of Fame Library, the New York Times Digital Archive, the San Francisco Chronicle Digital Archive, the Society for American Baseball Research, *Sporting Life*, the Sporting News Archives, *Sports Illustrated*, *Wall Street Journal*, and the Washington Post Digital Archive, among others.

For the fifth time, I am pleased to have worked with the staff at McFarland. Once again, I am deeply appreciative of the efforts by Gary Mitchem and other McFarland employees. Sophia Lyons gracefully facilitated matters related to photographic reproductions.

As always, I must thank my wife Sue and my daughter Jordan for abetting my immersion into this latest writing endeavor. At times, that becomes consuming, but they somehow tolerate me.

Preface

THE 1994 MAJOR LEAGUE SEASON, from its early stages, promised to be something special. Long-standing batting and pitching standards appeared threatened, including the most revered mark in professional sports: the single-season home run record. Matt Williams, Ken Griffey, Jr., Jeff Bagwell, Frank Thomas, Barry Bonds, and Albert Belle seemed poised to belt a minimum of 50 homers, a feat that had been accomplished by only 11 players. Jimmie Foxx, Ralph Kiner, Willie Mays, and Mickey Mantle—all legendary home run hitters—had done so twice, while Babe Ruth had achieved the feat four times. In 1927, New York Yankees slugger Ruth smashed 60 homers in the 154-game regular season. Thirty-four years later, another Bronx Bomber, Roger Maris, rapped his 61st homer in the Yankees' 162nd game, possible only because of the American League's recent expansion. Over in the National League, the record stood at 56, delivered by the Chicago Cubs' Hack Wilson in 1930, a very friendly year for batters.

During the first several weeks of the 1994 season, Seattle Mariners center fielder Ken Griffey, Jr., dubbed "the Natural" by many across the sport, seemed the prime candidate to soar beyond both Ruth and Maris. Later, San Francisco Giants third baseman Williams surpassed Griffey and looked ready to make a run at Wilson's NL record, at the very least. Overcoming a slow start and injuries that might have sidelined many, Williams's teammate, Barry Bonds, widely considered to be baseball's best all-around player, went on a tear throughout July that brought Williams, Griffey, and Thomas, the White Sox's behemoth, within striking distance. A broken bone in his left hand relegated Houston Astros first sacker Bagwell to the dugout, but Cleveland Indians outfielder Belle remained close behind the major league leaders.

According to sportswriters, other single-season batting records were endangered by the latest crop of big-league hitters. These included total bases, slugging percentage, doubles, runs batted in (RBI), walks, and, for a briefer time, batting average (BA), with Yankee right fielder Paul O'Neill hitting above .400 into June. By the middle of that month, O'Neill slipped below that average, although he was batting as high as .387 as late as July 8. Meanwhile, San Diego Padres outfielder Tony Gwynn was doing what he did best, seeking another batting title while making his own run at the elusive .400 average, something that hadn't been attained since Ted

Williams did so in 1941. The other records looked safer as the season progressed, although Wilson's home run total in the senior circuit remained primed for assault, as did Ruth's and Maris's historic seasons, certainly by Matt Williams.

Atlanta righthander Greg Maddux's wizardry on the mound also promised to be one of the finest in major league history. With particularly spectacular showings during April, May, July, and early August, Maddux was posting numbers that bested those of virtually every pitcher in the modern live ball era, the period beginning in 1920. Especially phenomenal were the sparse number of homers he gave up—four in 202 innings—and his earned run average (ERA), which stood at 1.56 as of August 11. With the exception of the St. Louis Cardinals' Bob Gibson's otherworldly 1.12 ERA in 1968, a season when batting averages dramatically plummeted, only the New York Mets' Dwight Gooden delivered a lower figure—1.53 in 1985—than Maddux. As matters turned out, Maddux posted a 1.63 ERA in 1995, easily establishing a two-year record for the non–Deadball Era period.

All of this was particularly significant, for baseball had long been the sport most focused, even fixated on statistics compiled by participants. The number 60, as in home runs, remained the holy grail, even after Maris did or did not nip Babe Ruth, depending on one's point of view. Ford Frick, while serving as commissioner of Major League Baseball, insisted that anyone compiling more homers than Ruth, who had been his close friend, had to do so within 154 games, or an asterisk should be attached to the new recordholder's statistic.[1] Others derided Maris because he batted only .269 the year that he smashed 61 and never hit more than 39 in any other season, while Ruth, a .342 lifetime batter, hit .356 during his record-setting year, shot past 40 homers 11 times, and set the single-season record four times. And that was after he had been baseball's best left-handed pitcher and a leading contributor to three Boston Red Sox teams that won the World Series (his Yankees won four championships).

In addition to astounding individual performances at the plate and on the mound, several teams were putting together remarkable campaigns in 1994. Seeking to end a title drought dating back to 1981, the longest stretch since Ruth came over from the Red Sox before the 1920 season, the 70–43 Yankees sat atop both the East Division and the AL after the games of August 11. The 67–46 Chicago White Sox led the Central, while the 52–62 Texas Rangers fronted the woeful West. New York was six and a half games ahead in the East, but both the Central and West were hotly contested. The 74–40 Montreal Expos, six games up on the Atlanta Braves, ruled the National League East with the majors' best record. The 66–48 Cincinnati Reds were only half a game ahead of the Astros. The 58–56 Los Angeles Dodgers led the paltry West.

A pair of wild-card teams, the squads with the best non-division winning league records, were slated to join the six division winners in an expanded three-round playoff series for the first time in major league history. At a minimum, 10 teams appeared to be vying for playoff spots, which promised that division and wild-card races would prove exciting throughout the season. The return of the Yankees to their formerly accustomed spot at the top of the American League thrilled many, certainly in the nation's greatest metropolitan area, while undoubtedly annoying others. Fascinating too was the play of the youthful Expos, who, across their 25-year history, had won only a single East Division crown. Fittingly, attendance totals were booming, with additional records destined to be shattered.

On August 11, Maddux and his Atlanta Braves shut out the Colorado Rockies at Mile High Stadium, a launching pad for batters, scattering three hits, all singles, making his ERA still more minuscule. Going three for five in a Padres win over the Astros, Tony Gwynn lifted his average to .394. The Mariners' Ken Griffey, Jr., swatted his 40th homer—a grand slam, in fact—in a win over the Oakland Athletics. The day before, Matt Williams had stroked his 43rd homer to help his Giants beat the Cubs at Wrigley Field.

However, the players and MLB's acting commissioner, Bud Selig, the owner of the Milwaukee Brewers, then officially shut it all down, calling a halt to the riveting 1994 season. This was the result of the acrimony that had beset Organized Baseball for over a century, leading to early retirements, walkouts, new leagues, and, more recently, lockouts and strikes. The latest labor strife, like earlier ones, was fundamentally about control: control of salaries, the ability of players to decide their own fates, and the game itself, particularly the professional edition.

From its earliest days shortly following the Civil War to the present, professional baseball has been idealized as the national game, supposedly representative of the nation's finest values. Poets, lyricists, sportswriters, and hucksters had extolled its graces and seeming embodiment of everything they suggested that both the sport and America stood for, as seen through a romantic lens. On April 7, 1889, Walt Whitman intoned, "The hurrah game! Well—it's our game: that's the chief fact in connection with it: America's game: has the snap, go, fling, of the American atmosphere." Remarkably, the very next day, Mark Twain asserted, "Baseball is the very symbol, the outward and visible expression of the drive and push and rush and struggle of the raging, tearing, booming, nineteenth century." More than a half-century later, the French-American historian Jacques Barzun insisted, "Anyone who wants to know the heart and mind of America, had better learn baseball."[2]

In a review of a book on Joe DiMaggio's fabled 56-game hitting streak, accomplished the same year Ted Williams batted .406, the paleontologist Stephen Jay Gould suggested in 1988 that the Yankee Clipper's feat was "the finest of legitimate legends because it embodies the essence of the battle that truly defines our lives. DiMaggio activated the greatest and most unattainable dream of all of humanity, the hope and chimera of all sages and shamans: he cheated death, at least for a while." A. Bartlett Giamatti, briefly MLB's commissioner, rhapsodized about baseball: "It breaks your heart. It is designed to break your heart. The game begins in the spring, when everything else begins again, and it blossoms in the summer, filling the afternoons and evenings, and then as soon as the chill rains come, it stops and leaves you to face the fall all alone. You count on it, rely on it to buffer the passage of time, to keep the memory of sunshine and high skies alive, and then just when the days are all twilight, when you need it most, it stops."[3]

The mythologizing about the national game had hardly been limited to America's foremost intellectuals. In poetry, song, novels, sports columns, plays, and films, baseball has been exalted. From Ernest Thayer's "Casey at the Bat" (1888), Jack Norworth's and Albert Von Tilzer's "Take Me Out to the Ball Game" (1908), and John Fogerty's "Centerfield" (1985), to F. Scott Fitzgerald's *The Great Gatsby* (1925), Ernest Hemingway's *The Old Man and The Sea* (1952), and Mark Harris's *The Southpaw* (1953), some of the nation's most creative writers wove baseball into their tales touching on the fabric of American life. On stage and the silver screen, the sport was similarly celebrated in works such as *Damn Yankees* (1958), *The Natural* (1984), and *Field of Dreams* (1989). Sportswriters from early 20th-century icons Ring Lardner, Damon Runyon, and Grantland Rice to Roger Kahn and Roger Angell waxed eloquently about events on and off the baseball diamond related to the game. Broadcasters ranging from Mel Allen, Red Barber, Dizzy Dean, and Pee Wee Reese to Vin Scully, Bob Costas, Duane Kuiper and Mike Krukow offered vivid images of baseball played at the highest level. Ken Burns's cinematic masterpiece, *Baseball*, captured something of its essence, undoubtedly for those who continued to revere it.

Against that backdrop and the growing recognition of Organized Baseball's real failings as explored by scholars and popular writers alike, particularly regarding deplorable racial exclusions and embittered labor clashes, major league baseball experienced a series of disruptions in the form of strikes and lockouts from 1972 up to the 1994 season. Those resulted from the persistent haughtiness, pettiness, and foolhardiness of team owners and league administrators in the face of demands made by the Major League Baseball Players Association (MLBPA), greatly strengthened under the stewardship of first Marvin Miller and then Donald Fehr.

Those two men, doing battle with Bud Selig, earlier commissioners, team owners, and their representatives, strove first to convince the players of the need for a strong union and foster their readiness at various junctures to threaten to walk away, albeit only temporarily, from the sport they loved. This was in keeping with earlier proponents of player organizations. Those included the late 19th-century New York Giants star pitcher and shortstop, John Montgomery Ward, who used the law he studied at Columbia University to help found a rival circuit to the established National League. Attorney Robert Murphy, whose bid to unionize players immediately following World War II fell short, nevertheless set the stage for improvements in labor conditions, including a $5,000 minimum salary and a pension plan. Star players Ralph Kiner, Bob Feller, Robin Roberts, and Jim Bunning helped to get the MLBPA off the ground, pushing for salary and pension improvements. But it was Marvin Miller, a labor economist, who helped to turn that association, which hired him as the MLBPA's executive director in early 1966 to represent major league players, into arguably the strongest union in the world.

Doing so required playing hardball at times as Miller went up against owners who, like their predecessors, had persistently held the upper hand in labor negotiations, especially through reliance on the reserve clause. That 19th-century concoction effectively bound players to their home teams for as long as those teams desired. It also allowed them to discard those athletes virtually at will or trade them to other ballclubs, without any input from the players themselves. Such an imbalance in labor relationships led Ward to charge in 1887 that baseball players were treated as chattel. That was the same argument Curt Flood, a seasoned major league veteran, made in 1969 when he demanded that Commissioner Bowie Kuhn allow him to carve out a deal with whichever team he—Flood—favored.

Hardly surprisingly, Kuhn turned down Flood, who proceeded to initiate litigation contesting the reserve clause, a case which eventually landed before the U.S. Supreme Court. While Flood's bid failed, it provided the impetus for other challenges by players, including pitchers Jim "Catfish" Hunter, Andy Messersmith, and Dave McNally, which ushered in free agency in the late 1970s. Throughout that decade and during the two that followed, team owners and the MLBPA, initially under Miller and then Fehr, feuded over the terms by which teams could compete for players' services. That struggle and others regarding escalating salaries and pensions, along with additional labor issues, led to four strikes and three lockouts prior to the 1994 season.

The announcement by Bud Selig on August 11 of that year was followed by another one the next month proclaiming dissolution of the rest of the season—hundreds of games altogether—the expanded playoffs, and the World Series. Thus, for only the second time since it was initiated in 1903, the World Series was not played. Scribes and fans alike were stunned and enraged by MLB's inability to reach an agreement to save what had promised to be an historic season. Even worse, as matters turned out, the strike lasted through spring training of the following year, imperiling the 1995 season as well. Some analysts and fans warned that major league baseball would never be the same, while suggesting a boycott of their own.

◆ ◆ ◆

In addition to the chase for the single-season home run record, the 1994 season, like all major league campaigns with the exception of one, had been building up to its climax, the World Series. *The Year Without a World Series* examines the factors, both recent and decades in the making, that led to the decision to call off the 1994 Fall Classic. The book begins by looking backward, to the World Series that was never played 90 years earlier and to various moments when the game appeared ready to grind to a halt or be shut down altogether, however temporarily. That included times of war, the 1989 Bay Area earthquake, and seeming calamities of a different sort: when team owners and players reached an impasse that threatened strikes, lockouts, and cancellations.

The introductory chapter is followed by chapters 2 through 4, featuring early labor struggles and the creation of both players' organizations and new leagues. Chapters 5 and 6 usher in the Major League Baseball Players Association and Marvin Miller, the labor economist who began to turn the previously largely futile MLBPA into a powerful instrument for the players it represented. Chapters 7 and 8 continue what I call the Miller Age, a period that eventually witnessed labor strife but also free agency, arbitration, and soaring salaries. Chapters 9 through 12 focus on two nemeses, Milwaukee owner turned acting commissioner Bud Selig and the MLBPA's Donald Fehr, Miller's eventual successor, in addition to the general state of the game as the 1994 season approached. Chapters 13 and 14 highlight arguably the majors' top two players—one from each league—who would be important figures during that year: Barry Bonds and Ken Griffey, Jr. Chapters 15 through 19 offer month-by-month tales of the 1994 season both on and off the playing field; long-standing records were threatened but so too was the very well-being of major league baseball. Labor discord continued into the spring of 1995 (Chapter 20). The final chapter reexamines major league baseball's enduring labor wrangling and the fate of several participants involved directly or indirectly in the 1994–1995 clashes between players and management.

1

The Strike

THE STRIKE OF 1994 MANAGED TO ACCOMPLISH what two world wars and the Great Depression could not. It led to cancellation of the World Series, something that had not occurred for 90 years. Since its beginning in 1903, only the petulance of New York Giants manager John McGraw and owner John Brush the next season had prevented the World Series from being played.

The 1903 World Series pitted the National League pennant-winners, the Pittsburgh Pirates, whose 91–49 record placed them six and a half games ahead of McGraw's second-place Giants, against the American League title-holders, the Jimmy Collins-managed Boston Americans, who ended up 91–47, 14½ games up on Connie Mack's Philadelphia Athletics.[1] Pittsburgh was led by its great shortstop, Honus Wagner—his .355 batting average topped the NL for the second time—and 25-game winners Deacon Phillippe and Sam Leever. Boston's best hitter was outfielder Patsy Dougherty, who hit .331, but its strength resided in its pitching staff, which included Cy Young, Bill Dinneen, and Tom Hughes, all of whom won at least 20 games, topped by Young's league-best 28 wins.[2]

Although the heavily favored Pirates raced off to a 3–1 game lead, Young and Dineen spearheaded the comeback that saw the Americans sweep four straight contests to win the first World Series. Boston followed up that triumph by again winning the AL in 1904, finishing 95–59 in what had become the standard 154-game regular season. With no ballplayer hitting .300, pitching again enabled the Americans to prevail, thanks to 20-game winners Young, Dinneen, and Jesse Tannehill. Young went 26–16, tossed a league-best 10 shutouts, struck out 200, and had a 1.96 earned run average.[3]

That season, however, was dominated by the New York Giants, who went 106–47, 13 games ahead of Frank Selee's Chicago Cubs. The previous year's titleholders, the Pittsburgh Pirates, fell to fourth place, 19 games back of the Giants. The Giants' best hitter was first baseman Dan McGann, who hit only .286, but the pitching was superb. Dummy Taylor won 21 games; Christy Mathewson went 33–12, with a league-leading 212 strikeouts; and Joe McGinnity was 35–8, with nine shutouts and a 1.61 ERA, all top marks in the NL.

Notwithstanding the Giants' dominance, manager McGraw and owner Brush, who despised AL president Ban Johnson, considering both him and the new league suspect, declined a chance to go head-to-head with the Boston Americans. McGraw recalled how Johnson had repeatedly suspended him due to tirades involving umpires. Now McGraw was furious that AL teams, offering higher salaries, had lured players from the National League. He was even unhappier when the new league placed a team in New York, the Highlanders, who thereby competed with the Giants for the allegiance of hometown fans. Brush had warned in early July that he would not allow his Giants to go against the cross-town Highlanders if the two teams prevailed in the pennant races.[4]

Hardly one to hide his feelings, McGraw vented in public. He asked why the Giants should compete against Boston or whichever team finished atop the AL, as his ballclub had already won the lone authentic major league race. As for Johnson and his stewardship, McGraw complained that the

Honus Wagner, the greatest National League player of the early 20th century. Wagner, an eight-time batting champion, led the pennant-winning Pittsburgh Pirates in 1903 (Bain News Service, 1915. Library of Congress Prints and Photographs Division, Washington, D.C.).

AL boss "has not been on the level with me personally and the American league management has been crooked more than once."[5]

Johnson lashed back, asserting that Brush and McGraw had wreaked more havoc on baseball than the game's worst enemies could have accomplished. McGraw's diatribe, he charged, was "only the latest of a series of vicious attacks and unfriendly actions" involving the American League by Brush and "such an irresponsible character as McGraw." The AL president's signed statement declared, "Sound sportsmanship, and not a sordid spirit influences the American League in a desire to make the world's series and other interleague post season games features each year."[6]

After Boston clinched its second straight pennant, its president, John L. Tyler,

Cy Young, the winningest major league pitcher with 511 victories, topped the World Series champion Boston Americans in 1903 with a 28–9 record. 1908 (Library of Congress Prints and Photographs Division, Washington, D.C.).

wrote to McGraw. "Dear Sir, as the Boston club today won the championship of the American league, I challenge your club to play for the championship of the world. Of course, if you refuse to play, we get the title by default, but I shall prefer to win it on the diamond in a series of five games or more."[7]

McGraw refused to reply, but Brush did. "Who are these people?" he asked. "We do not know them at all. The Giants do not care to play minor leaguers, so this absurd challenge from a lot of nobodies will be ignored." Brush also exclaimed, "There is nothing in the constitution or the playing rules of the National League which requires its victorious club to submit its championship honors to a contest with a victorious club in a minor league."[8]

His manager, Brush indicated, "stands alone and is without a rival," and the Giants were the strongest in the NL and "the most formidable ever brought together." Likewise, the NL was "the premier organization of America," establishing "the professional base ball championship of the United States." The Giants, Brush declared, stood ready to defend their title during the upcoming season. There was an additional consideration, one that McGraw and Brush wouldn't readily acknowledge. The two worried that the Giants would suffer the same fate as the Pirates had in dropping the previous year's World Series to the AL pennant winners.[9]

AL representatives slammed the refusal of the Giants to play the defending World Series champion Red Sox. Frank Farrell, treasurer of the New York Highlanders, accused Brush of "dodging a series" against Boston. The Highlanders' manager, Clark Griffith, charged that Brush was "hiding behind a bush" and that McGraw knew virtually any AL squad could whip the Giants. Hence, "it's no wonder that Mugsy is afraid to play." Chicago White Sox president Charles Comiskey couldn't understand Brush's snide comment about the AL being "a minor league."[10]

Denying that Brush or his ballplayers made the decision not to play the AL champs, McGraw accepted full responsibility while conveying his unwillingness to discard the NL pennant "like a rug." He expressed his readiness and that of the New York Giants "to be judged by our patrons and the supporters of honest sport." Taking him at his word, *Sporting Life*, a leading American weekly newspaper, took him to task for "preventing the playing of the world's championship series." The Giants' "blunder," *Sporting Life* insisted, was hardly helped by their manager's "bellicose statement." But that statement also provided "ammunition" about the Giants' concern regarding a Series matchup.[11]

Sporting Life delivered a devasting critique of the Giants' decision. "Messrs. Brush and McGraw have blundered and ... the failure to play a post-season series with the Boston American league and world's champions is regretted by the lovers of the game all over the land." First dismissing the Giants owner's notion that the American League was "a minor organization," the *San Francisco Chronicle* affirmed that baseball was "so thoroughly rooted in the affections of the American people that it can even withstand the blighting influence of John T. Brush."[12]

AL president Johnson hated McGraw, who had starred with the old Baltimore Orioles, declaring, "No thoughtful patron of baseball can weigh seriously the wild vaporings of this discredited player who was canned from the American league." Johnson had been enraged when McGraw, whom he had suspended for half a season, steered players over to the NL and accepted the position as manager of the Giants.[13]

Undoubtedly recognizing that his and McGraw's decision had resulted in unfavorable publicity, Brush made a belated concession, expressing a willingness to hold the World Series during the spring if various conditions were met that proved acceptable to the NL. Tim Murnane of the *Boston Globe* termed Brush's offer "absurd for many reasons," including the likely change of rosters and the lack of interest in such contests so far removed from the previous season.[14]

Sporting Life dismissed Brush's proposal, declaring that "the time to play any world's championship series is in the fall, when the issue is alive, public interest in keenest and the contending teams are at their best." Nevertheless, the paper deemed Brush's plan regarding future Series "novel, ingenious and equitable" as a means of insuring that the World Series would become "an annual compulsory event."[15]

Arguably, McGraw's greatest success occurred the next year, when his team faced the Philadelphia Athletics in the 1905 World Series. That followed a regular season in which the Giants' attendance fell by almost 10 percent despite another pennant as New York, having compiled a 105–48 record, finished nine games ahead of the Pirates. Catcher Roger Bresnahan hit .302, and Mike Donlin batted .356. McGinnity and Red Ames won 21 and 22 games, respectively, while Mathewson went 31–9 with a 1.28 ERA, 206 strikeouts, and eight shutouts, enabling him to win his league's pitching Triple Crown (most wins, lowest ERA, most strikeouts).

In the junior circuit, the Athletics' 92–56 mark put them two games up on the Chicago White Sox. Their light-hitting squad had first baseman Harry Davis post the best BA, .285, but four pitchers—Eddie Plank, Rube Waddell, Andy Coakley, and

Christy Mathewson and John McGraw, men with decidedly different temperaments, nevertheless guided the New York Giants to five pennants and the 1905 World Series title during the great pitcher's storied run (peak years 1901–1914). McGraw went on to capture five additional pennants and a pair of World Series championships. 1911 (Library of Congress Prints and Photographs Division, Washington, D.C.).

Chief Bender—won at least 18 games apiece. Waddell's 27–10 record bested Plank's 24–12, his 287 strikeouts were better than his teammate's total of 210, and his 1.48 ERA enabled him to match Mathewson's Triple Crown with one of his own.

The Athletics went into the Series with a severe disadvantage, having lost their ace left-hander, Waddell. While reports indicated that hijinks on a team train had led to a shoulder injury, the *Philadelphia Evening Telegraph*'s Horace Fogel and the

Philadelphia North American's Charles Dryden suggested that gamblers might have gotten to the pitcher.[16]

In the new best-of seven-game format, the Giants prevailed in five homerless contests, all shutouts, one by McGinnity and three by Mathewson, including the 2–0 finale against Bender. During the Series, Mathewson relinquished only 13 hits in 27 innings of work.

Ironically, given the McGraw-Brush refusal to participate in the previous year's World Series, the Giants' performance against the Athletics represented the pinnacle for both the manager and his peerless right-hander. McGraw, who went on to win seven more pennants but only two additional World Series, later acknowledged as much. Mathewson, in a career that saw him win 373 games, tying Grover Cleveland Alexander for the most in National League annals, would complete another Triple Crown three years later, when he garnered 37 wins, then won another ERA title the next year with a 1.14 mark.

However, both proved somewhat star-crossed in future postseason play. Despite remaining a stellar pitcher, Mathewson won only two of his next seven World Series decisions, dropping a pair of concluding games. McGraw lost three straight World Series (1911–1913) during the early 1910s, another one later in the decade, and then two more in the first half of the 1920s, after twice beating the crosstown New York Yankees, as the Highlanders came to be known. The Giants' regular season records never surpassed what the 1904 and 1905 squads starring Mathewson and McGinnity had accomplished.

One of the pennants the Giants won under McGraw's tutelage took place during wartime. The 1917 season ended with New York (98–56), absent Mathewson, who had retired after 15 full seasons with McGraw, 10 games ahead of the Philadelphia Phillies, but that team dropped the World Series (4–2) to the Chicago White Sox. U.S. involvement in the First World War led to a reduction in the number of major league games played during the next two seasons. Team schedules were sliced to fewer than 130 games in 1918 and to 140 the next year, followed by the World Series.[17]

In September 1918, players on both the Boston Red Sox—the team had changed its nickname from the Americans—and the Chicago Cubs threatened the first strike in the history of major league baseball. Demanding that those on the winning side each receive $2,500, with their opponents to get $1,000 apiece, the players were infuriated to learn that the National Commission, the sport's governing body, intended to share World Series receipts among the top four teams in each league, not just the World Series participants. The players on the Series championship squad would get $2,000 a man, $600 more than the runners-up, cutting their shares by over 40 percent from recent years.[18]

The war and the federal government mandate that players "work or fight" had caused the regular season to end abruptly on September 1. Interest in baseball waned, with attendance down 40 percent. It continued to lag even as the World Series opened. Fewer than 20,000 were present at Comiskey Park, where the first three games were scheduled, as the Red Sox's star left-hander, George Herman "Babe" Ruth, shut out the Cubs on six hits. Only slightly more fans showed up for the next game, won by Chicago to even the series. Saturday's Game 3, saw just over 27,000 in the stands as the Red Sox nipped the Cubs.[19]

Influenced by the weak attendance figures, the National Commission opted to cut player earnings still more than promised, with the winning players now slated to get only $1,200, $400 more than those who came up short. These amounts stood in stark contrast to the previous year's payments, with the winner's share of almost $3,700 and the loser's share of over $2,400, both totals actually several hundred less than the 1916 World Series participants received.[20]

As fans congregated at Fenway Park for Game 5, the players, who had failed to act the previous day when the Red Sox took the Series' lead under Ruth's stellar

Babe Ruth, the greatest player in major league history, was initially a southpaw pitcher with the Boston Red Sox, which he helped to lead to three pennants and the same number of World Series titles (although he only pinch-hit once during the 1915 World Series). Determined to play every day, he convinced the Boston owner to sell him to the New York Yankees, thereby pairing the game's most legendary hitter with what soon became its premier franchise. 1919 (National Photo Company Collection. Library of Congress Prints and Photographs Division, Washington, D.C.)

pitching, refused to leave the clubhouse. With just under 25,000 in attendance, no pre-game activities took place. There was no batting practice. No players were out on the field tossing the ball around. The starting pitchers failed to warm up. As game time passed, rumors floated through the air. Eventually, the players, although thoroughly displeased about the situation, agreed to play. John "Honey Fitz" Fitzgerald, the Boston mayor, whose most recent grandchild was named John Fitzgerald Kennedy, informed the gathered throng that the World Series would continue "for the sake of the public … and the wounded soldiers and sailors … in the grandstand waiting for us."[21]

Enraged by the player threats, many refused to show up for the Series finale the next day. Barely 15,000 watched as the Red Sox captured their third title in four years, their fifth overall. And remember: the 1904 World Series was never played due to the boycott by John Brush and John McGraw of the New York Giants. The National Commission piled on, refusing to award World Series emblems, typically given to World Series teams, to the Red Sox and Cubs players. Instead, it slammed "the selfish, mercenary and anarchistic actions" of the athletes, declaring them undeserving of such mementos. Full shares for the winning Red Sox amounted to only $1,108.45.[22]

J.V. Fitz Gerald, writing in the *Washington Post*, declared that baseball fans would long remember the threatened strike by the two teams competing in the recently concluded World Series. They had "put the dollar sign on baseball in unmistakable style," he bristled. The ballplayers, having made "fat livings" due to the American public's fascination with the national pastime, sought "to do a James boys' act," a reference to the notorious 19th-century outlaws. "It is impossible to kill baseball," Fitz Gerald wrote. "The sport will live as long as Americans." However, baseball acquired "another black eye" as a strike of the World Series almost occurred.[23]

◆　◆　◆

No reduction of major league baseball's schedule followed American engagement in the Second World War. Shortly after the twin congressional declarations of war that President Franklin D. Roosevelt sought against first Japan and then Germany, Commissioner Kenesaw Mountain Landis sent a letter to the Oval Office asking if major league baseball should be suspended. "The time is approaching when, in ordinary conditions, our teams would be heading for spring training camps," Landis wrote on January 14, 1942. Acknowledging that "these are not such ordinary times," Landis felt compelled to ascertain if FDR had determined "whether professional baseball should continue to operate."[24]

The president responded within a day, asserting that "the final decision" regarding MLB's immediate fate resided with the commissioner and team owners. Thus, Roosevelt indicated that his reply amounted to "solely a personal and not an official point of view." Then, FDR revealed,

I honestly feel that it would be best for the country to keep baseball going. There will be fewer people unemployed and everybody will work longer hours and harder than ever before.

And that means that they ought to have a chance for recreation and for taking their minds off their work even more than before.[25]

President Roosevelt underscored that baseball offered recreation that required only a couple of hours or 30 minutes longer than that and at low cost. He did express a desire that more night games be offered to enable day shift workers to take in an occasional game. Regarding the ballplayers, Roosevelt conveyed his belief that those "of active military or naval age should go, without question, into the services." He concluded with his observation that the players provided "a definite recreational asset to ... their fellow citizens."[26]

Over 500 players, including several of the finest stars in the game, eventually entered the American Armed Forces, with many experiencing combat. Those included the Detroit Tigers' slugging first baseman, Hank Greenberg; the Cleveland Indians' fireballing ace, Bob Feller; the Boston Braves' promising pitcher, Warren Spahn; and the New York Yankees catching prospect, Lawrence "Yogi" Berra. Players from the Negro Leagues also served, including Larry Doby, later an American League star outfielder.

The quality of play sometimes suffered, but baseball endured and legendary performances occurred. Detroit southpaw Hal Newhouser won two straight MVP awards, topped off with the Tigers winning the World Series in 1945, a feat made possible by the return from military service of Greenberg, appropriately enough the sport's first great Jewish star in an era that experienced a global battle against fascism.

Neither the Korean nor the Vietnam War proved as disruptive to the game, although many younger players were drafted into the military, thereby curtailing or delaying their entrance into major league baseball. Two young phenoms, the Giants' center fielder, Willie Mays, and the Yankees' left-handed pitcher, Whitey Ford, were each away from MLB for approximately two full seasons. Most notably, Boston Red Sox outfielder Ted Williams, who acted as a Navy Marine Corps pilot and aerial instructor for three years during World War II, was a fighter pilot in Korea in 1952 and 1953. A small number of major and minor leaguers served in the U.S. military during the Vietnam conflict, but the sport was scarcely impacted, actually undergoing expansion as the conflagration continued.

The labor wars of the 1970s and 1980s led to two shortened baseball seasons—1972 and 1981—and a one-day strike in 1985, when cancelled games were later played. Baseball suffered the most during 1981, when the players' strike led to about one-third of the regular season games being called off and never rescheduled. A lockout in 1990 pushed Opening Day back a week, but a full slate of games took place.

The previous season, a powerful earthquake, with a magnitude of 7.1, temporarily halted the World Series. Involving two teams in the Bay Area—the San Francisco

Giants and the Oakland Athletics—that year's championship bouts opened with two pitching gems by the A's Dave Stewart and Mike Moore in Oakland's home park. The third game was scheduled to be played on October 17 at San Francisco's Candlestick Park, with over 60,000 fans watching pregame activities.

At 5:04 p.m., severe tremors were felt, and broadcasts became dead airspace as buildings and roads began crumbling. Altogether, 67 people died and billions of dollars in property damage ensued. After the quake hit, baseball Commissioner Fay Vincent quickly postponed Game 3. Ten days passed before the Giants and A's met again, with similar results, Stewart taking that contest and Moore the next to complete the Series by the Bay.

Then there was 1994, when each team lost about 50 games and the postseason was aborted. For the first time since 1904, the World Series was cancelled, dashing the hopes of division-leading squads and players who were attempting to craft historic seasons. All of this included the New York Yankees' return to the front of the American League, after more than a decade, and the Montreal Expos' compiling the best record in the majors. Additionally, San Diego Padre Tony Gwynn approached a .400 batting average and San Francisco Giant Matt Williams and Seattle Mariner Ken Griffey, Jr., threatened the single-season home run record. Right-hander Greg Maddux of the Atlanta Braves produced a 1.56 ERA, over a run better than the second-best pitcher.

However, on August 11, MLB ground to a halt, due to the sport's eighth work stoppage, half of which occurred in the midst of the regular season. After the strike reached its 34th day, Acting Commissioner Bud Selig, who had maintained involvement in the affairs of the Milwaukee Brewers, which he ran as club president and owner, delivered the announcement baseball fans had feared. Blaming the players for the strike and their union's refusal "to respond in any meaningful way" to the need for cost containment, Selig had helped to convince team owners to shut down baseball for the duration of the season. That meant an end to the regular season, as well as no postseason play, ensuring that no World Series would occur for the first time in nine decades.[27]

Donald Fehr, executive director of the Major League Baseball Players Association, charged, "When people think back to what the final image of the 1994 season will be, it may be Bud Selig at a press conference in Milwaukee protesting pain and gnashing teeth but nevertheless going ahead and dashing the hopes and dreams of many people. It was their [the owners'] decision to make. They decided their circumstances were more important."[28]

Robert Lipsyte, an acclaimed sportswriter for the *New York Times*, delivered "In Memoriam," an ode to the game of baseball that began on the front page of the nation's most prominent newspaper. He wrote pointedly, "The National Pastime, which was buried yesterday, died a long time ago. Baseball, which survived, will live forever. And somewhere between the myth of the pastime and the glory of the game was the annual major league season, which seems to have collapsed of exhaustion toward the tail end of a century-long search for its soul." More readily, Lipsyte noted, the season would be most easily forgotten, but MLB would return in another guise.[29]

◆ ◆ ◆

The strike by the MLBPA and the effective lockout by team owners culminated in American professional sports' lengthiest work stoppage, the cancellation of over 900 games, and the failure to play any postseason contests, including the World Series. What two world wars and the Great Depression had proven unable to accomplish was managed by major league players, their union, team moguls, and the Brewers' owner-turned acting MLB commissioner.

Their inability or unwillingness to compromise continued throughout the postseason and the weeks when spring training for the next season would normally have occurred. Even President Bill Clinton's mandate that the two sides return to the bargaining table and resolve their differences by February 6, 1995, proved unavailing. Team owners began hiring replacement players, intending to use them during both spring training and the regular season. The MLBPA insisted that the labor dispute wouldn't end if replacement players appeared on Opening Day. Major League Baseball declared on March 26 that the impending season would be shortened to 144 games per team.

Federal court rulings went against the owners, leading union chief Fehr to state, "We hope that offer [to end the strike] will be accepted and accepted promptly." Expressing hope that the owners would not elect to lock out the players, he suggested, "The opportunity is there to begin rebuilding the game now, without waiting. Hopefully, we're learned something from the last seven or eight months."[30]

One of the lead negotiators for the players, pitcher David Cone of the Kansas City Royals, expressed his feelings. "It's nice to be talking about putting on a uniform. I haven't had much time to work out. I've been going to these damn meetings." But he affirmed, "The players are ready to go."[31]

The strike concluded with no new labor agreement. Approximately $350 million in player income had vanished, along with $800 million in team earnings. Still more costs would be borne in the period ahead. But Baltimore Orioles owner Peter Angelos expressed confidence that a resolution would be reached: "I believe there is a consensus among owners for a side understanding. The '95 season has to be completed and the World Series played. No work stoppage ... and no unilateral action by ownership."[32]

As the *Washington Post* reported, "Baseball, at last, is back, albeit with an uneasy labor peace." Players were slated to head to spring training camps. The start of the season was pushed back to April 26, with the owners having determined not to lock out the players. Acting Commissioner Selig indicated, "The players are back. The game is back, and we are very happy about that."[33]

2

The Players' League

MAJOR LEAGUE BASEBALL HAD THREATENED to head in the direction of a Doomsday scenario precisely because the game's overlords, who for a century held the upper hand in dealing with players, no longer did. In fact, the Major League Baseball Players Association—the MLBPA—was viewed by many as the strongest labor union in the nation, to the obvious dismay of team owners. That was a still relatively recent phenomenon, resulting from marked changes involving the reserve clause, devised by the attorney and later president (1883–1884) of the National League, A.G. Mills, which effectively bound a player to a team throughout his career before the advent of free agency.

Nevertheless, or perhaps accordingly, labor strife had characterized major league baseball since its early days in the latter stages of the 19th century. Some of that resulted from the National Agreement of February 17, 1883. That required teams in the two "major" circuits—the National League and the American Association—as well as the Northwestern League to honor existing player contracts and to sustain the reserve system under which NL squads promised not to attempt to sign players teams had "reserved." This was intended to prevent player raids and keep salaries in check.[1]

Established in 1885, the Brotherhood of Professional Baseball Players sought to improve salaries and, eventually, to challenge the reserve clause that thoroughly restricted player movement. The Brotherhood's charter, drawn by New York Giants shortstop John Montgomery Ward, pledged "to protect and promote its members collectively and individually, to promote a high standard of professional conduct, and to advance the interests of the 'National Game.'" Brotherhood members, who stood at 100 strong by 1887, ultimately insisted that the reserve system and minimum player salaries be terminated.[2]

Guided by 25-year-old Ward—initially a star pitcher, later an infielder, outfielder, and attorney but also a manager, team president, and league executive—the Brotherhood sought, generally ineffectually, to negotiate with representatives from the National League. Ward, cultural historian Robert Ross indicates, was no activist. "He didn't really have radical politics. He was really just looking out for his profession and his colleagues." Two years after the founding of the Brotherhood, Ward wrote an article that appeared in *Lippincott's Monthly Magazine*, a literary magazine based in Philadelphia, asking, "Is the Base-Ball Player a Chattel?" The deliberately provocative query was undoubtedly intended to stir up reminders of the nation's recent deadly struggle to eradicate slavery.[3]

Focusing largely on the reserve clause, Ward worried that "the system has become so rooted that heroic treatment may be necessary to remove it," based as it was on "great injustice and misuse of power." Who would rectify the situation? Would it be the ballclubs or the players or perhaps both? Likening the clause to the fugitive slave laws that had required an escaped slave be returned to his or her "owner," Ward asserted, "The reserve clause denies [the player] a harbor or a livelihood, and carries him back, bound and shackled, to the club from which he attempted to escape." Like a slave, the ballplayer "goes where he is sent, takes what is given him, and thanks the Lord for life." Referring to the sales of players that left them wholly uncompensated, Ward charged, "The whole thing is a conspiracy, pure and simple, on the part of the clubs, by which they are making money rightfully belonging to the players."[4]

John Montgomery Ward, a fine all-around player, became a leading advocate for players' rights, employing his legal training to help create the Players' League in 1890. Circa 1887–1890 (Benjamin K. Edwards Collection. Library of Congress Prints and Photographs Division, Washington, D.C.).

To Ward, it was apparent that the NL worried about "public sympathy, which is with the players." Hence, the league misrepresented the actions of the Brotherhood, casting aspersions regarding its motives. "Ball players," Ward noted, had "been cajoled for a long time by such methods, but they know their rights now and mean to have them."[5]

In November 1887, Ward indicated that the NL shielded

clubs altogether but provided "no protection" to the players. At that point, he did not favor abrogation of the reserve clause, acknowledging the sizable investments owners made at various points. When Brotherhood representatives soon met with owners, Ward responded to a question concerning the "object and the purpose" of the group. He stated bluntly, "It is no fault of ours if you do not know them. The constitution and by-laws of this organization are open to you at any time…. I have not the slightest hesitancy in telling you what they are. The objects are to protect its members in their right, to benefit a needy brother in distress—first, protection; second, beneficial." Ward then referred to "a fund for assisting the sick and to bury the dead," declaring it was "for the promotion of the National game." Fielding other queries, Ward denied wanting "to boom salaries," oppose the reserve clause, or hinder the levying of fines.[6]

Albert Spalding, the Chicago White Stockings owner and former star pitcher, declared, "I think the brotherhood is an excellent thing now. If they will only adhere to what they have laid down in their platform I am sure it will be a good thing for baseball all around. I guess I will join myself." He also declared, "I am inclined to think that we should recognize the Brotherhood." Agreeing to this motion, the National League formed a three-person committee to meet with the Brotherhood regarding a contract. League president Nicholas Young named Spalding, New York Giants owner John B. Day, and Philadelphia Phillies owner John L. Rogers to the committee.[7]

Writing in the October 1888 issue of *The Cosmopolitan*, Ward discussed "Our National Game." Exploring the National Agreement, he indicated that it guaranteed "to each club a monopoly of territory," while ensuring the National League and the American Association would honor each other's "contracts, reservations, suspensions, black-listments and expulsions." It set up a Board of Arbitration to resolve "all disputes and complaints" pertaining to the agreement.[8]

To Ward, the establishment of a "monopoly of territory" amounted to "a base-ball trust," like Standard Oil or other great combines. While new teams could arise, "club" members who joined "would be at once blacklisted and disbarred." The general public, Ward indicated, was unaware of much of this and of "base-ball law." That was "a law unto itself, and so reckless … in the undisputed exercise of … powers" with "little pretense to conformation with the rules laid down by courts of law and equity." By contrast, it was "hard-working, enthusiastic players who" ensured the game's popularity, wrote Ward.[9]

Ward, who had recently helped to steer his New York Giants to a second straight triumph in the "World's Championship Series," and his union long favored a conciliatory approach. However, a session with NL representatives failed to result in recognition of the Brotherhood. That was followed by implementation of the "Brush Classification Plan," which sought to determine particular wages with a top salary of only $2,500 annually; this was in keeping with a scheme concocted by Spalding to establish salary caps for minor leagues. Owners threatened to blacklist recalcitrant ballplayers. Consequently, in November 1889, again with Ward leading the way, a group of professional baseball players, some of whom had been tagged "outlaws" for refusing to be swapped to other teams, created another organization designed to afford them greater equity and financial opportunities.[10]

Announcing formation of the Players' League, initially called the United Baseball Association, that group produced a card with the following statement, while expounding a "Declaration of Independence":

> There was a time when the League stood for integrity and fair dealing, to-day, it stands for dollars and cents. Once it looked to the elevation of the game and an honest exhibition of the sports; to-day its eyes are upon the turnstile. Men have [gone] into the business from no other motive than to exploit it for every dollar in sight…. We believe that it is possible to conduct our National game upon lines which will not infringe upon individual and natural rights. We ask to be judged solely by our own work, and, believing that the game can be played more fairly and its business conducted more intelligently under a plan which excludes everything arbitrary and un–American, we look forward with confidence to the support of the public and the future of the National game.[11]

As their manifesto indicated, the players considered the new organization to be necessary, for "by a combination among themselves, stronger than the strongest trust, the owners were able to enforce the most arbitrary measures, and the player had either to submit or get out of the profession to which he had spent years attaining proficiency." A charter was drawn up, through which the players and their financial backers agreed to share power, discard the reserve clause, offer three-year contracts, and split gate revenues between home and away teams. Ward was compelled to agree that financial supporters would take the initial $10,000 in profits with any additional moneys to be placed in "the cooperatively managed League treasury."[12]

Sporting Life viewed the Players' League charitably. Deeming its plan "only partly co-operative," the publication contended that it "is really but little more than a change of employers with more privileges and liberties accorded to the players." Affording the Players' League front-page coverage on November 13, 1889, *Sporting Life* recounted the organization's recent gathering at the Fifth Avenue Hotel in New York City, where a manifesto was unanimously accepted by the players in attendance.[13]

It quoted from Ward's explanation regarding how they intended to obtain support from fans. "We will get it, in the first place, because of the mercenary and slipshod way the public has been treated by the management of the different National League clubs. This may be summed up in a general carelessness as to its comfort and a disposition to disregard its sentiment respecting the apportionment of both players and teams." Ward believed the players would be supported by the general public because they had the backing of labor organizations. He declared, "The movement is an experiment on our part to have the men who do the work participate in the profits of the pastime." Despite their higher salaries and shorter hours of labor, players were, after all, "workingmen. We are hired men, skilled in a particular employment, who work not only for the profit, but the amusement as well of our employers."[14]

Ward and like-minded players were obviously influenced by the sweeping changes the United States was undergoing. A process of rapid modernization was unfolding, with urbanization and industrialization advancing sharply, along with a marked expansion of the nation's gross national product. More and more corporations were appearing, including vast combines—pools, holding companies, and trusts, vilified above all else—tending toward monopolistic or, more accurately put, oligopolistic dominance. Great wealth was being generated, with a class of millionaires particularly benefiting but also, in a less spectacular economic fashion, a large middle-class and even comfortable members of the working class. But class inequities were mounting too, with a good portion of the population mired in dire straits. For many, both working and living conditions were simply abominable.

In response, labor unions emerged, the more militant ranging from the anarchistic Molly Maguires in coal fields to the Knights of Labor, whose members envisioned a cooperative commonwealth through which producers—the workers—reaped the bounty of what they produced. Farmers, affected by modernizing trends too, vacillated between determinations to leave the agrarian sector behind to battling institutions like banks, railroad companies, and warehouse owners. Many came together, forming granges and alliances, regional in scope. The more radical also favored something like the cooperative commonwealth the National Labor Union and the Knights, but not the more conservative American Federation of Labor, favored.

Based in St. Louis, *The Sporting News* began to give the new league considerable coverage. It quoted extensively from Will Johnson—his brother Albert would become owner of the Cleveland franchise of the Players' League—who declared that "every player in the [National] League with the single exception of [Cap] Anson has signed an agreement to join in the now talked of movement." Dismissing Anson, the star first baseman and manager of the Chicago White Stockings, as "an old horse" soon to be retired, Johnson declared, "Every one of the others have signed a pledge to stand by this agreement."[15]

Additionally, the Brotherhood needed to obtain control of "several base ball parks," including the Polo Grounds in Upper Manhattan. Predicting success for the new league, Johnson pointed to the fact that it would offer "the best ball in the country" and possess "the sympathy of the people." No one, he insisted, approved of how the National League operated, such as "the selling and trading of players" like chattel. Thus, "the time has come when the players must take the bull by the horns and do something for themselves."[16]

Employing parlance common to the era, *The Sporting News* predicted that "the fittest would survive" in a battle between the Brotherhood and existing baseball leagues. In a not unfriendly manner, an opinion piece suggested the Brotherhood could prevail if it possessed "the nerve to fight the battle to the last ditch." To accomplish that, players had to "fight together earnestly and well" as they bucked an organization boasting "money to spare at its back" led by men with "oceans of experience in the base ball line." *The Sporting News* went further, calling for the Brotherhood to link up with the American Association in order to place 10 teams on the baseball diamond, as the National League would.[17]

With the NL having refused to meet with Brotherhood representatives, the group revealed its determination "to play next season under a different management." The Brotherhood felt compelled to explain its decision to the public, emphasizing, as has been indicated earlier, the necessity of "integrity and fair-dealing."

Condemning the reserve clause and the National Agreement, the Brotherhood charged that they afforded "managers unlimited power." The managers in turn did not hesitate to employ such power "in the most arbitrary and mercenary way." They "bought, sold and exchanged" players as if "they were sheep instead of American citizens." As for "reservation," that amounted to "another name for property-right in the player." Thus, through a combination "stronger than the strongest 'Trust,'" baseball magnates could uphold "the most arbitrary measures," compelling the player to accede or retire.[18]

"Our National game," the Brotherhood believed, could be conducted in a manner that did "not infringe upon individual and natural rights." The players sought to be evaluated simply on the quality of their performance. Baseball, they reasoned, could "be played more fairly and its business conducted more intelligently" operating in a manner that excised "everything arbitrary and un–American."[19]

The *New York Times* called the players' effort "a very interesting experiment," through which they "virtually propose[d] to be their own managers, or rather, to manage their managers." They sought "more of the profits of the business of baseball" and hoped to avoid losses, including those doled out by "the unworthy manager" through fines and suspensions. Deeming these concerns "quite legitimate," the paper wondered if they were attainable and pointed to the necessity of considerable capital to back the enterprise.[20]

Henry Chadwick viewed the Players' League far more skeptically. An Englishman who came to reside in the United States, Chadwick helped to popularize baseball. He did so through editing *Beadle's Dime Base-Ball Player*, considered the first annual baseball guide; writing *The Game of Base Ball*, purportedly the initial hardcover book on the sport; editing Spalding's *Official Base Ball Guide*; writing a sports column for the *Brooklyn Daily Eagle*; and probably most significant of all, devising a box score. Called by many the "Father of Baseball," Chadwick castigated the players for having "seceded from the National League." Their new league, he predicted, would appeal to "base ball cranks in particular." While admitting this was "a very serious movement," Chadwick considered it "ill-advised and not warranted under the real circumstances of the case." He predicted it would "prove injurious to the best interests of the majority of the seceding players."[21]

Claiming no interest regarding the NL, Chadwick wrote that his only concerns involved "the future welfare of the national game." He did not seek to antagonize "the intelligent, temperate and gentlemanly class of players of the professional fraternity." But "looking through a national glass," he considered the players' action to have been "hasty," at the very least. Chadwick also questioned the players' arguments regarding the supposedly "oppressive enactments ... of a wealthy monopoly" against "base ball slaves." The great baseball enthusiast worried about the fate of the National Agreement, which he considered necessary for the well-being "of the national game."[22]

In a lengthy editorial, *Sporting Life* suggested that the "seceding" players would likely end up with "a new set of masters." Referring to "alleged grievances" and "vague" allegations, the paper deemed "the underlying motive ... a selfish but perfectly human desire to reap a still larger share of the revenue of the business" of baseball. Despite noting that the new league would exclude the reserve clause, *Sporting Life* commented that the players indirectly acquiesced to the need for "a similar measure." They did so in accepting three-year contracts allowing for ballclubs to determine the players' actual length of service.[23]

"A fierce life and death struggle" regarding public backing would ensue, the editorial predicted. "And one of the two must, it seems certain, go to the wall, as both leagues cannot live side by side in the same territory and thrive." *Sporting Life* suspected that the NL would likely come out on top of the newer, inexperienced, imperfectly run, and terribly costly Players' League. The latter might elicit public support initially, owing to the quality of play, but that would change with time. More fans would realize that "the grand old League," the one that "rescued the game from degradation and" strove diligently "to elevate it," deserved their backing.[24]

In a follow-up editorial several weeks later, Francis C. Richter, founder and editor of *Sporting Life*, offered a more positive analysis of the Players' League. Such an organization, Richter indicated, had been dismissed as "utopian" before being "belittled as the short-lived creation of irresponsible dreamers or schemers." Then, as the Players' League actually emerged, it was attacked for having violated the NL's "rights, privileges and business." Furthermore, it was called "a detriment to base ball." In fact, Richter stated, the new league had become "a mighty force in base ball, and must be treated as such alike by friends and enemies."[25]

The NL, through a committee made up of Albert Spalding, John B. Day, and John L. Rogers, slammed the Brotherhood. Claiming that their league had an "untarnished record" since its inception 14 years earlier, they extolled it for ensuring "the dignity" of the ballplayer's profession and his "munificent salary." Prior to the formation of the NL, they declared, baseball was riddled with "contract breaking, dissipation, and dishonesty." The NL proceeded to eradicate "pool selling and open betting upon its grounds," Sunday contests, and liquor sales. That resulted in attracting "a better class of people" as fans.[26]

As for the reserve clause, Spalding, Day, and Rogers insisted it had "proved beneficial to both clubs and players." The game had improved, salaries had increased more than three-fold, and great skill was exhibited. Demands made by the Brotherhood imperiled all of this and were made by "certain overpaid players" demanding control of the game, which had become "the most glorious and honorable sport on the green earth."[27]

Eventually, over 100 NL players inked contracts with the new Players' League. According to baseball historian Lee Lowenfish, the NL managed to convince 25 players to return to the senior circuit. But the two leading national sports weeklies, *The Sporting News*, based in St. Louis, and *Sporting Life*, situated in Philadelphia, welcomed commentary from Players' League representatives, including Ward. While admitting that ballplayers were paid more than the average worker, Ward insisted they remained "hired men" toiling for both pay and to amuse their bosses.[28]

In some ways, the Players' League proved remarkably successful. Because of the star power it had attracted, the quality of play was probably superior to that of the National League. Before the

Albert Spalding, like Ward, a former star player turned executive, helped to promote the game through his sporting goods business, a worldwide tour, and other promotions (Bain News Service, 1910. George Grantham Bain Collection. Library of Congress Prints and Photographs Division, Washington, D.C.).

season began, *The Sporting News* exclaimed, "The Players' League this year will contain the best crop of twirlers ever brought together in one organization." The paper referred to star pitchers like James "Pud" Galvin, Tim Keefe, and Charles "Old Hoss" Radbourne. Boasting better stadiums, including the Polo Grounds in upper Manhattan, it also probably resulted in higher attendance figures. Top players had jumped ship, led by catcher Buck Ewing, Keefe, catcher Mike "King" Kelly, who also managed the league championship Boston Reds, and Ward himself. Invoking the rhetoric common to the era's labor disputes, Kelly likened the competition between the two leagues to "a fight of a trust against the people."[29]

The labor wars proved costly to baseball owners from both the National League and the Players' League. *The Sporting News* predicted this, declaring their clash would amount to "a fight to the death." Albert Spalding, the former star pitcher and manager who had helped to establish the NL and presided over the Chicago White Stockings franchise, bluntly stated, "One league or the other must go to the wall, as they cannot go on as are now doing, each cutting the other's throat. The public is being overdosed with base ball, or rather, with the fight for patronage between the two leagues." He warned, "The two opposed leagues are waging a war for extermination. It cannot last. One or the other must give way." Spalding went further, seeking to vilify the rebel players at every opportunity, decrying them as "hot headed anarchists" determined to act in the fashion of "revolutionary movements."[30]

As the season wound on, Spalding demanded that the Players' League deliver "an unconditional surrender." The National Agreement, he insisted, had to "be maintained and reaffirmed" to enable baseball to become profitable yet again. Both the National League and the Brotherhood were losing money, Spalding acknowledged, but he asserted the NL's ability "to stand this fight for a long time yet." He also declared that the established circuit was "friendly disposed toward the players who revolted" and had no intention to "humiliate or dishonor their leaders." But "it is folly pure and simple, this Brotherhood sentiment of sticking together. It is always manliness to acknowledge it when you have done a wrong and are convinced of it."[31]

Spalding did more than issue analyses of the NL-Players' League clash. Along with other league executives, he encouraged Players' League investors to explore such options as selling their interests or joining the NL. The faith Ward and his colleagues had placed in their financial angels, the historian Robert Ross indicates, proved misplaced. "They believed that capital would act in the interests of labor. But building a league ... amid a political economy in which property does not come for free, is nearly impossible without an enormous initial sum of money, something the players did not have." Their defeat allowed the despised reserve clause to remain in existence for another eight and a half decades.[32]

As financial difficulties beset the Players' League, one of its strongest proponents, *The Sporting News*, backtracked rather dramatically. By the fall of 1890, as deals were being cut between NL and Players' League owners, the paper bemoaned the fact that the Brotherhood had "allowed itself to be controlled by a lot of capitalists ... who took the first opportunity to throw the players down."[33]

It also warned that the NL, which had seemingly soundly whipped the Players' League, "had better not push the players too hard." Many, *The Sporting News* warned, "still have a mind of their own." From the debacle that had transpired, the players might be goaded until "another uprising" occurred "that would do as much injury to the game as the last one."[34]

In something of a final paean to the Players' League, *The Sporting News* lauded John W. Ward, deeming him "the brilliant and brainy" instigator of the Brotherhood's effort. "No other man who has ever been identified with the national game ... has evolved a plan equal in magnitude, as broad in scope and whose features commended it to as successful an issue." Along with his associates Fred Pfeifer and Ned Hanlon, Ward created "the grandest of all modern baseball ball institutions." Much of the actual organizational work actually resulted from the endeavors of Al Johnson, who believed in the rightness and justice of the cause, and secretary Frank Brunell.

For a brief time, the two men attempted to keep the Players' League alive, but that effort soon became stillborn.[35]

In mid–January 1891, an agreement was made to meld "the remnant of the Players' League" into the National League or the American Association. The blacklisting of players officially ended. The reserve clause was maintained. Reports indicated that these and other decisions were intended to promote the game and bring about "justice and harmony between the players, managers and capitalists."[36]

3

From the Protective Association
to the Fraternity and Beyond

A DECADE PASSED BEFORE THE NATIONAL LEAGUE again confronted serious challenges to its hegemony. One involved the formation of the American League, led by Ban Johnson, which quickly set up teams in Boston, Chicago, and Philadelphia, thereby competing with NL ballclubs, but it also moved into cities that had recently lost major league franchises. The other regarded the Protective Association of Professional Baseball Players or the Players Protective Association, encouraged by AFL labor leader Samuel Gompers and viewed favorably by *Sporting Life*. That publication offered, "The wonder is that the union for self-protection against intolerable oppression has been so long delayed." The PPA's president, Charles "Chief" Zimmer, said, "The players realize that the sport needs a stirring up, and will cooperate with the club owners in the good work." Other veteran players, Clark Griffith and Hugh Jennings, served as PPA vice-presidents.[1]

By mid–1900, the *Washington Post* was reporting that "twenty-four members of the silent brotherhood," the PPA, had met and organized. This had to trouble the magnates, the newspaper indicated, "the magnates whose power has been even more despotic than that of the Czar of Russia." The PPA's counsel, Harry Taylor, claimed, "This is a conservative organization. There is nothing revolutionary about it, and we don't propose to keep men from playing ball." However, "the magnates ... can't afford to have their property be idle." The players' demands, Taylor said, "are just and modest and we do not anticipate trouble."[2]

Brooklyn shortstop Hugh Jennings declared, "Our organization today is strong, and we are ready to talk business.... We want justice, and we intend to get it in a straight above-board, and business-like way.... We are only fighting against methods in the contract system and the scheme of selling and farming players."[3]

Later, the PPA drew up its demands, which the American League accepted. The suspension of a player could last for only 10 days at a time. Teams had to cover medical expenses incurred for injuries that took place on the playing field. Services were to be rendered only to the team to which a player was contracted. The departure of a team from the league could allow for the player to end his contract after offering 10 days' notice. Teams agreed not to "sell, buy, 'farm' ... any player, or" seek to do so absent the written consent of the player. "No right of reservation for a" reduced salary was allowed "for the current year." A player's written consent was required for a reservation of greater than three season. A Board of Arbitration would determine disputes involving a player and team owner; the decision could not be appealed in court.[4]

In *Sporting Life*, Charles Zuber recognized that "the principal contention" pertaining to the PPA involved the reserve clause. Only Brooklyn president Charles Ebbets, Zuber indicated, had expressed opposition to the PPA's proposal that "a player shall be at liberty to sign where he pleases after he has been with one club for a period of three years." As the sportswriter predicted, other naysayers soon emerged. Ebbets's criticism of the proposed change revolved around his belief that the richer teams would "land all the star players." That could be avoided, Zuber suggested, by "placing a certain value on every player," thus preventing bidding wars.[5]

By contrast, Matt Killilen, who led the AL's Milwaukee franchise, viewed the PPA favorably. He predicted the players would not "jeopardize their own interests by making demands that are not within bounds." They also appreciated that owners could no longer dole out "some of the exorbitant salaries" they had in the past. The time, Killilen remarked, had "passed, that is where a few men draw all the money and the balance simply fill in."[6]

The Sporting News offered its own, somewhat ambivalent analysis of the PPA. The association could indeed "promote the business and welfare of its members" through the maintenance of order and an end to "rowdyism" on the playing field. That was necessary to "keep the game clean," or the public's confidence would dissipate. "Base ball is the people's pastime" and had to be kept "on a high plane," the paper insisted.[7]

The expressed willingness of President Zimmer and other PPA leaders "to revise their demands if it can be demonstrated that they are unreasonable" was pleasing to the editorial staff of *The Sporting News*. Baseball owners acknowledged that individual players had been mistreated, while insisting the prevailing system was "not responsible."[8]

In the middle of December, the National League summarily turned down the PPA's proposed changes that would have changed professional baseball's makeup. In "They Side-Stepped: Magnates Did Not Treat the Players Fairly," which appeared in the December 22 edition of *The Sporting News*, Baltimore sportswriter Frank Patterson wrote that baseball owners dealt with the PPA "unfairly and disingenuously." Another writer, J.L. Sweeney, worried about the game's future, fearing that the players, angered by the magnates' "contemptuousness," would strike.[9]

Sporting Life discussed the rejected demands in an article titled "Players Humiliated," which indicated that Taylor included contractual provisions containing "extraordinary and impossible conditions." Upon being handed the PPA's manifesto, Ebbets chuckled and declared, "They're only bluffing, and when the time comes around for advance money, they will all weaken." Calling the players' demands "simply preposterous," Ebbets stated, "Ball players have been well paid.

They have endured no hardships, and have an easy life." Harking back to the Brotherhood, he charged that "secret organization" had "killed baseball" a decade earlier and damaged baseball economics. Chicago White Stockings owner James Hart denied that owners would seek to dampen salaries, despite player complaints. The PPA warned that was precisely what NL owners intended to do. Taylor and Zimmer later explained that the PPA was designed "primarily and mainly to destroy the disposing of the services of professional baseball players without their consent."[10]

The PPA's attorney, Harry Taylor, a former player, delivered the union demands, which AL president Ban Johnson had accepted, to NL owners. Arthur H. Soden, owner of the Boston Beaneaters, soon declared, "The players made a mistake in having a lawyer. Had the boys come to the meeting and made reasonable demands they would have received due consideration." The NL went further, passing a resolution calling for all player salaries to be reduced for the upcoming season. Although discouraged, the players remained determined to prevent "farming," to restrict the time they were tied to a specific team, and to have "some say" in decisions regarding their being "sold or traded off ... by managers."[11]

Following a February meeting of the organization in Cleveland, the PPA reduced its demands to two: "the elimination of buying, selling or farming without the player's consent, and the submission of controversies between individual clubs and players to arbitration." Commending the PPA's "conservative action," Francis S. Richter, on February 16, urged the NL to give in "on these immaterial points and thus save itself and the sport some additional misfortune." Pleased that questions

Ban Johnson helped to create the American League, which he presided over and competed with the more established National League (Byron Bancroft Johnson Photographic Prints, 1910. Library of Congress Prints and Photographs Division, Washington, D.C.).

regarding the reserve clause had been removed, Charles Ebbets, previously a hard-liner regarding the PPA, indicated he was "favorably disposed toward the players."[12]

The following week, Richter, under the heading "The Sky Clearing," expressed his belief that the PPA and the NL had reached "a mutually satisfactory adjustment of [their] differences." Additionally, PPA president Zimmer was evidently siding with the NL in its dispute with the fledgling American League. While acknowledging that the PPA could not prevent players from moving over to the AL, doing so, Zimmer indicated, violated the Association's rules and brought a permanent loss of PPA membership. Further attempting to assuage the owners of the PPA's designs, he denied any intention "to seize ... power" from them or "to run the game" should any of the Association's demands be met. Zimmer sought instead "to correct certain abuses and see that they remain corrected." In fact, the Association soon tossed aside its insistence of arbitration and the NL accepted the PPA's demands concerning the "'farming,' buying and selling" of players. The NL also reduced "the option clause to one year," effectively making each contract valid for two years.[13]

Responding to criticisms of his actions, Zimmer issued a document articulating the PPA's goals and reach. The Association was created "for the express purpose

Charles Ebbets, owner of the Brooklyn ballclub, was a diehard opponent of players' organizations (Bain News Service, 1910. George Grantham Bain Collection. Library of Congress Prints and Photographs Division, Washington, D.C.).

of correcting certain evils that existed between employer and employed, not to tell this man where he shall sign, and that one what he shall receive for his services, nor to prevent others from jumping where they see fit." Zimmer continued, "There is not a word relating to these things in our constitution and by-laws, and it never was intended that there should be. Where they shall place, their price and all that is their own personal affair, and they should not drop it at our door." As for the existing war between the NL and the AL, Zimmer said, "The Players' Protective Association did not bring it on nor can we prevent it."[14]

For a time, the new American League afforded players a bargaining chip, which many employed. As the AL began constructing stadiums in Baltimore, Boston, Philadelphia, and Washington, D.C., the NL, recognizing the need "to conciliate the players," agreed to meet with Zimmer. His chief concerns remained the option clause and the reserve rule but also abolition of the "farming, selling, and the lending of players from club to club." A meeting in late February 1901 resulted in something of a reconciliation between the PPA and the NL, which upset many players.[15]

The vast majority of AL players in 1901 were, in fact, exiles from the older league, including star second baseman Nap Lajoie. His salary doubled when he switched from the Philadelphia Phillies to Connie Mack's Philadelphia Athletics. However, the AL agreed to accept the National Agreement, thereby once again solidifying the reserve clause and helping to restrain salaries. The joining of the two leagues also helped to destroy the PPA.[16]

◆ ◆ ◆

The next strong effort by players to organize didn't occur until more than a decade later, when the attorney David Fultz, an ex-player himself, helped to establish the Baseball Players Fraternity. On September 6, 1912, Fultz laid out the designs of the new organization. They included discouraging rowdy behavior from both spectators and players, providing financial aid to needy players, assisting players during grievance cases, and modifying the reserve clause. The *Los Angeles Times* neatly summarized the new organization's purpose: "the enforcement of the contract rights of the players, and the general welfare of the game of baseball in general." Its officers subsequently included Fultz as president and the Detroit Tigers' batting champion, Ty Cobb, and the New York Giants' Christy Mathewson as two of the four vice-presidents.[17]

American League president Ban Johnson and Chicago White Sox owner Charles A. Comiskey expressed no opposition to the Fraternity. "I am sure the leagues and owners will raise no objection to any such organization in the event that it is formed to better conditions for the players," declared the AL executive. "It looks good to me," agreed Comiskey. "I don't think any unreasonable demands will be made, and I don't believe the players intend to wreck the game, which just now is at the height of its prosperity."[18]

While insisting the ballplayer was "not oppressed," *The Sporting News* viewed the Fraternity somewhat favorably. It recalled the baseball war involving the Players' League and the NL, blasting the owners of that time as "arrogant" and insistent on receiving full credit "for the success of the pastime." A decade later, the players sought to organize yet again, resulting in laughter by the magnates but also a war. Now, fortunately, Ernest J. Lanigan, writing in *The Sporting News*, indicated, the "diplomatic Dave Fultz" headed the new players' association. The paper expressed additional pleasure that the Fraternity appeared determined to root out "rowdyism" from the sport.[19]

The Fraternity appeared as the 1912 major league season neared a close and received support from top major leaguers like Cobb, Mathewson, and the Washington Senators' incomparable right-hander, Walter Johnson. Like previous organizations seeking to band players together, the Fraternity called for higher salaries and better working conditions while attempting to avoid being labeled radical in the fashion of the Brotherhood. Calling itself an association, not a union, the Fraternity urged that "every reasonable obligation of the player's contract is lived up to by both contracting parties." The Fraternity sought elementary rights, among them the delivery of a copy of his contract to each player. It also asked for the center field fence area to be painted dark green to ensure that pitches were more visible, thereby precluding the possibility of serious injury. In 1920, Cleveland infielder Ray Chapman died soon after being beaned by a pitch from the Yankees' Carl Mays; Chapman, by

Dave Fultz, another former player turned lawyer, helped to establish the Baseball Players Fraternity in 1912 (Bain News Service, circa 1910–1915. George Grantham Bain Collection. Library of Congress Prints and Photographs Division, Washington, D.C.).

all accounts, failed to pick up the pitch as it soared toward his head, possibly because of the backdrop or due to the fact that balls, no matter how discolored, continued to be used in games at that point.[20]

Baseball magnates had other issues to contend with, including continued talk about possible legislation declaring major league baseball a trust, which could result in anti-trust activity. Illinois congressman Thomas Gallagher charged that baseball amounted to "the most audacious and autocratic trust in the world." While refusing to offer an opinion regarding that, Fultz acknowledged that many players believed they were "tied hand and foot by the terms of their contracts." By contrast, league officials, Fultz indicated, felt they held "an inalienable right to control ball players and dictate any terms they choose."[21]

Displaying a less than radical approach, the Fraternity, through Fultz, indicated that it had no intention of aligning "with any faction whatever in the baseball world." Obviously referring to a new league that had appeared, he declared, "If there is to be a war among baseball magnates, they must fight it out themselves. As an organization we refuse absolutely to be drawn into the controversy." Fultz's message was reported in an article in *Sporting Life*, "Fogel Proclaims Neutrality!" and in another piece in the *New York Times* titled "Does Not Seek War," with the subheading "Baseball Players' Fraternity Holds Aloof from Federal League Fight."[22]

The *Sporting Life* article also analyzed how Fultz's declaration was received in the baseball world. Some considered it to contain a hint that the Fraternity intended to employ "the war scare" to compel team owners to recognize it and agree to demands by the players' organization. Others saw Fultz's statement as treasonous, for the players had to "be either loyal or disloyal to organization ball." The newspaper itself was displeased with Fultz's statement and urged players to repudiate it.[23]

An editorial in that same issue of *Sporting Life* argued that players could not remain neutral should a war break out pitting Organized Baseball against the Federal League. As for the players, the editorial charged that since the Fraternity had first appeared, it was clear that they sought "to secure for themselves the greatest possible share of the increase of base ball prosperity, minus the responsibility and expense, and regardless of the ultimate consequences to themselves, their successors or the sport itself." Editor-in-Chief Francis C. Richter's editorial page asserted, "Everything else is beside this financial purpose, and such incidents as controversies, strikes, and wars will be only utilized as means to this selfish end."[24]

F.C. Lane, editor of *Baseball Magazine*, allowed Fultz to advocate for the Fraternity in a column that appeared regularly. By contrast, Albert Spalding, who had established a thriving sports equipment manufacturing company, continued publishing baseball manuals such as *Spalding's Guide*, where he blasted the latest effort of ballplayers to challenge team owners. While denying that "any grave disturbances" would occur, he admitted "dread" existed "that a selfish coterie of players might obtain control of the organization and retard for a moment the higher development of the game."[25]

The front page of the September 13 edition of *Sporting Life* featured a headline blaring, "Base Ball War Talk!" After indicating that Congress had refused to examine the supposed "nefarious base ball trust," sportswriter Joe Vila asserted that "enemies of organized sport headed by the Federal League" and the former NL manager and ousted team owner Horace Fogel were undertaking another effort. With advice from Fogel, those *Sporting Life* called "baseball outlaws," aware they lacked "first-class talent," had reached out to Fultz. The Fraternity, at this point, did seem desirous of "a pot of trouble." That could change, the paper feared, if the majors refused to raise player salaries.[26]

Later in the month, the Fraternity drafted a list of demands to be submitted to team owners. A 10-year major league veteran could only be given an unconditional release. The same was to hold true for a 12-year veteran of both the major and minor leagues. No player who remained on the big-league payroll through June would be optioned to the minors without waivers being obtained from all major league teams. A major league owner could not retain a player who possessed a chance to play for another big-league team before the season's final months, then option him to the minors. Many ballplayers appeared ready to refuse to sign future contracts without the fraternity's demands being met.[27]

By mid–October 1913, more than 700 players had joined the Fraternity. Two issues remained of paramount concern: the waiver rule and the reserve clause. Teams could ship a player to the minors because he had antagonized the owner or to receive payment from a team willing to exceed the waiver price. The players considered "too binding" and inequitable the ability of a team to tie "down hard and fast" a player "for his entire baseball career, to be traded, sold, or farmed as the club owners see fit." Soon presenting a larger list of concerns, the Fraternity added such demands as "ten days' notice before [he] can be released unconditionally" and a player becoming a free agent if no regular contract were offered prior to "expiration of the forty-five-day probationary period."[28]

Quite promptly, the National Baseball Commission, made up of the league presidents and a chairman, expressed no willingness to negotiate with Fultz even as talk could be heard that ballplayers were refusing to sign contracts. The commission conveyed a readiness "to arbitrate with a committee of players"; it refused to do so "with no one not active in baseball," obviously referring to Fultz. The players were displeased by the commission's pronouncement, with one warning, "We won't let the commission dictate to us whom we will have for our officers."[29]

The commission had other worries, particularly those involving the Federal League, which had begun operations with half a dozen minor league squads in 1913. Referred to as "an outlaw league," it attracted former star players like Sam Leever, "Deacon" Phillippe, and, most notably, the legendary Cy Young, as managers. The Federal League's impact became still more pronounced by the early fall, thanks to the refusal of the National Baseball Commission to deal with Fultz or to enact the reforms players sought. Should that state of affairs continue, the new league intended to conduct "a raid on" major league stars. Displaying its solidarity with the Fraternity, the Federal League purportedly offered Fultz its presidency, promising a three-year contract. But there was also talk that John Montgomery Ward, who had headed the Brotherhood, would be asked to guide the Federal circuit. In fact, James Gilmore, a Chicago businessman who had been acting president, continued to steer what now became a third major league.[30]

By early 1914, the *Sporting Life* was cheering Fultz's statement: "The Fraternity has no desire or intention of assailing the Reserve Rule." *Sporting Life* deemed the clause "indispensable for baseball's well-being. It also remained distrustful of all the players inside the ranks of their organization."[31]

As for the possibility of the Federal League's raiding major league teams, *The Sporting News* viewed that skeptically, contending that fans would remain "loyal to their favorite team." Nevertheless, scores of big leaguers joined the Federal League, and the threat to jump drove up salaries in the established majors. Baseball's top performers, such as Ty Cobb and Walter Johnson, particularly benefited, with the star hitter getting paid $20,000 by 1915 and the fireballer $17,500. Johnson first accepted and then reneged on a three-year, $75,000 deal with the Federals' Chicago franchise. The league did benefit from the signing of the great pitchers Chief Bender, Mordecai "Three-Finger" Brown, and Eddie Plank, along with infielders Hal Chase and Joe Tinker. All but Chase appeared to be near the end of their careers, although only Brown had a poor season immediately before joining the new league.[32]

Organized Baseball, writes Daniel R. Levitt, the foremost chronicler of the Federal League, "fought back furiously in the press, in the

Walter Johnson, the astounding Washington Senators pitcher who won 417 games, flirted with a move to the Federal League but remained with the generally woeful American League team (National Photo Company, circa 1909–1919. National Photo Company Collection. Library of Congress Prints and Photographs Division, Washington, D.C.).

courts, and on the field" against the upstart circuit. That battle took place as Dave Fultz attempted to sustain "a real players union." The new league clearly had an impact on the NL and the AL, which experienced a severe decline in attendance and a loss of revenue. The actual attendance figures for the Federal League "remain murky" at best.[33]

The Federal League, which operated as a major league in both 1914 and 1915, featured eight teams that first year, competing with the NL in Brooklyn, Pittsburgh, Chicago, and St. Louis. It also went up against the AL in each of the latter two cities. Additionally, the Federal League operated in Baltimore, Buffalo, Indianapolis, and Kansas City, all of which had featured AAA squads. Each Federal League team played in a new ballpark, the most outstanding of which was ultimately called Wrigley Field where the Chicago Whales were the home nine.[34]

Sporting Life, The Sporting News, and *Baseball Magazine,* which began publication in 1908, gradually became more supportive of the Federal League, after initially denying that it could prove viable or was necessary. Following its second season,

Judge Kenesaw Mountain Landis, the hard-nosed federal judge who became major league baseball's first commissioner, ruled with an iron fist while tolerating the stain of Jim Crow in the national pastime (Bain News Service, circa 1915–1920. George Grantham Bain Collection. Library of Congress Prints and Photographs Division, Washington, D.C.).

however, the Federal League suffered a pair of serious setbacks. A suit brought in federal court contending that the majors violated antitrust laws stalled because of the presiding judge, Kenesaw Mountain Landis, whose reverence for baseball evidently superseded his concern that congressional legislation be upheld. At one point during the proceedings, Landis admonished both sides: "I think you gentlemen here all understand that a blow at this thing called baseball—both sides understand this perfectly—will be regarded by this court as a blow at a national institution. Therefore, you need not spend any time on that phase of the subject." The NL and AL teams acted more forthrightly, buying out several Federal League owners and allowing the Whales' Charles Weeghman and the St. Louis Terriers' Phil Ball to purchase the Chicago Cubs and the St. Louis Browns, respectively.[35]

The Baltimore Terrapin owners also desired to join either the National League or the American League, but they were turned down by the major league bosses, who considered Baltimore too small a market with too many African American residents. The trial court accepted the Terrapins' contention that Organized Baseball had illegally conspired to restrain trade, with the Baltimore owners thereby entitled to treble damages of $240,000. The Court of Appeals issued a contrary ruling, declaring antitrust legislation inapplicable because baseball did not involve interstate commerce.

In 1922, the U.S. Supreme Court unanimously determined, with Justice Oliver Wendell Holmes, Jr., crafting the decision:

> The business is giving exhibitions of baseball, which are purely state affairs. It is true that, in order to attain for these exhibitions the great popularity that they have achieved, competitions must be arranged between clubs from different cities and states. But the fact that, in order to give the exhibitions, the Leagues must induce free persons to cross state lines and must arrange and pay for their doing so is not enough to change the character of the business.... That to which it is incident, the exhibition, although made for money, would not be called trade or commerce in the commonly accepted use of those words. As it is put by defendant, personal effort not related to production is not a subject of commerce. That which in its consummation is not commerce does not become commerce among the states because the transportation that we have mentioned takes place.

Somewhat astonishingly, Holmes concluded, "If we are right, the plaintiff's business is to be described in the same way, and the restrictions by contract that prevented the plaintiff from getting players to break their bargains and the other conduct charged against the defendants were not an interference with commerce among the states."[36]

◆ ◆ ◆

That same year, the Milwaukee attorney Raymond Joseph Cannon established the National Baseball Players Association of the United States. In an announcement on August 16, 1922, Cannon indicated that a players' union was intended to prevent them from becoming "pawns of the club owners." In a letter to the players, Cannon, a former semi-pro pitcher, indicated that many major and minor leaguers had asked him to set up "an association of professional baseball players ... connected

Justice Oliver Wendell Holmes, Jr., one of the greatest members of the Supreme Court, was the architect of the ludicrous 1922 ruling that deemed baseball was shielded from antitrust legislation (Harris & Ewing, photographer, 1932 or 1933. Harris & Ewing Collection. Library of Congress Prints and Photographs Division, Washington, D.C.).

with organized baseball." The purpose was to address "a great many unfair advantages … club owners are taking of the ball players … that must be remedied immediately." The players were asked to take a membership pledge demonstrating support for such "an association."[37]

The proclaimed purpose of the new union, *The Sporting News* explained, was to "improve the condition of the players." Sarcastically, the paper declared, "Poor slaves, they need improved conditions, no doubt," and would likely be welcomed by Gompers's American Federation of Labor. Regarding Cannon's involvement in the latest players' union, *The Sporting News* noted that he represented Hap Felsch, Joe Jackson, and others demanding their restatement into the game, having been banished by Commissioner Landis for their purported involvement in the 1919 "Black Sox" scandal that involved the dumping of that year's World Series.[38]

Baseball's barons responded as might have been expected. NL president John A. Heydler refuted the notion that such an organization was needed, for Judge Landis, recently appointed commissioner of Organized Baseball, ensured that "every player knows he can always get a square deal." The square deal comment involved Heydler's adopting the parlance once associated with President Theodore Roosevelt's progressive reform package. Referring to the majors, the league executive insisted that players had never been paid or "treated better." In his estimation, "no just grievances" had "not received prompt attention." Despite the recent High Court ruling, owners had not employed that as a club. Instead, "baseball today is conducted with proper regard for the rights of the players, the owners and the public."[39]

Brooklyn president Charles H. Ebbets warned, "I will not be black-jacked into meeting unreasonable demands by my players. If they go on strike next Spring, I will fight them with every means at my command. I know that the club owners have been very fair to the players. I know of no just grievances." Ebbets cited the example of one player, who had gotten $2,800 the previous season and been offered $4,500 but was demanding $500 on top of that. Connie Mack, owner-manager of the Philadelphia Athletics, revealed "no official knowledge of the plans for forming a ball players' union."[40]

NL president John A. Heydler dismissed the need for such an organization. "I never knew of a more inauspicious time to start a ball players' union. Salaries are higher now than ever before and playing conditions are better. The club owners have met virtually all the players' requests." But Heydler added, "I don't think the organization will hurt the game. The previous one did not and I don't see how this one will."[41]

New York Giants manager John McGraw stated, "I can see the need for such an organization in the minors, but for the life of me I can't reason out why big league players should want to band together. They are being treated better than at any other time in the history of baseball." McGraw declared, "Major league performers, getting fabulous salaries, are nothing less than ingrates when they enroll in such an association." McGraw was reportedly angry that several members of his world champion squad, among the best-paid and perhaps the highest-paid, had joined the union. The notion that the player might strike or demand a minimum salary of $5,000 was absurd, in McGraw's estimation. "In the last twenty years there haven't been five players who really went through with their threat to stay out of baseball unless their salary demands were met." He did think the union could do something worthwhile: "Raise a fund for impoverished players.... Many old-time stars have been discovered without a penny to their name." When asked about what had come to be known as the Baseball Players' Union, Commissioner Landis remarked "that there was nothing for him to say."[42]

The actual "constitution" of the players' organization proved largely innocuous, with the word "union" non-existent. One statement did offer that the association was intended "to protect the players in their dealings with the club owners." Others aspired to safeguard players' rights, bring about fair play, represent players in dealing with their bosses, and stave off "exploitation and unfair dealing." Additional professed aspirations included a desire to champion "clean, honest, sportsmanlike professional baseball" and "clean and high-class sport," as well as to avoid "clouds of suspicion" like those that had appeared recently, a clear reference to gambling and the tossing of games. The document contained no discussion of a possible strike or a minimum salary demand.[43]

An editorial in the *New York Times* sarcastically titled "Nothing to Lose but Their Chains" acknowledged that the Baseball Players' Union's "announced purpose" was "blameless enough" with its bromides regarding rights, fair play, exploitation, "clean, honest sport," and avoidance of scandals. But the newspaper refuted the need for a union, as the owner's "very human nature" provided "protection for the players."[44]

In 1924, a dozen former players established a charitable organization, the Association of Professional Ball Players of America. The APBPA, which soon received the backing of various dignitaries including Babe Ruth and Lou Gehrig, eventually provided assistance to ex-baseball personnel ranging from players and coaches to scouts and umpires.[45]

4

The American Baseball Guild
and Jumping

A FULL GENERATION PASSED before another concerted effort to organize base-ball players developed. That revolved around a Harvard-educated attorney who had assisted the National Labor Relations Board and was perplexed about the failure of baseball players to organize. On the evening of April 17, 1946, 35-year-old Robert Murphy, a former collegiate athlete, revealed that the American Baseball Guild had been established. Claiming that several ballplayers on 10 teams had joined, the Guild's labor relations director indicated that a number of "big name players" were serving as organizers for the new labor group.[1]

Headquartered in Boston, the Guild sought "to organize all professional baseball players in the United States." Initially, it did not intend to unionize players in the Mexican League. This was the fourth—or fifth, if one considered the Baseball Players' Union—serious attempt to unionize major leaguers. Most recently, the Congress of Industrial Organizations, the nation's leading labor instrumentality, had expressed interest in organizing ballplayers. Now, according to Murphy, the Guild possessed the following goals:

1. Freedom of contract so a player so a player would not be forced to join a particular club against his will.
2. Players sold or traded should receive a percentage of the purchase price.
3. Disputes between players and management regarding salary and other conditions of employment should be settled by collective bargaining.
4. Provisions should be made for security, insurance, bonuses and other matters.[2]

Through a statement, Murphy claimed, "Organized baseball no longer can rule with the iron hand of an absolute dictator.... Now it must deal with organized baseball players in the form of the American Baseball Guild. The Guild's purpose is to right the injustices of professional baseball and to give a square deal to the players, the men who make possible big dividends and high salaries for stockholders and executives."[3]

Organized Baseball was already confronting a challenge from the Mexican League, which was seeking to induce players to "jump" from the majors. By the early spring, the Mexican League, led by President Jorge Pasquel and his four brothers, was having some success. Brooklyn Dodgers catcher Mickey Owen, after initially changing his mind, opted to play across the border. Brooklyn president Branch Rickey sought to dismiss the import of Owen's departure, declaring, "I didn't figure on keeping him, anyway." An editorial in *The Sporting News*, "Jumpers in Mexico Make Pathetic Picture," piled on, declaring that departed players like Owen, Dodgers outfielder Luis Olmo, and Giants outfielder Danny Gardella "make a sad spectacle."[4]

Writing from Mexico City, sportswriter Jose Hanes suggested that Jorge Pasquel, who dismissively referred to "the Organized Monopoly of Baseball in the United States," might be benefiting from the controversy concerning player raids. The Mexican League appeared to have owners with considerable capital and community standing, although "shortcomings" abounded in the circuit setup. Showering facilities at the seven ballparks were not available for the ballplayers, who had to rely on taxis to transport them from hotels or homes. A lack of professionalism appeared present, with players smoking or drinking beer and consorting with rivals. Long train travel was required, such as from Mexico City to Monterey or Laredo, or buses, including regular passenger ones, carried teams from city to city. Fans, Hanes noted—perhaps in stereotypical fashion—"naturally are excitable," sometimes inclined to hurl "bottles, seat cushions or whatever is at hand," such as beer, at umpires. Few box seats were available, with the bulk of the seating no better than "bleacher seats in the States." Improvements were planned.[5]

Washington Senators owner Clark Griffith, a former

Branch Rickey, the former player and manager who became one of the game's greatest executives, is best remembered for his devising of the farm system and decision to integrate major league baseball through the signing, in 1945, of Jackie Robinson (Bain News Service, 1913. George Grantham Bain Collection. Library of Congress Prints and Photographs Division, Washington, D.C.).

great pitcher, leading force in the creation of the Players Protective Association, and part-founder of the American League, who had later personally battled against the Fraternity, now condemned the notion of another union for players. When asked about that very possibility, he responded curtly, "It can't be done." Griffith explained, "Dickering between owners and players just has to be carried out individually. There are big differences in players' abilities and I can't see a $40,000-a-year man refusing to play ball simply because another fellow wants $10,000." Players were "well paid right now," Griffith remarked. As for himself, he wanted to retain the ability to negotiate with each player individually.[6]

The reserve clause, Griffith said, provided "the foundation on which the game stands." It produced a "capitalistic condition" allowing the best-heeled owner to sign as many stars as he desired. Asserting that collective bargaining would prove impractical in the sport, Griffith called baseball a "matter of individual ability." Moreover, collective bargaining would invariably result in salary ceilings. Finally, he held that team owners had to retain the right to discard "unsuitable players ... to meet competition and keep the game alive."[7]

Clark Griffith, the former player and manager who owned the usually hapless Washington Senators. A former proponent of labor activism among ballplayers, he became a strident opponent of those like the attorney Robert Murphy, who, following World War II, created the American Baseball Guild (Harris & Ewing, photographer, circa 1940. Harris & Ewing Collection. Library of Congress Prints and Photographs Division, Washington, D.C.).

Almost immediately, the Guild announced its intention to follow up on accusations that major league executive were "intimidating" players interested in the new organization. Refusing to indicate which players had joined the Guild, Murphy also wouldn't name the club executives engaged in harassment. He did state, "They have absolutely no right to discuss with the players any matters concerning the union or union membership." Doing so violated the National Labor Relations Act, initially passed in 1935 to encourage union organizing. Murphy was willing to reveal that membership was "substantial" and included "several-high salaries players" or "stars." Presently, the players themselves were engaged in most of the union work.[8]

Both the Congress of Industrial Organizations and the American Federation of Labor encouraged unionization of pro ballplayers and affiliation by the Guild. CIO director of organization Allan S. Haywood said, "If baseball players want to form a union, I think that is a good thing." Club owners and officials generally declined to comment about the Guild, although Horace C. Stoneham, the New York Giants president and owner, stated, "The thing was tried twenty or twenty-five years ago with the baseball players themselves voting the thing out."[9]

Washington Post columnist Shirley Povich expressed grave doubts about the likelihood of organizing baseball players. The top players, drawing the largest salaries, wouldn't accept "any share-the-wealth" plan, he contended. A standardization of salaries didn't appeal even to the more-lowly-paid athletes, who hoped one day to make considerably more. If those ballplayers did seek to organize, team owners would likely dump them, Povich wrote. But suggesting that "organized baseball will never be unionized isn't smart, either."[10]

In an interview with *The Sporting News* on April 20, Murphy declared, "Obviously, I cannot give you any names at the present time. If clubs knew which players were interested in the movement, the players might be thrown open to criticism and possible financial injury." But he revealed that players from most of the major league teams had joined, and that a majority "on some clubs" had.[11]

Indicating that the latest union effort would be different from previous ones, Murphy stated, "Back in the old days, there was no National Labor Relations Board. Today, we have the law behind us, and if ball players continue to be as interested in the Guild as they have been to date, there is no question in my mind that it will be accepted." He expressed hope that some baseball legend like Babe Ruth, Ty Cobb, Tris Speaker, or Jimmie Foxx would serve as the organization's chair. Murphy also pledged that no strikes would be forthcoming, for the arbitration board could resolve any dispute. He also promised that the Guild would "establish a minimum wage for players in the majors."[12]

"Ruth May Head Mex Loop" read a front-page headline in *The Sporting News*, which dismissed those who had bolted to the Mexican League as "has-been and never-were ball players." The aging home run king was said to have been invited by the Pasquel brothers to visit Mexico, where, as throughout Latin America, his fame remained "great." However, Ruth soon denied any knowledge about a position with the Mexican League, indicating that he had spent little time with Jorge Pasquel. The Bambino seemed more interested in a possible managerial job at the Triple-A level.[13]

In the meantime, one unnamed American League player expressed doubts about the Guild's viability. "I can't see how the Guild could help the high salaried players as, for example, Ted Williams, Hank Greenberg or Bob Feller." As for himself, the player noted that his decade-long experience made him more knowledgeable "about negotiating over salary than any union boss." He received "a pretty good salary … usually" what he sought. While the union might aid "the ordinary worker," the player said, "I don't see any place for it in baseball."[14]

The Guild soon filed charges alleging that the Senators and Clark Griffith had engaged in unfair labor practices. A statement by Robert Murphy accused Griffith of seeking, through coercion and intimidation, "to dissuade the Washington players from joining the Guild." The organization, according to its labor relations director, had been conducting "a clean fight in the interest of American baseball." It did "not intend to countenance any unfair tactics on the part of club owners." Most owners, Murphy acknowledged, had not acted in a similar manner, notwithstanding their opposition to the Guild.[15]

In response, Griffith termed the accusations "ridiculous." He stated, "I don't know this fellow Robert Murphy or anything about his outfit, and furthermore I don't know what he's talking about when he says I have violated the players' right to organize if they like." Griffith dismissed the complaint: "The whole thing is silly." While declaring Murphy "a smart cookie and not to be underrated," Shirley Povich thought Murphy's maneuver regarding Griffith was "a transparent bid of publicity seeking."[16]

Murphy soon indicated that the Guild would seek a minimum salary of $7,500, which would amount to a sharp increase for rookies, who generally averaged around $3,000 less. At the same time, he denied that unionization would result in a salary ceiling. "There shall be no standardization of salary—no maximum salary—and a player shall receive as much as he is worth." The Guild's eight-point plank also included provisions for players to receive half of the purchase price when they were sold, peaceful resolution of conflicts without resorts to strikes, arbitration to resolve grievances, expanded freedom of contract, and insurance coverage.[17]

The major leagues themselves began seeking legal redress, with Larry MacPhail, one of the owners of the New York Yankees, obtaining a restraining order targeting Mexican League officials. In granting the request, New York Supreme Court Justice Julius Miller wrote, "No real proof that Organized Baseball is an illegal monopoly is submitted on behalf of the defense." Miller did note, "The facts … at most show that an individual ball-player's freedom of contract is restricted and limited." But the judge offered that even if Organized Baseball were considered "a monopoly, it would seem that it is not a combination in restraint of trade."[18]

The Pasquel brothers' latest gambit involved an attempt to lure former NL batting champion Pete Reiser, the Brooklyn Dodgers' outfielder, dangling a three-year offer amounting to $100,000. Reiser informed the press, "I've told the Mexican representative that I'm not going."[19]

Dodgers president Branch Rickey also obtained a temporary injunction to prevent the Mexican League from undertaking additional raids on his team. Rickey stated, "These continued proposals are bad for our morale. It takes the players' minds off the game. I don't mind a fly bothering me, but if a wasp keeps buzzing around, I've got to make the attempt to brush it off." Concerning the Mexican League's unsuccessful attempt to corral his star outfielder, Rickey declared, "Pete Reiser remained with the Brooklyn club because I don't believe he wanted to be a man without a country." The Dodgers' top executive added, "Moreover, I don't look on the Mexicans as a permanent threat. They can't go on paying such huge sums where it doesn't come in at the gate." Rickey added, "The players already in Mexico are going to be dissatisfied with Mexican baseball."[20]

Former Dodger Mickey Owen thoroughly refuted Rickey's declaration regarding former major leaguers being dismayed by their stay South of the Border or by how they were being treated there. Talking to Stan Musial, the Cardinals' batting star then being heavily recruited by the Pasquel brothers, Owen "told him that anyone who thinks Jorge doesn't know his baseball has been badly informed." Alfonso Pasquel was intensifying the bidding war, offering Musial "$130,000 for five years, with half of it … payable in cash on the spot if he wanted it." Musial admitted, "They made me an offer that was hard to turn down." But choosing to remain in St. Louis, Musial commented, "Let's consider this Mexican thing a closed matter for the present. Let's say no more." He also said, "I do not intend to use the Mexican offer as a club over the Cardinals."[21]

According to the *Los Angeles Times'* Dick Hyland, Ted Williams turned down an offer of $70,000 a year from Bernie Pasquel. Having recently left the U.S. Armed Forces, where his $40,000 salary was reduced to $85 monthly, the Red Sox's hitting genius said: "It's just the same as before. Look, how many players like me are there in baseball? None. I am Ted Williams. There is no other. There is only one Bob Feller, only one Joe DiMaggio. There are a lot of baseball players but only about a dozen or so of us are, well, we're symbols. We're baseball. Baseball is our national game. Little kids and the same men and women I knew in uniform are baseball fans. We play for them. If we go to Mexico, what becomes of baseball in our country, what becomes of our fans who are our people?"[22]

In a lengthy article in *The Sporting News*, editor Edgar G. Brands explained that Organized Baseball performed a delicate balancing act regarding "personal freedom" and "property rights." Lower court judges often ruled in favor of players, seen to be at a competitive disadvantage in their dealings with ballclubs. However, federal courts, including the highest court in the land, ultimately had ruled in favor of Organized Baseball on player contracts, the reserve clause, and charges of monopoly. Notwithstanding "rumblings of player dissatisfaction," which "'brotherhoods,' 'fraternities,' 'unions,'" sought "to capitalize on," court renderings and Commissioner

Landis's "unswerving support" had "served to strengthen, rather than nullify, the contract relations." The game's "few experiences in court" had "taught players, officials and club owners that differences could be better settled outside of judicial chambers." But Brands feared that 1946 might prove "turbulent" for Organized Baseball.[23]

While Larry MacPhail was battling the Mexican League, he also offered opinions about the Fraternity. As Robert Murphy declared, "We have signed up 90 percent of the player personnel of the Pittsburgh club," MacPhail agreed that a players organization was necessary. As *The Sporting News* recalled, the Yankees president "long ago warned" that a failure to provide the players with "a voice" would only "invite trouble." The paper likewise indicated that the major leagues should have offered a minimum wage "long ago."[24]

Ty Cobb, who had retired from the majors with the highest lifetime batting average ever, doubted whether a labor union for baseball players was viable. "For most occupations you can set a standard of performances and a pay scale for attainment of that standard," he said. For ballplayers, however, it was different. Some entered the majors ill-prepared for what confronted them. Some tried to run around, and others "eat themselves out of the big leagues." Cobb did indicate that a player who had amassed a reputation due to his lengthy stay with a ballclub should be financially rewarded.[25]

The American Baseball Guild and Robert Murphy suffered a pair of devastating defeats in early June 1946. On Friday, June 7, the Pittsburgh Pirates refused to agree to a strike of that evening's contest against the New York Giants. Sportswriter Oscar Ruhl acknowledged that "for a few hours the Pittsburgh players had President Bill Benswanger of the Pirates—and baseball in general—over a barrel, while they fiercely debated the virtues of striking or not striking." Starting an hour before gametime, they held a closed-door meeting in their clubhouse, talking for 75 minutes, past the time when batting practice was to begin. The "FOR PLAYERS ONLY KEEP OUT THIS MEANS YOU" sign even applied to Murphy, who was photographed at the dressing room door.[26]

In a secret ballot, the players voted 20 to 16 to strike. That majority vote, however, didn't come close to reaching the three-quarters mark the players had determined necessary to carry out the action. A three-quarters tabulation would have led to more than a single-game walkout. Explaining their decision, infielder Lee Handley underscored the players' high regard for Benswanger. He admitted, "I don't think we gave Murphy a square deal. We let him down and I was one of those who did it. We're not radicals. We don't want to be affiliated with any labor organization. We want our own group, like the Professional Golfers or the Actors' Guild. We believe thoroughly in some plan for representation." Third baseman Bob Elliott, Pittsburgh's top-paid player, said, "I don't like the idea of going on strike.... I say this as one who believes in the principles of the Guild."[27]

The National Labor Relations Board, in a ruling issued on June 12, dealt another blow to Murphy's American Baseball Guild. It refused to conduct formal hearings regarding jurisdiction over professional baseball squads, and it dismissed charges involving unfair labor practices by the Pirates. Both Benswanger and Pittsburgh's farm director, Bob Rice, had shared a few thoughts in the clubhouse before the players gathered alone. Benswanger told them, "I haven't had any trouble with a ball player since I became president fifteen years ago, and they cannot refute that statement. I have never hurt a ball player. I am leaving up to them to decide whether to play."[28]

Many sportswriters offered support to various player demands, especially the idea of a minimum salary. The *Detroit News'* H.G. Salsinger pointed to "some injustices" such as the underpaying of certain players or their shabby treatment, setting the stage for the Pasquels' raids and Murphy's Guild. "These invasions," Salsinger wrote, could have been prevented through the institution of a minimum salary scale and the offering of a percentage of sales to the players. The *Brooklyn Eagle's* Tommy Holmes agreed with Salsinger's suggestions and indicated that in keeping with most employers, baseball bosses "rarely see the light until they are properly sandbagged." Criticizing baseball's "archaic legislative structure," *PM's* Tom Meany charged that it turned players into "peons" lacking any security or promise about a square deal. He backed a minimum wage and a pension for 10-year players.[29]

"Setback for Guild but Problems Remain" read the headline for an editorial in *The Sporting News*. Dated June 19, 1946, it referred to the twin setbacks endured by Murphy but warned that baseball's labor difficulties remained unresolved. Referring to the labor strife besetting the nation in the aftermath of World War II, the column pointed to several issues of continuing concern. These included "the ten-day notice of release clause" and the lack of a minimum salary. The players, *The Sporting News* noted, would look forward to the return of the Players' Fraternity.[30]

By the end of the following month, *The Sporting News* reported that Organized Baseball's "social revolution" was nearing completion. The two major leagues appeared to be welcoming a second edition of the Players' Fraternity, which supposedly would operate harmoniously with team owners. That would lead, the paper predicted, to a $5,000 minimum annual salary, a new contract removing the 10-day release notice, training camp allowances, and the ending of salaries being cut when major leaguers were farmed out to the minors. NL president Ford Frick confessed, "I am chagrined and ashamed that I did not bring about these changes before the players sought them. But I plead inertia. Not a good excuse, but the only one we have."[31]

As the Baseball Guild withered, the major leagues presented a 90-page report on player demands. The magnates agreed to several concessions, including establishing minimum annual salaries throughout Organized Baseball, setting the level at $5,500—subsequently reduced to $5,000—for the majors. Tossed out was "the ten-day notice of release clause." An allowance was promised for preseason sessions; the players would refer to payment for spring training as "Murphy money." No major league player's salary would be reduced if he was sent to the minors. A pension system, with both players and teams contributing monthly, was to be established. Some barnstorming would be allowed. Moving expenses up to $500 would be given to a "player with a family who is sold or traded" in the midst of the playing season. Reporting to training camp before March 1 would be voluntary, starting in 1948.[32]

Robert Murphy believed that the owners' willingness to introduce "a welfare fund" was an acknowledgment that "the guild is correct in its claim the baseball contract is unfair to the players." He declared, "It is obvious that efforts of the guild to correct injustices to the player are in a large measure responsible for this action by the baseball barons." Murphy went on to say, "This is proved by the fact that never before in the long history of baseball was such a measure suggested by the owners."[33]

Significant too was the decision to change the Advisory Council, which had operated since 1921, when it replaced the National Commission. For the first time, one player each from the two major leagues would be added to the sport's governing body, now to contain seven members.[34]

A series of disputes arose, including the proposal for a 168-game season. By December, big league owners made additional concessions, including prohibiting any team from seeking "waivers on more than seven players at one time." The owners accepted the players' demand that doubleheaders not be scheduled following night games, which would affect the two St. Louis teams the most. The two leagues agreed to match $250 annual player contributions for a pension plan, which would also be given World Series broadcast money and All-Star Game proceeds.[35]

Several players—a number of them prewar stars—soon confronted the reality of massive pay cuts. Under the terms of new contracts, no player's salary could be "less than 75% of the rate stipulated for the preceding year." Unfortunately, that only applied starting with the 1948 season.[36]

◆　◆　◆

Neither the altered contractual arrangements in major league baseball nor the collapse of Robert Murphy's Baseball Guild meant that labor or legal issues in Organized Baseball were fully settled. The status of players who jumped to the Mexican League remained in flux. In addition to Mickey Owen, Luis Olmo, and Danny Gardella, the Pasquel brothers snared the front-running Cardinals' ace southpaw pitcher, Max Lanier, a former ERA champion and ace of two World Series championship squads, and Sal Maglie, a promising right-hander with the Giants. At the time he jumped, Lanier sported a 6–0 win-loss record with a 1.93 ERA. His teammates, pitcher Fred Martin and second baseman Lou Klein, were among the other MLB players—27 altogether—who bolted to the Mexican League.[37]

Several quickly regretted what they had done. All, however, confronted a five-year ban placed by Commissioner Happy Chandler on any player who played in the Mexican League and failed to return before an April 1, 1946, deadline. Vern Stephens, a power-hitting shortstop for the St. Louis Browns, only avoided the ban because he came back home having appeared in but two Mexican League games.[38]

After receiving word of Chandler's edict, Danny Gardella, the former New York Giants outfielder who jumped to the Mexican League, hired an attorney, Frederic Johnson. The attorney brought suit against MLB for $300,000, contending that his client was being deprived of his livelihood through an illegal restraint of trade. The legal action thus challenged the reserve clause and other facets of player contracts. It also brought up the question regarding whether Organized Baseball necessarily was part of interstate commerce owing to its ties to radio and television. The *Washington Post*'s Shirley Povich foresaw a ruling going against "Operation Baseball" concerning "antitrust and interstate commerce laws."[39]

A.B. "Happy" Chandler, former Kentucky senator and governor, became MLB's second commissioner (1945–1951) and helped to bring about the game's desegregation (Harris & Ewing, photographer, May 13, 1940. Harris & Ewing Collection. Library of Congress Prints and Photographs Division, Washington, D.C.).

Criticized for his lawsuit, Gardella, at that point making $36 weekly as a hospital orderly, referred to contentions that he was "undermining the structure of the baseball contract." He said, "I can't see it that way. Let's say that I'm helping to end a baseball evil." Regarding the way he had been treated, Gardella offered, "They persecuted me. I was terribly mistreated."[40]

While a federal judge, relying on the U.S. Supreme Court's ruling in 1922, held against the ballplayer, a federal appeals court, in February 1949, mandated a jury trial. In a settlement, Gardella received $60,000 to withdraw from the lawsuit.[41]

In June 1949, Commissioner Chandler ended the ban on the jumpers. Most notably, that enabled Maglie, known as "the Barber" for his brushback pitches, to help lead the Giants to a pair of pennants and, in 1954, to the World Series title. In a final bid for glory, he helped the Dodgers win the 1956 NL pennant.[42]

Organized Baseball's antitrust exemption appeared threatened once more, as a series of minor league players and officials, following Gardella's lead, brought suits in federal courts. During the spring of 1951, Senator Carl Johnson of Colorado, who happened to be president of baseball's Western League, urged the majors, especially, to seek federal legislation to sustain the reserve clause and baseball's infrastructure. He warned, "The door is open to every disgruntled player, every pipsqueak phony, every trouble maker, to go into court and attack the reserve clause in order to extract … valuable considerations from baseball." To Johnson, "a sport which is so vital to this nation ought not to present an Achilles heel."[43]

That July, the House Judiciary Committee's Subcommittee on Monopoly Power undertook hearings into Organized Baseball. Subcommittee chair Emanuel Celler, from New York City, had recently stated, "If baseball is illegal, then we must prosecute the owners or change the law." Responding quickly, MLB created an Open Classification status for a league with the requisite criteria—substantial population, attendance, and ballpark capacity—to be considered "a superior minor league." That in turn would result in additional money for drafted players and greater representation in baseball circles.[44]

In 1953, the U.S. Supreme Court again handed down a decision involving Organized Baseball. This resulted from a lawsuit brought by George Toolson, a minor league pitcher with the Yankees, charging antitrust violations culminated in his blacklisting. In a 7–2 decision, the Supreme Court effectively sustained the earlier ruling by Justice Holmes and his colleagues, declaring that Congress had not seen fit to apply antitrust laws to Organized Baseball.[45]

5

The Major League
Baseball Players Association

DURING THE SUMMER OF 1953, as the top big leaguers gathered for the annual All-Star contest, two of the very best, Yankees right-hander Allie Reynolds and home run king Ralph Kiner, recently traded from the Pirates to the Cubs, discussed the players' pension fund. Serving in their capacity as player representatives, they wanted to bring up the question of the fund's sustainability, a proposed increase in the minimum salary, and the ability of low-paid players to participate in winter ball in Latin America before a meeting of team owners. Shortly afterward, Reynolds and Kiner reached out to Jonas Norman Lewis, an attorney in New York City, who had written about "Baseball Law" but hardly in a manner favorable to the players. No matter—the owners' immediate response was hostile. One of the Yankees partners, Del Webb, a major real estate developer, demanded of Reynolds, "What are you attempting to do, start a union?" Reynolds replied, "That's the farthest thing from my mind," then explained that the players required an organization to deal with the issue of the pension.[1]

Lewis was equally emphatic regarding the players' intentions. "There is absolutely no contemplation of a union. The players don't want it and I don't advise it. There is a loose association of players now that is going to be closer knit for the exchange of ideas and mutual help, but definitely no unionization."[2]

Kiner stood as a stark reminder as to the imbalance between players, even the game's finest, and management. During his first seven seasons in the majors, he led the NL in homers each year, twice belting over 50 homers, while driving in and scoring more than 100 runs five times. On three occasions, he hit over .300 and compiled a slugging percentage greater than .600. Nevertheless, following the 1952 season in which his batting average admittedly slid to .244 but he still tied for the lead in homers, Kiner received word that his contract for the next year would be sliced by the maximum 25 percent that was allowed. When he reminded Branch Rickey that fans came out to watch the team only because of his slugging, the Pirates' GM, coming off a 50–104, last-place finish, stated, "We can finish last without you." With his salary reduced from the $90,000 mark that had been the NL's highest, Kiner suffered another indignity when, just prior to a game with the Chicago Cubs, he was informed that he had been traded to the visiting team.[3]

Former commissioner Happy Chandler, who had possibly been denied an extension of his term due to his investigation of two owners for purported gambling interests, accused team bosses "of doing a horrible thing" in seeking to reduce the funding of the players' pension. By contrast, he expressed admiration for both Roberts and Kiner, saying they were "fighting for the other players."[4]

Shirley Povich viewed the player-owner meeting more favorably than Reynolds and Kiner apparently did. "Everything went along just swimmingly in the conference rooms this time," the *Washington Post* sports columnist reported. The players were allowed to play winter ball if they chose to, and the owners agreed to formally acknowledge "an official players' group" and "their legal counsel." The owners also admitted that the pension fund necessarily had a large stake in television and revenues proceeds from the World Series and the All-Star Game.[5]

Povich lauded the "intrepid leadership" of Kiner and Reynolds, who would not "be bluffed or intimidated by" threats of retaliation by the owners. "It required more than a bit of courage for [the two men] to lead the fight. Theirs was a completely unselfish project." As two of the game's top-paid players, they "had less to gain, more to lose, than any of the athletes they represented." The two had recently sought an increase from $50 to $80 monthly for players with five years of service and from $100 to $150 for those with a decade in the majors. They also wanted annuities to start at age 45, not 50, and for player contributions to be reduced. Ford Frick, who had replaced Chandler as baseball commissioner, indicated that such changes were prohibitively expensive.[6]

A committee of owners and players came to an agreement on February 16, 1954, that the pension plan's funds would be increased from $450,000 to about $2,000,000 annually. "Full and complete control" of the funds would be undertaken by a committee made up of two owners and two player representatives. The

Allie Reynolds, a great pitcher with the postwar New York Yankees, became an important player representative, paired with Ralph Kiner, during the early 1950s. Ca. 1952 (National Baseball Hall of Fame Library. Cooperstown, NY).

Ralph Kiner, the Pittsburgh Pirates' slugger who won seven home run crowns before being traded to the Chicago Cubs, served alongside Allie Reynolds in representing players during the early 1950s. Ca. 1953 (National Baseball Hall of Fame Library, Cooperstown, NY).

funds would be derived from 60 percent of the receipts from All-Star Game ticket sales and television and radio payments, along with 60 percent of those media funds from World Series games. Cleveland general manager Hank Greenberg declared, "We gave them everything they wanted."[7]

♦ ♦ ♦

Following the Toolson decision, the owners clearly appeared emboldened, refusing to allow Lewis to attend the owners' annual winter gathering. Angered, the players got together on their own, while Lewis informed the press that the owners declined to provide accountability regarding the pension fund. Consequently, player representatives voted to create the Major League Baseball Players Association, whose first president was the longtime Cleveland Indians pitching great, Bob Feller.[8]

Over the next few years, the MLBPA made little headway other than getting the minimum salary bumped to $6,000, while players "seethed," indicates Lee Lowenfish. In late 1954, for instance, players were displeased on receiving word that team owners had dismissed several of their demands. They were especially "irked" by the rejection of their proposal that the major league salary minimum be raised from $6,000 to $7,200.[9]

One year later, player representatives again expressed displeasure regarding "the uncooperative attitude" displayed by owners toward player proposals. This time, they were particularly unhappy that their employers summarily rejected a request to have representation during contractual negotiation over All-Star Game and World Series radio and television rights. With millions of dollars at stake, Feller indicated, "It seems only reasonable … that we should have some voice in the establishment and administration of the new contract."[10]

At times, sportswriters celebrated the changes Organized Baseball made to benefit players. For instance, alterations induced *The Sporting News*, on February 13, 1957, to proclaim, "Players' Pension Plan Now 'Finest Anywhere.'" Associate Editor

Bob Feller (right), the Cleveland Indians' fire-balling ace, headed the Major League Baseball Players Association by the mid–1950s. He is shown here with Bucky Jacobs, the Washington Senators' rookie pitcher (Harris & Ewing, photographer, August 2, 1937. Harris & Ewing Collection. Library of Congress Prints and Photographs Division, Washington, D.C.).

Oscar K. Ruhl referred to "benefits so lucrative," including a $550 monthly stipend for 65-year-old former players with 20 years in the big leagues. Joined by pension committee member Joe Cronin and MLBPA head Feller, Commissioner Frick referred to "a 75 per cent increase in payments, including a rise from $100 a month to $175 for ten-year men at age 50 and from $50 to $88 for five-year men." Calling the new plan, which became retroactive to 10 years earlier when the initial pension was devised, "a tremendous forward step in management-player relations," Ruhl also mentioned "insurance, hospitalization and disability benefits."[11]

Feller, recently retired from the Indians, lauded the new plan, declaring it "will make baseball all the more attractive to the youngsters of America." He stated, "I am not asking the boys to substitute a baseball career for an education. But, if they want to play ball, the pension payments should make for greater allure." Less happily, team owners still refused to lift the $6,000 salary minimum, which troubled the MLBPA president.[12]

Despite that discordant note, *The Sporting News* sang the praises of the accord between ballplayers and MLB. "What a great break for the players!" exclaimed an editorial, which asserted, "We know of no comparable arrangement in any industry." The sports weekly continued in that vein: "Obviously, the players never had it so good…. The greatest of their predecessors had no such protection against want in later years." Sportswriter Jimmy Powers's column, "The Powerhouse," also exulted while pointing to the fact that "so many labor unions and corporations these days have retirement setups and most of the millions of insurance policies have annuity options." Former manager Frank Frisch, who had been one of MLB's best during his playing days, encouraged sports-minded youngsters to stick to baseball. After all, big leaguers now received "fine pay … the finest pension plan … stay at the finest hotels and have the finest modes of travel."[13]

During June 1957, the House Judiciary Committee's Antitrust Subcommittee, which Emanuel Celler chaired, met to explore why antitrust legislation did not apply to baseball. A recent U.S. Supreme Court decision, *Radovitch v. National Football League*, did not extend the antitrust exemption that shielded Organized Baseball to other sports. The hearings of the Celler subcommittee proved inconclusive, although the chair remained concerned about baseball's singular protection from antitrust law.[14]

Democratic Congressman Emanuel Celler, a representative from New York City, held hearings on MLB's antitrust exemption (New York World-Telegram and the Sun staff photograph, 1951. New York World-Telegram and the Sun Newspaper Photograph Collection. Library of Congress Prints and Photographs Division, Washington, D.C.)

♦ ♦ ♦

If past developments portended later ones, talk of a new baseball circuit might have been expected to spur greater organizational efforts by major league players. The relocation of the Dodgers and the Giants to the West Coast following the 1957 season convinced New York attorney William Shea of the need for a new National League franchise in the nation's largest metropolitan area. A lack of support for expansion from big league owners led Shea and Branch Rickey to pursue another course: the creation of an eight-team Continental League. To ward off the threat, team owners agreed to add four teams, two in each league. Shea would be awarded an NL franchise in New York City, with his New York Mets eventually playing in the ballpark named after him.[15]

◆   ◆   ◆

Rather than talk of expansion inducing player militancy, over the course of the next several years, the MLBPA limped along, beset by inadequate legal representation. That proved true throughout Norman Lewis's tenure as the players' attorney and that of his eventual replacement, Judge Robert Cannon. Unhappy that Lewis did not appear fully devoted to their cause, the players fired him in March 1959, although he had helped to get the minimum salary raised to $7,000 15 months earlier and a pension fund established. Later in the year, Frank Scott, the Yankees' former traveling secretary, became a part-time executive director, establishing an MLBPA office in New York City. The Philadelphia Phillies' star pitcher, Robin Roberts, and Tigers outfielder Harvey Kuenn had insisted such an office was required to "make it feasible for ball players to register their views and opinions on any matters pertaining to association policy of player welfare." Urged to do so by Scott, the players selected their new legal counsel, choosing Cannon, whose father had represented several of the Black Sox, including Buck Weaver and Shoeless Joe Jackson, in their futile requests to be readmitted to Organized Baseball.[16]

Throughout his service to the MLBPA, Cannon remained most devoted to what he considered the good of the game. His warm relationships with team owners, in fact, resulted in his name being tossed around as a possible commissioner. As baseball chronicler Brian McKenna notes, Cannon "never met an owner he didn't like." The owners in turn invited Cannon, who declared the reserve clause to be a "necessary evil," to meetings, a courtesy they had denied his predecessor. He urged players not to hire a lobbyist to argue their case before Congress or to "jeopardize the fine relationship existing between [them] and the club owners." Astonishingly, Cannon offered a thumbs-up when owners illicitly raided the pension plan of $167,400 for tax purposes. Ballplayers, boasting the world's finest pension plan, were so privileged they "don't know what to ask for next," he informed a congressional committee. Starting in 1959, two All-Star Games were played, with virtually all of the proceeds ending up in the pension fund, strengthening it considerably, leading Cannon to crow, "I don't think there ever has been a better feeling between the owners and the players. We are perfectly happy."[17]

◆   ◆   ◆

By the mid–60s, the minimum salary in MLB remained stuck at $7,000, while even the addition of four new teams had not pushed up pension benefits. Despite new 162-game regular seasons and territorial expansion, player salaries remained stagnant. Increased television revenues also greatly benefited team owners alone.[18]

The players, led by Robin Roberts and Jim Bunning, another longtime right-handed pitching ace, determined that a director and an attorney, both full-time, needed to be working on their behalf. Like many of the players, Roberts was particularly concerned about the pension fund, with the current plan slated to expire in early 1967. Joining them on a search committee were yet another right-handed starting pitcher, Bob Friend, and outfielder Harvey Kuehn. All, except for Bunning, were at the tail end of their playing careers, and Bunning was himself an 11-year veteran.[19]

Various possible executive directors were considered, among them Robert Cannon, Bob Feller, and Hank Greenberg. Also discussed was 48-year-old Marvin Miller, an economist with the United Steelworkers of America, whose headquarters could be found in Pittsburgh. Miller's name had been suggested to Roberts by Professor George Williams Taylor of the Wharton School of Finance. Taylor, who had chaired the War Labor Board for which Miller, a graduate of New York University in economics, worked during World War II, informed Miller that when asked about possibilities, "the first person I thought of was you." After his wartime service, Miller worked for the International Association of Machinists and the United Steelworkers of America. He became the latter union's lead economic adviser.

Marvin Miller (pictured here around 2000), serving as the MLBPA executive director, helped to make that union one of the strongest in the world, especially through the ushering in of free agency. (National Baseball Hall of Fame Library, Cooperstown, NY).

Miller knew, or soon discovered, that the minimum salary had barely budged for years and that the average salary was only $19,000. Only the game's brightest stars, a select few—Hank Greenberg, Ted Williams, Stan Musial, Joe DiMaggio, Willie Mays, and Mickey Mantle—had ascended to the $100,000 annual salary range. The players, Miller quickly determined, "had no rights."[20]

Over three hours, Miller met with three of the committee members—Friend wasn't present—in Cleveland just prior to Christmas Day 1965. In response to Miller's queries regarding working conditions, Bunning indicated that "playing fields and locker rooms were often lousy, even dangerous, the travel schedule brutal, and the season much too long." The pension fund was clearly foremost in the minds of the ballplayers, worried that the owners would discard the "60–40" arrangement that placed the bulk of All-Star Game and World Series radio and television proceeds into it. Already mulling over offers from Harvard and the Carnegie Endowment for International Peace, Miller listened to Roberts inform him, "If you are elected executive director … your general counsel will be Richard Nixon." Miller replied, "Sorry. It won't work." Looking displeased, Roberts asked, "Why not?" After a pause, Miller responded, "First off, Nixon is an owners' man" who had "no background whatsoever in representing employees and wouldn't know the difference between a pension plan and a pitcher's mound." Moreover, "he's going to run for president again."[21]

Although he left the meeting believing he had blown it, Miller maintained interest in the job. He wrote to Roberts, declaring, "I am impressed with the virtually perfect fit between your needs and my skills." He received a call from Roberts several days afterward asking about the possible appointment of Nixon as the MLBPA attorney. Questioned how strongly he was opposed to working with the former Republican presidential candidate, Miller responded, "Very." Roberts indicated that he still wanted to forward Miller's name and to "rethink this general counsel setup."[22]

The committee, goaded by Friend, recommended that Judge Cannon, who had recently almost been elected commissioner, be hired. Fortunately for major leaguers, Cannon didn't care to move to New York City from Milwaukee; he also demanded too much money. The owners agreed to pay a large portion of his salary—although this violated the 1947 Taft-Hartley Act—but Cannon, seeking to retain his judgeship and concerned about a pension, eventually declined the position as full-time executive director. Hedging his bets, Cannon hoped that the players would agree to his demands, but the players' executive committee withdrew its support.[23]

In a telephone conversation, Roberts sought to explain to Miller that the selection process was beginning anew. When Miller coldly declared, "I'm no longer a candidate," Roberts attempted to persuade him otherwise. Calling every day, Roberts maintained the pressure before finally asking, "Would it help if Friend called you himself?" Despite Miller's indicating "Probably not," he soon heard from Friend, who charged Cannon with having misled him. Within a couple of days, Miller returned the call to Friend and said, "If the players elect me, I'll accept the job."[24]

◆ ◆ ◆

As matters turned out, the exit of Cannon could not have been more fortuitous for big league ballplayers. They were about to be represented by a man who would become, inarguably, one of the most important figures in the history of the game. Nineteenth-century titans include William Hulbert, who helped to establish the National League in 1876; Albert Spalding, a former great player whose sporting goods company and world tour helped to spread the gospel of baseball; and the Englishman Henry Chadwick, who emigrated to the United States, where he created several of the game's most indelible statistics. Their younger contemporary, John Montgomery Ward, the star player-attorney, was instrumental in setting up the first strong union in major league baseball. Babe Ruth's slugging theatrics forever transformed major league baseball and helped to make it far more popular. His sometimes nemesis, Judge Kenesaw Mountain Landis, became the majors' first commissioner. Rube Foster, the legendary pitcher and manager in blackball, founded the Negro National League. Branch Rickey effectively created the farm system, later ushered in sabermetrics, and above all else, signed Jackie Robinson to a minor league contract, helping to break down the appalling color barrier. Robinson's brilliant play and unparalleled character, along with the stellar performance of other Negro League veterans, did still more to end Organized Baseball's own insidious brand of apartheid. Just young enough to have missed the Negro Leagues, Curt Flood became another pioneer, challenging the reserve clause at the expense of his own superb playing career.[25]

First the screening committee, then the Executive Committee, opted for Miller, with the contingency that a majority of the association's members agree to the selection. Miller started off with some disadvantages. He was not an attorney, unlike both Lewis and Cannon. He was a liberal Democrat, again unlike many players. He sported a mustache, which was becoming fashionable among younger men but not those of his own age. He was also a Jew from the Bronx in a time when very few of his religious brethren had entered the big leagues, although Hall of Fame inductee Hank Greenberg, former Cleveland home run champ Al Rosen, and the game's greatest pitcher at present, Sandy Koufax, had all excelled at Organized Baseball's highest levels.[26]

Ironically, major league owners might well have been able to squelch Miller's appointment if they had done their due diligence. According to Miller biographer Robert Burk, the man who soon headed the Players' Association had a decidedly left-wing background, including support for former vice-president Henry Wallace's quixotic third party presidential bid in 1948. The ability to redbait, particularly in a still decidedly conservative industry like major league baseball, had hardly fully diminished by the mid–60s. But MLB's representatives proved desultory in this moment as they did during so many of their labor battles with players, particularly those soon to involve Miller.[27]

Some reports did quickly emerge of Roberts and Bunning supposedly having railroaded the choice of Miller as MLBPA's executive director. One ballplayer charged, "Roberts knows he's nearing the end-of-the-line and he's trying to establish a full-time job for himself. He's selfish. Robin knows he can't handle Judge Cannon, so he's trying to ax the judge in favor of some union guy he can lead around by the nose." The player was accusing Roberts of plotting to replace Miller following the expiration of the new executive director's two-year contract.[28]

According to sportswriter Dick Kaegel, "loud-voice opposition" almost immediately sprang up against Miller, with many upset by his union ties and one player representative dismissing him as a "labor boss." Seeking to dispel such concerns, Miller informed *The Sporting News*, "The whole question of union is irrelevant. The players have had their own association for several years; the only change is the addition of a full-time administrator." He denied being a labor organizer, declaring himself "a professional economist with a background in pension plans and mediation," which, although Miller didn't express that openly, the MLBPA sorely required.[29]

Although he wasn't surprised by team owners vilifying him, Miller discovered that Judge Cannon had engaged in a scurrilous campaign of his own. Confronting that backdrop, Miller undertook an extended tour of most major league teams. According to him, the players' initial response proved "favorable," including among the Angels, who had previously exhibited staunch opposition. The Angels' catcher and player representative, Bob Rodgers, offered, "The club was very impressed by Miller and may have a change of heart." Regarding the tour itself, Miller insisted he was not "campaigning" for the position but had initiated it at the behest of player representatives and to allow him to meet ballplayers.[30]

Also confronting Miller was the anti-union mindset long cultivated by the owners and accepted by a large number of the players. "Players were not only ignorant about unions, they were positively hostile to the idea: They didn't know what a union was, but they knew they didn't want one. There was a reason for this attitude. From time immemorial, the baseball powers-that-be force-fed the players propaganda: The commissioner (although appointed and paid by the owners) represented the players; players were privileged to be paid to play a kid's game; and (the biggest fairy tale of all) baseball was not a business and, in any case, was unprofitable for the owners."[31]

Tim McCarver, at the time a young catcher with the St. Louis Cardinals, later acknowledged, "We were naïve. We had no idea about unions…. More than that, we had no idea of how powerful we were." As for himself, McCarver reflected, "I was stupid enough to swallow the idea once that 'I'd be taken care of.'" He came to appreciate, however, "there is no taking care of you."[32]

Speaking to the players forthrightly enabled Miller to begin to gather support. Recognizing that they were most concerned about the pension, he informed them, "I've been told that players feel that you have a great pension plan. I disagree." It was true that in certain regards "it was a landmark." But due to inflation, Miller said, "You are actually worse off in 1966 in terms of benefits than you were in 1947 when it was established." That drew attention.[33]

Continuing, Miller offered, "In determining the value of a pension plan you must project to when you are fifty, sixty, or older, when you will be drawing benefits. Unless a monthly retirement benefit is adjusted regularly to reflect higher living costs, it's unlike to be enough to buy a full tank of gas in thirty years."[34]

Having promised to field questions or listen to comments, Miller opened the floor but "an uneasy silence" followed. He affirmed, "This is your organization. I want you to feel free to ask anything you want." The fiery Jimmy Piersall asked if

Miller would call a strike, something the other ballplayers feared. Adopting baseball parlance, Miller replied by declaring that a player dissatisfied with a contractual offer could only resort to holding out, to withholding "his services." He then presented a query of his own. "What is a strike but a withholding of services?" However, Miller added, "*individual* holdouts are ignored and ineffective." As for strikes, they had to be employed "sometimes … but only as a *last* resort, much like going to war."[35]

Miller spoke still more openly.

I want you to understand that this is going to be an adversarial relationship. A union is not a social club. A union is a restraint on what an employer can otherwise do. If you expect the owners to like me, to praise me, to compliment me, you'll be disappointed. In fact, if I'm elected and you find the owners telling you what a great guy I am, fire me! Don't hesitate, because it can't be that way if your director is doing his job. The owners loved Judge Cannon. Don't make that same mistake with your new executive director.[36]

Whether ironically or fittingly, the controversy regarding Miller's appointment occurred while two of the game's top hurlers were engaged in a serious contractual dispute. The twin Los Angeles Dodgers aces, southpaw Sandy Koufax and right-hander Don Drysdale, were coming off the 1965 season when they led their team to the World Series championship, their second title in three years. Guiding Los Angeles to the NL pennant with a 97–65 win-loss record, Koufax grabbed his second Cy Young Award and his second pitching Triple Crown, winning 26 games while losing only eight, striking out a major league record 382 batters, and compiling a 2.04 ERA, taking that crown for the fourth straight year. Drysdale went 23–12 with a 2.77 ERA and 210 strikeouts, while tossing seven shutouts, one fewer than Koufax, and completing 20 games, seven fewer than Koufax. Koufax finished second in the NL MVP race, behind the Giants' Willie Mays, who smacked 52 homers, drove in 112 runs, batted .317, and slugged at a .645 clip.

With Koufax having made $85,000 for the 1965 season and Drysdale $5,000 less, both pitchers considered themselves underpaid. The great left-hander's salary battles with the Dodgers were not new and included bitter dealings during which Buzzie Bavasi, LA's general manager, threatened to slice his salary as much as he could, rather than accede to another $5,000. This followed a year—1963—during which Koufax went 25–5 with a 1.88 ERA and 306 strikeouts, all league-leading totals, topping all of that off with two brilliant winning performances against the Yankees in the World Series. One of those was a Game 1 outing during which Koufax whiffed 15 batters, a Series record. Due to his severely arthritic pitching arm, Koufax also recognized that his playing career was likely nearing an end, despite his having pitched at an historic level during the past four seasons. With Mays signed for $125,000 a year, the Dodgers offered Drysdale a $5,000 raise and Koufax another $15,000, which would bump him to $100,000.[37]

Displeased by the initial offers and determined not to allow the Dodgers to play one against the other, their top two pitchers elected to link up, seeking three-year contracts that would pay each $167,000 annually, a $1 million package. Only heightening the Dodgers' displeasure, Koufax and Drysdale, in all but unprecedented fashion, insisted that their agent would represent them. They supposedly explored other options, such as appearing in a movie and on a television program. In the end, the Dodgers signed Koufax to a $125,000 deal, placing him alongside Mays at the top of player salaries, while Drysdale received $110,000. Bavasi was less than thrilled, stating that the pitchers' holdout only succeeded because "one of the two was the greatest pitcher I've ever seen (and possibly the greatest anybody has ever seen)."[38]

Don Drysdale and Sandy Koufax, the two great Los Angeles Dodgers pitchers, threatened a two-man strike before the start of the 1966 major league season. Ca. 1966 (National Baseball Hall of Fame Library, Cooperstown, NY).

Most media members and much of the public sided against Koufax and Drysdale during their contractual dispute with the Dodgers. Murray Robinson of the *New York Journal-American* bitterly assailed their holding out, asserting that "the greed which has become the ruling passion of today's professional athlete never showed its ugliness more unpleasantly." Noting that he had always backed players in their clashes with owners, whom he accused of having "practically invented greed," Robinson now feared that the Dodgers' movie deal threatened to display "the modern star athlete's completely selfish attitude toward the very sport which has made him valuable to outside promoters."[39]

Sportswriter Jack Mann explored "The $1,000,000 Holdout" in the pages of *Sports Illustrated*. During the past three seasons, Koufax had compiled a .795 winning percentage, going 70–18, while Drysdale had won at a .571 clip, putting up a 60–45 record. Mann referred to the "outlandish, enormous" chance that "the most famous, highest-paid and greatest lefty-righty entry in" baseball history might sit on the sideline this season or permanently. He also appreciated that the Dodgers, sans the pair, were "virtually an un-team," having batted .245, the poorest mark for an NL pennant winner.[40]

Refusing to cast aspersions on the two Dodgers aces, Mann castigated the sport's "legal-fiscal structure" as "multifariously unfair for half a century." Perhaps "a shake of the foundation is in order." Koufax and Drysdale appeared to have considerable strength in their bargaining position, more even than "Ruth and Gehrig, Mize and Medwick, Hubbell and Ott" in days past. The Houston Astros alone would lose $200,000, Bill Giles, who shaped their public relations, admitted. But Walter O'Malley, the Dodgers owner, acknowledged receiving calls from other team leaders. "Nobody wants it to happen."[41]

After Koufax and Drysdale came to terms with the Dodgers, Bob Feller, who had once led the MLBPA, displayed no sympathy for his fellow pitchers. "They were putting on the squeeze and it looked like a union deal to me," Feller declared. "I'm all for a ball player getting what he can as an individual, but I don't go for this collective bargaining. Just imagine what would happen if a team's entire infield decided to hold out as a group."[42]

Notwithstanding Feller's criticisms of Koufax and Drysdale, their action, like the turn to Marvin Miller as executive director of the MLBPA, foreshadowed ever more contentious relationships between big leaguers and team owners.

6

Miller Time

THE MAY 28, 1966, EDITION OF *THE SPORTING NEWS* offered a lengthy article by Frederick Klein titled "No Nonsense and Fact-Packed—That's Miller." A steel executive who had often negotiated with him discussed Miller's approach and makeup: "Marvin is a non-nonsense guy. He does his homework and he knows how to present his facts. He listens and he expects to be listened to. At the same time, he's a gentleman. I've never seen him lose his temper or pound the table." As for the MLBPA itself, Miller contended it had never been run in a professional manner, lacking an office or a full-time employee. "With proper guidance and player support," he believed, nevertheless, that it possessed "great potential for improving the status of the players and the game generally." He hoped for "dignified and constructive" interactions with the owners, carried out in "a climate of mutual respect, with the full understanding that I am working for the players."[1]

First, Miller had to resolve various contractual issues of his own, including the length of his initial contract as MLBPA executive director, and to find an apartment in New York City, site of the Players Association's headquarters. Then, he had to contend with the stark reality that the Players Association had assets amounting to but $5,400, with players contributing $50 apiece in dues annually. Additionally, following Miller's selection, team owners backed out from their promise, however illegal it had been, to fund the executive director's salary and the Association to the tune of $150,000 yearly.[2]

Recognizing that the pension plan was contributory, the cost shared by players and team owners, Miller realized that the $344 payment by each athlete funded the Players Association. The owners agreed to finance the pension as Commissioner William Eckert informed Miller; only two players refused to participate. But Bowie Kuhn, who served as the NL's associate counsel, told him, "The 60–40 formula has been shelved." That was a reference to the divvying up of All-Star Game and World Series proceeds, which were mushrooming, from radio and television. Such a unilateral decision, Miller warned Eckert, would violate labor law.[3]

Even the 60–40 apportioning, Miller recognized, relied on the honesty of the owners, something the players could not take for granted. He told the player representatives, "What also must be understood is that the formula itself has large holes in it which could encourage fraud. In any case, what players are going to have to rely on is their own group strength to obtain adequate funds from the owners to finance a healthy and improving pension plan into the future."[4]

Miller finally received his contract from the player representatives, which offered him a $50,000 annual salary over a 30-month time span. "That's ample time for the players and myself to determine the wisdom of our mutual decision," Miller indicated. He also appointed Dick Moss, a graduate of Harvard Law who had served as associate general counsel at United Steelworkers of America, general counsel of the MLBPA, but only after meeting with Richard Nixon at Roberts's urging. He continued to encounter Bowie Kuhn, who served in his capacity first as assistant NL counsel and then as MLB's fifth commissioner. Kuhn, to put it mildly, hardly impressed Miller, particularly as he assisted the owners' ceaseless attempt to destroy or badly damage the MLBPA. Thanks to Miller and the players' unflagging support, those efforts proved futile, although at times injurious to the reputation of the Association and Organized Baseball as well.[5]

By August 1966, it was clear that the dealings between Miller and club owners would prove contentious. He accused them of greed, warning their hostility toward the Association "will make the players more militant against them." He was displeased about the owners' determination to discard the existing formula for funneling money into the pension fund, opting instead to deliver "a flat sum of $4 million" annually. Miller also indicated that the payment of Association dues by the players "will give us a much more militant organization which I think is fine."[6]

As the owners stretched out the time before automatic deductions of union dues would help to make the MLBPA solvent, Miller searched for another means to fund its operations. Beginning in late 1966, the union signed an agreement with Coca-Cola, which helped with short-term financing, and then Miller worked to establish a licensing agreement, apart from Major League Baseball, that proved highly beneficial to the players. The MLBPA's near impoverishment rapidly disappeared, thanks to the Coca-Cola deal and other commercial arrangements; it was soon comfortably in the black. Notwithstanding Miller's initial opposition, the Association agreed to accept a $4.1 million pension contribution from team owners in lieu of the 60–40 split for TV and radio revenue. The Association also pushed for a $10,000 minimum annual salary.[7]

In its February 12, 1967, edition, the *New York Times*' David R. Jones offered an analysis, "New Era Looms in Baseball Player-Club Relations." Jones opened with a quote from Marvin Miller: "This idea that a baseball player is a piece of property that can be owned, traded, sold or released, and that his only recourse is to take it or quit, has been accepted for too long." The MLBPA executive director declared, "Sooner or later the players will want to get into this question of whether they are someone's property, or whether they are not. When that happens, there will have to be some fundamental changes in the thinking of baseball club owners." During the interview with Jones, Miller also discussed the need for an impartial arbitrator to resolve player grievances, which presently were handled by the commissioner. Asked about resorting to a strike to accomplish the Association's demands, Miller admitted to not having a full sense of how militant the players were.[8]

In his column in the *Washington Post*, Red Smith explained that Miller was already transforming the MLBPA from "a company union" into a genuine one. To the famed columnist, Miller appeared "an eminently reasonable man," who was already winning the respect of team owners. Eventually, Smith warned, "the great bugaboo, the reserve clause," would have to be addressed. A ballclub, he wrote, needed "to protect its investment, but it doesn't have to be an out-and-out slave trade." Owners must "recognize the players as partners in their business, not livestock to be bartered." Smith predicted, "The change of view will come hard."[9]

During the spring, team owners established the Players Relations Committee to tackle labor matters, selecting John Gaherin, a top negotiator for the New York Newspaper Publishers Association, to contend with Miller. While sports historian Charles P. Korr suggests that a mutually respectful relationship developed between the two men, Gaherin believed his adversary "intended to destroy the whole goddamned temple that I was paid to hold up." In Korr's estimation, Miller considered Organized Baseball's entire makeup to be "evil."[10]

Buzzie Bavasi, the Dodger executive forced to handle the holdouts by Koufax and Drysdale, also considered Miller to be a formidable foe: "Marvin may be a no-good son of a bitch to a lot of people … and there were lots of times I wanted to knock him on his ass." And yet, Bavasi admitted, "he never lied to me and I don't think to anyone else." Importantly too, from the start, the MLBPA boss understood the problems ballplayers faced, "and they followed him…. He guided them where they wanted to go."[11]

Tim McCarver, a longtime catcher and later television broadcaster, explained how Miller dealt with the players. "The most remarkable thing to me, looking back, is what a patient man Marvin Miller was," McCarver indicated. Understanding "how disparate his knowledge of" labor negotiating was from that of the players, he strove to school the player representatives, who in turn "educated the rest." This proved to be "a very slow, methodical process." Miller was fortunate that the MLBPA leaders were among "the best, the brightest, and the stars." They eventually included Don Baylor, Jim Bunning, Reggie Jackson, Mike Marshall, Brooks Robinson, Tom Seaver, Ted Simmons, and McCarver himself.[12]

With club owners meeting in early August, Leonard Koppett discussed a change in player attitudes regarding contractual matters. The players demanded they be included in genuine collective bargaining talks. "Historically," Koppett wrote, baseball tycoons had responded to any collective action by players "with intransigence." Should that happen again, he warned, "a chain of trouble will begin." The major change at work, Koppett noted was the involvement of "a full-time, salaried professional labor negotiator." Also different was the unity being displayed by the players.[13]

The changing nature of management-player relations became increasingly apparent. In a column dated January 18, 1968, Robert Lipsyte of the *New York Times* opened his opinion piece, drawing on language from *The Communist Manifesto*, penned 100 years earlier. "A specter is haunting the capitals of sport—the specter of unionism." He then wrote, "Athletes are groping seriously toward some kind of representation more effective than the present players' association." According to Lipsyte, Miller pointed to "three basic areas of common interest" for baseball players. Legislation was required to overcome baseball's antitrust exemption. Players needed to counter the "inaccurate" images regarding athletes and unionization. Television proceeds needed to be apportioned much more equitably.[14]

Lipsyte recognized that the individual owners and players were both similar and dissimilar to those who came before them. He saw many of the former as "holdovers from another era" due to their "frontier spirits," particularly those with "family-owned clubs" purchased some time ago. The players on the other hand, were "quite different from their forebears," having close relatives who belonged to unions, viewing the labor movement favorably, and becoming influenced "by the personal militancy of the times." Those athletes loved the sport but refused "to play for love alone."[15]

A short time afterward, near the end of February, team owners and ballplayers agreed to the first collective bargaining agreement in the history of American professional sports. Miller recognized that this was a "landmark" settlement. The Basic Agreement, which helped to legitimize the MLBPA, resulted in an increase in the major league minimum salary from $7,000 to $10,000, and reduced the maximum salary cut to 20 percent. Players who were released got 30 days' pay. Spring training weekly stipends went up to $40; they had been stuck at $25 since 1947. Daily allowances increased by three dollars to $15. Players were entitled to first-class travel and hotel accommodations. The agreement also established a grievance arbitration procedure to tackle labor disputes; Commissioner Eckert served as the final arbiter. And owners and players agreed to set up a study group to explore possible changes to the reserve clause.[16]

Although the initial pension plan Miller helped to negotiate was due to expire in March of the following year, the collective bargaining agreement led to the owners' contribution increasing from $4.1 million to $5.45 million annually. Also, the eligibility for player pensions was reduced from five to four years.[17]

Finally, MLB's initial CBA prevented owners from doing what they long had: unilaterally effecting whatever changes they chose to without input from the players. Any such alterations in the future would necessitate collective bargaining. Thus, it's not unreasonable to suggest this agreement amounted to MLB's Magna Carta regarding rights for ballplayers.[18]

Steadily looming over discussions between players and management was the threat of a strike, the possibility of which Miller dangled at not infrequent moments. Helpful in that regard was the support of several leading stars, including Bob Gibson, Al Kaline, Mickey Mantle, and Willie Mays. By late 1968, for instance, headlines warned, "Baseball Strike Moves Nearer." Players, led by a number of the game's

finest, delivered a statement before spring training camps were to open, urging players not to "sign individual salary contracts" or to report to those sites "until the
negotiations are satisfactorily concluded." Miller indicated, "If there is a ray of hope
that there will be a ball season this year, it is coming from the owners' recognition
that the players are sticking together." Fears arose of a "sitout." Players appeared
ready to boycott spring training. Both sides appeared unwilling to back off their
hardline stances. The owners often appeared determined to contest any demands
the MLBPA presented, while hoping that the union would fold. Paul Richards, the
Atlanta Braves' executive vice president, dismissively stated that Miller "speaks only
for a few rabble-rousers and greedy ball players." Finally, a compromise involving
a $5.45 million contribution to the pension fund for each of the next three years,
in addition to slicing qualifying time to four years, terminated talk of a strike in
February.[19]

"The next baseball storm," Leonard Koppett soon prophesied, could make
the recent battle regarding the pension fund seem "like the mildest of zephyrs." It
involved the game's "touchiest subject, the reserve clause." But the *Washington Post*'s
Bob Addie indicated later in the year that the players remained split about "the wisdom of attacking the time-honored reserve clause."[20]

◆ ◆ ◆

Curt Flood, the top-flight St. Louis Cardinals center fielder, challenged MLB's reserve clause
in federal courts. His unsuccessful effort nevertheless helped open the doors toward free
agency and the empowerment of major league players. Ca. 1967 (National Baseball Hall of
Fame Library, Cooperstown, NY).

In early 1970, Miller issued a memorandum to ballplayers, indicating that prolonged discussions regarding the reserve system had proven "fruitless." While the MLBPA had not called for an abolition of that system, it had sought changes which had been summarily rejected. Why? Because team owners desired "to inhibit competition by restricting a player to one market for his services during his entire career," Miller reasoned. He emphasized the lack of control players possessed regarding their livelihoods. The "fact that some players are 'treated well'" hardly mitigated "the lack of dignity in the relationship."[21]

One star player, Curt Flood, had begun to threaten the very foundations of major league baseball as it had operated for nearly a century. A veteran with 12 full seasons as the center fielder for the St. Louis Cardinals, including three pennant winners, Flood was a three-time All-Star, who batted over .300 six times and twice compiled over 200 hits. But following the 1969 campaign, for which he won his seventh straight Gold Glove and hit .285, Flood was traded to the Philadelphia Phillies as part of a several-player deal.[22]

Refusing to accept the transaction, Flood spoke with his personal attorney regarding options. The aggrieved ballplayer also talked to Miller, indicating that he intended to sue MLB. Although not attempting to dissuade Flood, Miller informed him that "he didn't have a chance in hell of winning" due to "the courts' history of bias towards the owners and their monopoly." He also warned Flood that "even if he won, he'd never get anything out of it—he'd never get a job in baseball again." Undaunted, Flood questioned if a suit would assist his colleagues. Miller replied, "Yes, and those to come." Flood responded, "That's good enough for me." Miller retorted, "You're a union leader's dream."[23]

Influenced by an impassioned speech by the great Pirate hitter and outfielder Roberto Clemente, who hailed from Puerto Rico and was viewed by fellow Latino ballplayers as a role model, the MLBPA agreed to back Flood. Still, Miller warned Flood that even a legal victory could result in the end of his playing career. The suit would take time, which could itself rob Flood of his final playing days. He would also likely confront a blacklist for the owners were, Miller said, "a mean, vindictive bunch."[24]

Leonard Koppett, one of the nation's top sportswriters, spoke to Miller who helped the ballplayer obtain former Supreme Court Justice Arthur Goldberg as his attorney, regarding Flood's situation. "What would you think of a suit by Curt Flood challenging the reserve clause?" Miller asked. Koppett responded, "You'll lose in court. But by losing, you may really win in the long run, because the only way you'll ever weaken the reserve clause is by striking for it, and only after all your players are convinced that there's no other way will they be ready to do that. Losing in court may convince them, and once they prove they are willing and able to strike, I think they can get pretty much whatever they want by negotiation."[25]

Within a short while, Flood fired off a letter to baseball Commissioner Bowie Kuhn. He stated that as a 12-year MLB veteran, "I do not feel that I am a piece of property to be bought and sold irrespective of my wishes. I believe that any system which produces that result violates my basic rights as a citizen and is inconsistent with the laws of the United States and of the several states." While desiring to play ball in 1970, he felt entitled to field "offers from other clubs before making any decisions." Flood requested that Kuhn apprise all big league teams of his impending availability. In an interview that took place after he wrote to the commissioner, Flood listened as broadcaster Howard Cosell wondered how a $90,000 ballplayer could be enslaved. "A well-paid slave is nonetheless a slave," Flood answered.[26]

The MLBPA agreed to back Flood provided he would "fight to the finish," the Yankees' player representative Steve Hamilton offered. "We're not interest in helping Curt Flood make more money. We're interested in modifying the reserve clause." The union became "convinced of his dedication and agreed to help him." Hamilton explained, "We want a checks-and-balances thing" regarding when a player could achieve free agency. "We do think there is a time, 5 years, 10 years, or some point. That can be worked out."[27]

In March 1970, Flood declared, "I don't think that one of the 24 men (owners) in baseball will touch me with a 10-foot pole. In my own mind, I don't really expect to play again." Expecting his suit to take two years, at which point he would "be 34 by then and it would be very difficult to come back from that," Flood said. Believing his case would land in the U.S. Supreme Court, Flood refused to consider signing a contract containing the reserve clause. Flood's case, Marvin Miller agreed, involved a matter of principle. "In the final analysis," he said, "if you can't disagree with your employer and be able to tell him you are going to work elsewhere dignity is impossible."[28]

Red Smith foresaw Flood prevailing at lower court levels, compelling team owners and their attorneys to appreciate "that the reserve system cannot stand up in law." At that point, but not before, Organized Baseball would accept "the inevitable and frame a modified emancipation proclamation." Smith also recognized that players and owners were at odds regarding impartial arbitration.[29]

In his *Los Angeles Times'* column, Charles Maher criticized Bowie Kuhn's defense of the reserve system. The MLBPA, Maher noted, was backing Curt Flood but not seeking total free movement of players. They understood, he wrote, "such freedom would destroy the stability of the game." He quoted an earlier statement by the Association's executive director, Marvin Miller: "The reserve clause binds a player to a club for life. We are asking to discuss something less than life. We suggest that after a certain number of years a player could become a free agent. The number of years is negotiable."[30]

◆　◆　◆

Despite the predictions he had earlier delivered to Miller, Leonard Koppett never actually thought Flood would receive a trial, let alone have his case advance to the Supreme Court. But if that happened, he couldn't foresee the Court reaching "the same conclusion that made it ridiculous in the first place." He had believed that Congress would change various antitrust exemptions pertaining to sports of all kinds.[31]

None of that had occurred, and yet Koppett now predicted, "The Flood case will prove to be a turning point in the battle against the reserve clause, not a defeat." Already, it had educated both the players and the public about "the real issues and real alternatives," and it had compelled the team bosses to offer to negotiate about the reserve clause. This only became possible, Koppett noted, due to the Flood case.[32]

The trial began in the Federal Court in New York City, where, on May 19, 1970, Judge Irving Ben Cooper presided with no jury present. Sitting at the table for Flood, Arthur Goldberg, and the ballplayer's personal attorney, Allan Zerman, were the MLBPA's Marvin Miller and Dick Moss. Following Flood's testimony, Miller spoke of the reserve system and his attempts to bring about a modification through negotiations.[33]

Although Flood had received little vocal support for his lawsuit from ballplayers—Hall of Famers Jackie Robinson and Hank Greenberg were notable exceptions—the closeness of the decision demonstrated that change was in the offing. Testifying during Flood's antitrust trail, held in Federal Court in New York City, Robinson declared, "Anything that is one-sided is wrong in America. The reserve clause is one-sided in favor of the owners and should be modified to give the player some control over his destiny." Absent such a modification, "I think you will have a serious strike by the players."[34]

A longtime club official, general manager, and team owner following his playing career, Greenberg pulled no punches. "The reserve clause is obsolete, antiquated and definitely needs change." Expressing his love for the game, Greenberg declared, "We need more harmonious relations between players and owners, and we need to repair baseball's image with the public." It was necessary "to abolish the existing reserve clause and work out a substitute." Conveying hope that moderation would prevail, Greenberg said, "I'd rather see the owners do it voluntarily than in court, but it has to be worked out somehow. I can't see anything detrimental happening to baseball without it."[35]

In his column for *The Sporting News*, Leonard Koppett assailed MLB's testimony during the Flood case. Terming it "a disaster," he commented on Bowie Kuhn's presentation, which established a pattern followed by virtually all defense witnesses. The reserve system should only be changed—and that was highly unlikely—through collective bargaining. "History" demonstrated that "chaos" ensued when no reserve system remained. Baseball's uniqueness included the massive costs of player development. In discussing possible changes, the sport's "integrity," "balance of competition," "workability," and "economic impact" had to be considered.[36]

In fact, Koppett indicated, the reserve system had hardly resulted in balance with the Yankees, Dodgers, Giants, and Cardinals winning almost two-thirds of the past 100 pennants. A player emancipated from the reserve clause could readily resign with his old team. Several means could be employed to stave off monopolization of the best players. Thus, Koppett concluded, "baseball's defense" presented "an image of self-righteous rigidity, clinging to the past, fearful of change, crying for special privileges, confessing weaknesses, spouting sophistry."[37]

A federal district court judge turned down Flood's request for an injunction designed to eradicate the reserve clause. Judge Irving Ben Cooper agreed that from the player's vantage point, the reserve clause did "deny him throughout his career freedom to choose his employer." Despite such an admission, Judge Cooper deemed the system "reasonable and necessary to preserve the integrity of the game, maintain balanced competition and fan interest, and encourage investment in the player development." The ruling, Marvin Miller stated, left determination of the reserve clause's validity to the U.S. Supreme Court.[38]

On June 19, 1972, the U.S. Supreme Court issued its narrowly decided—5–3—ruling in the case of *Curt Flood v. Bowie Kuhn*, et al. Issuing the majority opinion, Justice Harry Blackmun declared professional baseball to be a business engaged in interstate commerce. He also acknowledged that the exemption from antitrust legislation accorded Organized Baseball amounted to "an exception and an anomaly." Therefore, "*Federal Baseball* and *Toolson* have become an aberration confined to baseball." While others might deem that "unrealistic, inconsistent, or illogical ... the aberration is an established one." Then, Blackmun largely blamed Congress for having failed to rectify the situation.[39]

Both Justice William O. Douglas and Justice Thurgood Marshall delivered dissents, with Justice William Brennan concurring in each instance. Justice Douglas wrote, "Baseball is today big business that

Justice Harry Blackmun delivered the U.S. Supreme Court's 5–3 ruling in 1972 against Curt Flood, thereby seemingly sustaining MLB's reserve clause (Robert S. Oakes, January 26, 1976. Harry A. Blackmun Collection. Library of Congress Prints and Photographs Division, Washington, D.C.).

is packaged with beer ... broadcasting, and ... other industries. The beneficiaries of the Federal Baseball Club decision are not the Babe Ruths, Ty Cobbs, and Lou Gehrigs." Rather, "the owners, whose records many say reveal a proclivity for predatory practices, do not come to us with equities. The equities are with the victims of the reserve clause." Justice Marshall indicated, "To non-athletes it might appear that petitioner was virtually enslaved by the owners of major league baseball clubs who bartered among themselves for his services. But, athletes know that it was not servitude that bound petitioner to the club owners; it was the reserve system."[40]

Ballplayers and much of "the liberal segment of the press," sports columnist Merrell Whittlesey noted in *The Sporting News*, were hardly enthralled with the decision. The Cubs' player representative, pitcher Milt Pappas, denied that his colleagues were seeking "utter chaos" through the reserve clause's eradication. They sought instead "some freedom in negotiating" for veteran players. The Braves' player rep, pitcher Cecil Upshaw, sounded more mournful: "The purpose of the case was to decide whether this was legal or illegal under American law. It looks to me like someone failed to live up to his responsibility."[41]

Finding "no internal logic in the decision," Marvin Miller also defended Flood from criticism for the suit, some of it apparently emanating from players. He indicated they "likely will benefit in the long run through increased chances of successful negotiation on the reserve system." Miller went on to say, "The baseball player remains the lone pro athlete with no protection whatsoever if he finds himself working for an employer he considers unfair." Pro football, basketball, and hockey players, by contrast, had competing leagues that could vie for their services.[42]

Over the course of the next several years, the MLBPA, led by Marvin Miller and his successor Donald Fehr, brought about such change, although it hardly came easily and involved a series of unfortunate lockouts and long dreaded, much feared strikes. The pioneer, Curt Flood, who had briefly joined Washington during the 1971 season, appearing in only 13 games, never played in the major leagues again. He owned a bar in Majorca for a time, served for one year on the Athletics broadcasting team, got involved in a pair of baseball organizations, and painted. Afflicted with throat cancer, 59-year-old Curt Flood died on January 20, 1997, of complications caused by pneumonia. No matter how gradually but for far too long, his heroic, largely lonely stance received too little recognition.[43]

◆　◆　◆

A new three-year contract was agreed to on May 23, 1970, with the minimum salary going up to $12,000, then $12,750, and finally $13,500. Tackling the reserve clause was put on hold until the Flood case was resolved. An impartial arbiter was to handle "nuts and bolts" labor issues that didn't impact the integrity of the game; the commissioner remained the final arbiter of those that did. Severance pay and expense money became more generous. Players could employ agents to handle contract negotiations, as owners finally acknowledged.[44]

In early July 1971, the MLBPA filed charges with the National Labor Relations Board of unfair labor practices by the big league ballclubs, including their refusal to provide specific information about the latest television contract. Team owners, Marvin Miller maintained, behaved "arrogantly" and in a "challenging and insulting" fashion toward the players. "It is unfortunate that recent history has taught the club owners so little," Miller declared.[45]

Not disagreeing with Miller's assessment, Red Smith warned that the owners were telling the players, "It's none of their business." He wondered about the baseball bigwigs: "Do they have some kind of death wish? Do they set out deliberately to antagonize their players, to stir discontent, foment strife, invite strikes, just for the pleasure of making trouble for themselves and damaging their own business?"[46]

An impasse remained, which led to a 13-day strike that resulted in cancellation of 86 games at the start of the 1972 season. Rip Sewell, a Pirates' starting pitcher for about a decade beginning in 1939, slammed the ballplayers. "First the players wanted a hamburger and they (the owners) gave them a hamburger. Then they wanted a filet mignon and they gave them a filet mignon. Then they wanted the whole damn cow and now that they got the cow, they want a pasture to put him it. You just can't satisfy them and I have no sympathy for any of them."[47]

By contrast, Jackie Robinson backed the strike wholeheartedly. "I congratulate the players. It's high time they stood up in this manner. The owners are going to respect the ballplayers a little more." Because the average player's career was short-lived, "they want to get something so their future is secure."[48]

Sports Illustrated headlined its April 10 cover: "Baseball's Troubled Season." Inside that issue, William Leggett discussed the tumultuous nature of the national pastime. He opened with the defending World Series champion Pirates gathered in Pittsburgh's spring training clubhouse to decide whether to support "action" unless MLB bosses agreed "to sweeten an already fat pension plan." Pitcher Dave Giusti, the Pirates' team representative, responded to a query regarding why the meeting had been so lengthy. "The main problem I had was to tell some of the players how to spell the word strike." According to Leggett, the owners appeared "united and militant in their stand"; the ballplayers were united too. Team owners finally agreed to boost their funding of the pension plan to $5.95 million annually.[49]

The front-page of the *Washington Post* dated April 14 heralded "13-Day Baseball Strike Ends." The companion article referred to "the first general major league baseball strike in the nation's history." Commissioner Bowie Kuhn disclosed that none of the 86 canceled games would be played. Team owners also demanded that the ballplayers "not be paid for make-up games," something Marvin Miller indicated had never been requested. The shortened season, Miller proposed, might establish a pattern, one that players had long desired.[50]

Sportswriter Ron Rapoport spoke to David Feller, who taught law at the University of California and had served as the United Steelworkers of America general counsel when Miller was among its lead negotiators. Feller admitted to not always believing his former colleague's contention that the owners always made "the wrong choice." He instead anticipated a certain amount of rationality. He had been informed by Miller that the players were generally "conservative and independent, not at all collective-minded, and the last ones you'd think would call a strike." Their employers had managed to turn them into strikers. To Feller, the owners apparently had no conception of what they were facing or how to respond to the players. When the players did strike—and Miller knew how "to run a strike"—the owners attempted to destroy the MLBPA.[51]

Displaying perplexity, Miller quickly warned that another impasse threatened. To his amazement, the same issues—"the Basic Agreement, pension plan, reserve clause and a shorter season"—could foment "another dead end" if the owners failed to adopt a new approach to collective bargaining. "It's insane that all these subjects should come up for renewal and discussion at the same time, but that's the way the owners want it," he declared.[52] The failure to make up lost games led to an unequal number of appearances on playing fields in 1972. That in turn resulted in Detroit and Boston each losing 70 times, but the Tigers nipping the Red Sox by half a game in the AL East by having one more contest in the win column.[53]

As spring training was about to begin the following year, a 17-day lockout ended with another three-year contract concluded. That agreement boosted the minimum salary to $15,000 and then another $1,000 for the 1975 season. A salary arbitration procedure was established, to become effective after the 1973 season. Players who had a minimum of two years in the majors could participate. Owner contributions to the players' pension fund would reach $6.45 million in 1975.[54]

Following the resolution of the latest labor dispute, *Washington Post* sportswriter Dave Brady presented an opinion piece, "Curt Flood's Fight Was Not in Vain." The settlement, he wrote, was not lacking in "special irony for Curt Flood." One of the provisions allowed a 10-year player, five with the same team, a say in whether he would be traded. "That is roughly what Flood was demanding before he sacrificed his career" in conducting his legal fight, Brady wrote. "Flood himself was a martyr to his conviction that the reserve clause amounted to involuntary servitude, but now a seam has been opened for other players."[55]

7

Free Agency and Arbitration

EACH SPRING, MARVIN MILLER VISITED SPRING TRAINING CAMPS, talking up the MLBPA. One year, he went to the San Francisco Giants' site in Phoenix, Arizona. Viewing right fielder Bobby Bonds, "a really prime ballplayer" who possessed both power and speed in abundance, Miller was stunned to learn what Bonds made. Speaking to the players, Miller stated, "I want to tell you something. Take any one of you—take Bobby Bonds. I'm going to make a prediction." Then, Miller referred to Bobby's son Barry, whom he knew well and realized already "that he was something special." Miller said, "If we can get rid of the system as we now know it, then Bobby Bonds's son, if he makes it to the majors, will make more in one year than Bobby will in his whole career." That grabbed the players' attention.[1]

A series of events occurred before the CBA expired that transformed the game. Jim "Catfish" Hunter, the Oakland Athletics' star pitcher on three straight World Series championships, a 20-game winner in four consecutive years, and the soon-to-be Cy Young recipient, charged following the 1974 season that a contract breach made him a free agent. As required under a two-year contract agreed to with Hunter, the A's owner, Charles O. Finley, was to place half of the pitcher's $100,000 salary into an annuity with a specified insurance company. He had failed to do that. During the season, the MLBPA and Marvin Miller delivered warnings to Finley about the breach. Although Commissioner Kuhn subsequently refused to emancipate Hunter, MLB's arbiter, Peter Seitz, proclaimed him a free agent. A bidding war ensued, with Hunter signing with the Yankees, receiving a five-year deal worth $3.75 million.[2]

Montreal Expo southpaw pitcher Dave McNally, a four-time 20-game winner with the Baltimore Orioles, and Los Angeles Dodger righthander Andy Messersmith, a two-time 20-game winner, seemingly at the top of his game, proceeded to undertake the 1975 season without having signed contracts. They claimed to have played out their option year, thereby affording them free agency. Thus, they were more directly contesting the reserve clause, and, in contrast to Curt Flood, had the complete support of the MLBPA.[3]

On December 23, speaking in New York City, arbitrator Seitz sustained the Association's argument that the two pitchers were now free agents. He ruled against the owners' contention that a player's contract was unilaterally renewable for as long as a team desired. Instead, he upheld the MLBPA's argument that such a contract could not "be extended more than one year beyond its original expiration date." That effectively ended the reserve clause or the manner in which it had been interpreted by team owners for nearly a century.[4]

The outraged owners immediately fired Seitz, declaring they "no longer have confidence in the arbitrator's ability to understand the basic structure of organized baseball." In fact, that very structure was called into question more completely than ever. Wholly cognizant of that, the game's magnates planned to appeal Seitz's ruling. Nevertheless, both they and the players, sportswriter Ralph Ray indicated, soon appeared ready to discuss the reserve system and the soon-to-expire CBA.[5]

For now, the commissioner and team owners

Jim "Catfish" Hunter, Cy Young Award–winning pitcher with the Oakland Athletics, effectively became MLB's first prominent free agent, leading to a great increase in player salaries. Ca. 1973 (National Baseball Hall of Fame Library, Cooperstown, NY).

bemoaned what had transpired. Bowie Kuhn declared, "I am enormously disturbed by this arbitration decision. If this interpretation prevails, baseball's reserve system is eliminated by the stroke of a pen. That would be a disaster for the great majority of players, for the clubs and most of the fans." Joe Brown, general manager of the Pirates, asserted, "It's the worst thing to happen to baseball in a long time."[6]

Others pointed to the ruling as Marvin Miller's "biggest victory" as union chief. Miller himself warned, "Time is running out," referring to the latest bargaining for a new CBA. He hoped for "a more constructive attitude on the other side when" talks began again in early January. "I don't think it's becoming to see the commissioner and others wringing their hands just because what they had held basic for 100 years is no longer applicable." The ruling, Miller pointed out, only positioned baseball "closer to other team sports," with professional basketball, football, and hockey already having one-year options.[7]

When Seitz's ruling was quickly sustained by a federal appeals court, McNally proceeded to retire, which he had been planning to do. Messersmith signed a three-year contract with the Atlanta Braves for $1 million, blowing past the $90,000 salary he had previously received. It also easily surpassed the three-year, $540,000 deal offered by the Dodgers. American League president Lee MacPhail acknowledged, "It's incumbent upon us to sit down and try to work out an agreement on the reserve system that both players and owners can live with."[8]

As the arbitrator's ruling was being appealed, team owners responded defiantly, again locking players out of spring training. "What we have is an owners' strike," said Marvin Miller. "It is a strike against the fans and against the players and it is without justification." He warned that April 25 was the deadline. The players remained under contract to play, but if that became impossible due to the lockout then "each player has the right to demand to be paid on April 10." Unless payment were forthcoming within 10 days, "they are free. Either they will be paid, or the franchises will have no players." At that point, the ballplayers "could seek alternatives," including community ownership. Miller predicted, "I think there will be a baseball season, one way or another."[9]

Like the previous one, this lockout lasted 17 days before Commissioner Kuhn called for an opening of camps on March 18, then seemingly "went into hiding" before reappearing three days later only to state, "We do not have a final agreement." Contending with owners still determined to retain stringent controls over players, Miller thought the MLBPA's agreeing to cede court-won rights might induce liability on its and his part, while acknowledging such concerns could possibly be addressed. *Sports Illustrated* nevertheless cheered the announcement that the lockout was over through an article titled "At Last, Spring Is Sprung." With camps opening, it seemed as if labor acrimony had dissipated, Douglas S. Looney wrote. Yet he also indicated that neither side could "agree on what to do about the Big Bugaboo, the reserve clause."[10]

No cancellations occurred as players began the season without a new CBA. On July 12, 1976, a four-year deal was accepted by both team owners and players. It lifted the minimum salary to $21,000 by the 1978 season, and owners increased their payment to the pension fund to $8.3 million. Players with two years of service were again eligible for salary arbitration, while a five-year veteran could demand a trade. If such a trade were not forthcoming, the player became a free agent.[11]

Most significantly, this CBA allowed for players with six years in the big leagues to become free agents but also freed several players whose contracts for the 1976 season had been unilaterally renewed. Among the players set free were outfielder Reggie Jackson, recently traded from the A's to the Orioles, and two of his former Oakland teammates, outfielder Joe Rudi and pitchers Ken Holtzman and Rollie Fingers. Draft-choice compensation was afforded a team that lost a free agent.[12]

Marvin Miller declared, "I'm very happy over the settlement. Anytime a just and equitable settlement can be reached, I think it's a good thing." While Commissioner Kuhn termed the CBA "bold and imaginative," Oakland owner Charles Finley considered it "ridiculous" and said, "We've been hornswoggled." His St. Louis Cardinal counterpart, Gussie Busch, muttered, "We have been kicked in the teeth."

Pittsburgh's boss John Galbreath indicated his belief, "We can live with it." Several individuals from both camps referred to the deal as "experimental."[13]

Marvin Miller participated in one more CBA negotiation as the MLBPA's executive director, prior to his retirement. Those became heated as spring training began on March 4, 1980. The MPBLA's executive board voted unanimously to recommend that its members authorize a walkout by players on or following April 1. This was only the second time the union board had issued such a recommendation, having done so back in 1972. "We're getting our guns in position," declared Miller. He mentioned that negotiations had been deadlocked for 16 weeks. "We don't even know what management really wants yet. It's all been a stall." Miller complained, "In an era of unparalleled prosperity for baseball, there is no need for this confrontation."[14]

On March 27, MLB's lead negotiator, Ray Grebey, declared, "In an effort to continue the collective bargaining and to avoid the work stoppage threatened by the players' association, we have asked the mediation service to enter the bargaining." Explaining the owners' decision to resort to federal mediation, Grebey said, "There is no reason for a strike in the absence of a signed agreement, especially in the light of high player salaries and the increased benefits offered to the players in the current negotiations." After all, "in 1976, baseball was played half a season with no agreement. A settlement was reached without interruption of the season."[15]

Completing his latest tour of big-league camps, Miller spoke to the players about negotiations, receiving their virtually unanimous support for a strike if no deal had been obtained by April 1. The vote in favor was 971–1. Although not informed about the mediation service, Miller expressed no opposition but questioned what a mediator could do at this late date. "In fact, it is ludicrous. Federal mediation can be helpful as an aid to bargaining. It is not a substitute. I fear that the owners are leaning on it as a substitute."[16]

With the previous collective bargaining agreement having expired and a new one yet to be agreed to, players walked out during spring training on April 1. The eight-day strike ended, but threats of an in-season strike beginning on May 23 loomed. Angered by the players' cancellation of all exhibition contests, California Angels' owner Gene Autry threatened, "Frankly, if I had my say and the other owners agreed with me, I'd close down for the season. What's the sense of going out again? It's a waste of time, their time and a lot of money. There's no reason for it and I would just as soon forget the season."[17]

The *Washington Post*'s columnist Shirley Povich presented his own analysis of the owners' "unsinkable adversary": Marvin Miller. Under his watch, Povich noted, the players' average salary had gone from $16,000 to $121,000. The pension fund had mushroomed, enabling a former player, coach, and manager like Leo Durocher to pull down $23,000 annually.[18]

Also in the *Post*, staff writers Jane Leavy and Peter Mehlman delivered an article shortly before the strike-date deadline, "Witching Hour for Baseball Is Just Days Away." Cleverly, they began with the following observation: "Karl Marx probably did not have Jim Palmer and Reggie Jackson in mind when he went to bat for the proletariat." No matter, "a called strike three" would ring out absent a negotiated settlement between players and team owners. Drawing on baseball history, Leavy and Mehlman referred to John Montgomery Ward's stewardship of players walking away from the National League in 1890 and the more recent MLBPA's strike that began "on April Fool's Day." Once more, workers—the players—were uniting. Militant player representatives like Mark Belanger and Doug DeCinces, both Baltimore Orioles, were upset and frustrated, believing their employers desired a strike. Yet another Oriole, Rick Dempsey agreed. "It's almost as if they want it to happen."[19]

The MLBPA's Marvin Miller considered it ironic that "many people who are exploited in their own jobs are siding with the millionaire owners." As for Miller, Mike Littwin of the *Los Angeles Times* urged, "Believe [him] when he says something. He does not issue idle threats." This was a lesson that team owners had learned, no matter how slowly. By now, "they're come to respect him, or at least fear, him," Littwin wrote. He quoted Dodger outfielder Reggie Smith, who said, "Just look at all that Marvin has done for us. We don't follow Marvin like sheep, but I can't remember when he ever led us astray."[20]

Miller, Littwin indicated, might be soft-spoken but was "nevertheless hard." Yet he retained his cool. Discussing negotiating sessions, one player revealed, "I get so angry I'm about to go crazy, but there's Marvin cool and calm and in control." As for the owners, Miller believed they "want to go back in time," issuing proposals they had to know wouldn't be well-received.[21]

On May 23, team owners and players accepted a preliminary four-year package, with the issue of free agency postponed until the next year. The latest CBA raised the minimum salary to $30,000 and, following additional increases, to $35,000 in 1983. Players with two years of service retained the right to arbitration, and those with five years of service could again demand trades. Owner contributions to the pension plan went up to $15.5 million annually, and owners also increased player life insurance coverage.[22]

Ralph Ray, writing in *The Sporting News*, feared that the latest settlement "appeared to be more of an armed truce than a peace pact." Miller was said to be enraged by the owners' suggestion they could put in place "their latest compensation plan, as of next March" should no compensation plan be accepted. According to the agreement, Miller said, the owners could declare in mid–February their intention to enact "their compensation plan nine months later." As for the players, they possessed the right to inform management of their determination to "strike over the compensation issue no later than June 1." Charging management with operating in "bad faith and looking for trouble," Miller said the players would explore "the joint study of free agency in good faith."[23]

Chicago Sun-Times sports columnist Jerome Holtzman also discussed the owners' attitude regarding the latest CBA. He emphasized how readily the owners admitted that five of their own opposed the settlement, instead desiring to refuse to adhere to the just agreed to contract. This may have been designed, Holtzman suggested, to warn the MLBPA that various teams remained dissatisfied and the players should anticipate "a continuing hard-line stand on free agency compensation."[24]

The next February, the MLBPA's executive board targeted late May, well into the 1981 season, for a strike, as owners demanded compensation for free agent losses. Miller declared, "This time the gun is in the hands of the owners," who appeared to be "attempting to turn back the clock." Each time a labor controversy occurred, he stated, some people, including journalists, asked, "Well, what do the players want now?" He answered, "Nothing." The players were willing to maintain the reserve system as it presently existed. However, if the owners were to "pull the trigger," he said, "we reserved the right to shoot back. And we almost certainly will."[25]

As the possibility of a strike lengthened, Fred Rothenberg of the Associated Press commented that Miller, having "led baseball kicking and screaming into the 20th century," was ready to retire. But he refused to do so while the question of free-agent compensation remained unresolved. He would not leave the MLBPA as management sought to sharply restrict free-agent rights achieved through the arbitration decision involving Andy Messersmith and Dave McNally. Free agency had resulted in soaring player salaries. Thanks to Miller, players had also achieved pension increases, better working conditions, medical coverage, higher minimum salaries, and the right to pursue grievances. In contrast to when he first spoke to the players about heading their association, Miller, a "soft-spoken, patient" man but one with "an iron-fisted, strong-willed bargaining demeanor," had won "their fervent support." He was proudest of the fact that every player belongs to the association, which lacked compulsory membership.[26]

Later, the strike deadline was pushed back two weeks to June 12. On that date, another player strike was planned, but one that would be far more prolonged began. The New York Mets' player representative Rusty Staub confessed, "There is a total roadblock." The cover of the June 22 issue of *Sports Illustrated* displayed a glove with a ball inside, superimposed against a backdrop with a hazy but clearly empty stadium. The headline read, "STRIKE!" Below that, a subheading indicated, "The Walkout the Owners Provoked."[27]

Inside, Jerry Kirshenbaum's "Scoreboard" opened with a dig at "the lords of baseball," referring to the way the U.S. Supreme Court had treated them "as special characters." But they had also "been indulged by their players," Kirshenbaum insisted. Five years earlier, the players had relinquished, of their own accord, "their newly acquired freedom to sell their services to the highest bidder," something that most Americans were allowed. Still not satisfied, the owners demanded more in the way of compensation for free agents. The players' unwillingness to deliver "another whopping concession," Kirshenbaum wrote, resulted in the strike that halted the major league season.[28]

Jim Kaplan's "No Games Today" called this "a struggle in which the workers fought to preserve the status quo and avoid a strike, while the bosses sought radical change and courted a walkout." In the lead article for *Sports Illustrated*, Kaplan wrote, "The issue wasn't just high salaries; it was freedom." Cleveland Indian pitcher Bert Blyleven declared, "We have something we won in the courts and they're trying to take it away." While insisting they desired to maintain the game's "competitive balance," team owners were dismayed by the ever-escalating player salaries. In 1976, the average MLB player received just over $52,000; four years later, that figure had nearly tripled, approaching $144,000. Another year later, the average salary stood at around $175,000. Owners had proven unable to restrain themselves in bidding wars, probably due to concerns about antitrust legislation in addition to sheer competitiveness. And, obviously unable to best the MLBPA's top negotiator, owners depicted the strike "as the ultimate showdown with Miller" over "control of the game." But Miller, following owners' accusations he was preventing an agreement, allowed the Association counsel, Don Fehr, to replace him during negotiations.[29]

Wrapping up his essay, Kaplan wrote, "So there's your scenario for a prolonged strike. Marvin Miller, the man who taught baseball about collective bargaining, won't be at the table. And the owners he should be speaking to will remain in the dark. Play ball."[30]

By July 1, the *Washington Post*'s Jane Leavy was asking the question baseball fans dreaded: When to call off the season? Chicago White Sox owner Jerry Reinsdorf admitted to not knowing "what the cutoff is" but said, "once you get below 100 games, it is a flat-out farce. I'd personally be in favor of calling off the season." Oriole right fielder Ken Singleton appeared to agree: "Anything less than 100 games would be a shame." The MLBPA's general counsel, Donald Fehr, soon expressed his lack of confidence as well: "I am pretty close to being ready to believe that there will be no agreement this season." Near the end of the month, Marvin Miller charged, "I became convinced tonight that they [team owners] do not want a settlement."[31]

Acting unilaterally, the owners instituted a plan that required any team signing a free agent to relinquish both a draft pick and a roster player. Given the hardball tactics, it's hardly surprising that the strike lasted for virtually two full months, leading to "first half" and "second half" standings. That, unfortunately, led to the Cincinnati Reds, with the major's best overall record, 66–42, and the St. Louis Cardinals, with the East Division's top season-long mark, both missing the playoffs.[32]

On July 31, the strike officially ended, although the games did not resume until 10 days later. Writing on the front page of the *New York Times*, sports columnist Murray Chass noted that players had lost about $28 million in salaries, while teams had experienced $110 million in losses, with about $44 million of that covered by insurance. As Chass suggested, teams attempted to recoup some of their losses by splitting the abbreviated season in half, thereby added another round of playoff games. The Baltimore Orioles infielder Doug DeCinces, who served on the players' negotiating committee, optimistically stated, "I seriously doubt that the owners will try to challenge the players again."[33]

Also, in the *New York Times*, Jane Gross discussed the heavy financial repercussions experienced by the players, team owners, and major league communities. The majors' most financially successful franchise, the Los Angeles Dodgers, was out about "$7.6 million in ticket revenues and concessions alone." New York Yankee outfielder Dave Winfield, the top paid ballplayer, had lost nearly $400,000 in salary. Cities across the land had been hit hard, with reduced revenue in a variety of industries directly or indirectly related to major league baseball. Gross noted that there were adverse effects more difficult to measure—"the residual hard feelings felt by owners, players and fans."[34]

Yet another account in the nation's leading newspaper, this one by Al Harvin, featured comments by fans, some of them clearly disgruntled, others relieved that baseball would soon be back. An-ex cop, now retired, indicated he was not dismayed by the strike's cold-blooded nature. "I've always known that baseball is a business." He did indicate, "I'll tell you one thing. I think the players should have a Curt Flood Day when they come back because he made all of this possible for them and he gave up his whole career."[35]

Due to the agreement that enabled major league baseball to restart, with the loss of 713 games, a somewhat complicated system was enacted affording greater compensation for free agents ranked in a top tier. The loss of such players, for instance, required compensation in the form of both "professional players" and amateur draft choices; each team could protect only 24 players from throughout its organization.[36]

Most observers believed that neither side prevailed in the latest skirmish. The NL's pension representative, Montreal pitcher Steve Rogers, worried: "We gained little other than solidarity. We accepted to avert irreparable damage to the game." Kansas City star batter George Brett warned, "I think the fans will stay away. I would." But Marvin Miller predicted, "The owners won't underestimate the players anymore. That's probably the most important think to come out of the strike. If there was any victory, it was a victory for the spirit of the players."[37]

The following year, Marvin Miller's retirement as the MLBPA executive director became effective. During his 16-year tenure, Miller helped to reshape major league baseball inalterably. He empowered the players and helped to make the MLBPA into, as many called it, the most powerful union in the world, never having been bested by baseball commissioners, team owners, unsympathetic media figures, disgruntled fans, and the very occasional displeased ballplayer.

In Lee Lowenfish's estimation, the backing of major league baseball's top stars helped to explain much of Miller's success. St. Louis Cardinal catcher Ted Simmons referred to Miller as "essential." Roger Angell, author of numerous eloquent essays on baseball for *The New Yorker*, would seemingly prove more critical—although quite possibly tongue-in-cheek—of both the players, whom he argued were receiving "too much money for their own damned good," and Miller. "Look at the way they all vote one way as soon as Marvin Miller gives them his spiel. They're country boys and he's a fast-talking city slicker who can outsmart them all. Hell, he's outsmarted us, so far."[38]

Several years later, the author Malcolm Gladwell delivered a lengthy essay on "Marvin Miller's revolution" for *The New Yorker*. Through the mid–60s, baseball players, with few exceptions, were not terribly well paid. That began to change dramatically during Miller's stint as MLBPA executive director. He recast the Players Association, transforming it into a genuine union, one that became increasingly powerful in the very period when unionization was waning in the United States. In the process, he triumphed in the battle for television revenue, immeasurably boosted player pensions, compelled the owners to engage in collective bargaining, had salary disputes and various grievances resolved through arbitration, and won free agency for the players. He convinced players that the reserve clause reduced them into "pieces of property," stole "all their dignity as human beings," and ensured they lacked any effective bargaining power.[39]

None of that was easy, either the battles with team owners or educating players about their inherent worth as workers, no matter how unusually skilled, even gifted. To Gladwell, Miller's "great insight" involved carrying "trade unionism to the world of talent." By the end of his tenure as MLBPA boss, baseball revenues going to player salaries exploded from 10 percent to almost 50 percent. Moreover, in subsequent years, player minimum and average salaries would only continue to surge. So too would player-management squabbles.[40]

8

We're on Strike!
No, You're Locked Out!

MARVIN MILLER'S IMMEDIATE REPLACEMENT, KEN MOFFETT, lasted only 11 months on the job before being fired. The 50-year-old Moffett, who had unionism "ingrained" from family members who included a Molly Maguire and union leaders, graduated from the University of Maryland before becoming a union organizer. In 1961, he began a career with the Federal Mediation and Conciliation Service. As the FMCS's acting director, Moffett dealt with an array of labor conflicts, including ones involving air traffic controllers, postal workers, and ballplayers. In January 1982, he became the FMSC's director but was replaced by an appointee of the Reagan administration.

Highly regarded, Moffett helped resolve the lengthy 1981 strike in major league baseball. He was unanimously elected to fill Marvin Miller's shoes. Asked about "labor peace," which Commissioner Kuhn had recently suggested the need for, Moffett stated, "I'm all for it. I've spent the last 21 years of my life trying to foster labor peace. I like to think I'm pretty good at it. I just hope there is the same feeling on the other side, that the owners want to get along, that everything doesn't have to be a battle."[1]

Moffett's seeking "a more cooperative relationship with management" enraged his predecessor, who remained a consultant for the MLBPA. Moffett attributed his removal to an attempt to construct a "tough, impartial drug policy" in the midst of a drug scandal involving widespread cocaine usage by players. He also admitted, "I was trying to build a bridge to management. However, the union is determined to be confrontational on every issue. They're still back on a 1930s tack."[2]

Miller briefly served as the Association's executive director once again. Major league players soon selected 34-year-old Donald Fehr, an attorney who had helped the MLBPA when Dave McNally and Andy Messersmith were fighting for free agency. Fehr's parents, Irene Sylvia (née Gulko) and Louis Alvin Fehr, were both of German-Jewish ancestry. Donald attended Indiana University, where he belonged to a fraternity, before enrolling at the University of Missouri–Kansas City School of Law.[3]

Fehr worked side-by-side with Miller as an Association counsel, a job he was hired for in 1977. Thus, he was intimately involved during the negotiations pertaining to the 1981 strike. In fact, Fehr later indicated that he and Miller effectively ran "a two-man office" for over five years. But Miller elected not to influence the selection of his replacement, which Fehr deemed "a disaster" as no one knew what the position of executive director entailed like Miller did. As Fehr analyzed matters, "Marvin, for all intents and purposes, *created* the union. In a sense, he was the only one justified to say precisely what the job involved." Perhaps predictably, during Moffett's brief tenure, Miller became so displeased with attempts to restrict the advice he was giving to the MLBPA that he told Fehr, "I want nothing more to do with the Players Association."[4]

First holding the title of acting director of the Association, Fehr, aided by Associate General Counsel Gene Orza and special assistant Mark Belanger, the recently

retired Baltimore Orioles shortstop, negotiated the next CBA, a five-year package, for the MLBPA. Major league baseball was operating under a new commissioner, Peter Ueberroth, who had received plaudits for helping to orchestrate the 1984 Olympic Games in Los Angeles. Team owners, facing the possibility of a strike by umpires as postseason play loomed, unanimously elected Ueberroth commissioner. His arbitration was credited with staving off the threatened strike.[5]

No doubt pleasing to Miller was the agreement to discard the free agent draft, thereby enabling free agents to negotiate openly with any ballclubs they selected. Teams seeking to retain free agents had to allow them to engage in salary arbitration if they chose. Compensation of only amateur draftees remained. Earlier calls for "an average payroll plan" to cap salaries were eliminated, as was a plan

Don Fehr, who replaced Marvin Miller as the MLBPA executive director, led that organization for over a quarter of a century (1983–2009), helping players achieve ever greater salary and pension increases. Ca. 1991 (National Baseball Hall of Fame Library, Cooperstown, NY).

"to cap salary arbitration awards." Three years of service, not two, were now required for salary arbitration eligibility, something of a give-back or loss for the MLBPA, arguably its first real setback. But the minimum salary rose to $68,000 by 1989, players got more World Series money, and team owners agreed to pay $39 million annually into the pension fund, also by 1989. The two sides agreed to a joint committee that would explore means for handling drug or alcohol-related issues. The MLBPA retained the ability to contest disciplinary action for such offenses.[6]

Those negotiations, like earlier ones, hardly went smoothly, with a two-day strike taking place during the thick of divisional races, on August 6–7, 1985. The walkout revolved around both the pension fund, in the wake of a mammoth television contract major league baseball had inked, and a cap pertaining to salary arbitration. Neither side came away satisfied, but the owners and players agreed to make up the 25 games that had been cancelled. Murray Chass did note that the largest issue causing the 1981 strike, compensation involving professional ballplayers, was simply dropped.[7]

But all was hardly well with major league baseball. Notwithstanding profits which had tripled to $625 million in the eight years prior to the tenure of Commissioner Ueberroth, the demand for free agents began to slacken almost immediately after players and team owners agreed to the latest CBA. Players charged that team owners, led by Ueberroth, colluded to restrict free agent bidding following each of the 1985, 1986, and 1987 seasons. Ueberroth had indeed helped to orchestrate the collusion to keep costs down, notwithstanding soaring profits. They only continued to surge, thanks to massive television revenue. At the same time, players were experiencing tremendous salary growth due to both salary arbitration and free agency.[8]

Contending that owners were "damned dumb" in desiring a World Series title over profits, Ueberroth also pushed general managers to restrict long-term contracts. His imploring proved effective in the sense that fewer free agents were pursued, and at one stage, big league salaries actually dipped considerably. Star players like Detroit Tigers outfielder Kurt Gibson and Montreal outfielder Andre Dawson scarcely attracted nibbles from interested parties. That was particularly egregious in the case of former Rookie of the Year Dawson, a five-tool player with great power and speed. He was a four-time All-Star and two-time MVP runner-up. Dawson was also a six-time Gold Glover (given to the premier defensive player at each position in both the AL and the NL). And he was a three-time recipient of the Silver Slugger Award (given to the premier offensive player at each position in both the AL and the NL).

There were other excellent ballplayers, some award winners themselves, who seemed unable to attract suitors. New York Yankees pitcher Ron Guidry was a former Cy Young Award winner and a four-time All-Star, with five Gold Gloves and three 20-win seasons. Yankees knuckleballer Phil Niekro, a five-time All-Star, four-time Gold Glover, and five-time top six Cy Young Award competitor, had also won 20 games three times and was approaching 300 lifetime victories. Another three-time 20-game winner, four-time All-Star, and two-time Cy Young Award runner-up, Tommy John was also known for the reconstruction surgery that revitalized his pitching career.

Atlanta Braves third baseman Bob Horner, a bona fide slugger, was yet another former Rookie of the Year and All-Star. The Tigers' power-hitting catcher, Lance Parrish, had been selected to five straight All-Star teams and had won three Gold Gloves and five Silver Slugger awards. California Angels catcher Bob Boone had been named to four All-Star squads and won four Gold Gloves by 1986. Chicago White Sox catcher Carlton Fisk was a 10-time All-Star who had won a Rookie of the Year Award, a Gold Glove, and a pair of Silver Slugger awards. He had finished as high as third and fourth in MVP races. Yankees second baseman Willie Randolph was a four-time All-Star and former runner-up for the Rookie of the Year Award. Coming off a season in which he led the NL in batting and on-base percentage, outfielder Tim Raines had been chosen for six consecutive All-Star teams and had just been named a Silver Slugger.[9]

Not one of these players received offers of the kind that might have been expected. Some did attract interest initially, with the Yankees going after Fisk and the Royals reaching out to Gibson before pulling back. The mindset of the owners was captured by Lee MacPhail, as he prepared to end his term as head of MLB's Player Relations Committee:

> We must stop daydreaming that one free agent signing will bring a pennant. Somehow, we must get our operations back to the point where a normal year for the average team at least results in a break-even situation, so that clubs are not led to make rash moves in the vain hope that they might bring a pennant and a resulting change in their financial position. This requires resistance to fan and media pressure and is not easy. On the other hand, the future health and stability of our game depend on your response to these problems.[10]

The *Los Angeles Times*' Ross Newhan began a series of reports calling attention to the owners' failure to bid for free agents. Beginning in late 1985, he asserted that "the market" was "being picketed by" team owners, leading agents to charge that collusion was taking place. Los Angeles attorney-agent Tom Reich said, "I foresee a glut of unsigned and released players. There's [sic] serious war drums. It's hardball." Donald Fehr declared, "To say the least, the market is non-existent."[11]

Marvin Miller referred to the collusion regarding free agency as "the greatest scandal in baseball history." Team owners, operating at Ueberroth's behest, were clearly in violation of Article 18 of the CBA adopted 1976. It read, "The utilization of non-utilization of rights under [the free agency provision] is an individual matter to be determined solely by each Player and each Club for his or its own benefit. Players shall not act in concert with other Players and Clubs shall not act in concert with other Clubs." As the legal scholar and MLB arbitrator Roger I. Abrams notes, management, in 1976, requested the clause's inclusion amid negotiations to alter the reserve system following Andy Messersmith's receipt of free agency. Management also wanted to prevent a repeat of the Koufax-Drysdale holdout of a decade earlier. Issuing a demand of their own, the players insisted owners also not be allowed to collude.[12]

For three straight years, in February of 1985 and 1986 and January of 1987, the MLBPA filed grievance charges against team owners, regarding their failure to bid on free agents. The union's executive director, Donald Fehr, grumbled, "This is the arrogance of robber barons who say: 'We're rich guys. We have a monopoly. We can ignore the labor agreement you signed and you can't stop us.'" The initial pair of decisions by arbitrators Thomas Roberts and George Nicolau, handed down in September 1987 and August of the following year, was in favor of the players. Those cases and the next one came to be known as Collusion I, Collusion II, and Collusion III, respectively. Collusion I ended with seven players, including Kirk Gibson and Carlton Fisk, being named free agents yet again. They were also awarded "$10.5 million in back pay," the money considered to have been lost because of a rigged marketplace.[13]

Gibson's agent, Doug Baldwin, reported, "It opens up a lot of options for him. It gives him more flexibility. He doesn't want to make a sideshow of this. We're not going on a caravan. There are a few teams he'd like to talk to, especially in light of the trade talks involving him last December." Donald Fehr, the MLBPA executive director, termed the ruling "a good, solid first step," although he offered, "I'm disappointed we didn't get it for the other players, but I understand it."[14]

Prior to the 1988 season, Gibson signed a contract with the Los Angeles Dodgers. He immediately proved a sensation with the NL team, helping lead LA to the pennant. Then a badly injured Gibson limped to the plate in Game 1 of the World Series to face the Oakland Athletics' seemingly unhittable reliever, Dennis Eckersley, in the bottom of the ninth inning. This would be his lone appearance at bat during the World Series. With the Dodgers trailing, 4–3, and a man on second base, Gibson, having worked the count full after falling behind 0-and-2 and looking badly outmatched, golfed a slider, virtually one-handedly, into the right field stands. The improbable victory catapulted the Dodgers to the World Series championship. That fall, Gibson received word that he had been named NL MVP.[15]

In an exclusive interview conducted by *The Sporting News*' Dave Nightingale, Commissioner Ueberroth defiantly declared, "I still think each owner will do what he damned well pleases and, when people finally see that, the collusion talk will stop." He referred to earlier comments by players regarding their salaries such as "If they're dumb enough to pay us that much, then we'd be dumb not to accept." In Ueberroth's words, "now, some of those quotes are coming home to roost."[16]

Apparently unflappable until the end of his single term as MLB's top boss, Ueberroth appeared proud of his role in strengthening the game's financial makeup. While 21 teams were purportedly losing money when he began as commissioner, none were losing money only four years later. Television revenue alone doubled, giving each team almost $15 million annually, and licensing income related to merchandise tied to MLB had increased "16-fold." Furthermore, only one strike-day had occurred, drug cases seemed to have plummeted, ticket prices lagged behind inflation, attendance was exploding, and baseball finally appeared more attentive to the paucity of minorities in front offices.[17]

A master at working public relations, Ueberroth presented himself as not doing the bidding of the owners and as willing to laud the MLBPA, particularly in wrestling with the game's drug problems. However, the writer Daniel Okrent pointed to "two significant blots on Ueberroth's record," discussion of which angered him. He refused to acknowledge that collusion had occurred on his watch, although the player salary increases slowed "to their lowest rate in the free-agent era." During one year in which the commissioner insisted that collusion didn't take place, salaries actually decreased. The other criticism involved his supposed lack of a love of the game, which appeared more striking still in comparison to the reverence his successor, A. Bartlett Giamatti, clearly exuded.[18]

◆　◆　◆

With the collusion issue still unresolved, discussions regarding the next CBA proved far more contentious and culminated in another lengthy lockout. The eventual four-year agreement resulted in the minimum salary being lifted to $109,000 by 1992. Players again had to have three years of service to be eligible for salary arbitration, with the exception of the top 17 percent of ballplayers possessing two years of service having that opportunity, starting in 1991. Owners raised their contribution to the pension fund to $55 million yearly. Each side was allowed to opt out after three years of the contract.[19]

The immediate sticking points remained free agency and compensation for free agents. The Washington Post's Richard Justice wrote an article titled "For the Boys of Summer, It Looks Like Silent Spring." After meeting with ballplayers in Phoenix, Donald Fehr said, "They're getting a little more resentful and they're beginning to show a sign of anger." This time the owners refused to open spring training camps until the players agreed to revenue sharing. Fearing fixed salaries and a salary cap, the players opposed that idea. Although the owners avoided referring to a "lockout," that was precisely what they immediately accomplished. Following a meeting of the MLBPA's executive board, Fehr reported, "It's safe to say there's no sentiment among any of the players here that they should roll over and concede to the owners."[20]

In both Florida and Arizona, where spring training camps were situated, "everyone from peanut vendors to tourism officials winced at the bad news," said Sports Illustrated in a writeup titled "Victims of Greed." Team owners, economically fattened due to large profits, appeared little concerned about the huge financial impact on those two states, nonprofits, municipalities, and private businesses.[21]

A month later, Sports Illustrated contained a four-page photo essay of sorts, "Silent Spring." The first image was of an empty ballfield. The second had a sign, "Field Closed," and a small image with a billboard indicating "BASEBALL FANS ENDANGERED SPECIES." The next two showed players attempting to get into shape.[22]

On March 19, Commissioner Fay Vincent, while acknowledging that "damage has been done," announced that a new, four-year contract had been concluded, thereby ending the 32-day lockout of spring training camps. Those camps were to open the following day, with the initial exhibition games to be played on March 26. Deputy Commissioner Steve Greenberg, son of the great Hall of Fame slugger, expressed hope that a full 162-game schedule would be possible.[23]

Despite the extended lockout, the MLBPA executive director Donald Fehr stated at the conclusion of the latest negotiations, "There is a measurably lower degree of hostility" compared to the three earlier ones he had attended. Regarding Vincent's expressed hope that labor relations would improve under his watch, Fehr indicated, "The answer is yet to be told. After a passage of time under this agreement, under the administration we have in baseball now, if the players perceive an attitude of genuine respect and an effort to be fair, if there is respect[ing] the agreements that are made, then the respect will come back and be genuine. That remains to be seen. The effort will be made. We certainly hope it turns out that way."[24]

Oakland pitcher Scott Sanderson, who served on the MLBPA's negotiating committee, ended a news conference: "The players express their appreciation for Mr. Vincent and his part in all these negotiations and his respect for all the players and their respect for him." That might have been a fateful blessing for the new commissioner, who had replaced A. Bartlett Giamatti, the beloved but short-term head of major league baseball, the previous year. The former president of Yale University, Giamatti had become president of the National League before being unanimously elected commissioner, like his immediate predecessor Ueberroff. Beset by a gambling scandal involving Pete Rose, MLB's all-time hits leader, Giamatti succumbed to a fatal heart attack only five months into the job.[25]

In September of that year, arbitrator George Nicolau awarded players $102.5 million for lost salary related to the 1987 and 1988 campaigns covered in the case of Collusion II. It was estimated that about 300 ballplayers would be affected. Each team would be forced to pay around $4 million. MLBPA executive director Donald Fehr declared, "Protest as they will, the owners can no longer downplay either the significance or the effect of their intentionally wrongful conduct." He expressed uncertainty how much individual players would obtain or what type of allocation procedure would follow. "It will have to be done as part of an ongoing process," he said. "Some sort of procedure will be developed whereby individual claims will be asserted. We've had some discussion with the arbitrators, but nothing has been formalized."[26]

On December 5, MLB owners agreed to a $280 million payment to conclude the collusion cases. Only the Houston Astros' John McMullen voted against the deal. The agreement also granted free agency to 15 players, among them Detroit Tigers pitcher Jack Morris, Minnesota Twins third baseman Gary Gaetti, and San Diego Padres outfielder Jack Clark.[27]

Like Thomas Roberts earlier, Nicolau had determined that team owners were in violation of the CBA rule stating, "clubs shall not act in concert with other clubs."

Fehr emphasized, "This decision represents a substantial win for the players." He declared: "When coupled with arbitrator Tony Roberts's decision, total damages awarded to players in the collusion cases now stand at $113 million, and counting. There will be much more to come when the remaining damages are determined, including lost salary for the 1989 and '90, interest and other damages. Protest as they will, the owners can no longer downplay either the significance or the effect of their intentionally wrongful conduct."[28]

Even before Collusion III was fully resolved, major league teams engaged in a spending frenzy, bidding for free agents. In an article titled "What Price Success?," sportswriter Tim Kurkjian discussed the whopping sums doled out to players like NL batting champ Willie McGee, recently traded from the St. Louis Cardinals to the Oakland Athletics; New York Yankees reliever Dave Righetti; and Toronto Blue Jays left-handed starter Bud Black, with an 83–82 career mark; they were all signed by the San Francisco Giants for $10 million or more apiece. The total amount? $33 million. "The 1991 Giants are much more expensive," wrote Kurkjian. One pitcher with a lifetime .395 winning percentage, Matt Young, got a three-year, $6.35 million package from the Boston Red Sox. Giants general manager Al Rosen worried: "For 100 years, we've been trying to find a way to destroy this game, and we finally found the key."[29]

Refuting such a notion, Donald Fehr declared, "With all the collusion, the owners will get no sympathy from the players by complaining about hypothetical poverty." He also dismissed the notion that television ratings or revenue would continue to slip. "Why would anyone even assume that?"[30]

With the 1991 major league season fast approaching, the MLBPA was repeating what it had done just recently: building a strike fund for the players to draw from if "labor peace in baseball" vanished. The MLBPA's associate general counsel, Gene Orza, suggested such a nest egg made "it foolhardy for clubs not to engage in meaningful and appropriate negotiations." Meanwhile, the Association's executive director, Donald Fehr, having to contend with the handling of claims associated with the $280 million settlement, indicated, "It seems unspendable. But when you begin to divide it up, that changes pretty quickly." He foresaw as many as 800 ballplayers, including several who were retired, putting in claims. Ultimately, 843 players filed 3,173 claims totaling $1,321,948,295, leading to Fehr to exclaim, "It indicates the magnitude of the task we have ahead of us."[31]

◆ ◆ ◆

Fehr was compelled to endure inevitable comparisons with his predecessor. In mid–1991, Marvin Miller undoubtedly piqued more such analyses through the release of his largely autobiographical book, *A Whole Different Ball Game: The Sport and Business of Baseball*. An analysis in the *New York Times Book Review* opened by pointing to a 1983 book by the historian David Q. Voight that referred to Miller as "the liberator." Miller had converted "a ramshackle player's association … into

America's most successful union of the post–World War II era." While unionism in the United States was in full "retreat," Miller and major leaguers "were rewriting the rules of labor-management relations to their advantage," resulting in "enormous salaries." In the process, as Miller emphasizes over and over again, their union pushed baseball "to new heights of fan interest and profitability."[32]

The review referred to Miller as "the domineering union chief" but a "baseball rarity" as well, "a hardheaded statesman." Miller operated under the belief that large profits would benefit all concerned parties. Thus, he told Dodgers owner Walter O'Malley that profitable teams alone could "enrich the players." However, the review maintained, the owners failed to understand their adversary, angered by his determination to end the sport's paternalism. Consequently, they opposed collective bargaining and refused to consider any alterations of the reserve clause. That resulted in their losing "both the reserve system and their advantage at the bargaining table." They also piqued the "intensely personal fighting" that produced "the extreme adversarial relationship" shaping union-team owner relations.[33]

By the summer of 1991, the MLBPA was in far different shape than it had been a quarter of a century earlier when Miller became its executive director. One source of its financial well-being was through its administering of the vastly increasing royalties obtained by licensing "players' faces on products like trading cards, posters and board and video games," the journalist Richard Sandomir reported. During the past year and a half alone, that had amounted to $124.7 million. As Fehr noted, "The increased revenues simply track baseball's increased popularity," in addition to ending the monopoly on playing cards held by the Topps trading card company until a decade earlier. The MLBPA's executive board determined each year precisely how such royalties were passed along to ballplayers. One option, adopted recently, was to withhold a substantial sum as a lockout or strike was anticipated. The union had various expenses too, including costs incurred during negotiations and various salaries, including Fehr's now substantial one of $500,000 annually and Miller's $90,000 yearly pension.[34]

During spring training the next year, Fehr made the rounds of camps, warning players of what to expect from team owners over the course of the ensuing months. Their employers would likely revisit the year-old CBA in December, which either side was entitled to do. They would proceed to lock out spring training camps in February. Following his meetings with ballplayers, Fehr said, "It's almost a here-we-go-again thing. You don't take it as a certainty because a lot can happen between now and then, but at the moment, I assume they will re-open and I assume they will lock out." Fehr further explained, "They have clearly left the impression with the players that they intend to lock out. If they do, it'll be a long one so you have to prepare for it. You plan for the worst-case scenario."[35]

In addition to such developments, the MLBPA was continuing to amass its own large fund projected to reach $125 to $140 million. Owners indicated that discussion of a labor clash was premature. Milwaukee Brewers owner Bud Selig, who presided over the board of directors for the Player Relations Committee, which handled labor issues for the owners, offered, "We're a long way from making any of those decisions." Chicago White Sox owner Jerry Reinsdorf, who sat on the PRC, indicated that reopening was a distinct possibility. Should labor issues remain unresolved, Reinsdorf admitted, "a lockout is something that would have to be considered."[36]

9

The Adversaries

Donald Fehr vs. Bud Selig

THUS, LOOMING OVER THE UPCOMING SEASON were the labor wars that had long riven baseball, seldom more fiercely than during the past two decades. Two strong-willed men stood at the center of the latest labor battles: Donald Fehr, a baby boomer turned 46, who served as MLBPA's executive director, and Allan Huber "Bud" Selig, the soon-to-be 60-year-old acting commissioner of MLB.

Selig first landed on the pages of the *New York Times*, albeit hardly close to the front part of the sport section, through a small article, "Baseball Back at Milwaukee but It's Only Exhibition," as the 1967 season approached. An exhibition contest between the White Sox and the Twins was slated for County Stadium on July 24, reported Selig, head of the Milwaukee Brewers Baseball Club, Inc., which the *Times* noted "doesn't have a team." Following that year's World Series, the White Sox announced a plan to host nine regular-season contests and another exhibition game in what the *Times* referred to as "baseball-starved Milwaukee." Yet again, Selig was referred to, along with his baseball association.[1]

One week later, Selig again made national news. His group, the Milwaukee Brewers, had tendered an offer to the National League, promising an annual television contract of $1.1 million and stadium rent of $1 annually for 25 years, covering attendance up to a million patrons in return for a major league franchise. Milwaukee had lacked such a ballclub since the Braves moved to Atlanta after the 1965 season.[2]

Born in Milwaukee on July 30, 1934, Bud Selig was the child of Jewish immigrants, his father Ben from Romania and his mother Marie from Ukraine. While Marie became an elementary school teacher, Ben was a car salesman who later ran Wisconsin's largest Ford dealership. Bud was raised in a largely Jewish neighborhood on 52nd Street. After finishing at Washington High School of Information Technology, Bud attended the University of Wisconsin–Madison, majoring in history and political science. While in college, he attended the first games played by the Milwaukee Braves in County Stadium, 80 miles from Madison. After two years of service in the U.S. Army, he began working for his father, eventually succeeding him as head of a Ford dealership. Eventually, Selig began selling Chevies and operated a car-leasing enterprise.

Following the lead of his mother, who took him to Borchert Field to see the minor league Brewers or to Chicago to watch the White Sox, Bud Selig was an avid baseball fan. He began purchasing stock in the Milwaukee Braves franchise, then led a group of investors seeking a new franchise for the city in the wake of the team's relocation. After failing to acquire the Chicago White Sox, Selig's group, paying $10.8 million, purchased the financially flagging Seattle Pilots, who had lasted a mere year, shifting the team to Milwaukee.

After struggling for several early seasons, like most new major league teams, the Brewers became a force to be reckoned with in 1978, posting their first winning season with a 93–69 record, placing them in third place in the AL East, only six and a half games out of first. The next year saw the Brewers, who went 95–66, finish second, although eight games back. Another third-place finish was followed by the Brewers' first title in 1981, as they went 62–47 in winning the AL East before losing the AL Division Series in five games. Milwaukee (95–67) captured the pennant in 1982 but dropped the World Series in seven games to the St. Louis Cardinals. Loaded with power, the Brewers featured catcher Tim Simmons, first baseman Cecil Cooper, MVP shortstop Robin Yount, third baseman Paul Molitor, left fielder Ben Oglivie, and center fielder Gorman Thomas. The pitching staff was led by 18-game winner and Cy Young Award recipient Pete Vuckovich.

Over the next decade and longer, Milwaukee generally featured solid but non-competitive units. The two exceptions were in 1988, when the 87–75 Brewers finished fourth but only two games back, and four years later, when Milwaukee, at 92–70, finished second, four games behind. The 1993 season had been terribly disappointing as the Brewers fell to seventh place, 26 games back, winning only 69 games.

By that point, Selig had become a key figure within MLB ownership ranks. During 1990, in fact, his fellow owners turned to the Brewers' boss to help resolve yet another labor dispute, which had led to the seventh halting of major league games in 18 years. In February of that year, owners instituted a lockout, which all but precluded the holding of spring training. Controversy swirled around the Basic Agreement, a five-year contract that had recently expired.

Writing in the *Los Angeles Times*, Ross Newhan indicated that baseball's "health and stability" could "be measured in dollars—but not a lot of sense." The owners expected the upcoming season's revenues to be as high as $1.5 billion, while the players had salaries averaging "more than $600,000." In spite of all that, the former appeared beset by greed and the latter by hubris.[3]

Nevertheless, on the early morning of March 19, 1990, Commissioner Fay Vincent revealed an "agreement in principle" regarding a four-year labor contract, allowing for a start to the major league season on April 9, a few days after the scheduled date. American League president Bobby Brown also indicated that an abbreviated spring training would begin shortly. The greatest bone of contention, the *New York Times*' Murray Chass indicated, involved salary arbitration. That, even more than free agency, had resulted in the dramatic increase in player salaries, or so owners believed.[4]

As for the lockout, Selig explained, it had been "designed to produce an agreement before the season started. It was designed to prevent the interruption of the season, all the sadness of 1981, the heartache that we went through. It put pressure on both parties to get something done."[5]

To Richard Justice of the *Washington Post*, the latest "long, bitter labor dispute" came to a close as had the previous conflicts—those "in 1976, 1981 and 1985"—following the owners' inability to break the MLBPA. A recognition of that fact led to concessions and the eventual signing of a deal, despite the owners' also failing to get a desired revenue-sharing agreement. It was helpful, Justice believed, that Donald Fehr, the MLBPA head, and Commissioner Vincent, who had fully participated in the negotiations, got along well together. Sharing his thoughts about Vincent, Fehr revealed, "He was a refreshing change, and I can't say too much about it. Commissioners have a history of presenting themselves as something they're not. He made no pretense of

Fay Vincent, MLB's eighth commissioner, was ousted in a coup led by team owners Bud Selig of the Milwaukee Brewers and Jerry Reinsdorf of the Chicago White Sox. Ca. 1991 (National Baseball Hall of Fame Library, Cooperstown, NY).

who he represented, in addition to the fans and the best interests and all of that. Yes, I do like him." Deputy Commissioner Steve Greenberg went further: "To a person, there was tremendous respect for Fay and that's something you can't say of former commissioners."[6]

The following year, Vincent issued a policy indicating that "the possession, sale, or use of any illegal drug or controlled substance by Major League players and personnel is strictly prohibited.... This prohibition applies to all illegal drugs and controlled substances, including steroids." More happily, Vincent foresaw the further expansion of MLB, with the addition of franchises in Denver and Miami.[7]

◆ ◆ ◆

However, Vincent's tenure as commissioner remained

troubled until it ended just over halfway through his term. It had begun following the death by a sudden heart attack of A. Bartlett Giamatti, the former president of Yale University, who became MLB's seventh commissioner. Lacking Giamatti's appeal, Vincent never won the allegiance of team owners. This despite Vincent's having to contend with a massive earthquake that disrupted the 1989 World Series, labor strife, the percolating of drug issues, and George Steinbrenner's shenanigans. Vincent's banning of both drug-riddled Yankees reliever Steve Howe and Steinbrenner hardly endeared him to the Yankees "Boss."

The Philadelphia Phillies owner, Bill Giles, worried about the state of the game. "Things are in a mess right now. Baseball is kind of paralyzed. That's why I'm hoping we can convince [Vincent] to resign." The office of the commissioner, Donald Fehr remarked, was initially intended to safeguard the game's integrity, along with "the long-term interests of fans, players and management." To Fehr, it was "a unique post. Seventy years after Judge Landis started it, the owners appear ready to destroy it." Fehr's analysis was in line with Vincent's thinking, as the commissioner indicated in a letter to team owners. "The position is too important to baseball for me to abandon it by resigning," although doing so would save him a lot of grief.[8]

Refusing during the summer of 1992 to resign or to relinquish his right to participate in MLB's labor negotiations, Vincent received a vote of "no confidence" from 18 team owners on September 3, who demanded his resignation. His strongest opponents, believing Vincent didn't adopt a strong enough pro-owner stance during labor negotiations, included the Cubs' Stanton Cook, the White Sox's Jerry Reinsdorf, Milwaukee's Bud Selig, and Philadelphia's Bill Giles. Texas Rangers boss George W. Bush, Jr., a Vincent supporter, asserted, "We are dealing with a man, who is a man of principle and integrity. He's not going to leave, because he believes it is, not what's right for him, but what's right for baseball." The *New York Times'* Claire Smith also suggested that Vincent "will not die by his own hand," as a majority of owners desired.[9]

◆　◆　◆

While Vincent's fate as MLB commissioner was yet to be determined, Donald Fehr undertook yet another tour of major league teams. The players, as the *New York Times'* Murray Chass noted, had "a vested interest in" how the clash between the commissioner and team owners concluded. It might well affect the owners' decision to reopen the CBA and undertake a lockout when spring training was scheduled to begin. Chass wondered about the impact should the new commissioner operate in the manner of league presidents by acting "as the owners' high-paid messenger boy."[10]

Most team owners, Dave Kindred reported, no longer had faith in "Vincent's ability and/or willingness to do what they pay him to do." In the sportswriter's estimation, the owners had to "clean up the Vincent mess because they have a bigger mess coming out." Their determination to devise a new CBA led Donald Fehr to declare, "I have heard rumors that a significant number of owners want to try to break the union." Rumors had emerged that owners might shutter ballparks for the full 1993 season.[11]

Such talk certainly hindered the cultivating of necessary trust from fans. Kindred charged, "For a century, [team owners] have abused the naïve customer's trust. They have wanted the customer to believe players' greed would kill the game." But it was the owners who "conspired to commit what may be the greatest crime in the game's history": their collusion regarding free agents.[12]

Despite such analyses, Vincent submitted his resignation, effective immediately, on September 7. "A fight based solely on principle does not justify the disruption when there is not greater support among the ownership for my views," Vincent indicated in his letter to the owners.

> Litigation does nothing to address the serious problems of baseball. I cannot govern as commissioner without the consent of the owners to be governed. I do not believe that consent is now available to me.
>
> I can only hope owners will realize that a strong Commissioner, a person of experience and stature in the community, is integral to baseball. I hope they learn this lesson before too much damage is done to the game, to the players, umpires and others who work in the game, and most importantly, to the fans.[13]

The outgoing commissioner directed other barbs at his critics, indicating that some owners had desired that he relinquish "the responsibility to act in the 'best interests of baseball'" or "represent only owners, and … do their bidding in all matters." Refusing to operate in such a fashion, Vincent had agreed to serve as commissioner, believing the sport's top boss had "a higher duty" and "unique power" to uphold the integrity of the game. As for team owners, they held "a duty to take into consideration that they own a part of America's national pastime—in trust. This trust sometimes requires putting self-interest second."[14]

Even before Vincent tendered his resignation, Selig was being called "the only powerful owner in baseball," as Jerry Reinsdorf indicated. Selig, the White Sox chieftain noted, could collect the votes of other owners, perhaps because he was "one of the nicest guys in baseball" and remained in touch with his colleagues weekly.[15]

Several of Vincent's supporters among the team owners sang his praises, while bemoaning his departure. Texas Rangers owner George W. Bush declared, "If anybody can find any winner in this mess, it's my friend because he showed that among the rubble, there rose a dignified human being with a lot of class. He's clearly the winner as far as I'm concerned." Baltimore Orioles owner Eli Jacobs termed Vincent "an unselfish decision-maker, not once failing to act in the best interests of baseball." Houston Astros boss John McMullen viewed the now former commissioner as "personally ethical and correct."[16]

Major league ballplayers were uncertain about the impact of Vincent's ouster regarding labor relations. "There was a certain amount of resignation," Fehr revealed. "The sentiment is, 'They want another war again? Nice that they told us. Too bad. What can we do?'" Union officials warned players that if the owners reopened the CBA, then a lockout was apt to occur. "And if there is, it will likely be for a long time," Fehr noted. "So, as we have been, we assume it and we prepare for it."[17]

"The commissionership," Claire Smith declared, "is dead," leaving in its wake "an erupting volcano" amid "turbulent metamorphosis." The likely winners of this new state of affairs, she indicted, included team owners Reinsdorf, Selig, the Los Angeles Dodgers' Peter O'Malley, and the Tribune Company, in charge of the Chicago Cubs. They appeared to have attained what they sought. They grabbed "control of the game with the opposition badly outnumbered and all but silenced," along with a clear means to supplant the commissioner with "a chief executive officer … answerable … only to the owners."[18]

◆　◆　◆

On September 9, the major leagues' executive council unanimously selected Selig the council's chair. While lacking the title of commissioner, Selig was, "in effect, an interim commissioner," Murray Chass argued. The search for Vincent's replacement supposedly continued. But Selig had considerable support among the owners, including some of Vincent's backers. "A healing process" was necessary, the Boston Red Sox's Haywood Sullivan insisted. He revealed that Selig had "been given the authority to act on all matters." Selig, who already headed the owners' labor relations committee, expressed his determination "to lead by consensus."[19]

Claire Smith suggested that the 58-year-old-Selig, no matter his title, was now "in the hot seat." All his colleagues agreed that he would diligently strive to address the tasks at hand, while Smith referred to him as "the worker bee of owners." She also warned, "Failure to be perfect, failure to produce, failure to please all of the owners all of the time can be fatal in this day and age, in this game."[20]

Almost immediately, Chass and Smith predicted the owners were heading toward "a self-inflicted shutdown" for the following spring. A meeting of the owners led one participant to declare, "I'd be surprised if there isn't a lockout. No votes were taken, but they were certainly feisty enough about it." No decision regarding collective bargaining would be undertaken "for a while," Selig was quoted as indicating.[21]

Many club owners, Chass acknowledged, appeared desirous of acting before the present contract expired after the upcoming season. They wished, he wrote, "to, in their terms, take back control of the game from the players." The owners would be led by Selig, who had been named chair of the executive council, amounting to his selection as "the temporary replacement for the commissioner," Chass again contended. Selig also served as board chair of the PRC, represented the owners on an economic study committee, sat on the ownership committee, and headed the executive council, thus placing him in a position to shape the committee that would choose the next commissioner. He declined only to serve on the restricting committee that would explore possible alterations regarding that position.[22]

According to Smith, Selig was "the closest thing to a commissioner baseball has these days." But presently, he was befuddled, unable to understand why Vincent's ouster was seen as setting the stage, in a fashion desired by management, to compel "such a confrontation so as to shut down the game for a very long time." Expressing her obvious belief that the American public either didn't care any longer about baseball or was "so war-weary," Smith turned to Donald Fehr for his analysis. His clients, Fehr indicated, were not merely "wary" of the owners but hacked off, "angrier" than they had been since the spring 1990 lockout.[23]

As Fehr saw matters, the owners had demonstrated no intention of "doing anything except fighting a war for the sake of fighting a war, or reestablishing their prominence, of making clear their primacy." Consequently, they discarded Vincent and made "clear they have utter disdain for the public. And so, the next group they beat up upon is the players."[24]

Admitting that the commissioner may have been let go for other reasons, Fehr noted that the owners most desirous of Vincent's removal were "the people most interested in fighting a conflict with the players for purposes of fighting a conflict with the players. This way they have no one in position to interfere with that, to raise questions." Encouraged to do so by Selig and other owners, Vincent had helped to end the last lockout but then had riled the league presidents because of his negotiations with the umpires' union. Now Fehr worried that "the owners no longer perceive a difference between the P.R.C., the owners as a group, the executive council or Reinsdorf's living room."[25]

Newsday's Marty Noble also indicated that the owners were "ready for war." He quoted Fehr's analysis of the situation: "I just think it's interesting that no one on the ownership side is talking about—even remotely about—things like reconciliation and healing and trying to work out problems. They're just beating tom-toms. I know what that means. We'll do what we have to do. It's just sad that it's going this way again." Canadian journalist Craig Daniels wondered if Vincent had been canned "to prepare for an all-out war." Fehr certainly worried that the owners desired a lockout. "It's one thing to engage in a labor dispute because the circumstances require you to," he stated. "It's another thing to go in with your trumpets blaring, merely for the glory of the fight. And this one is for the glory of the fight."[26]

"Who was acting in the fans' best interests when the owners got rid of Fay Vincent?" the author and economist Andrew Zimbalist asked. "It was all done for the bottom line, like it always is in baseball. And you have to ask, how long can the sport go on like this? It's been five years since a World Series game was played in the afternoon. The old traditions are disappearing, and somewhere along the line you lose people."[27]

Writing in *Sports Illustrated*, Duncan Brantley discussed the owners' evident determination "to turn on the Players Association." They appeared desirous of terminating arbitration, thereby markedly reconfiguring baseball finances. Brantley also feared that the "newfound togetherness" of the owners, displayed in their unanimous backing of Selig as "quasi-commissioner," would enable the "ugly charade" to lead to "a negotiating charade" only to conclude with an impasse at the bargaining table and a lockout. The sportswriter recalled the greeting by Baltimore owner Edward Bennett Williams as Peter Ueberroth readied to attend his first meeting with team owners: "Welcome to the den of the village idiots."[28]

Ron Brown, who headed the Democratic National Committee, expressed no interest in the commissioner's job. His was among the most prominent names, which included that of former Secretary of State James Baker, bandied about by the news media.[29]

As the 1992 major league season wound to a close, another *New York Times* reporter, Ira Berkow, discussed Selig's interim appointment. Regarding the search for the new head of MLB, Berkow quoted Selig as indicating, "We should look at it not in terms of 1920, when the commissioner's role was first defined, with Judge Landis, but in the realities of 1992." What beckoned, Berkow indicated, was not the granting of "the broad powers" afforded Landis or those his successors, like Vincent, believed they possessed but actually didn't. What was clear to Berkow was that baseball's rulers would "not endure a new commissioner stepping on any of their toes."[30]

Refuting the notion that this made for difficult circumstances, Selig asserted that "plenty" of well-regarded individuals would become applicants. Looking to David Stern, the NBA commissioner, Selig indicated that "a strong ... imaginative" leader was required. "We've got to improve our game to make it more appealing." While attendance records had recently been set, television ratings had dipped, and a large majority of ball clubs ended up with deficits, or so Selig claimed.[31]

In his "Sports of the Times" column appearing in the Sunday, October 4, edition of America's foremost newspaper, Dave Anderson indicated that MLB's commissioner had been "lynched by a posse of club owners ... now ... thinking about locking the players out of Spring training, if not locking them out of the 1993 season." As commercial consideration enveloped the game, "Not many people will care," Anderson warned.[32]

His colleague Murray Chass hardly disagreed, worrying that as the World Series between the Braves and the Blue Jays wrapped up, "the business side of baseball's dual personality" would once more predominate, "coloring the public image of the game." He too feared that the owners might institute a lockout in the spring that could lead a cancellation of some "or all, of the 1993 season." Below the second and larger portion of Chass's essay was a poll, taken from responses to the question, "What is your favorite sport?" indicating that baseball stood a distant second to football, amassing less than half as much support.[33]

With the conclusion of the World Series, Glen Macnow of the *Philadelphia Inquirer* wrote, "The boys of summer wrapped things up last weekend. On deck: the fools of winter." Discussing the sport's "corporate season" with its "traditionally acrimonious contract negotiations," Macnow worried, "This off-season promises a nastiness not seen in years." Enraged by what they considered "a horrid escalation of salaries," team owners appeared ready for a lockout of spring training camps.

That, Macnow prophesied, might result in "no major-league baseball in 1993 at all." Such timing, in his estimation, couldn't be worse with attendance already down and "abysmal" television ratings.[34]

Donald Fehr acknowledged, "I really don't know what fans should think right now. I don't want to say that baseball will definitely shut down next year, but the odds greatly favor it. The owners seem hellbent on forcing a confrontation. These are not happy times for fans." White Sox owner Jerry Reinsdorf, one of the largely uncompromising owners, declared, "The way to get the players' union to move is by taking a position and telling them we're not going to play unless we make a deal. And we have to be prepared not to play for one or two years if it comes to that."

In early December, a delayed but much-anticipated economic report on baseball finally appeared. It called for players with three years of service to reach free agency, thus halving the time presently required. It also urged an augmenting of revenue sharing to help shore up more financially vulnerable teams. Operating revenues and expenses had both risen, but club projections seemingly portended major losses for the next two years. Neither Donald Fehr nor Bud Selig responded to the report's release, although the MLBPA head was said to be angered that it had been made public. Selig acknowledged, "It wasn't supposed to be out for a while." Both sides, he believed, needed time to explore it.[35]

Newsday's Marty Noble discussed the economic report. He quoted an NL general manager threatening, "Maybe we'll just kill player development." Explaining his rationale, the baseball executive said, "If we're going to make free agents of players with three years service, why bother developing talent? We'll never get to see our players realize their potential." A dissenting opinion by Henry J. Aaron, a Brookings Institute economist, offered another perspective, claiming that the report had been unable "to clarify the nature of the disputes between players and owners and fails to explain the structure underlying this unfortunate relationship."[36]

The report, Noble remarked, did goad both players and team owners to "arrest the decline and embitterment of baseball in American life." It suggested that a series of occurrences made a partnership between the two sides "more urgent and more possible than at any time in recent years." Those included the approaching end of the massive financial gains for owners and ballplayers characterizing the previous decade, possible reductions in revenue from national broadcasting, particular problems related to the more financially strapped teams, and acknowledgment by both owners and ballplayers "that something is amiss."[37]

Aaron obviously thought as much, asserting that Organized Baseball was "in political chaos, bereft of any governing mechanism by which clubs can agree to share revenues … in a fashion that will permit clubs both to compete equally on the field and to have an equal chance to make positive operating revenue." But Aaron also noted that a baseball study committee could not determine, simply through examining statistics, "the weight that owners attach to making profits, fielding winning teams and having fun." After all, "running a baseball club is probably more fun for most people than selling cars, beer or shipping services." Thus, "owners may be prepared to sacrifice profits or even pay for the pleasure of bearing losses."[38]

Coming on the heels of the announcement of the economic report, the owners, by the narrowest of margins, voted to reopen negotiations pertaining to the CBA, thereby threatening a delay to the start of the 1993 regular season. When asked if the 15–13 tabulation made any difference, Fehr replied, "I don't treat it with any particular significance." He did express concerns about hardline owners, a clear reference to Selig and Reinsdorf. As for the reopening of the labor contract, Fehr indicated, "The mere fact this step was taken makes a confrontation possible when it otherwise wouldn't have been."[39]

◆ ◆ ◆

As if enough drama was not taking place—over the course of three days, 35 free agents had signed contracts amounting to $225 million—the Senate Antitrust Subcommittee was looking into major league baseball's seven-decade-long antitrust exemption. Democratic senator Howard M. Metzenbaum from Ohio warned, "Congress is more serious about repealing the antitrust exemption or limiting it than it has ever been before in my recollection." The firing of Fay Vincent led Wyoming's Alan Simpson, a Republican, and Delaware's Joe Biden, a Democrat, to call for hearings, at which both Donald Fehr and Bud Selig were expected to testify.[40]

While Selig stated that MLB was operating in a more efficient manner than many believed, several members of Congress refuted that contention. Regarding the antitrust exemption, Senator Metzenbaum asserted that if it "does provide some benefits to the fans and the game, the owners are going to have to prove it." Referring to allegations that Cincinnati owner Marge Schott had tossed out racist and anti–Semitic verbiage and the threats of yet another lockout, Patrick J. Leahy, a Democratic senator from Vermont, declared, "Owners have a broader responsibility than treating baseball like an exclusive Rotisserie league."[41]

Fehr and Selig offered contrasting notions regarding hearings. The union head stated, "I would say that in the fifteen years I've been around baseball, this is by far the most pointed and serious inquiry about the way baseball governs itself. Unlike some of the other hearings, I sense that there is very deep and continuing interest in the matter." Discussing the recent refusal of MLB to allow the San Francisco Giants to relocate to Tampa-St. Petersburg, Selig said, "I can understand the heartbreak and sensitivity of the people" there but refused to promise the awarding of an expansion team in the not-too-distant future to that area.[42]

10

The State of the National Game

DEMOCRATIC SENATOR TIMOTHY E. WIRTH OF COLORADO, who both put together and headed the Senate Task Force on the Expansion of Major League Baseball, expressed his belief "that if the national pastime can't get its act together," Congress would respond. He worried that team owners, beset by the very kinds of changes they had long resisted, appeared ready for "a final confrontation with their own product—the players who make the game." That risked "alienating their market once and for all." Municipalities and whole areas witnessed "a valuable asset ... being torn down." Deeming baseball "an integral part of our heritage and therefore ... important to preserve," Senator Wirth believed that the antitrust exemption promoted restraint of trade.[1]

Sportswriter Tim Kurkjian wrote about hard economic times in major league baseball, with attendance having declined for all but eight of the 26 franchises in 1992. Reliever Steve Howe, despite having repeatedly violated MLB's drug policy and coming off a season when he threw only 22 innings, received a new two-year deal valued at $4.2 million, which amounted to "a 250% raise per year." Both CBS and ESPN eagerly awaited release from a four-year contract with the majors that cost $1.5 billion.[2]

Minnesota general manager Andy MacPhail, a third-generation front office executive, was also concerned about baseball's general well-being. "We're infecting the game with acrimony—and there's no reason for it. Someone has to take the first step. Someone has to have the courage to say, 'Hey, this is wrong.'" He explained, "What got us into this mess is all parties acting in their own self-interest. If we keep doing that, this game is going right down the toilet."[3]

All the squabbling by owners, players, agents, and the MLBPA, *Chicago Tribune* columnist Bob Verdi chided, wasn't "going to do it.... You're not going to destroy baseball. That might upset you, because you certainly are trying, but that's tough. You've caused those of us who love the game a lot of aggravation lately, so it's your turn to squirm." Verdi could foresee the bickering parties ushering in another lockout, thereby pushing the beginning of the upcoming season. Or they "may cancel the entire 1993 season. Maybe the 1994 and 1995 seasons, too."[4]

There was immediate damage being done. Presently, baseball felt "like fingernails on a chalkboard.... Baseball has shut out every kid who wants to watch the

World Series but can't because the damn games end at midnight for the sake of tele-vision ratings—which are terrible anyway. Baseball has lost the kid who wakes up on a sunny morning in July and wants to sit in the bleachers but can't because he has only a buck in his hand. And heaven forbid, if the kid can jam his way into the ball-park, that he asks for an autograph when one of those fat-head millionaires is in a bad mood."[5]

To Verdi, the recently ousted Fay Vincent was "the one guy … who wanted to start a dialogue toward peace." Instead, he "was thrown out of office so you all could keep fighting.… You're selfish and stubborn and greedy and arrogant, and we prob-ably helped make you that way. We'll give you that." In closing, Verdi wrote, "But that's all you get. Baseball is ours, and you can't have it."[6]

In mid–January 1993, Marty Noble analyzed the issue of arbitration, which team owners were determined to eradicate for their sport. That was both unlikely and would be insufficient, contended Richard Ravitch, MLB's lead negotiator and head of the Player Relations Committee. "The basic economic issues in baseball," he said, "require much more fundamental changes in the player compensation system." Noble suggested that a compromise, leading to revised arbitration, was essential. To date, while ballclubs, over 341 cases, had prevailed most of the time, the arbitrator had actually reduced a player's salary on only nine occasions.[7]

Disagreeing with the notion that big league teams were hurting financially, Donald Fehr stated, "This industry—if you look at the economic numbers—it's not in bad shape." He continued, "But if you listen to the whining and complaining and bickering and misery and if you look at how they try to do things and the abso-lute ineptitude they're brought to bear on all of this so far, it looks like a problem." Fehr pointing to the owners' disagreements about revenue sharing, their problems in negotiating a favorable national television deal, and their inability to handle Reds owner Marge Schott.[8]

Deputy Commissioner Steve Greenberg, formerly a player agent himself, recog-nized problems in the arbitration process. The "evidence" presented could result in a souring of player-team relationships. Arbitration forced teams "to say terrible things about players." Instead, he said, "We should market our players." Baseball needed "to take advantage of its resources—the players."[9]

With negotiations set to begin regarding a new CBA, management's labor representative, Richard Ravitch, declared, "I will recommend to the owners that under all circumstances baseball should be played in 1993." At the same time, he intended to request the MLBPA consider shortening the present contract by nearly two months to November 1, befitting economic circumstances. The union would likely not be amenable to such a proposition as the new date would allow teams, under various instances, to proclaim "an impasse … and unilaterally change terms and conditions … for 1994."[10]

Believing the owners would accept his recommendation, Ravitch mentioned having discussed the issue with Bud Selig, who "was agreeable to what I informed the players." On being informed that Donald Fehr was not recommending that the players accept a no-strike pledge, Ravitch stated, "What you just heard makes it clear that if there is a disruption, if the public is deprived of baseball in 1993, it will not because of the owners."[11]

On February 17, team owners unanimously agreed to link revenue sharing with a salary cap. "We're saying today there is linkage between these two things," Selig remarked to a group of journalists. "It's often said by the Players Association, let them solve their own problems first. Let them go to revenue sharing. The clubs took a step today to acknowledge there is a linkage." Admitting that "we don't have a specific plan," Selig added, "But I'd say it's more than philosophical."[12]

Responding skeptically, Fehr declared, "Just because they said so doesn't make it so." Speaking by telephone from his New York City office, he indicated, "Maybe one day they'll explain to us what the linkage is. I'm glad they did it; I'm sure they got an enhanced feeling of solidarity. I hope they feel better. But the real linkage is the big-market owners won't share with small-market owners unless the players give them back the money. That's the only linkage we've heard about."[13]

The March 8 issue of *Sports Illustrated* offered an extended treatment of Donald Fehr, perhaps aptly titled, "The Perfect Square." Writer E.M. Swift described a recent address by Fehr at the union's inaugural Comic Relief fund-raising dinner to assist low-income and homeless children nationwide. Following a brief, joke-free talk, Fehr departed the stage. Calling his subject "a private man, reclusive when possible, even antisocial," Swift wrote that Fehr, who regularly worked 55–70 hours weekly, would rather be alone on a beach reading non-sports related books. "The more you're around me, the more you'll find that 99 percent of the time I talk about things other than sports," Fehr disclosed.[14]

Bud Selig, the interim commissioner of major league baseball during the 1994 strike and lockout, and later longtime commissioner (1998–2015). Ca. 1991 (National Baseball Hall of Fame Library, Cooperstown, NY).

Notwithstanding his taciturn nature, Fehr, like Marvin Miller before him, had achieved major victories over baseball barons, including regarding mandatory drug tests and collusion. He had carved out deals with baseball-card companies that had seen revenues leap from $2 million annually in 1981 "to $70 million in '92." Free agency under his watch had seen the players' average salary surpass $1 million. Aiding him was his replicating of a pattern Miller had adopted. He responded to queries from journalists with one design in mind: "to inform, even persuade, the interviewer of the union's way of thinking." He also followed Miller in telling "the truth—always. You don't make up things. You don't chisel with the press. If you can't tell the press something, you say that." And like Miller, Fehr's devotion to the union was drawn from his progressive sensibilities.[15]

◆　◆　◆

The acclaimed writer Richard Ford, in an article in the *New York Times Magazine*, "Stop Blaming Baseball," opened with the statement, "Major League Baseball, whether we like it or not and, lo, for better or worse, has permanently changed." Among the unfavorable differences included the waning interest of young people, particularly those of color. Attendance was down. The most popular sports video lacked any connection to baseball. The heralded All-Star Game was rapidly being surpassed by the NBA's midseason extravaganza. National television broadcasts would likely become less frequent. "Baseball, always a rather delicate game of cyclical popularity," Ford wrote, "seems once again to be wearing rather thin."[16]

The author expressed uncertainty whether it was the nation or baseball itself that was to blame. As "America gradually became a country of litigation, investigation, contract disavowal, mortgaged futures and egregious excess," did "baseball just began to seem bland by comparison—a game like another?" Or did "baseball ... damage ... itself," become "its own enemy so that two decades of bad decisions, large and small, about playing surfaces, inhospitable parks, moronic mascots, players' strikes, owners' arrogance, hypocritical rule applications plus the rise of free agency over team loyalties, the persistence of systemic racism, all that and a good deal more?"[17]

During the early stages of the 1993 season, Murray Chass delivered a column, "Buy the Crackerjacks While It Lasts." Play on the baseball diamond, he worried, could be subsumed by "off-field elements ... 'The Commissioner,' 'Revenue Sharing,' 'Salary Cap,' and 'Strike/Lockout.'" Team owners had yet to pick the new man to lead MLB. They also had come to no agreement regarding revenue sharing, but without it, Richard Ravitch warned, the players would never accept a salary cap. Evidently, Ravitch's own attempts to reach out to players preparing for the regular season merely made Donald Fehr's job "easier." Influenced by Ravitch, owners didn't believe players would walk out during the season, owing in part to a perception that it would sully the union's reputation with the general public. Chass concluded, however, "The union's position is that public relations doesn't [*sic*] win negotiations. Players have always been better at knowing how to win than the owners."[18]

In a cover article for *Sports Illustrated*, Tom Verducci discussed a worrisome aspect of recent American popular culture related to baseball: the replacement of heroes like Joltin' Joe DiMaggio with "No Way Jose" Canseco. The piece opened with 12-year-old Buddy Selig discovering a hero in the Yankees' center fielder. Now MLB's "quasi commissioner," Selig was searching "for another hero," who could perform the feats Magic Johnson, Larry Bird, Michael Jordan, Patrick Ewing, and Charles Barkley had for the National Basketball Association. This was necessary because— and Verducci was playing on the ditty from Simon and Garfunkel's hit "Mrs. Robinson"—"Joltin' Joe has left and gone away."[19]

During the 1940s and 1950s, major league baseball featured "DiMaggio, Williams, Musial and Jackie Robinson," Selig said. By comparison, "Many of the best players in the game have tarnished reputations," Verducci noted. The Mets' slugging outfielder, Darryl Strawberry, was in a rehab center. Red Sox star pitcher Roger Clemens was a "lighted fuse." The powerful Athletics outfielder Jose Canseco had been busted for driving at 130 miles an hour and for packing a gun in his vehicle. Ken Griffey, Jr., seemingly refused to "run out ground balls." Barry Bonds, considered "his sport's best player," was also viewed as "too ornery." Fittingly, three issues later, *Sports Illustrated* featured Bonds on the cover, with the headline "I'm Barry Bonds, and You're Not."[20]

Verducci pointed to another area of concern for major league baseball. His article, "Have You Seen This Man?," explained Organized Baseball's difficulty in finding a new commissioner. The latest scuttlebutt touted Richard Thornburgh, former governor of Pennsylvania and current Attorney General of the United States. Other names bandied about included Lee Iacocca, a media favorite during his time as chairman of Chrysler, and General Colin L. Powell, chairman of the Joint Chiefs of Staff. One AL owner admitted, "There is no clear-cut front-runner." But the game's magnates were, Verducci said, seeking "the *perfect* commissioner."[21]

Search committee head Bill Bartholomay, who chaired the Atlanta Braves, indicated, "We need someone dedicated to the game, with no other agenda but to roll up his sleeves and get the job done. We need someone capable of expanding our game and bringing it into the 21st century. There's lot of room for expanding our game in foreign markets." Viewing that as a tad too ambitious, Verducci wondered "about first waking up the bored and disenfranchised fans right here at home."[22]

◆ ◆ ◆

The *Chicago Sun-Times*' Dave Van Dyck complained that baseball owners were concocting a new scheme "to bail them" out of the financial mess they were encountering. They intended to rearrange teams into three divisions in each league, with the winner in each, along with a wild-card team, participating in an expanded round of playoffs. Van Dyck preferred that they reduce both salaries and ticket prices. While baseball had given fans the movie, *Field of Dreams*, the owners, caring nothing about the sport's traditions, were selling "the Field of Schemes."[23]

That summer, nearly four months into the regular season, Murray Chass was again warning about the possibility of a strike. Concerned about the apparent stalling by owners regarding a new CBA, Donald Fehr informed players that their employers might be attempting to shape the timing of labor talks. "Regrettably, it is for this reason that players must now begin to consider a work stoppage late this season." Calling a strike a last option, the union head asked, "Do the owners put you in a position where that option is more viable than the others? You hope you never get there, but we'll have to see." Fehr worried that management's "behavior is certainly consistent with, if it is not in deliberate furtherance of, a strategy to delay the negotiations long enough to get past any possibility of a strike at the end of the 1993 season." At that point, ballclubs, Fehr remarked, could usher in a salary cap for the next year. "In effect, the owners would then dare the players to strike next year."[24]

Tensions between the MLBPA and baseball owners failed to abate, with the relationship of Donald Fehr and Richard Ravitch continuing to deteriorate. After Ravitch indicated that the owners would not lock out the players at any point in 1994 or unilaterally alter free-agency or salary-arbitration directives, Fehr stated, "That's the minimum they had to do." But he refuted the notion that it would stave off a strike. "I can't make that judgment. It has to be decided by the players."[25]

Sportswriter George Vecsey wrote, in early August, "What baseball needs right now is more Nolan Ryans and Robin Venturas and fewer Bud Seligs and Donald Fehrs and Richard Ravitches." Vecsey was referring to a recent dustup between the 46-year-old strikeout out king and the White Sox third baseman, angered after getting hit by Ryan's second pitch of the game. As Ventura raced to the mound, Ryan awaited him, quickly placing his much younger opponent in a headlock where he proceeded to pummel him. But Vecsey was also pointing to the possibility of a preemptive strike by the MLBPA the next month, which would outwit the owners, who were evidently plotting a lockout. "This would be dumb. This would be really dumb," wrote Vecsey.[26]

Instead, he argued, the players should comprehend that "they have the owners right where they want them—clueless and divided." Yes, baseball had both small-market and big-market teams. But Ravitch's revenue sharing was "not how these guys got rich in the first place." There was a difference too, Vecsey indicated. "Baseball is subsidized by the public, tolerated by good will, tax breaks, municipal stadiums, sweetheart contracts." Failing to appreciate this were the owners who possessed "the blood avarice and intelligence quotient of sharks. Or bulls." Major league ballplayers, for their part, "would be fools to strike," Vecsey contended. "Matadors do not strike. They wave their capes and let the bulls make the mistakes. Nolan Ryan could demonstrate."[27]

In early September, Donald Fehr sat down with John Rawlings for an interview about the state of the game, published in *The Sporting News*. When asked why players seemed opposed to another round of playoffs, Fehr indicated they held several concerns. They needed to be convinced that fans would support the additional games. Most were adamantly opposed to automatically having a pair of runner-up teams from each league make the playoffs, believing that would effectively negate the regular season. Fehr declared, "They want to be sure winning a division championship means something."[28]

Rawlings indicated that team owners considered the added playoffs economically necessary. Pushing back against that notion, Fehr explained, "The industry as a whole has no financial difficulty. There is plenty of money to go around." That would continue to be the case even if television revenue dropped. Ballclubs were generating greater revenues locally and setting attendance records. Although there might be individual teams having difficulties, overall, they were "well-managed and ... cater to fans well." He was skeptical of talk of financial problems, Fehr noted, because the union hadn't received "current financial numbers."[29]

The union remained troubled by continued talk of a linkage between revenue sharing and a salary cap. Sarcastically, Fehr stated, "Apparently, big clubs will share with little clubs, as long as the players repay to the big clubs what they lose." He indicated that if difficulties existed in the present revenue sharing setup, it should be changed. That, however, "has nothing to do with players," Fehr insisted.[30]

Rawlings referred to the owners' recent pledge not to lock out the players or make changes to the present CBA upon its expiration. That seemingly assured that the beginning of the 1994 regular season was not jeopardized. Fehr expressed doubt whether that was so, although admitting, "There is certainly no reason to consider any action this year." However, he emphasized, "What happens next year is too soon to say."[31]

"Life will go on" following baseball's realignment, *The Sporting News'* Peter Pascarelli prophesied. He considered 32 teams, allowing for 16 in each league, to be ideal. But should that happen, adding four additional expansion squads "would dilute the product." That in turn might enable "such sluggers as Juan Gonzales, Frank Thomas, Ken Griffey, Barry Bonds, and Albert Belle" to "push 60 home runs against the thinned-out pitching staffs."[32]

◆　◆　◆

Major league baseball actually appeared to be thriving, both on the playing field and at the box office. Attendance was suddenly up 22.5 percent in 1993, assisted by the addition of two expansion teams, the Colorado Rockies, on a pace to draw nearly five million fans, and the Florida Marlins. The Toronto Blue Jays seemed ready to shoot past the four-million mark for the third straight year. Five more teams would likely attract more than three million fans each, and no team would end up with fewer than one million fans.[33]

What Tim Kurkjian and *Sports Illustrated* called a "New Power Supply"—which Peter Pascarelli had also recently commented on—helped to explain some of the renewed and heightened fan interest. Young, dynamic sluggers were pounding balls over the fence in a manner that had often been absent for the past two decades or longer. While batting averages during the decade had eventually dropped precipitously, home run bashing had characterized the 1960s thanks to Harmon Killebrew, Willie McCovey, Mickey Mantle, Willie Mays, Henry Aaron, and many of the game's greatest all-time sluggers. The 1990s now threatened to become another era of prodigious power thanks to the likes of Juan Gonzalez, Albert Belle, Gary Sheffield, Frank Thomas, Mark McGwire, Jose Canseco, Matt Williams, Ken Griffey, Jr., and Barry Bonds. Besides McGwire and Canseco, the others had become, at least recently, relatively high average hitters.[34]

"There are lots of 'em, and they're going to be around a long time," said the Reds' outfielder, Kevin Mitchell, a former home run champ and MVP himself. "I love watching them bash." While referring to the Rangers' Juan Gonzalez as "the best of the new guys," Mitchell most admired the Mariners' Ken Griffey, Jr., "I've seen the man on the bench, in a tie game, say to me, 'Do you want me to hit a home run?' Then he does it." During spring training, Griffey told Mitchell, "The game is too easy for me, Mitch."[35]

"At Long Last, Game's the Thing" read the headline in the *Boston Globe* on September 10. "For the first time in 30 years," Peter Gammons wrote, "baseball has a generation of superstars who stagger the public imagination." He referred to Frank Thomas, Juan Gonzalez, and Junior Griffey, whom he referred to as "this generation's Willie Mays," among others. But Gammons cautioned that baseball remained in peril because "owners and players cannot agree on how the spoils should be divided." Fay Vincent had been dumped, Gammons asserted, "because he underestimated the acrimony between the haves and have-nots."[36]

◆　◆　◆

In addition to the power surge, baseball was blessed during the 1993 season with competitive races in all divisions until the final few weeks. Famed Detroit Tigers broadcaster Ernie Harwell said, "I've never seen a season like this, as far as the streak factor. It's been such a seesaw year for everybody. In our division, it's been a roller-coaster for everybody." Long-standing rivalries continued to attract interest. The Dodgers were scheduled to host the Giants for the last four games of the regular season, with San Francisco, led by Barry Bonds, nipping at the heels of the front-running Atlanta Braves.[37]

Mark Newman, a senior editor with *The Sporting News*, wrote about attendance records being set but also about a resurgence of offense, leading to talk about the balls being juiced. Both John Olerud and Andres Galarraga hovered around .400 at the plate before descending to the range of mere mortals, however superlative their seasons proved to be. The young slugger, Ken Griffey, Jr., tied Dale Long's nearly four-decade-long record of smashing homers in eight consecutive games. That record had been matched by Don Mattingly during the 1987 campaign.

The 1993 MLB season concluded as the previous one had, with the Toronto Blue Jays winning the World Series. The Blue Jays again finished first in the AL's East Division, this time with a 95–67 record, seven games ahead of the New York Yankees. The West was won by the Chicago White Sox, whose 94–58 mark put them eight games up on the Texas Rangers. Over in the senior circuit, the Philadelphia Phillies took the East Division, going 97–65, three games ahead of the Montreal Expos, while the Atlanta Braves, who had dropped the previous World Series, went 104–58, nipping the San Francisco Giants by one game to land atop the NL West.

All three postseason series went six games, with Toronto winning the American League championship series over Chicago and Philadelphia capturing the National League title by whipping Atlanta. The Blue Jays then bested the Phillies, twice beating their ace reliever, Mitch Williams, including in the finale on Joe Carter's three-run homer over the left field fence. This was only the second walk-off homer in World Series history, the first occurring in 1960 when Bill Mazeroski belted a home run off Ralph Terry in Game 7, enabling the Pirates to defeat the New York Yankees, who had been overwhelming favorites thanks to slugger Mickey Mantle and ace hurler Whitey Ford. The Pirates prevailed despite being outscored in the Series, 55–27, having lost games by 16–3, 10–0, and 12–0 counts but winning four times by a margin of seven runs altogether.[38]

With the Blue Jays repeating as titleholders, the 1993 season offered continuity, but change was in store as well. Heading Toronto's pennant drive was first baseman Olerud, who batted .363, rapped 54 doubles, and had a .478 on-base percentage, top marks in the AL. Sixteen-year veteran Paul Molitor, who signed with the Blue Jays as a free agent during the off-season and led the AL with 211 hits while batting .332, was the Most Valuable Player in the World Series, hitting .500 with a pair of homers and eight RBI. CBS's Andrea Joyce was the first woman to serve as host, alongside Pat O'Brien, of a World Series broadcast.

Carlton Fisk of the Chicago White Sox played in his 2,226th game as a catcher, breaking Bob Boone's record. Sparky Anderson's Detroit Tigers (85–77) finished tied with third in the AL East, which turned out to be the venerable manager's last winning campaign. After four straight losing seasons, the New York Yankees, under manager Buck Showalter, displayed promise, although like the Tigers, they did so by relying largely on veteran talent. New York made key acquisitions, snaring right fielder Paul O'Neill in a trade and starting pitcher Jimmy Key through free agency.

Yankees general partner George Steinbrenner was permitted to resume his duties with the team following a suspension due to shady operations involving a gambler. On the other hand, Cincinnati Reds owner Marge Schott got banned for a full season following complaints about her use of racial and ethnic slurs. Slamming team owners for engaging in discriminatory practices, civil rights leader Jesse Jackson threatened a boycott unless MLB devised a plan to place more minorities in front-office positions.

In the National League, the Montreal Expos, led by manager Felipe Alou, built on an impressive second half during the previous season, putting together their second-best record in franchise history. The NL West featured the year's top divisional race with the Braves, having picked up first baseman Fred McGriff and starring pitchers Greg Maddux and Tom Glavine, barely coming out ahead of the Giants, who had signed MLB's top free agent, outfielder Barry Bonds. Free agency decimated the Pirates, who also lost outfielder Bobby Bonilla and their top pitcher, Doug Drabek. A 12–1 blowout loss in the season finale left San Francisco a win short, notwithstanding Bonds's heroics. Bonds hit 46 homers, produced 365 total bases, drove in 123 runs, and had a .677 slugging average, all league bests, while hitting a then career-best .336.

MLB determined to expand the playoffs, splitting each league into three divisions and adding a playoff round that would display a pair of wild-card teams; the recent exclusion of the 103-win Giants was one seeming justification for the additional round. That made Pat Gillick, who had put together the team in Toronto that captured consecutive World Series championships, uneasy. "Next year, you get a five-game series," he noted. "Next year, you could get one hot pitcher in the first round. He could knock you out."[39]

George Vecsey of the *New York Times*, referred to the World Series competitors, the Blue Jays and the Phillies, as "legitimate champions who had survived long division races. No wild cards among them. No lucky losers." However, Vecsey indicated, "we will never be able to say that again. Paul Molitor and Joe Carter won the last true World Series," before asking, "Do you think the owners and the television barons understand any of this?"[40]

11

Commissioner-Less Baseball

Baseball historian John Thorn offered his own take on the state of the game in a column, "Stop Me If You've Heard This One Before," which appeared in *The Sporting News*'s October 18, 1993, issue. Written as the World Series was taking place, the essay began with the flat statement, "Baseball is in bad shape." The game remained without a commissioner, Fay Vincent having been ousted "in a palace coup." Corporate dominance of the sport appeared to be mounting. Revenues seemed to be heading in one direction, skyrocketing player salaries in another. A number of major-market teams were in disarray and uncompetitive. Smaller-market teams were beset by "magical thinking" concerning operating deficiencies.[1]

The dismay about major league baseball, Thorn noted, was hardly unique. During the 1970s, talk could be heard about the game's demise. Sportswriters decried the supposedly "sluggish play by roving mercenaries who had no loyalty to the teams or their fans." Those "knights of the press box" blasted ballplayers' ready resort to illicit drugs and not infrequent dalliance "with gamblers and low-lifes." Owners seemed "inept" as well as divided among themselves.[2]

Yet baseball rebounded in the 1980s, once again labeled "the national pastime" thanks to fresh icons, competitive races, and escalating revenues piquing talk of expansion, even global in scope. With the arrival of the new decade, team owners, worrying that players had accumulated too much power, strove to rekindle profits through "running the game like a business." Coming on the heels of collusion during the last half of the 1980s, the tycoons desired to destroy the MLBPA, prop up big-market teams, and obtain "real estate fortunes from ballparks."[3]

All of that was still "not enough." Despite efforts to spruce up baseball, which helped bring about "the spectacular hitting" in 1993, owners still doubted that the sport could remain profitable. Looking back to the late 19th century, Thorn recalled the labor strife that led to the short-lived Players' League, the financially difficult times during the 1890s, and the eventual emergence of the American League, which helped to "save Major League Baseball from itself."[4]

Thus, to Thorn, "the past is prologue." Contemporary baseball would also experience "hard times," as would various franchises. Economic problems would puncture "the baseball bubble" yet again. No matter, "the elements of salvation" existed, including the internationalization of the game; the minor leagues with their "human scale" framework and "connection to the spirit of play"; and "our children, to whom baseball is just a game."

♦   ♦   ♦

Pairing his earlier interview with Donald Fehr, John Rawlings conducted one with Bud Selig. This time, Rawlings began by asking, "Is the game as romantic now as it was to you as a young boy?" Selig responded, "I have always loved the romantic aspect of this game. That's one of the reasons I was so fond of Bart Giamatti. He was a great Red Sox fan and I loved the Yankees." He recalled walking in New York City with the late commissioner one evening, talking for hours about the historic baseball summer of 1949. Wondering if people still viewed the game in the same way, Selig thought they did, despite the massive changes society had undergone.[5]

When asked about the present state of the game, Selig responded, "The only thing left to debate is how dynamic baseball is." He appreciated that the sport had problems and that "a lot of negativism" existed, but MLB was hosting "more than 70 million people in a season." Declaring "it's a magnificent game with a fantastic history," Selig insisted, "That's something no other sport has." In fact, he thought baseball might be greater than previously. "The focus ... is back on the field and that's where it belongs. People are tired of hearing about all the acrimony."

Responding to a query about the job of commissioner, Selig expressed belief in that system but said, "This is a new era." Owners had been forced to achieve consensus. They had redefined the commissioner's role, affording him or her "more power than before." MLB, which lacked a television policy the previous year, now had one. The charge that owners simply sought control to bring about a strike or a lockout hadn't proved accurate. Revenue-sharing, which was viewed as impossible until recently, was being considered. Altogether then, those who complained that baseball was "wandering aimlessly ... don't have a clue." As for the upcoming season, Selig expressed optimism that a full complement of games would be played.[6]

♦   ♦   ♦

With both the 1993 regular season and the playoffs wrapped up, a number of noteworthy retirements occurred. George Brett, long the face of the Kansas City Royals, left the game after 21 seasons with that team, during which he hit 665 doubles, 137 triples, and 317 homers, while driving in 1,596 runs, scoring 1,583, amassing 88.6 WAR (indicates how many more wins a player is "worth" than a replacement player at the same position), and compiling a .305 batting average.[7] He was a three-time batting champion and former MVP, who hit .390 during an injury-plagued 1980 season. Catcher Carlton Fisk, who had split his 24-year career almost evenly between the Boston Red Sox and the Chicago White Sox, knocked out 421 doubles and 376 homers, while driving in 1,330 runs and ending with 68.4 WAR. Two-time MVP and home run champion Dale Murphy, after 18 seasons, most with the Atlanta Braves, departed two home runs shy of 400, having driven in 1,266 runs. Shortstop-center fielder Robin Yount, who played his entire 20-year career with the Milwaukee Brewers, also retired with a pair of MVPs, 1,632 runs scored, and 3,142 hits. Twelve-year veteran George Bell, who had starred with the Toronto Blue Jays, winning an MVP, wrapped up his tenure in the majors with 265 homers and 1,002 RBI.[8]

Top pitchers also were departing from the game. John Candelaria, a 19-year vet, just over half of that time with the Pittsburgh Pirates, had a 177–122 record, an excellent .592 win-loss percentage, a 20-win season, and an ERA title. Fastballer turned junkballer Frank Tanana put up early outstanding numbers, winning an ERA title and a strikeout championship, on his way to 240 victories spread over 21 seasons. Then there was Nolan Ryan, who had particularly shone with the California Angels, the Houston Astros, and the Texas Rangers, hurling seven no-hitters, winning 11 strikeout and a pair of ERA titles, twice winning 20 games, setting a single-season strikeout record, and six times whiffing over 300 batters. Ryan began the season holding "52 official major league records." Altogether, the seemingly ageless—until the 46-year-old star blew out his right elbow in the final game he pitched in the major leagues—Ryan won 324 games, threw 61 shutouts, had 83.6 WAR, and struck out 5,714 batters. And he had easily bested Robin Ventura in their infamous clash.[9]

During the postseason, player movement, often prevalent since the advent of free agency, proceeded apace, despite the lukewarm assessment by Tony DeMarco, a sportswriter for the *Fort Worth Star-Telegram*, about the quality of available choices. The latest crop, he argued, didn't compare to the previous one, which included Barry Bonds, Greg Maddux, and Paul Molitor. It did possess a couple of sure-fire Hall of Famers, but they were "in the twilight of their careers." Notwithstanding DeMarco's analysis, a number of very fine ballplayers were about to become available to the highest bidder.[10]

After the World Series, nearly a dozen top players were allowed to negotiate with whichever teams they chose to, a fact that continued to grate on team owners. Doing so were lifetime .300 hitter and first baseman Will Clark of the San Francisco Giants, NL batting champion Andres Galarraga of the Colorado Rockies, pitcher Dennis Martinez of the Montreal Expos, speedy outfielder Ricky Henderson of the Toronto Blue Jays, first baseman Rafael Palmeiro and infielder Julio Franco of the Texas Rangers, outfielders Ellis Burks and Tim Raines of the Chicago White Sox, shortstop Alan Trammell of the Detroit Tigers, designated hitter (DH) Harold Baines of the Baltimore Orioles, and first baseman Eddie Murray of the New York Mets.

On November 19, the Los Angeles Dodgers dealt pitcher Pedro Martinez to the Montreal Expos in exchange for second baseman Delino DeShields. Just turned 22, Martinez, a frail-looking right-hander from the Dominican Republic who stood an inch short of six feet, had gone 10–5 with a 2.61 ERA during his first major league season. Despite striking out 119 batters in only 107 innings, Pedro, the younger brother of another slim hurler, 6'4" Ramon Martinez, who had recently won 20 games with the Dodgers, was viewed by his first team as too slight to withstand the rigors of major league baseball. Hence the trade for the light-hitting DeShields.

Three days later, the Texas Rangers inked Will Clark to a contract. The former Rookie of the Year and four-time top-five MVP contender, 29-year-old Clark appeared to be in the prime of his career. The Rockies kept Galarraga and pirated Burks from the White Sox, who got Julio Franco of the Rangers and resigned Raines. The Orioles resigned designated hitter deluxe Baines, after he hit 20 homers and batted .313, and added Palmeiro following a season in which he put up 37 homers, drove in 105 runs, and batted .295 for the Rangers. The Cleveland Indians signed both Dennis Martinez and Murray, who had contributed 27 big flies and 100 RBI to the Mets. Henderson went back to Oakland Athletics, after a short stint with the Blue Jays.

◆ ◆ ◆

In an article titled "Another Awful Offseason," Peter Pascarelli discussed the upside of recent baseball events. The past season had proven successful both on the playing diamond and at the box office, with attendance mushrooming across the country and the Braves and the Giants waging "the best pennant race in a decade." Helpful in displaying baseball's prowess and piquing its popularity was "a dynamic new generation of stars," among them Barry Bonds, Juan Gonzalez, Ken Griffey Jr, Randy Johnson, and Greg Maddux. To Pascarelli, those players matched up well against stars from previous eras.[11]

Despite the game's buoyancy, however, its commercial makeup "teeters on the brink with potentially disastrous brush fires starting to crackle throughout its vast landscape," wrote Pascarelli. Almost 18 months after the owners compelled Fay Vincent to resign, they appeared to be in no great hurry to name a new commissioner, although possible candidates included television executive Dick Ebersol; the well-placed attorney Paul Kirk; and Democratic senator George Mitchell from Maine. Many owners were exhorting Selig to agree to serve as the permanent commissioner, for however short a term as he wished.[12]

Other problems included the possible sale of several franchises and decaying stadiums in Detroit, Milwaukee, San Francisco, and New York (two there). The threat of congressional action regarding MLB's antitrust exemption remained. Talk of revenue sharing by the owners had "sputtered for months." The CBA was about to expire. The MLBPA had to agree to playoff realignments. National television revenues were anticipated to drop sharply. Ratings for the Toronto-Philadelphia World Series were the second-poorest ever.[13]

Such areas of concern, Pascarelli believed, had produced "an overwhelming sense of uncertainty over the game" as borne out by a series of interviews with all kinds of "baseball people." Publicly, Selig insisted he didn't want to be commissioner, although other owners were urging him to accept the position. The appointment of Kirk, who formerly chaired the Democratic National Committee, might be well-received in congressional circles, where talk could be heard about the need for a commissioner to be selected "from outside the ranks." The actual loss of baseball's antitrust exemption might lead to additional franchise moves.[14]

By December, with the expiration of the CBA approaching, more than a year had passed without negotiations. Moreover, none were scheduled. While Ravitch maintained his belief in a linkage between revenue sharing and a salary cap, Fehr declared, "Our basic view of a salary cap hasn't changed. The only salary cap the owners want is one where they're not paying players the market value. The players aren't interested in that."[15]

♦ ♦ ♦

At the start of the new year, Peter Pascarelli, in *The Sporting News*, again reflected on the state of major league ball. Regardless of "all the greed, arrogance and stupidity" exhibited by both players and their employers, "there's a lot of good being done," he maintained. This had been forgotten at times, due to baseball's association "with boorish millionaires arguing about the size of their pay raises."[16]

That was unfortunate because baseball, through engagement by both teams and individual players, had assisted with a variety of charitable efforts. Cincinnati Reds shortstop Barry Larkin raised funds to provide health care for indigent young people. Cleveland Indians slugger Albert Belle aided the Mayor's Crime Commission. Boston Red Sox star pitcher Roger Clemens was involved with over "a dozen charitable efforts." In impoverished sectors of the nation's capital, Baltimore Orioles center fielder Mike Devereaux helped to establish more than a score of Little League teams. Los Angeles Dodgers pitcher Orel Hershiser solicited large sums of money to battle cystic fibrosis. Philadelphia Phillies first baseman John Kruk's program offered "outings for cancer victims and their families." Baltimore's Eddie Murray assisted a community center. St. Louis Cardinals shortstop Ozzie Smith's foundation aided area charities. He also took the lead in guiding MLB's involvement in helping Midwest flood victims. The MLBPA had joined forces with MLB to sponsor a program tied to the National Education Association. Teams throughout the majors were involved with programs tackling a host "of urban and community issues—illiteracy, child abuse, drug abuse, the handicapped, research for various health problems, crime prevention, stay-in-school efforts, disaster relief, the homeless and on and on." MLB was acting to fund baseball programs for inner city youth and, partnering with Coca-Cola, renovating baseball parks across the United States.[17]

♦ ♦ ♦

Writing in *The Sporting News* one week later, Pascarelli posed the question, "Has the dawn of a baseball new year ever been shrouded in more uncertainty than 1994?" Referring to baseball's "murky" financial state, he noted that many team rosters remained unsettled and "dozens of free agents" were still unsigned. At long last, owners did seem primed "for momentous decisions on revenue sharing and a commissioner." A new collective bargaining agreement, Pascarelli noted, might soon be ready, but salary arbitration beckoned. From what he had learned, the decision about the commissioner's job was unresolved.[18]

Pascarelli conveyed other observations regarding the game on the field, including the projected top rookies. Among those were Atlanta catcher Javy Lopez, infielder Chipper Jones, and outfielder Ryan Klesko; Chicago White Sox pitchers James Baldwin and Scott Ruffcorn; Cleveland outfielder Manny Ramirez; Montreal outfielder Clifford Floyd; New York Yankees third baseman Russell Davis; Oakland pitcher Steve Karsay; Philadelphia reliever Ricky Bottalico; San Francisco first baseman J. R. Phillips; Seattle outfielder Marc Newfield; and Toronto catcher Carlos Delgado and shortstop Alex Gonzales.[19]

Regarding which team was likely to replace the Blue Jays as MLB's best, Pascarelli first emphasized how the additional playoff round made repeating still more difficult. He pointed to Atlanta, saying the Braves were "too good and too classy to go forever without a World Series championship." Like Pat Gillick, Toronto's general manager, Atlanta's John Schuerholz always appeared ready "to pull the trigger on an over-the-top, in-season deal," as he had in acquiring Fred McGriff late in the 1993 season.[20]

Predicting who would succeed Barry Bonds if he didn't win yet another MVP Award in the National League, Pascarelli put Atlanta outfielder David Justice at the top of his list, followed by Philadelphia catcher Darren Daulton, Cincinnati shortstop Barry Larkin, Montreal outfielder Larry Walker, and Houston first baseman Jeff Bagwell.[21]

As matters turned out, their peers duplicated the votes of sportswriters in selecting Barry Bond and Frank Thomas as the Major League Baseball Players Association Players Choice Award recipients. Reporting the results, the *Orlando Sentinel*'s Barry Cooper tagged Bonds, who now had gone two for two in winning the award, which had only been initiated in 1992, "the most dominant player in the sport."[22]

◆　◆　◆

MLB also stayed in the news thanks to three new additions to the baseball Hall of Fame. One top candidate, former star slugger Orlando Cepeda, admitted to *The Sporting News* how much he had invested in his possible selection. In "One More Chance," sportswriter Mark Newman indicated that this was "more important to Cepeda than ever. Each morning, before he prays, he has the pangs of anxiety that have caused his stomach to ache for the past month or so."[23]

For this was Cepeda's 15th year on the ballot. If he didn't get in this time, he'd have to wait three more years before the Veterans Committee would vote on his admission. The likelihood of his entrance into the Hall of Fame had obviously been dampened when, prior to his first year of eligibility, the seven-time All-Star received a 10-year prison sentence for drug smuggling.[24]

On January 12, 1994, the Baseball Writers of America elected 329-game winner Steve Carlton, a four-time Cy Young Award recipient, to the sports' Valhalla. Excluded from only 19 of 455 ballots, the taciturn yet often surly left-hander received 95.8 percent of the votes cast, easily exceeding the 75 percent threshold required for admission. Carlton, a six-time 20-game winner and only the second pitcher to strike out more than 4,000 batters, thus became only the 25th player chosen to enter the Hall of Fame during his first year of eligibility. Despite an often-stormy relationship with the press, Carlton, on receiving word of his impending induction, acknowledged, "I'm touched to be elected to the Hall of Fame."[25]

By contrast, first baseman-outfielder Cepeda, who ended up as a designated hitter, came up seven votes short. This despite a home run crown, two RBI titles, 10 seasons batting over .300, a lifetime .297 average, 379 homers, and 1,365 RBI, along with a Rookie of the Year Award and an MVP Award. Failing to hide his emotions, Cepeda acknowledged, "It is heartbreaking. It's like losing a ball game, 1–0, after having so many opportunities to win." Cepeda hoped the Veterans Committee, three years down the road, would view his possible selection differently. "They saw me play good baseball in my prime. So, they'll have an idea of what I did on the field."[26]

William C. Rhoden, a columnist for the *New York Times*, wondered "what level of vindictiveness would compel a baseball writer to exclude Orlando Cepeda from the baseball Hall of Fame?" The decision had convinced Rhoden, even more than before, that his fellow sportswriters should not be allowed to participate in the granting of sports honors. Holding fast "to some mythic notion of what an athlete should and should not be," various members of his profession had voted against Cepeda.[27]

Rhoden obviously considered it unfortunate that the criteria for election to the baseball Hall of Fame included "consideration of character, integrity and sportsmanship." That seemed absurd to Rhoden and caused him to recall that many of the same naysayers had first refused to admit Negro League stars and then supported creation of a separate wing for Black ballplayers. Angered about the treatment of Cepeda, Rhoden also recalled the exclusion of other outstanding players like Nellie Fox and Roger Maris. He wouldn't be as troubled if former players and baseball personnel were deciding, for they had fought to make the big leagues. In closing, Rhoden repeated a quote by Jim Dwyer, who had played with the Minnesota Twins: "The Hall of Fame is for baseball people. Heaven is for good people."[28]

Other star players receiving a thumbs down from baseball writers included pitchers Phil Niekro, Don Sutton, Bruce Sutter, and Jim Kaat, along with everyday players (sometimes turned DHs) Tony Perez, Steve Garvey, Tony Oliva, Ron Santo, Dick Allen, and Joe Torre.

Some weeks later, the Veterans Committee voted in Phil Rizzuto and the late Leo Durocher, both former shortstops who acquired greater notoriety when their playing days had ended. A one-time MVP and one-time runner-up for that award, Rizzuto made five All-Star teams while anchoring nine pennant-winning squads, seven of which went on to win the World Series. Afterward, he served as a Yankees radio and television sportscaster for four decades. On being informed of his selection, Rizzuto characteristically exclaimed, "Holy Cow!", before nearly falling to the floor.[29]

The tempestuous Durocher, who played alongside Babe Ruth during his first two major league seasons and then on the Gashouse Gang of the Dizzy Dean–led

St. Louis Cardinals during the 1930s, had become one of the game's top managers. While winning over 2,000 games, Durocher guided the Brooklyn Dodgers to the

1941 pennant and the New York Giants to NL titles in 1951 and 1954, blanking the Indians in four straight games in the 1954 World Series.

One of baseball's most controversial figures, suspended for the 1947 season due to his involvement with unsavory sorts like gamblers and underworld figures, Durocher became embittered as each season passed without his election to the Hall of Fame. At one point, he stated, "if they don't think I belong there, so be it." Durocher's win-at-all-cost sensibility was displayed when he explained in 1951, "My mother's on second. The ball's hit out to short center. As she goes by me on the way to third, I'll accidentally trip her. I'll help her up, Brush her off, tell her I'm sorry. But she does not get to third."[30]

Phil Rizzuto, the Hall of Fame Yankees shortstop and longtime announcer with his former team. Ca. 1949 (Library of Congress).

The Sporting News found much to appreciate regarding the selection of Rizzuto, although admittedly less so in Durocher's case. Its staff indicated, "If Ted Williams and Joe DiMaggio say Rizzuto was the best shortstop of his era, that's good enough for us." Additionally, Rizzuto was one of the sport's favorite personalities. However, The Sporting News noted that the latest Hall of Famers "made their marks performing in New York." The city dominated the voting for the Hall of Fame. That hardly mattered when it came to a star like Tom Seaver. But it did make a difference in the cases of Don Sutton and Phil Niekro, also 300-game winners, shortstop Larry Bowa, and outfielder Richie Ashburn, both of whom only ended their playing days in New York City.[31]

◆　◆　◆

In the midst of the elections for the Hall of Fame, sports fan learned to their amazement—and to the annoyance of some—that Chicago Bulls superstar Michael Jordan was leaving the National Basketball Association to pursue a career in baseball. Jordan, already a three-time regular season MVP and winner of seven consecutive scoring titles, indicated that he was done with basketball, having led the Bulls to three straight NBA titles. A gold medalist with the 1984 U.S. men's Olympic team, Jordan had also spearheaded the Dream Team that captured gold in Barcelona amid an unprecedented international media frenzy eight years later.

Having experienced the recent death of his father and with controversies swirling about his gambling habits, Jordan, recently retired from the Bulls, expressed his determination to play for the Chicago White Sox. Bulls owner Jerry Reinsdorf also ran that team, which had finished first in the AL West before losing the League Championship Series to Toronto in six games. Jordan had been working out for several hours a day at the recently constructed Comiskey Park.

Encouraged by Reinsdorf, White Sox trainer Herm Schneider was assisting Jordan with a series of hand exercises to enable him to make the transition to baseball. White Sox players, including reigning AL MVP Frank Thomas and former batting champ Julio Franco, were showing up to help Jordan round into baseball shape.

Dave Kindred, sports columnist with the *Washington Post*, quoted Jordan explaining why he was participating in regular batting practice sessions: "I'm trying to see how good I can get. I haven't seen live pitching yet, but I'm driving the ball against the machine."[32]

Jerry Reinsdorf had said about Jordan, "If he was 18 and you were scouting him, you'd say he has great tools. But he's 30." Still the owner also explained that Jordan loved being at the ballpark and around the batting cage and could be involved in spring training if he desired. Moreover, Reinsdorf stated, "I know Michael well enough to know he would not do anything to make a fool of himself. And he would not ask us to let him come to spring training unless he's proved himself."[33]

The Bulls' general manager, Jerry Krause, who had a complicated relationship with the team's unrivaled star, said, "You can never say Michael can't do anything. But the hardest thing in the world to do is to hit a baseball—harder than anything in basketball." As Krause saw matters, "If Willie Mays had played only basketball from the time he was eight years old, he'd have been Michael Jordan. and if Michael Jordan had only played baseball, he'd have been Willie Mays."[34]

Speaking to Bob Greene, a columnist with the *Chicago Tribune*, basketball's greatest phenom explained, "I want to go to spring training for one reason, and that's to make the team. This is no fantasy. I plan to be in Sarasota by mid–February." Jordan, who hadn't played organized baseball since he was a teenager, continued: "If the White Sox were to tell me that they didn't think I was good enough to make the team, and that they don't want me at spring training, then I would accept their wishes and not go. But my enthusiasm for doing this is so great that if they wanted me to pay my own way, then I'd pay my own way down there just for the chance to show what I can do."[35]

When asked why he was pursuing this new path, Jordan replied, "First of all, it's fun. I'm not doing this for a fantasy camp experience." Moments later, he reflected, "And this is something my father always wanted me to do. He started me in baseball when I was six years old. Two years ago, he told me that I should go for it." Then Jordan told Greene, "I'm serious. My father thought I could be a major league baseball player, and I'm sure that right now he can see me trying. He's watching every move that I make." Regarding a possible return to the sport that had made him internationally famous, Jordan bluntly stated, "That's over. That's the past. I don't miss it at all."[36]

As for those who thought he couldn't pull this off, Jordan acknowledged, "I think a lot of people want me to fail. Good. Let them keep saying it. The person who is going to have to succeed or fail, is me, not them."[37]

◆ ◆ ◆

What a growing number of sportswriters considered MLB's dysfunctionality proceeded apace. One of the game's most astute observers, the *New York Times'* Murray Chass, maintained his sharp-honed analyses. Although the 1994 regular season was fast approaching, team owners and the MLBPA had yet to determine the makeup of projected divisions or whether an additional round of the playoffs should take place. Another stumbling block involved the number of playoff games that would provide proceeds for the pension fund. "Why aren't we getting paid the same way the clubs are?" wondered the MLBPA's associate general counsel, Eugene Orza. "Why don't the players get paid for every game when the clubs are getting paid for every game for the first time?"[38]

On January 18, owners voted unanimously to institute a revenue sharing plan. Donald Fehr, still head of the union, reacted less than enthusiastically to news of the agreement. "Now I guess the thing to do is for me to go and negotiate with the players for about the same amount of time it took the owners to negotiate their new deal—about two years," Fehr remarked. "We just have to wait to see what it is. For two years, they've been saying that if they reach such an agreement, the next step is for players to accept a cap." Fehr cast doubt on the MLBPA's willingness to go accede to the owners' demands. "There has not been the slightest suggestion that the players were invited to do anything except say, 'Yes, sir.' You don't make friends and influence people by saying for two years that we will decide this and the players will have to take it."[39]

The next day, an accord was carved out between MLB and the players' union. The two sides approved of the realignment of the National and American Leagues, carving them into three divisions each. Playoff participants would double to four in each league, including a wild card—the team with the best non-division-winning record. Somewhat perplexed that the MLBPA had not been invited to participate in announcing the new divisional configuration and the additional round of playoffs, Fehr said about the new schema, nevertheless, "We think it's good for the game or we wouldn't have agreed to it."[40]

Indicating that the realignment was the first in a quarter of a century, Peter Pascarelli emphasized that MLB had yet to resolve two overriding issues. The selection of a commissioner had been postponed yet again. The owners, despite their evident delight in having reached consensus on revenue sharing, understood "that the main event still lies ahead—a big-money showdown." That would "pit Dick Ravitch and his merry band of newly united owners against Don Fehr and his iron-willed union."[41]

Pascarelli delivered a warning: "No one should lose sight of the fact a divisive labor war that results in a strike or any bitter interruption to the season could render much of what the owners accomplished meaningless." With the owners, through Ravitch, having promised that no lockout would be forthcoming, "the onus of shutting down the industry," Pascarelli wrote, "is on the players." He added, "Push probably will not come to shove until August." Should the talks be foundering then, the ballplayers could threaten both "pennant races and the postseason with some kind of job action." They would not have much to lose, with the bulk of their salaries already paid by that point.[42]

◆ ◆ ◆

While negotiations for a new labor accord were supposed to have begun 14 months earlier, the MLBPA and team owners agreed on March 7, 1994, as the starting date for talks, less than a month before the opening of the regular season. Previous discussions had been put on hold as Richard Ravitch sought to convince the club bosses to accept revenue sharing. With that feat finally accomplished, he was ready to meet with MLBPA representatives. The baseball executive remained determined to link revenue sharing with a salary cap, which the players continued to oppose.[43]

The players readied for what they anticipated: another clash with baseball management. "There's always some reason for concern because the owners kind of seem to be in disarray," Yankees first baseman Don Mattingly explained. "So, we're always cautious and conservative and hope for the best, but expect the worst." Regarding the possibility of a strike, Donald Fehr declared, "It always comes down to the following: If you're in a position in which you can't get an agreement and there don't appear to be any reasonable options open, and the owners could unilaterally impose a salary cap in the off season or something, then you've got problems."[44]

After the negotiations opened, Ravitch told those in attendance, including 73 ballplayers but no owners, that their employers desired "cost certainty." To that end, he promised to provide the financial data relied on in the owners' decision to back revenue sharing. "Dick said there is nothing they won't turn over," Fehr reported. "Given the kind of proposal they want, it would be difficult not to give us everything."[45]

The initial negotiating sessions didn't go well, leaving Fehr to ponder what lay ahead. "At this point, it's hard to see things coming to a closure," he stated following those meetings. "History is not with us." Fehr was unhappy that the owners failed to appear during the encounters and because of their refusal to indicate precisely what they desired.[46]

The sputtering labor negotiations occurred precisely when Congress was again exploring baseball's antitrust exemption. The exchanges between Bud Selig, MLB's de facto commissioner, and Howard Metzenbaum, chair of the Senate Judiciary Committee's subcommittee on antitrust, proved contentious. Making his stance clear, Metzenbaum opened with a thunderbolt. "In my view, any slim justification that baseball might have had for keeping the extraordinary privilege of antitrust immunity was lost when they gutted the office of the commissioner." Chastising Selig and other team owners, the senator declared, "You have absolutely made the commissioner into a figurehead. Whereas before he had great authority and wasn't necessarily on either side, he was able to move in where there was a problem. Instead, you now say, 'You're a lackey. You're worthless. Go out there and negotiate a labor agreement.'"[47]

Drawing on a romantic view of baseball history and the commissioner's office, Senator Metzenbaum stated, "My view is that the Congress should move to reclaim

From left: Senators Edward M. Kennedy (MA), Strom Thurmond (SC), and Howard Metzenbaum (OH). Senator Metzenbaum battled with Bud Selig regarding baseball's antitrust exemption (Marion S. Trikosko, photographer, February 7, 1979. U.S. News & World Report Magazine Photograph Collection. Library of Congress Prints and Photographs Division, Washington, D.C.).

our national pastime for the fans before the barons of baseball become too cozy, too comfortable and too cocky with their newly acquired powers. By refusing to hire a commissioner and by downgrading that job, the owners have broken their word to the Congress and breached faith with the fans."[48]

When Selig indicated that the new commissioner would be granted greater powers, Metzenbaum countered, "I say B.S." Selig continued to insist that the commissioner held large powers designed to safeguard MLB's integrity and public confidence. Metzenbaum appeared particularly upset by Selig's unwillingness to indicate that the next commissioner would be empowered to prevent a lockout. Donald Fehr admitted that Selig was "in a tough position," forced to confess that the commissioner's post never amounted to much or declare that despite the new agreement's "plain language and … clear intention … it doesn't mean what it says."[49]

Topping all concerns regarding major league baseball was the fear that a player strike might well take well place, curtailing or ending the 1994 season. Donald Fehr offered, "As of now, we have no indication when or if the owners will make a proposal or tell us what they want to do other than utter the word salary cap. It appears it will be a long negotiation and a difficult one."[50]

12

It Happens Every Spring

WITH SPRING TRAINING IN THE WORKS, fans in two cities looked forward to new ballparks. This stood in sharp contrast to many other locales, including some whose stadiums had been constructed decades earlier. The oldest existing venues were famed Fenway Park (Red Sox, 1912), Tiger Stadium (1912), and Wrigley Field (Cubs, 1914), constructed during the first great era of stadium building. The Indians' Municipal Stadium dated back to 1931, the Brewers' County Stadium in Milwaukee to 22 years later. The 1960s resulted in a profusion of new ballparks, including for the Giants (Candlestick, 1960), Dodgers (Dodger Stadium, 1962), Astros (Astrodome, 1965), Rangers (Arlington, 1965), Braves (Atlanta-Fulton County, 1966), Cardinals (Busch, 1966), Angels (Anaheim, 1966), Padres (San Diego, 1967), and A's (Oakland, 1968), with just Dodger Stadium remaining a baseball-only facility. The Blue Jays started out in Exhibition Stadium, which had opened in 1959, while the Washington Senators had played in Robert F. Kennedy Memorial Stadium, known as RFK Stadium and renamed District of Columbia Stadium, until the team was moved to Texas in 1971.[1]

The 1970s and 1980s witnessed the construction of largely soulless, multi-purpose stadiums, with the exception of Kauffman Stadium, built on the outskirts of Kansas City, Missouri (1973); the majestic Yankee Stadium also underwent a major renovation that removed many of its distinctive qualities. Then there were Riverfront (Cincinnati, 1970), Three Rivers (Pittsburgh, 1970), Veterans (Philadelphia, 1971), Stad Olympique (Montreal, 1976), Kingdome (Seattle, 1976), and Hubert H. Humphrey Metrodome (Minneapolis, 1982).[2]

A new wave of stadium building began in 1989 with the completion of the futuristic-appearing Toronto SkyDome, MLB's first facility with a retractable roof. Also designed for multi-purpose usage, it served as home turf for the Blue Jays, the NBA's Toronto Raptors, and the Canadian Football League's Toronto Argonauts.[3]

In 1991, the White Sox relocated to the charmless new Comiskey Park, which despite the intentions of the architect, Philip Bess, hardly exuded the "pragmatic idealism" he envisioned. Bess's hopes for Armour Field were guided "by a concern that it be a genuinely urban building, constrained by its block, with an architectural presence, scale, and monumentality, befitting its status as a public building." In other words, Bess aspired to lay plans for a genuine neighborhood baseball park.[4]

Fenway Park (Bain News Service, circa 1910–1915. George Grantham Bain Collection. Library of Congress Prints and Photographs Division, Washington, D.C.).

The Astrodome, baseball's first multipurpose domed stadium, held its first regular season game in 1965 for the hometown Houston Astros, an expansion team then beginning its fourth year of operation. Ca. 1965 (Historic American Engineering Record Collection. Library of Congress Prints and Photographs Division, Washington, D.C.).

Washington, D.C.'s RFK Stadium, named after the late Senator Robert F. Kennedy. Initially called District of Columbia Stadium, it opened its doors in 1961 for the National Football League's Redskins. The next year, the Washington Senators began hosting games there (Marion S. Trikosko, photographer, July 29, 1963. U.S. News & World Report Magazine Photograph Collection. Library of Congress Prints and Photographs Division, Washington, D.C.).

Far more aesthetically pleasing was Camden Yards, the first of a series of retro ballparks that harked back to vintage stadiums while offering modern amenities. The Kansas City–based architectural firm HOK Sport (renamed Populous in 2009), which had botched the new White Sox stadium, slammed a home run with the innovative ballpark designed to help resuscitate the Inner Harbor, downtown Baltimore's waterfront. Expertly designed, Camden Yards offered seating near the field of play, low outfield fences, and wrought iron, all associated with baseball during the first half of the 20th century. But it also contained luxury boxes, which all MLB owners wanted, and vividly displayed the massive B & O railroad warehouse, stationed beyond the right field fence.[5]

Even the site of the new ballpark resonated with students of the game. Center field was located where Babe Ruth's father once owned a tavern and had an outhouse. The stadium was situated only a couple of blocks from the Babe's birthplace.[6]

Two new stadiums—Jacobs Fields in Cleveland and The Ballpark in Arlington, Texas—followed Camden Yards' retro approach but with their own distinctive flavor. Whereas Camden Yards featured a warehouse look, Jacobs Fields had an industrial feel, and The Ballpark exuded an obvious Texas flavor, in contrast to the symmetrical stadiums that had recently been built and were designed for multipurpose usage.[7]

A baseball-only facility, Jacobs Field, like the Gateway Sports and Entertainment Complex it was part of, was intended to help renovate downtown Cleveland.

The city, still among the 10 largest in the nation as late as 1970, had lost over 400,000 inhabitants since 1950 and had slipped below half a million by 1994. It had gone into default in 1978, the largest major city in the nation to do so since the Great Depression, only just escaping that fate again nine years later.[8]

Nevertheless, Cleveland had recently received, for the fifth time, the All-America City Award, which saluted communities that demonstrated constructive citizenship. Mayor Michael R. White and real estate developer Richard E. Jacobs, owner of the Cleveland Indians, envisioned Jacobs Field providing momentum to revitalize the city. The new stadium, also designed by HOK, had an exposed steel framework intended to conjure up images of industrial Cleveland. It offered a scaled-down version of Fenway Park's Green Monster in left field, different distances to and heights for outfield fences, and vertical light towers, thus allowing for a view of Cleveland's downtown skyline. Additionally, Jacobs Fields promised a warmer, more inviting backdrop than the massive, multipurpose Municipal Stadium, where professional football's Cleveland Browns also played.[9]

The Ballpark in Arlington, stationed at the midpoint between Fort Worth and Dallas, was constructed in suburbia, not at the heart of one of the nation's aging industrial cities. The exterior displayed red brick and Texas granite, while stone steer heads stood atop exterior arches and aisle seats featured wrought-iron lone stars. Portions of the Ballpark replicated facets of older classic baseball stadiums: the original Comiskey Park's arched windows, Ebbets Field's asymmetrical makeup as well as its arches and red brick façade, Fenway Park's manual scoreboard, Tiger Stadium's right field porch, Wrigley Field's center field bleachers, and Yankee Stadium's parapet encircling the upper deck. Thanks to a reduction in foul territory alongside the playing field, fans were close to the action.[10]

◆   ◆   ◆

As spring training loomed, Lewis H. Diuguid of the *Kansas City Star* reflected on preseason baseball. During the past few years, he noted, large crowds had congregated in the "little parks" where major league teams readied for the start of the season. That was owing, in part, to the number of older fans who had chosen retirement abodes where their favorite teams played winter ball, and to those who undertook trips to partake of the Grapefruit League in Florida or the Cactus League in Arizona.[11]

The luckiest fans and the most fanatical could take in almost 30 games, half of them of the "home" variety. Or they might pick and choose, trying to see as many teams and visit as many ballparks as possible. Diuguid reported that he had gone to spring training in Florida in 1992 and then headed for Arizona the next year. An indiscriminate viewer could watch 20 teams in Florida but only eight in Arizona.[12]

For the 1994 version of spring training, however, Phoenix offered a convenient cluster of seven squads with as many venues to be had "within an hour's drive." There were doubleheaders, split-squad games, and contests throughout the day and into the night. With games starting in the early afternoon, fans could spend their mornings watching games of pepper. As for Diuguid, he spent a week in Arizona, visiting five ballparks and seeing a half-dozen games.[13]

Central Florida, where 10 teams were stationed, boasted one noticeable advantage over Arizona when it came to spring training. A "small-town feel, even in the 8,000-seat ball parks," was present, in Diuguid's estimation. Local, tasty, cheap cuisine was another attraction, as were the "local merchants' corny ads on the outfield fences" that made "fans feel at home between innings." Another eight teams were stationed down the Florida peninsula before one reached Miami. Unfortunately, prices were continuing to rise for "what used to be free not so many seasons ago," Diuguid bemoaned.[14]

On February 27, 1994, Steve Marantz of *The Sporting News* offered his take on spring training. "Baseball comes not a moment too soon this year," he began, before noting wintry weather conditions as well as the recent magnitude 6.7 earthquake that rattled Los Angeles' San Fernando Valley, leaving 60 dead, more than 900 injured, and property damage in the tens of billions of dollars. He also alluded to the Winter Olympics in Lillehammer that was just ending and the scheduled release of a made-for-television movie about the rivalry between figure skaters Nancy Kerrigan and Tonya Harding that led to Harding's directing an attack on Kerrigan.[15]

"Baseball, 1994" would be a new version, Marantz acknowledged. There would now be six divisions, three in each league, and eight teams would make the playoffs, the division winners and two wild cards, the non-division winning team in both the NL and the AL with the best record. Two teams would play their opener on a Sunday, additional day games were scheduled, and no new teams had been added to MLB.[16]

Before spinning the tale of 15-year-old Ryan Sherman playing hooky from his high school in Sarasota, Marantz wrote, "Boys love baseball. This politically incorrect observation is not meant to offend girls. It does not scientifically refute a trendy theory that baseball has been abandoned by youth. It simply recognizes what is."[17]

However, Ryan, who had sneaked into the ballpark, was accompanied by his mother. "Moms love baseball, too," Marantz indicated. Furthermore, "boys and moms also love Michael Jordan," which was fortunate as "his Airness" entered the playing field shortly after Ryan and his mother took their seats along the first-base line. Following two hours of warmup activities, Ryan observed, "I feel sorry for the other players. Nobody is paying attention to them."[18]

In *Baseball America*, Mark Ruda presented a look at the experiment by the man called Air Jordan, "Scouting Michael Jordan: Can His Airness Make It in Baseball?" Acknowledging that Jordan was following his childhood dream and that of his father, Ruda wondered if the quest would devolve into "the White Sox' spring-training nightmare." Another question that came to mind for the sportswriter was whether the 30-year-old Jordan, having not played organized baseball for over a decade, could even make it in the minor leagues.[19]

In mid–January, White Sox outfielder Michael Huff indicated, "As of right now, he knows and everyone in here knows that at a major league level, he would not succeed. But to see how far he's come in a month-and-a-half, everybody believes he could."[20]

Ruda proceeded to deliver what he called "the Michael Jordan scouting report." White Sox broadcaster Ken Harrelson, a former power hitter in the major leagues, offered, "Hitting is timing and rhythm, and what athlete has better timing and rhythm than Michael Jordan?" Harrelson added, "If Michael's goal is trying to play in the big leagues this year, then he's fighting a real uphill battle. For this year, it'd be very remote. But I would never count Michael Jordan out of any scenario. We're dealing with the greatest athlete we've ever seen."

Billy Williams, the Hall of Fame outfielder now coaching the same team—the Chicago Cubs—he long starred for, indicated, "I think he could hit a fastball, but I don't think he could hit a curveball…. I've seen good athletes who don't know how to hit a baseball. He's going to get knocked down by pitchers, and he's going to have to stand in there."[21]

Others questioned Jordan's power and even his fielding, with another Cubs coach, Jimmy Piersall, a former two-time All-Star outfielder, contending, "He would hurt any big league team he was on. Natural ability only goes so far."[22]

By contrast, Jordan's arm caused White Sox general manager Ron Schueler, himself a former MLB pitcher, to admit, "I wish my arm was as loose as his." His speed also impressed those who watched Jordan's workout sessions that had been held in secret at Comiskey Park.[23]

On the other hand, Jordan's hyper-competitiveness caused some concern. NBA star Danny Ainge, who briefly played in the majors, warned, "great players go through 0-for-15 slumps, 2-for-32 slumps. I don't think Michael's used to that."[24]

While the "greatest athlete in the world" was confident he could make the majors as an outfielder, "hardly anyone else believes it," wrote Tim Kurkjian. Pirates outfielder Andy Van Slyke said, "Baseball has as good a chance of having a salary cap as Michael Jordan has of wearing a White Sox cap; neither is going to happen." Phillies pitcher Larry Anderson admitted, "I'm pulling for him, but I can't see it. If I hang a slider, and it comes up there as big as a basketball, he'll hit me good. But if I'm throwing well, he'll have a rough time." An anonymous member of the White Sox declared, "Everyone is pulling for him, but he has no chance."[25]

Jordan struggled during the start of spring training, going hitless in his first 14 times at bat. On March 14, he finally notched his first hit, the byproduct of a grounder glancing off the third baseman's glove. That same day, the cover of *Sports Illustrated* contained a headline, "Bag It, Michael: Jordan and the White Sox Are Embarrassing Baseball," along with a photograph of the great athlete whiffing at a pitch that darted under his bat. The accompanying article by Steve Wulf, "Err Jordan—Try as He Might, Michael Jordan Has Found Baseball beyond His Grasp," was equally dismissive. "Err Jordan," which its author later admitted was "snarky," appeared following two spring training games.[26]

◆　◆　◆

Bud Selig, president and chief executive officer of the Milwaukee Brewers, was operating as chair of MLB's executive council. In that capacity, he had assumed many of the duties normally handled by a commissioner. The position had remained officially vacated since Fay Vincent, having received a no-confidence vote from the owners, resigned in early September 1992. Refusing to serve as a "figurehead" as some of baseball's owners desired, Vincent submitted his resignation in the "best interests of baseball."[27]

That left MLB's executive council, which normally functioned as an advisory board to the commissioner, in charge of the game's operations. Subsequently, Selig became *de facto* acting commissioner. In an essay in *The Sporting News*, Selig refuted the notion that MLB's commissioner was "all supreme or omnipotent … [or] almighty." Instead, such power only resided in ensuring the game's integrity and maintaining the public's confidence, he indicated.[28]

"The labor question," Selig noted, had proven "particularly vexing" due to the ill-defined nature of the relationship involving MLB's top official and the player relations committee, established 26 years earlier. At that point, reported Selig, the owners set up the PRC to make certain "they were fairly and professionally represented" in negotiations conducted with the Major League Baseball Players Association. The PRC had also been designed to "keep the commissioner out of labor negotiations."[29]

As Selig saw matters, the owners were "legally responsible for" labor policy devised by their ballclubs due to the fact that teams had to adhere to federal labor legislation. And in line with MLB's constitution, the commissioner was afforded broad powers to operate "in the best interests of the game." However, to Selig, the uncertainties surrounding employment of such powers had hindered previous collective bargaining efforts.[30]

Consequently, MLB, near the end of the 1992 regular season, established a restructuring committee intended to ascertain what responsibilities and authority the commissioner actually possessed. Ultimately, the owners determined that their sport's top official "should retain full power to protect the integrity and public confidence in the game." Furthermore, the commissioner now held jurisdiction over the National League, the American League, and the PRC. He was authorized to approve the selection of league presidents and "to develop and negotiate the clubs' labor strategy."[31]

To Selig, this meant that the commissioner, acting in his capacity "as protector and promoter of the game," would prove more influential, depending on his leadership and persuasive capabilities. Three-quarters of a century earlier, Judge Landis was given the job "to protect and promote the game for the benefit of the fans."

Present-day followers of MLB were possibly still better represented now that the commissioner's powers were "clear and unmistakable."[32]

♦ ♦ ♦

Sports Illustrated's Baseball Preview for the 1994 season featured Ken Griffey, Jr., on the cover, with the caption "So Good … ," alongside the Dodgers' catcher, Mike Piazza, who was paired with the rest of the caption, "So Young." The accompanying story, "Kids: A Proliferation of Exciting Young Stars Has Put a Fresh Face on the Game," by Tom Verducci, called Griffey "the best of them" but also quickly referred to White Sox first baseman Frank Thomas, Rangers left fielder Juan Gonzalez, White Sox pitcher Alex Fernandez, Astros first baseman Jeff Bagwell, Cubs outfielder Sammy Sosa, Angels outfielder Tim Salmon, and Rangers catcher Ivan Rodriquez. Verducci tossed in another bunch of 25-year-olds and younger: Piazza, Blue Jays first baseman John Olerud, Indians second bagger Carlos Baerga, Tigers third sacker Travis Fryman, Giants shortstop Royce Clayton, Orioles righthander Mike Mussina, Braves lefty Steve Avery, and Giants relief pitcher Rod Beck.[33]

To Verducci, these players were the future of the game and were already "invigorating" major league baseball and expanding its appeal. With stars like Nolan Ryan and George Brett, both 20-plus-year veterans, having just retired, "poster boys for the geriatric generation" no longer served as "baseball's ambassadors." There was already talk that this could be a historic group, one that Verducci compared with "history's four best" groups. The 1912 cohorts included Ty Cobb, Walter Johnson, and Tris Speaker. The 1928 gang had Lou Gehrig, Al Simmons, and Paul Waner. The 1957 youngsters particularly shone with Henry Aaron, Roberto Clemente, Mickey Mantle, Eddie Mathews, Willie Mays, and Frank Robinson, with stardom still awaiting Don Drysdale, Harmon Killebrew, Sandy Koufax, and Brooks Robinson. The 1970 contingent included Johnny Bench, Reggie Jackson, and Jim Palmer.[34]

In MLB history, a mere half-dozen players had belted more than 120 homers by the age of 23, with Gonzalez and Griffey having just accomplished that feat; the others were Hall of Famers: Mantle, Mathews, Frank Robinson, and Mel Ott. Gonzalez and Griffey had joined Thomas in becoming among the sixth threesomes to hit .300 with 40 home runs, while driving in 100 runs "in the same league in the same season." They were the first to pull that off prior to their 29th birthdays.[35]

The Baseball Network, a new joint consortium involving MLB and two of the major television networks—ABC and NBC—set out to promote these young stars. Ken Schanzer, who headed the new broadcasting venture, which *Sports Illustrated* called "a novel National tv-triple play," indicated, "Every time we talk to an advertiser, we talk about the young players in the game and the excitement they're generating. We're encouraging clients to take a look at these guys."[36]

This was in line with the promos ABC and NBC had aired during the National Football League's recent playoffs. Three individual players were featured: Gonzalez, Griffey, and Barry Bonds. Schanzer revealed that after he agreed to his new post, he first put a call into players association executive director Donald Fehr. "I told him our operating principle is this: The players are the game. We will do everything we can to promote our stars front and center. And they're there."[37]

This made perfect sense to Verducci, who agreed that players like Griffey were "the best advertisements for the game," particularly because advertisers worried about the older demographic audience attracted to baseball. Worrisome too was the fact that older players, meaning those who had reached their 30s, had created "an enormous vacuum," no longer dominating the sport. The longevity of the young stars from only seven years before had proved lacking. Verducci ticked off such a group, before indicating that none had been in the previous year's All-Star contest, with many saddled by injuries: Jose Canseco, Roger Clemens, Eric Davis, Dwight Gooden, Wally Joyner, Don Mattingly, Darryl Strawberry, and Danny Tartabull. Only Clemens still seemed destined for eventual induction into the Hall of Fame.[38]

What Verducci failed to note was how many of the once-promising careers of erstwhile stars—other than Clemens—had been derailed by drug abuse or alcoholism. An addiction to cocaine proved particularly poisonous for several of these young stars, as it had for others. Among those recently forced to endure rehabilitation, prison, suspension, or loss of reputation were Cy Young Award winners Ferguson Jenkins, LaMarr Hoyt, and Vida Blue, the latter also a former MVP; outfielders and one-time batting champions Tim Raines and Willie Wilson; first baseman Keith Hernandez, another ex-MVP and batting champ; and reliever Steve Howe, just to name a few.

The Pittsburgh Pirates, having won the 1979 World Series, went into the new decade not knowing that several players on the team's roster would be brought down by cocaine. Those included pitcher Rod Scurry, shortstop Dale Berra, former MVP and batting champion Dave Parker, and first baseman John Milner.[39]

Money alone, Cincinnati Reds manager Davey Johnson worried, had been enough to damage the previous young group of baseball stars, "the first wave" that received "the really big money." Johnson hoped that players were again aspiring to MVPs, HR titles, batting crowns, and the like. Many pointed to Jose Canseco as an example of where it could all go wrong, a player who became more concerned about being a celebrity and received more attention for his non-baseball antics. One American league general manager reflected about Canseco, "There was a player who could have done anything he wanted in this game."[40]

When asked who the top young player was, the one they wished they had for the next decade, several managers and top baseball executives pointed to Griffey. Doug Melvin, Cleveland's assistant general manager, suggested, "Nobody else can do all the things Griffey does. Not only does he give you so much production at the plate, playing center field the way he does, he takes runs away too."[41]

An AL general manager expressed great affection for Thomas but then said, "I'd take Griffey because of his body. You look at his dad and see that he had such a long career, and Junior has the same genes." Noting that Gonzalez had experienced back ailments, the GM added, "you worry about pure power hitters. Frank is already big, and you worry about him getting hurt or getting bigger as he gets older. But Griffey has the kind of body you think will hold up over a long period of time."[42]

Thomas didn't question the choice of Griffey. "All around, I would say Griffey's the best. Junior's getting better and better, and his defense in incredible. There are only three guys in the game I'd pay to see play: Junior, Juan and Barry Bonds."[43]

Others disputed Thomas's analysis, referring to Griffey as a slacker. One GM indicated, "I don't see him as serious about the game all the time the way he should be. I still see him silly." Some were disturbed by Griffey's failure to run out every ground ball when it appeared an out at first base was inevitable. Or because he wore his cap backward. Or due to his fraternizing with players on other teams. Or the obscene gesture he directed at Sparky Anderson, Detroit's manager, the previous year after belting a homer. Additionally, Junior was "usually the first one out of the clubhouse," as he acknowledged.[44]

Griffey's relaxed attitude also bothered some, which he understood. "I've heard all the things said about me…. I take my game seriously, but I don't play like I'm serious. I play to have fun. You play better when you're loose. All I want is to be the best player I can be, not what people think I can be. When I'm done playing, I want people to say about me, 'He could flat out play. He had fun while he played. And I enjoyed watching him play.' That's all."[45]

Mackey Sasser, who played 37 games alongside Griffey in the Mariners' outfield, offered, "He doesn't even realize his own talent yet. He's still a kid. I've watched Barry Bonds play, and he's every bit of Barry Bonds—only younger. He's the only guy I've ever seen who can call his shots." On both Mother's Day and Father's Day, Griffey had said he intended to knock out a homer. He did exactly that. On other occasions, Sasser reported, Griffey had done that as well.[46]

According to Verducci, Tim Kurkjian, and Steve Wulf, the Braves, Reds, and Giants were favored in the NL, while the Orioles, White Sox, and Mariners were expected to come out on top in the AL. Having won three division titles and nearly 300 regular-season games over the past three seasons, the Braves possessed baseball's finest starting pitching: Greg Maddux, Tom Glavine, John Smoltz, and Steve Avery. The Reds had ace pitcher Jose Rijo and a potent lineup that now included shortstop Tony Fernandez, formerly of the world champion Toronto Blue Jays. The Giants could put on the playing field pitcher Mark Portugal, second baseman Robby Thompson, and most of all, Barry Bonds.[47]

Over in the American League, the Orioles had added "four high-profile free agents," including first baseman Rafael Palmeiro and third baseman Chris Sabo, while retaining shortstop Cal Ripken (fast closing in on Lou Gehrig's consecutive games played record), starting pitcher Mike Mussina, and reliever Lee Smith. The White Sox were led by first baseman-designated hitter Frank Thomas, left fielder Tim Raines, and pitcher Jack McDowell. The Mariners included third baseman

Edgar Martinez, right fielder Jay Buhner, Griffey, and the wickedly fast left-hander Randy Johnson.[48]

◆ ◆ ◆

In its April 4 issue, *The Sporting News* also discussed "Baseball 94." Its cover contained the smiling face of Ken Griffey, Jr., with the headline "The Son Also Rises." An opinion piece by Bob Verdi, "No baseball news will be good news in 1994," worried about seemingly endemic problems. There was the continuing threat of congressional revocation of the antitrust exemption. There was word of a forthcoming book by Fay Vincent referring to Bud Selig as a "small town schlepper." There was the continuing resistance of the players to a salary cap. There was Donald Fehr's warning that "another work stoppage" could take place. There was Nelson Doubleday, the Mets' chair, denying anti–Semitic comments attributed to him. There was, Verdi wrote, "George Frankensteinbrenner warning Jim Abbott to give more to the Yankees and less to charity."[49]

13

The Best Player in Baseball

Barry Bonds

As the 1994 season approached, two players—Barry Bonds and Ken Griffey, Jr.—appeared poised to outshine all others, both in terms of potential and based on their previous accomplishments on the playing field. Each was the son of a major leaguer who had achieved prominence in his own right. But the two sons had already exceeded what their fathers—Bobby Bonds and Ken Griffey—had done on baseball diamonds and were poised to become two of the most gifted ever to play the game.

At one point, Bobby Bonds, who was born in March 1946, in Riverside, California, had promised to pick up the mantle from both Willie Mays and Willie McCovey, his teammates on the San Francisco Giants. While Bonds was still in the minors, his manager, Max Lanier, a top pitcher with the World War II pennant-winning St. Louis Cardinals before he jumped to the Mexican League, talked to his son, Hal, the Giants' second baseman, about Bobby.

"The guy can hit, huh?"

"A ton."

"Can he run?"

"He doesn't run, he flies."

"Has he got an arm?"

"Like a cannon."

"Has he got power?"

"He can hit the ball a mile."[1]

By 1969, the year Bobby Bonds began to shine in major league baseball, Mays was in the third year of a descent from what had been a sustained, even historic career. A genuine five-tool player, Mays could do it all with grace and style. He was a four-time home run champ, twice having belted over 50 homers, with four other seasons of 40 or more. A brilliant base runner, he had thrice led the league in triples, once hitting 20, and had captured four stolen base titles too. Rookie of the Year for Leo Durocher's 1951 New York Giants, Mays had helped the team win the NL pennant, which it did again in 1954, after he spent nearly two full seasons in the U.S. Army. That latter season resulted in his lone batting crown, the first of two MVP awards, and a sweep of the Cleveland Indians in the World Series. The first game featured Mays's over-the-shoulder catch of a towering shot by Vic Wertz that also saw the Giants' center fielder toss a perfect strike to second base to prevent Indians runners from scoring.

With his power and speed both waning, Mays limped to his worst season in 1969, although he edged closer to both the 3,000-hit and 600-homer career marks that few players had attained, with nobody managing both feats. By contrast, McCovey was riding high, putting up the best totals of his 22 years in the big leagues. As Mays hit only 13 homers and drove in but 58 runs while batting .283, McCovey, another former Rookie of the Year, delivered an MVP season, leading the league with 45 homers, 126 RBI, an on-base percentage of .453, and a slugging average of .656. He also hit .320, fifth-best in the NL.

Twenty-three-year-old Bobby Bonds, in his first full campaign, led the league with 120 runs scored while knocking out 32 homers, tied for the sixth-best total, and driving in 90 runs. Seldom a high-average hitter, he batted only .259, and, also all too characteristically, struck out a ton, 187 times in fact, topping the majors. Possessing a rare combination of power and speed, Bonds stole 45 bases, behind only St. Louis' Lou Brock and Houston's Joe Morgan. His 6.3 WAR was seventh in the league, which McCovey and Atlanta's Henry Aaron led with 8.1.

With 21-game winner Juan Marichal, whose ERA was 2.10, both totals only a bit better than the Giants' second-best pitcher, 19-game winner Gaylord Perry, who had a 2.49 ERA, the team went 90–72, finishing runner-up in the NL West, three games back of the Braves.

Although McCovey had another huge year in 1970, Bonds soon became the Giants' biggest star, finishing one homer shy of becoming the majors' first 40–40 player, while compiling a 7.8 WAR in 1973, when *The Sporting News* named him NL Player of the Year. Bonds remained in San Francisco only until 1974, when he was traded to the New York Yankees, whom he played for but one year before undertaking a baseball odyssey.

Like many players of his era and earlier ones, Bonds's prowess was undoubtedly hindered at times by his fondness for cigarettes and alcohol. Nevertheless, he completed a 14-year career in the majors, having scored 1,258 runs, driven in 1,024, batted .268 with 302 doubles, 66 triples, and 332 homers, and compiled 57.9 WAR. He led the league in runs scored twice and in total bases once, scored more than 100 runs six times, twice had over 100 RBI, swatted more than 30 homers on five occasions, and stole more than 40 bases six times. He was a 30–40 player four times and had another season when he hit 32 homers and stole 30 bags. A three-time All-Star who appeared to be on a possible path to the Hall of Fame during his first seven full years in the majors, Bonds finished as high in the NL MVP race as third and fourth during his San Francisco stint.

A little more than four years younger than Bobby Bonds, Ken Griffey, born in April 1969 in Donora, Pennsylvania, played with the Cincinnati Reds for the first nine years of what became a 19-year career. While never the powerful force

Bonds was, Griffey, a three-time All-Star once named All-Star Game MVP, was a base-stealing threat in his prime and a regular .300 hitter often plagued by injuries. Twice he scored over 100 runs, he hit as many as 21 homers, and he stole as many as 34 bases in a season. In seven full seasons, Griffey hit over .300, including in 1975 when the Reds won their first World Series title in 35 years, and he batted .336 during his second season as a regular in 1976, when the Reds swept the Yankees in postseason play. His career ended with Griffey having compiled 1,129 runs scored, 2,143 hits, a lifetime .296 batting average, and 34.5 WAR, far below Bonds.

◆ ◆ ◆

Born on July 24, 1964, in Riverside, his father's birthplace, Barry Bonds possessed a baseball pedigree, which included Reggie Jackson, a distant cousin of Bobby's, and Willie Mays, who acted as his godfather. Athletic excellence abounded in the Bonds family, with an uncle a former state hurdles champion and an aunt an ex-Olympic hurdler. While in high school, Bobby recorded a 9.5 mark in a 100-yard race and won the state broad jump championship.

His son, Barry, went to Junipero Serra High School, located in San Mateo, California, becoming a three-sport star in baseball, basketball, and football. Both longtime major leaguer Jim Fregosi and Hall of Fame receiver Lynn Swann of the Pittsburgh Steelers had attended Serra High, as later would quarterback Tom Brady. Like his father, Barry exhibited both power and speed on the baseball field. A .467 batting average his senior year resulted in Barry's being chosen a prep school All-American, but his arrogance precluded his receipt of the team's most valuable player honor. His coach insisted, nevertheless, that he "was a very easy man to coach, an extremely hard worker.... I never had any problems with Barry.... When you give Barry his space, you couldn't be around a nicer kid." The Giants drafted Bonds in the second round but failed to come to terms with him, offering $70,000, $5000 less than he demanded.[2]

Undoubtedly, it hardly helped that Commissioner Bowie Kuhn had banished Mays from MLB in 1979, forcing him to leave his post as hitting instructor for the New York Mets. That followed Mays's agreeing to serve as a goodwill ambassador for an Atlantic City hotel and casino. Kuhn thundered, "A casino is no place for a baseball hero and Hall of Famer." Four years later, Kuhn would direct the same kind of edict at Mickey Mantle, who had been hired to serve in a similar capacity.[3]

Encountering no pressure from his godfather and miffed at the Giants' refusal to fork over a relatively small amount of money, Bonds accepted a scholarship to play ball at Arizona State University in Phoenix. Coach Jim Brock led one of the nation's top collegiate programs, having been named NCAA Coach of the Year in both 1977 and 1981, when he guided the Sun Devils to College World Series titles.

During three years of playing for Brock, Bonds batted .347, hit 45 homers, and drove in 175 runs. He twice helped the Sun Devils reach the College World Series; in 1984, he tied a CWS record, rapping out eight consecutive hits. It hardly hurt that several other Sun Devils eventually reached the major leagues. While at Arizona State, Bonds attained All-American honors and was named the Sun Devils' most valuable player. A year after he became a professional baseball player, Bonds would complete his degree in criminology.

In what was becoming too familiar, Bonds had proven controversial, even among his fellow players at ASU, who, at one point, all but unanimously called for him to be booted from the squad. Years later, Coach Brock informed *Sports Illustrated*, "I liked the hell out of Barry Bonds. Unfortunately, I never saw a teammate care about him. Part of it would be his being rude, inconsiderate and self-centered. He bragged about the money he turned down, and he popped off about his dad. I don't think he ever figured out what to do to get people to like him."[4]

Following his junior year, Bonds awaited the 1985 baseball draft, which proved to be remarkable. Five players were grabbed ahead of him: B.J. Surhoff (Brewers), Will Clark (Giants), Bobby Witt (Rangers), Barry Larkin (Reds), and Kurt Brown (White Sox). Other noteworthy selections in the first round included Pete Incaviglia (Expos), Walt Weiss (Athletics), Serra High alum Gregg Jefferies (Mets), and Rafael Palmeiro (Cubs). During subsequent early rounds, the following future major leaguers were picked: Randy Johnson (second, Expos), Tino Martinez (third, Red Sox), Bobby Thigpen (fourth, White Sox), David Justice (fourth, Braves), Jeff Brantley (sixth, Giants), and Brady Anderson (10th, Red Sox). Auburn's Heisman-winning halfback, Bo Jackson, was a 20th-round selection of the Angels. Two rounds later, the Tigers named John Smoltz, and a pair of rounds after that, the Cubs chose Mark Grace. In round 36, the Blue Jays tagged Jim Abbott, a top-flight high school pitcher who had been born without a right hand.[5]

Within a couple of days of being drafted by the Pirates, Bonds signed for $150,000. He was assigned to Prince William of the Class A Carolina League. He played in 71 games, hitting .299 with 13 homers, scoring 49 runs, knocking in 37, and stealing 15 bases in 18 attempts. Displaying a good eye, he also walked 37 times, putting together an on-base percentage (OBP) of .383, while slugging .547; his OPS (on-base plus slugging percentage) was .930. Promoted the next spring to the Hawaii Islanders in the Triple-A Pacific Coast League, Bonds competed in 44 games, in which he hit .311 with seven homers, scored 30 runs, drove in 37, slugged .527, and had a .435 OBP and a .963 OPS.[6]

That resulted in his transfer to the Pirates' roster, led by manager Jim Leyland, and he immediately became a regular in the outfield. Despite exhibiting promise, he struggled mightily, perhaps for the first time in his baseball career. No matter, the Pirates' "superscout," Howie Haak, exclaimed about the rookie center fielder, "He can do everything Darryl Strawberry can do except throw," referring to the Mets' slugging outfielder. In 413 plate appearances, spread over 113 games, Bonds collected only 92 hits, batting a mere .223. Yet he again displayed both power and speed, amassing 26 doubles and 16 homers, scoring 72 runs, batting in 48, and pilfering 36 bases in 43 attempts. Walking 65 times, he whiffed on 102 occasions but managed a .330 OBP, a .416 slugging average, and a .746 OPS. Despite his inconsistent start, Bonds still finished sixth in the Rookie of the Year balloting, won by Cardinals reliever Todd Worrell.[7]

During the next three seasons, stardom beckoned Bonds while not quite arriving. He approached 100 runs scored, hit 30 or more doubles, twice stole 32 bases, and put up just under 60 RBI each year, not bad numbers for a leadoff hitter. His homer totals were solid if not spectacular—25, 24, and 19—and his batting average reached as high as .283 but fell as low as .248. His OBP was in the .350 range—despite the lower batting average in 1989, he walked 93 times that year—his slugging average twice just missed .500, and his OPS ascended, at its peak, to .859.

The Pirates as a team were returning to respectability during Bonds's first years with the club, albeit inconsistently, sliding back down in 1989, as its young slugger-speedster did. That changed the following year, when Bonds became a genuine superstar, as Pittsburgh went 95–67, posting the NL's best record in winning the East Division by four games over the Mets. Third baseman Bobby Bonilla and center fielder Andy Van Slyke shone at the plate, alongside Bonds, while Doug Drabek went 22–6 with a 2.76 ERA, winning the Cy Young Award.

Generally slotted behind cleanup hitter Bonilla, Bonds raised his batting average to .301, while gathering 32 doubles, 33 homers, 93 walks, 52 steals, 104 runs scored, 114 RBI, and a .406 OBP. He amassed league leading totals in slugging (.565), OPS (.970; on-base plus slugging percentage), and OPS+ (170; OPS adjusted for the ballpark and the league in which the batter played). But he also finished in the top 10 in doubles (10th), homers (fourth), runs scored (sixth), RBI (fourth), total bases (293, sixth), walks (second), stolen bases (third), and extra-base hits (68, fourth). Remarkably, he was runner-up in both Offensive WAR (6.5) and Defensive War (2.5). His total WAR, 9.7, easily beat out the Phillies' Lenny Dykstra (8.9) and was far ahead of the third-place finisher, the Cubs' Ryne Sandberg (7.1).

Named to the All-Star team for the initial time, Bonds was voted NL MVP, winning all but one of the first-place votes; the other went to teammate Bonilla. *The Sporting News* chose Bonds as its Player of the Year. Terming him "a second-generation major league star," the paper recognized that he was "envied for the advantage of his bloodlines, but he is also expected to fulfill all of their promise." Seemingly welcoming that, Bonds asserted, "I want to put my father and myself in an untouchable class as a father-son combination. I want us to be the best ever in baseball." He pointed out that they had already reached "30–30 five times, and … 30–50 once. We're not finished yet."[8]

Other honors came Bonds's way, including his first Gold Glove and Silver Slugger awards. Working hard at his defense, Bonds had become an elite outfielder, the game's finest in left field. The Pirates' center fielder, Andy Van Slyke—his earlier receipt of a Gold Glove evidently spurred Bonds on—later indicated, "He willed himself to become great."[9]

Unfortunately, in what also became something of a pattern, Bonds struggled in postseason play. In the NL Championship Series, which the Pirates lost to the Reds in six games, he batted only .167, with no extra-base hits and only a single RBI.

Then, in something of a precursor and demonstrating MLB's changed nature, Larry Doughty, Pittsburgh's general manager, revealed that 13 teams asked during winter meetings about the availability of Bonds, who wouldn't attain free agency for an additional two years. The Pirates also soon demonstrated no inclination to negotiate a multiyear contract with either Bonds or their top starting pitcher, Doug Drabek. Both, along with Bobby Bonilla and four other players, were soon mired in arbitration. Eventually, Bonds and Bonilla each lost his arbitration case; this was Bonds's second defeat in salary arbitration.

His resulting anger spilled over to training camp, leading to a shouting match involving coach Bill Virdon, manager Jim Leyland, and Bonds. Accusing his star of "sulking" and displaying a "lackadaisical attitude," Leyland declared, "I don't give a damn what his problems are, he's not going to run this camp.... He can just go home." Bonds had recently pledged not to reup with the Pirates following the 1992 season "if they offered me $100 million." Referring to "the current financial circus" with players and management battling over salaries and contracts, *San Francisco Chronicle* columnist Bruce Jenkins charged that Bonds was "quickly becoming the biggest prima donna in sports."[10]

Another stellar year for the supremely talented Bonds was 1991, when he batted .292, hit 25 homers, scored 95 runs, drove in 117, stole 43 bases, and walked 107 times. He led the league in OBP (.410), OPS (.924), and OPS+ (160), while finishing in the top 10 in runs (eighth), RBI (second), walks (second), total bases (262, 10th), and slugging (fourth, .514). His offensive (second, 5.8) and defensive (10th, 1.5) WARs were both top 10, while his overall WAR (8.0) was second only to that of the Braves' Cy Young Award winner, Tom Glavine (9.2). During one tight game against San Diego, after Bonds was walked twice with the contest in doubt, he stared into the opponents' dugout, leading Padres manager Greg Riddoch to holler, "I can't help it if you're the best player in the game. That's your fault, not mine." Despite winning his second Gold Glove and Silver Slugger awards, Bonds finished runner-up in the MVP tabulation, receiving 259 votes, 15 behind the Braves' third baseman, Terry Pendleton, who led the league with a .319 average.[11]

Putting together the best record in the majors, 98–64, Pittsburgh ended up 14 games ahead of St. Louis in the NL East. Bonds had another miserable NLCS, batting only .148, driving in no runs, and managing only three singles and a double in 27 at-bats. Pittsburgh lost the pennant in a seven-game series against Atlanta, getting blanked in the last two contests as their star managed but one single.

The 1992 regular season proved to be another brilliant one for Pittsburgh's star, indeed his finest yet, which *Sports Illustrated* all but predicted, placing him on the cover of its May 4 issue with the headline "Bonds Away!" Leading the Pirates to their third straight NL East title, Bonds smacked 36 doubles and 34 homers, accumulated 295 total bases, batted .311, his top average to that point, drove in 103 runs, and stole 39 bases. His league-best marks included runs scored (109), walks (127), intentional bases on balls (32), slugging percentage (.624), extra-base hits (75), OBP (.456), OPS (1.080), and OPS+ (204). Among his other top 10 numbers were doubles (ninth), homers (second), stolen bases (ninth), RBI (fourth), and batting average (seventh).[12]

His Offensive WAR (8.3) easily topped the NL, while his total WAR (9.0) was slightly below Atlanta right-hander Greg Maddux's. Winning his third straight Gold Glove and Silver Slugger awards, Bonds grabbed his second MVP, swamping the previous year's recipient, Terry Pendleton. Not wanting anyone to consider his previous MVP Award "a fluke," Bonds set out "to win it," he admitted. "Once you climb the mountain, it's harder to stay. I want to stay." The Associated Press also named Bonds Player of the Year. Bonds acknowledged, "I had the best manager and coaching staff in the major leagues. Jim Leyland was like my other pair of eyes."[13]

The Pirates (96–66) again captured the NL East, beating out the Expos by nine games. Despite holding a 2–0 heading into the bottom of the ninth inning, Pittsburgh failed to prevent Atlanta from scoring three times. Former Pirate Sid Bream slid into home, just beating Bonds's throw to the plate. Undoubtedly reflecting on what might have been, Bonds remained in the field for minutes after the game ended. He had performed somewhat better in the series, belting his first postseason homer, scoring five runs, walking six times, and batting .261.

On December 4, 1992, Bonds signed a record $43.75 million contract with the San Francisco Giants, spread over six years. While the slugger denied it was important to be MLB's highest-paid player, his agent, Dennis Gilbert, insisted, "The best should be paid the best." The *Washington Post*'s Mark Maske indicated that Bonds, displaying a rare combination of power and speed, was "widely regarded as the best all-around player in baseball." The Yankees had actually offered slightly more on an annual basis but refused to budge from a five-year offer. The Red Sox also declined to agree to Gilbert's demand that a six- or seven-year package be tendered. The executive vice president of the bid-winning team, Larry Baer, said, "What this is, more than anything, is a statement that [new owner] Peter Magowan is dedicated to exciting baseball at Candlestick Park."[14]

In "Sports of The Times," his column for the *New York Times*, Dave Anderson pondered what would have transpired if the Giants had followed the Yankees and Red Sox in declining to offer Bonds a lengthier contract. Anderson recognized that had such a scenario, in which all teams agreed that Bonds was too pricey, occurred, charges of collusion would have been forthcoming. But the new owners of the Giants, led by Peter Magowan, who headed Safeway Inc., "clearly wanted to make a statement," indicating their readiness to "create a pennant contender" while drawing more fans to cold and windy Candlestick Park. Bonds, Anderson indicated, might have chosen the Giants because Bobby Bonds would now become their batting coach. This apparently superseded Barry's recognition that "the Candlestick Park chill might reduce the numbers he put up in Three Rivers Stadium" for the Pirates.[15]

Asking "Is Bonds a Jerk?" Craig Marine of the *San Francisco Examiner* indicated yes, but depicted him as an artist. "He runs like a gazelle, hits for average, for power and with runners on base. He's the best defensive left-fielder in the league and an incredibly hard worker who keeps his body prepared to play." His friend, Bobby Bonilla, now playing with the Mets, expressed no doubts about good his former Pirates teammate was. "Barry is the best player in the game. Sure, he knows it. But he is." During the past three seasons, his on-base percentage alone was .456, close to the range of Ted Williams and Babe Ruth over their fabled careers. Orlando Cepeda, who had starred with the Giants alongside Mays and McCovey, declared about Bonds, "He can swing a bat. He can play the game of baseball. Barry can compete with anybody in any era."[16]

That summer was when *Sports Illustrated* again placed Bonds on its cover, this time displaying him leaning against a bat held with his right hand, his left hand on his hip. The magazine featured that headline, "I'm Barry Bonds, and You're Not." The accompanying, in-depth article, "The Importance of Being Barry," by the sports journalist Richard Hoffer, contained a subheading, "The Giants' Barry Bonds is the best player in the game today—just ask him." Spending time in the clubhouse, Hoffer commented that it was "redolent of the perfume of entitlement."[17]

Present in one corner was Willie Mays, now a special assistant to the team president and general manager but known as "the greatest Giant there ever was." That very morning, Glenn Dickey, columnist for the *San Francisco Chronicle*, had compared Mays and Bonds, acknowledging that both were incredible ballplayers but asserting that each could "be a royal pain in the rear." Asked about Dickey, Mays referred to the sportswriter as "an asshole." Offering to get Bonds, Mays said, "He's not as bad as you think." As matters turned out, Bonds was napping in the trainer's room.[18]

With the Giants' slugger having begun the season at a "torrid" pace, the Mets' manager, Jeff Torborg, declared, "Bonds belongs in a higher league." The Pirates' general manager, Ted Simmons, jokingly indicated, "Let's think of the things he can't do." Bonds's teammate, shortstop Royce Clayton, offered, "I've never seen anyone like him. Barry is like Magic Johnson—he makes everyone around him better." In fact, it almost seemed as though he could "just turn it on and off" when he chose. Absent his poor playoff performances, Hoffer suggested, "it would be reasonable to suspect that he was playing with the game."[19]

There were concerns about Bonds that Hoffer noted. Notwithstanding his undeniable talent, "his complaining, his rudeness, his insensitivity to teammates can wear a franchise out." One unnamed Pirate once stated, "I'd rather lose without Barry Bonds than win with him." Pittsburgh center fielder Andy Van Slyke submitted, "If Barry is guilty of anything, it's of not attaching meaning to his words." As for Bonds's performance, Van Slyke affirmed, "He is the greatest player I ever played with, or will ever play with." But hardly helping matters was Bonds's toxic relationship with the press.[20]

In an article in the *Washington Post* titled "The Best Player in Baseball," Thomas Boswell indicated that his subject desired "to know every nuance of anything than can happen in a baseball game." The gifted ballplayer, he wrote, was a "chip off the old block," having a "chip ... on his shoulder" like his father had. At the same time, he was "the best all-around player since Mays.... Since Mays, nobody has been able to blend the five basic skills-running, throwing, fielding, hitting and hitting with power—as well as Barry Bonds."[21]

The cover of *The Sporting News* issue of June 14 displayed Bonds in his classic swing mode, alongside the query, "HOW DO YOU PITCH THIS GUY?" The accompanying three-page article by freelance writer Bruce Schoenfeld referred to Bonds's performance in April and May, "if extrapolated," as the game's "finest all-around ... since Mickey Mantle's thunderous 1956." Having altered his approach at the plate, the Giants' star was "choking up farther on the bat and shortening his stroke," becoming in the process a threat to collect both a batting championship and the Triple Crown.[22]

Referring to his phenomenal streaks, Marcel Lachemann, the Marlins' pitching coach, indicated, "When you get a hitter as good as Bonds is and he gets this hot on top of it, it's as close as you're ever going to see that" continuing over a full season. Throughout the baseball campaign, Bonds had been "waiting for a pitch he knows he can handle," Schoenfeld wrote. "At his hottest a few weeks ago, observers marveled to see him passing on pitches just an inch or two above the strike zone. But he had the patience to realize letting those go would get him a better pitch later in the at-bat, or at worst a walk." The Cardinals' pitching ace, Chris Carpenter, admitted, "There's not really any way to pitch him; you just have to hope when he comes to the plate, he's aggressive. You hope he doesn't make you throw a strike to him, because if he does it suddenly gets a lot harder."[23]

Barry Bonds, one of the game's greatest all-around players, starred for first the Pittsburgh Pirates and then the San Francisco Giants. Ca. 1994 (National Baseball Hall of Fame Library, Cooperstown, NY).

As the All-Star game approached, the *Baltimore*

Sun's Ken Rosenthal declared, "He's F. Robby in '66, Reggie in '77, Rickey in '89." In fact, "Barry Bonds is doing them all one better. No player changing teams has ever had as great an impact, and this season is only half over." His brilliant play was even "overshadowing his abrasive personality." He had become "the Michael Jordan of baseball, a player transforming an ordinary team into a monster." Bonds was "the straw that stirs the drink. And sips it all himself."[24]

The *Orlando Sentinel*'s Brian Schmitz appeared to be in complete agreement with Rosenthal. He wrote, "There's the American League and the National League, and then there's the Barry Bonds League. Bonds simply is in a league of his own." The 28-year-old Bonds, who had received the most votes from fans in tabulations for the All-Star Game, was "now the player his father, Bobby, only hoped to be" and could, eventually, be compared to Willie Mays, his godfather, both offensively and defensively. He was presently "the game's greatest player, a one-dude dynasty." He also attracted "buzzzzz" from fans expecting a Jordan-like performance.[25]

On its August 1993 cover, *Baseball Digest* asked, "Barry Bonds: Best All-Around Player in Majors?" Editor John Kuenster noted that Barry was appearing on the front of his magazine nearly two decades after Bobby Bonds had initially been featured there. The article on Bobby called him "baseball's best run producer," with a rare combination of power and speed. Kuenster then repeated the adage attributed to wordsmith Yogi Berra, "It's like déjà vu all over again." Barry also possessed the twin attributes of power and speed but also "a much better eye for the strike zone." Bobby was faster and possessed a better arm, but Barry had "reached double digits in assists four times" and made up for an average throwing arm with "the quickness with which he gets to the ball." Giants pitcher Jeff Brantley declared, "He can pretty much do it all. His baseball instincts are unbelievable."[26]

Mike Downey of the *Los Angeles Times* called Bonds "baseball's stick of dynamite. At the plate he has become Barry the dinosaur, big as Barney. Nobody knows how to attack him." Downey stated, "He's the greatest player in the game today and is in a terrible rush to get wherever he is going next. Here is someone for a true baseball fan to appreciate."[27]

Throughout the 1993 season, Bonds, as if sliding into a new gear, attained unprecedented heights for him. His .336 batting, the league's fourth-best, was easily the finest of his now eight-year career. For the first time, he led the NL in homers (46), RBI (123), and total bases (365). He was also first in slugging (.677), OBP (.458), OPS (1.136), and OPS+ (206) percentages, as well as intentional bases on balls (43). He was in the top 10 too in doubles (eighth, 38), runs scored (second, 129), and bases on balls (second, 126). His Offensive WAR (8.8) was tops, and his overall WAR (9.9) was just a shade behind Cincinnati pitcher Jose Rijo's.

It was hardly surprising, then, when Bonds received another MVP Award, along with usual Gold Glove and Silver Slugger honors. Somewhat amazingly, four voters cast first-place votes for the Phillies' Lenny Dykstra, but Bonds outpointed him, 372–267. *Baseball Digest* also selected Bonds for its Player of the Year Award, as did the Associated Press, whose vote was determined by broadcasters and sportswriters. That group chose Bonds for the second straight year.[28]

Led by Bonds, third baseman Matt Williams, and second baseman Robby Thompson at the plate and 20-game winners John Burkett and Bill Swift, the 1993 Giants rebounded from the previous year's 72–90 record to win 103 games, equaling the most in their San Francisco era. But they came up one win short, finishing behind the Atlanta Braves in the National League West. Thus, San Francisco, with the second-best record in the major leagues, missed out on the playoffs.

◆　◆　◆

With the 1994 regular season still weeks away, *The Sporting News* analyzed one of the two top all-around players in the game. Along with Seattle Mariners center fielder Ken Griffey, Jr., another son of a former three-time All-Star, Barry Bonds, the two-time reigning MVP, who had now won three of those awards, appeared to be in "a league of his own."[29]

San Francisco Examiner sportswriter Larry Stone began his piece by stating the obvious and asking a question, "Barry Bonds faces his annual quandary, one that never touches the lives of mere mortals in his profession: just how do I top myself this time?" By this point, the eight-year veteran was already a four-time All-Star and four-time winner of both the Gold Glove and the Silver Slugger awards. He had scored over 100 runs three times, batted in more than 100 on four occasions, hit better than .300 three times, and led the league in scoring, homers, total bases, RBI, walks, on-base percentage (3), OPS (4), and OPS+ (4). Over the past four years, he had never finished worse than second in the NL MVP vote, and the one runner-up decision hardly made any sense.[30]

As for his own goals, Bonds explained, "Every time, I try to keep the same pace, and every year, I end up doing something better than the year before." However, recognizing what drove him, Bonds admitted, "But I'm starting to dig a hole for myself. You can't do that forever. I've got to find something to piss me off, or fire me up, and then I can do better." Someone seemed to understand this, posting a sheet of paper on his spring training locker that read, "You ain't _____ till you win no. 4." Stirring himself up, Bonds said, "The guys in here don't think I can do it, so I'm going to have to show them. At least they know what makes me tick." If he were to obtain an unprecedented fourth MVP Award, Bonds predicted, "you won't see the fifth. I wouldn't want to go through that kind of pressure again…. I'd just chill and let someone else have it."[31]

For now, Bonds was targeting another MVP and 40–40 performance, meaning 40 homers and stolen bases in the same season, something only Jose Canseco had accomplished to date. Additionally, Bonds desperately wanted the World Series title that had so far eluded him, with first the Pirates losing three straight years in the playoffs, and then the Giants dropping the final contest of the regular season to come up a game short.[32]

Also, to motivate himself, Bonds reflected about what Michael Jordan had achieved in basketball and Joe Montana in football. "Something has to keep you going, because you can easily say, 'What else can I do?'" Then there was the fact that he soon would turn 30 and believed he had perhaps four more seasons at the top of the sport. "Something has to slack off. It's mother nature. Then I'll have to help in other ways. I'm always studying the game."[33]

14

The Natural

Ken Griffey, Jr.

KEN GRIFFEY, JR., WAS BORN IN DONORA, PENNSYLVANIA, on November 21, 1969. His 19-year-old father, Ken Griffey, like Bobby Bonds, possessed athletic excellence in his own family. Griffey Sr.'s father, Joseph "Buddy" Griffey, was a stellar athlete, playing alongside Stan Musial in high school before receiving a scholarship to play football at Kentucky State University. In high school, Griffey was a four-sport star, excelling in baseball, basketball, football, and track. Drafted in June 1969 by the Cincinnati Reds in the 29th round of the amateur baseball draft, the speedster Griffey turned down offers to play college football, signing for $500 a month.

While Griffey Sr. took six years of professional ball to become a major league regular, his son's path was far smoother. His performance on the playing field while at Moeller High School, which Cincinnati's star shortstop Barry Larkin had attended and where Griffey played during his junior and senior years, attracted scouts from throughout the major leagues. His coach at Moeller, Mike Cameron, who watched Griffey bat .478 and display considerable power at the plate, later indicated, "He was very natural, very graceful, I think he hit some of the longest balls ever recorded.... Then in the field.... I don't think people really appreciated it because he made it look so natural."[1]

Considered a five-tool player, Griffey, as anticipated, became the first selection in the MLB draft. As Tom Mooney, a scout for the Seattle Mariners, acknowledged, "His skill set was easy to identify. He really was, at age 16 or 17, a man playing against boys." Bob Harrison, another Seattle scout, saw that "the game was easy for him." His colleague, Roger Jongewaard, went further, extolling the young ballplayer's "rare combination of speed/power/instincts" that allowed him to be "much better than Barry Bonds" when Barry was 17.[2]

A leading evaluator for the Mariners, Steve Vrablik, wrote,

Son of Ken Griffey now playing with the Atlanta Braves. Ken Griffey, Jr., just 17 years old, will not be 18 until Nov. of this year. Has above-avg to outstanding tools in all 5 categories. Future hitting ability above avg. Over-anxious at times at the plate when he wants to go for the long ball. Will drop his hands with a slight hitch and a tendency to uppercut. Quick stroke with good bat speed and outstanding power potential. Gets a late start out of the box with his big swing, but he has good running ability. Very good instincts in the OF, gets a good jump with above avg. range. Top prospect for me with outstanding skills.[3]

In June 1987, Seattle handed Griffey a signing bonus reputed to be as high as $175,000.

Assigned to Class A Bellingham in the Northwest League, 17-year-old Ken Griffey, Jr., proved stellar from the outset, hitting 14 homers, scoring 43 runs, driving in 40, stealing 13 bases, slugging .604, and compiling a .445 OBP and a 1.049 OPS in 54 games. *Baseball America* chose him as the top prospect in the minor leagues.

But following the season, the troubled 17-year-old ingested 277 aspirin pills in an attempt to kill himself. That ended with a stay in Providence Hospital's intensive care unit in Mount Airy, Ohio. Griffey later explained, "It seemed like my father and I were always fighting. I know a lot of kids go through that with their families, but it was hard for me. You see, I'm real stubborn."[4]

The pressures of being a baseball phenom—he was referred to as "The Natural"—also wore on young Griffey, who considered killing himself one other time, possibly with his father's gun. "It seemed like everyone was yelling at me in baseball, then I came home and everyone was yelling at me there. I got depressed. I got angry. I didn't want to live." A reputed racially-charged incident during which one of the team bus driver's teenage sons called him "Nigger" and another went after him with a gun didn't help. Nor did Griffey's propensity for staying out "until 3 or 4 in the morning," according to his father. Griffey Sr. insisted his son "pay rent or get" his own place. "I was confused. I was hurting and I wanted to cause some hurt for others," Griffey Jr. recalled. Amazingly, while Jr. was in the hospital, the two got into it again, which only stopped when he tore the IV out of his arm. The family agreed that Jr. should get a condominium of his own.[5]

Transferred that spring to Class A San Bernardino in the California League, Griffey Jr. again hit for both power and average—11 doubles, 11 homers, and a .338 average—in 58 games. He scored 50 runs, drove in 42, had a .431 OBP, a .575 slugging average, a 1.007 OPS, and stole 32 bases. He struggled a bit more on moving to Class AA, playing for Vermont in the Eastern League, where he knocked out only a pair of homers and batted .279 in 17 games but managed to both score and drive in 10 runs during his abbreviated venture. No matter, *Baseball America* again picked Griffey as its leading major league prospect.

Marty York, writing in *The Globe and Mail* out of Toronto, offered his analysis of the young ballplayer, "Griffey Jr. Destined for Stardom, Scouts Contend," before spring training. Several scouts indicated that Griffey possessed "the most natural talents since Willie Mays. Or, at least, Eric Davis," a reference to the Cincinnati center fielder at the time considered to have preternatural skills of his own. Sheldon Bender, a superscout for the Cincinnati Reds, declared, Griffey "has tremendous ability and all the tools you're looking for. He has tremendous makeup. He can hit and hit with power. And he's a great outfielder."[6]

Griffey was expected to begin the season in the high minors, but as Seattle manager Jim Lefebvre indicated during spring training, "Every day, he shows you something that tells you he's going to be an incredible player." *Newsday*'s Peter King referred to the "Man-Child Ken Griffey Jr.," who in one eight-game stretch pounded out 16 hits in 31 at-bats, as "Mariners' teen sensation." Lefebvre admitted, "As the competition in the spring gets better, he has gotten better. That's a sign of a great talent."[7]

His promise was great enough to win a spot with the Mariners in 1989, where, as a 19-year-old rookie, he managed, despite breaking a bone in his left hand, 23 doubles, 16 homers, 61 RBI, and a .264 average in 127 games. His .329 OBP, .420 slugging average, .748 OPS, and 108 OPS+ paled by comparison with the upcoming years but enabled him, nevertheless, to finish third in the Rookie of the Year competition. Beating him out were the runaway winner, Orioles reliever Gregg Olson and Royals starter Tom Gordon, but Griffey did receive one first-place vote.

Griffey Jr.'s joining Seattle's roster occurred while his father had returned to the Cincinnati Reds. This was the first time that a father and son were playing in the big leagues simultaneously, as a cover story in *The Sporting News* indicated. While Ken Griffey had been a fine ballplayer, his son threatened to become a "megastar."[8]

The next year, the 20-year-old Ken Griffey, Jr., did indeed become something of a star in the major leagues, which *Baseball Digest* seemed to predict. Its March 1990 issue displayed Griffey on its cover, indicating that he was following "in His Dad's Footsteps." The companion article by the *San Antonio Express News*' Kevin O'Keefe mentioned that he already had "a candy bar named after him … a line of T-shirts," an impending book, and "a father-son poster." Griffey was quoted as saying, "I want to surpass my father because then I'd know that I accomplished a lot."[9]

The May 7 cover of *Sports Illustrated* featured Ken Griffey, Jr., with the headline "The Natural" and a lowercase reference to "Seattle's 20-year-old Wonder." Sportswriter E. M. Swift's "Bringing Up Junior" analyzed the young phenom, with a remarkable opening statement. "You kind of want to put the whole show under glass and preserve it forever, before it changes, the way people wanted to do when Willie Mays first came up and the Say Hey Kid won everybody's heart. Now there's *this* kid: Junior. It's more than just the breathtaking baseball skill you want to capture—his great arm, his fluid stride, his viperlike upper-cut swing. It's the whole darn affair."[10]

That included his father, now a 40-year-old, 18-year veteran of the major leagues, grabbing a plane to watch his son replicate his own "dazzling over-the-wall catch" in the same ballpark five years ago. There were his teammates, who appeared to lack jealousy as they watched his wondrous feats. There was his mother Alberta, whom he called each evening, reversing the charges. There was "the pure joy" Griffey displayed while turning "this big-buck, high-pressure business called baseball back into a playground game."[11]

Still the game's youngest player, Griffey was all but certain to become even better. His hitting coach, Gene Clines, indicated, "He's a big kid, a baby. When he finally buckles down and gets serious about his game, there's no telling what kind of numbers he will put on the board." Clines added, "I don't think anybody's ever been that good at that age. He's in his own category. He is a natural." Indeed, at this point of the major league campaign, Griffey was leading the AL in batting and was close to the top in hits, homers, total bases, and RBI.[12]

The *Hartford Courant*'s Bob Sudyk delivered his own commentary on Ken Griffey, Jr. He began his piece memorably: "It is not true that the skies parted and Ken Griffey Jr. floated down on a cloud, nor that a voice of a prophet came out of an Iowa cornfield and told of the coming of the perfect ballplayer, one who would dominate the national pastime during the last decade of the 20th century." Still, "such cosmic entrances," Sudyk proposed, might be fitting due to "the real-life achievements of Junior Griffey," already "the cornerstone of the franchise and the darling of Seattle." Not many would question that Griffey was the game's "most salable commodity" at present. Jim Lefebvre, the Mariners' manager, submitted, "Junior's the best prospect I've ever seen. I've told the coaches, 'We're going to be able to go through our lives and say we were there at the start of Ken Griffey Jr.'s career, a once-in-a-lifetime kid to come along.' He's so far ahead of his talent, it's frightening. He's got God-given instincts."[13]

Seattle general manager Woody Woodward certainly didn't disagree with that assessment. "When you talk about superstars, I think you talk about players like Willie Mays and Henry Aaron, players who had done it consistently over the years," Woodward said. "Ken Griffey Jr. has the potential to be that kind of a player." The Mariners' batting coach, Gene Clines, termed him "a natural," while manager Jim Lefebvre referred to his "good genes."[14]

Batting .300 during the 1990 season for the first time, while hitting 28 doubles, 7 triples, and 22 homers, Griffey scored 91 runs, drove in 80, stole 16 bases—he was thrown out 11 times—and compiled other impressive statistics, particularly for such a young ballplayer. Those included a .366 OBP, a .481 slugging average, an .847 OPS, a 136 OPS+, and 287 total bases. He made the All-Star team, won his first Glove Glove for superb center field play, and finished 19th in the MVP balloting, which admittedly amounted to only seven points. Griffey finished seventh in Offensive WAR (5.2), seventh in batting average, eighth in triples, fifth in hits, seventh in extra-base hits, sixth in intentional bases on balls, fourth in total bases, ninth in runs scored, ninth in slugging average, and eighth in OPS.

In late August, the Ken Griffeys—father and son—played together, becoming the first to do so in the history of the major leagues. Both singled and scored a run in a 5–2 win over the Royals. Having been nailed by a toss from Griffey Sr. as he attempted to turn a single into a two-bagger, Bo Jackson mused, "I'd have been mad if anyone else had thrown me out, but it was a piece of history. Those Griffeys were messing with me."[15]

Although his Mariners regularly foundered in the AL West, Griffey's own stardom continued to ascend in 1991. At season's end, the *Washington Post*'s Thomas Boswell indicated he "has proved to be almost as good as his hype." He was the league's leading vote getter for the All-Star Game. Griffey batted .327 with 42 doubles, and 22 homers, while stealing 18 bases in only 24 attempts. He scored 76 runs and batted in 100 for the first time. Totaling 289 bases, he finished with a .399 OBP, a .527 slugging average, a .926 OPS, and a 155 OPS+. He finished in the top 10 in batting (fourth), doubles (fourth), extra-base hits (ninth), intentional bases on balls (21, third), RBI (eighth), OBP (eighth), slugging average (seventh), OPS (fourth), OPS+ (sixth), and total bases (10th). His 7.1 WAR was fourth-best in the AL, where he finished a respectable ninth in the MVP balloting. He made the All-Star team again, repeated as a Gold Glove winner—drawing comparisons with Willie Mays in the process—and also won a Silver Slugger Award.[16]

The next season was similar, with Griffey, said to have "the league's sweetest swing," hitting .308 with 39 doubles, and 27 homers, while scoring 83 runs and driving in 103. Amassing 302 total bases, he had a .361 OBP, slugged .535, and put up .896 OPS and 149 OPS+ numbers. He was in the top 10 in batting (eighth), doubles

(fifth), homers (seventh), total bases (sixth), intentional bases on balls (15, third), slugging (.535, fourth), OPS (.896, fifth), OPS+ (149, fifth), and Offensive WAR (6.2, sixth). A repeat All-Star and the winner of that year's All-Star Game MVP as he went three for three with a double, a homer, and a pair of RBI, he also won another Gold Glove Award, was viewed as "spectacular in the field," and finished 17th in the MVP count. On top of all that, he remained a fan favorite.[17]

Like Barry Bonds, Griffey transformed into a legitimate superstar during his fifth year in the major leagues. As Thomas Boswell wrote, "This season, Ken Griffey Jr., Frank Thomas, and Juan Gonzalez truly and totally arrived." Previously, Griffey had elicited "comparisons to Mays as a swift, thrilling center fielder with every known baseball

Ken Griffey, Jr., called "The Natural," was another great all-around player, particularly during his tenure with the Seattle Mariners. Ca. 1994 (National Baseball Hall of Fame Library, Cooperstown, NY).

skill." One question remained: "Would he ever hit home runs?" As Griffey answered that, Boswell asked, "Honestly, is there anything he might not do?"[18]

During 1993, Griffey, like Bonds, slammed over 40 homers for the first time, ending up with 45, while also belting 39 doubles, and batting .309 with a league-best 86 extra-base hits, 113 runs scored, 109 RBI, and 359 total bases. His .408 OBP, .617 slugging average, 1.025 OPS, and 171 OPS+ were personal bests too. Griffey's top 10 totals included doubles (sixth), homers (second), hits (eighth), runs scored (sixth), RBI (10th), bases on ball (96, eighth), intentional bases on balls (25, second), slugging (.617, second), OBP (.408, sixth), OPS (third), and OPS+ (third). Topping all American League position players with an 8.8 WAR, Griffey, somewhat surprisingly, ended up only fifth in the MVP race. An All-Star once more, he did receive a fourth straight Gold Glove and a third Silver Slugger Award.

With several weeks left during the 1993 season, Jim Thomas of the *St. Louis Post-Dispatch* talked about Griffey's having already broken the home run franchise record for the Seattle Mariners by smacking his 33rd against Kansas City reliever Tom Gordon. "I never thought I'd hit 30 homers. I never thought I'd hit 20 home runs. I've seen the George Fosters, Tony Perez, those type of players, hit 30 and 40. And George hit, what 52? When he did that, I was 7 years old." His father, now the Mariners' hitting coach, spoke of his son. "He wants to get better every year, so he just tries to improve on each category as he goes along."[19]

To Thomas, "the scary part is contemplating when—if? —Junior will level off." Seattle manager Lou Pinella indicated, "He's going to be a great player." Quickly, he continued, "He's one now. You measure greatness over the years. All he needs to do is maintain. He doesn't need to get any better." Pinella added, "We just let him play. He doesn't need to improve on anything." Griffey's father said, "He's maturing. It's getting better every year. He's understanding himself a little more."[20]

Minnesota star outfielder Kirby Puckett sang Griffey's praises: "I think Junior's the best player in the league, with the potential to be better. He can do anything he wants." Griffey appeared even better than Bonds was at a comparable age, although as Bob Sherwin of the *Calgary Herald* noted, "In the past few years, though, Bonds's numbers have soared." Red Sox outfielder Andre Dawson, a veteran of both leagues, said about Griffey, "He's nowhere near what his potential could be. He's a guy who has power, can hit for a high average … has pretty good speed. He has all the tools to do everything, and he's only 23 years old." Yet to attain his peak, Griffey "has a long way to go. His work habits will dictate how good a ballplayer he'll be."

Comparing Griffey and Bonds, Dawson stated, "Both are possibly franchise players. It's any manager's dream to have either of them." Then he added, "But I think there's something special about Junior, given the fact that he's just 23 years old. He's going to get a lot better." Dawson added, "He'll [Bonds] tell everyone how good he is … whereas Junior plays the game and keeps his mouth shut." Bonds didn't disagree regarding the superlatives spun about Griffey. "The Kid can play baseball. I think if Junior ran more than he does, he would be considered the best. I've gotten to run more and I've driven in more runs." The Giants' star continued: "There's no lack of talent between the two of us. You're got to admire a kid like that, 18, 19 years old in the big leagues. At 18, I was trying to figure out which college I'd attend. He could have 20 years in the bigs and not even be 40. That's amazing."[21]

Yet all was not easy for one of MLB's naturals, as Mark Maske of the *Los Angeles Times* reported. Still confronting a learning curve, Griffey continued to discover "how someone who's done more than all but a select few in the history of the game came be regarded by so many baseball people as obnoxiously immature and too often disrespectful—to the game and to his immense talent." Maske saluted the ballplayer called "perhaps the best … in baseball not named Barry Bonds." Admittedly lacking maturity at times, Griffey nevertheless appeared ready to respond to new manager Lou Piniella's imploring to "give me more." Still, one of Piniella's counterparts suggested, "He's young. But he just doesn't play the game right all of the time. It'd be a shame for any of that talent to go wasted. You're talking about possibly one of the greatest players ever—if he grows up." In full agreement, the *Houston Chronicle*'s Milton Kent indicated that "Griffey continues to amazes" and "looks like a player for the next century."[22]

During the 1993 season, Griffey achieved other feats, becoming only the fifth MLB player to slam 100 homers before turning 23. He also tied Dale Long (1956) and Don Mattingly (1987) as only the third player to smack a home run in eight straight games. He and Bonds were the first left-handed batters in nearly a quarter of a century—the Red Sox's Carl Yastrzemski and the Cubs' Billy Williams in 1970 were the last—to have 100 RBI, score 100 runs, smash 40 homers, and bat .300 in the same season. But at 23, Griffey was the youngest major leaguer to deliver 100 RBI for three straight years; in the process, he beat out Ty Cobb, Mel Ott, Joe DiMaggio, Ted Williams, and a contemporary, Juan Gonzalez. Demonstrating his all-around prowess, Griffey established a record for AL outfielders in handling 573 consecutive chances without committing an error.[23]

Alan Solomon of the *Chicago Tribune* contended that the new season might demonstrate that Ken Griffey, Jr., was "the league's best all-around player." Dwight Jaynes of *The Oregonian*, published in Portland, wrote, "If Barry Bonds drops off at all this season, Griffey will become the best player in the game." Griffey was being counted on for "another monster season" to enable the Mariners to contend. Including Junior in their "Center Field of Dreams," sportswriters in the *Seattle Times* waxed poetic: "From Ty Cobb's tenacious play in the early 1900s to Willie Mays's defining catch in 1954 to Ken Griffey Jr.'s spectacular defense today, center field has always been center stage for baseball's greatest athletes."[24]

In its spring baseball feature, *The Sporting News* honed in on Griffey, a superstar evidently shaped by his "sense of family." Calling his subject "a work in progress," Steve Marantz referred to him as "a man-child, young enough to wear his cap backward and blast his rap music as loud as he pleases, old enough to inspire and lead his Mariners' teammates." Having been touched by "the dark side," Griffey conjured up images of the flawed protagonist Roy Hobbs in Bernard Malamud's novel *The Natural*. But according to Marantz, a more apt comparison seemed to be Alfred E. Newman, the everyboy of *Mad* magazine, whose motto was "What, me worry?"[25]

At present, "life hardly could be better for Junior," Marantz suggested. "A player of nearly seamless skill, his career is on a Hall of Fame trajectory" with "superlatives quickly ... exhausted." Griffey, the word went, "bats with the ease of Williams ... fields with the grace of DiMaggio ... banters with the wit of the comedian Arsenio Hall." Fellow Mariner Jay Buhner said, "He's so good, it gets a little irritating. Like it's so effortless, I think, 'Is it that easy, man? Is it that easy?'" Teammate Edgar Martinez, a former batting champ, admitted, "His swing is perfect. I would love to have his swing." On top of it all, Griffey, unlike many superstars—Barry Bonds immediately came to mind—dealt easily and openly with all he encountered, the press and fans alike.[26]

15

Opening Days

THE 1994 MAJOR LEAGUE SEASON, with an abundance of stars and regular players alike, began during the first week of April. Highlights included Chicago Cub Karl "Tuffy" Rhodes smashing three homers during his first three trips to the plate against New York Mets righthander Dwight "Doc" Gooden in the opener on April 4. Among those present at Wrigley Field was the First Lady, Hillary Rodham Clinton, an avid Cubs backer. Sporting a Cubs jacket and cap, Hillary joined Harry Caray and Ron Santo in the radio booth and Caray and Steve Stone on television. Gooden and the Mets wound up with the victory in a 12–8 slugfest. In another Day One appearance, the Red Sox's Roger Clemens, like Gooden, got bombed. Third baseman Matt Williams slugged two homers, helping San Francisco beat Barry Bonds's former team, Pittsburgh.[1]

Then there was the opening in Cleveland on April 4 of Jacobs Field, which cost $175 million and was largely paid for by a "sin tax" levied on cigarettes and liquor and funds contributed from Dick Jacobs, the team's owner. Over 41,000 were in attendance. Present were President Bill Clinton; Ohio governor George Voinovich; and the Indians' greatest pitcher in team history, Bob Feller. The president extolled the new stadium, "Beautiful, man," before stating, "There isn't enough federal money to rebuild the cities. It takes efforts like this one to bring in jobs and housing."[2]

During the early postwar era, the Indians had experienced a remarkable nine-year stretch when they finished first or second in the American League each year with two exceptions. They took the pennant in 1948 and 1954, capturing the World Series on the first occasion and winning an American League–record 110 games on the second, although they got swept in the World Series by Willie Mays's New York Giants. Notwithstanding a second-place finish in 1959, they entered a long dry spell prior to the 1994 season.

Attendance at mammoth Cleveland Stadium, with its seating capacity well past 70,000, soared during 1948, shooting up to 2,620,627. But by the mid–50s, it had slipped far below 1,000,000, including a game in late 1956, when 356 showed up. "I remember the place was so empty and so quiet that from the pitching mound I could hear the clacking of the typewriters up in the press box," Herb Score recalled of the contest when teammate Bob Lemon won his 20th game of that campaign. Many soon referred to "the curse of Rocky Colavito" following the trade of the young home run king to the Tigers for AL batting champ Harvey Kuehn.[3]

Despite the team's remaining mired in undistinguished play, attendance finally pushed back past the 1,000,000 standard in 1986, never again falling below that level. A 76–86 record, placing Mike Hargrove's Indians sixth in the AL East in 1993, didn't prevent them from drawing over two million fans for the first time since 1949. In recent memory, Cleveland had lost "Joe Carter, Brett Butler, Julio Franco, Tom Candiotti, Bud Black and Greg Swindell," to actual or impending free agency. But more lately, the team, guided by general manager John Hart, had managed to amass a group of fine young players, including second baseman Carlos Baerga, catcher Sandy Alomar, Jr., center fielder Kenny Lofton, and left fielder Albert Belle. Promising too were third baseman Jim Thome and right fielder Manny Ramirez. The Indians also added important free agents of their own, among them starting pitchers Dennis Martinez and Jack Morris and first baseman-designated hitter Eddie Murray.[4]

The improved makeup of the Cleveland roster was duplicated by a sharp increase in salaries, now approaching $1.1 million per player, just below the major league average. That amounted to a 6.1 percent increase during the past year, "a problem for at least 12–15 franchises," according to Bud Selig, chair of MLB's executive council and the acting commissioner. Skeptical as ever of management's analyses, Donald Fehr asked, "How can an industry that's had this kind of sustained growth be in a crisis situation?"[5]

GM Hart pledged, "I will not allow to happen in Cleveland what happened in Pittsburgh." Predicting that the Indians would "be a very competitive team," Hart believed that would continue to be the case "down the line." Dick Jacobs, the Indians owner, declared, "Fans are gonna love us. Fans are gonna adopt this team. This has been ten years in the making. It's been like giving birth to an elephant, with about eight years of gestation."[6]

President Clinton tossed out the first pitch for the home opener in 1994, setting the stage for the contest between the Indians and Lou Piniella's Seattle Mariners, who finished fourth in the AL West the previous season. Taking the mound for the Indians was Dennis Martinez, having signed with Cleveland after a 15–9 campaign with the Montreal Expos. Starting for the Mariners was their 6'10" southpaw, Randy Johnson, the tallest man in the majors, who had made the All-Star team for the second time in 1993. Despite uncharacteristically striking out only two batters during the first seven innings, Johnson had a no-hitter and a 2–0 lead going into the bottom of the eighth. But the Indians tied the score, following a walk, a single by Sandy Alomar, a wild pitch, and a double by Manny Ramirez, clearing the bases. Both teams notched a run in the 10th inning, then Wayne Kirby drove in Eddie Murray with a single to left field in the 11th, enabling Cleveland to win the first regular season game ever played at Jacobs Field.

The Ballpark, which cost $191 million—nearly three-quarters covered by a half-cent sales tax in the city of Arlington—welcomed fans for the Texas Rangers' home opener one week later. The team's president, Tom Schieffer, referred to the soon-to-be demolished previous ballpark, Arlington Stadium, as "a backwater stop, the worst facility in baseball." Now, Tim Kurkjian wrote, they "have one of the best … an open-air, natural grass, 49,292 seat, asymmetrical, baseball-only masterpiece." This was "another stadium that combines the look of an old-time ballpark with the latest fan-friendly features." Each of its seats—all angled—faced home plate.[7]

Derived from the second version of the Washington Senators, an expansion squad added to the American League in 1961, the team moved to Arlington a decade later. Usually terrible throughout its brief tenure in Washington, D.C., the team, renamed the Texas Rangers, rested at the bottom of the AL West for its first two seasons, then spent several years flirting with respectability before moving from cellar-dwelling status to never quite becoming truly competitive. The past season had been one of the franchise's best, with an 86–76 record leaving the Rangers eight games behind the White Sox in the AL West. The 1994 Rangers were led by two-time home run champion Juan Gonzalez; two-time All-Star and two-time Gold Glove catcher Ivan Rodriguez; third baseman Dean Palmer; former Giants first baseman Will Clark; and DH Jose Canseco, the former Rookie of the Year, MVP, home run champ (two times), and Silver Slugger Award winner (three times). Texas also had on its roster a pair of budding stars: second baseman Jeff Frye and right fielder Rusty Greer. The pitching staff was led by left-hander Kenny Rogers, having completed a 16–10 season, and Kevin Brown, a right-hander with a wicked sinker and a hard, heavy fastball, who had won 21 games two years earlier and finished 1993 with a 15–12 record.

The *Los Angeles Times'* Ross Newhan analyzed the new-look Rangers, following the retirement of Nolan Ryan, the replacement of Rafael Palmeiro by Clark, and Canseco's attempted comeback. Clark had signed a five-year deal worth $30 million to move over from the Giants. Additionally, the American League West now contained only the Angels, Athletics, Mariners, and Rangers, with the White Sox shifting to the Central Division. Rangers GM Tom Grieve stated, "I think we can win and will win. I think every team in the division believes it has a better chance without the White Sox, but I think we'd win even if the division was the same. We have the best team."[8]

Manager Kevin Kennedy admitted, "We no longer have any excuses for not winning the division." He hoped that Gonzalez, signed to a new seven-year package amounting to $45.45 million, would assume a leadership role. Some of his teammates had expressed concerns when he sat out a number of important contests late during the previous season. Kennedy had also appeared ready to suspend the slugger for missing a therapy session due to oversleeping.[9]

Along with their new ballpark, the Rangers also had new uniforms, discarding their previous blue-and-white apparel for a red-and-white makeup with a new logo. Van Cliburn, the renowned classical pianist raised in East Texas, joined with the Fort Worth Symphony Orchestra in delivering the national anthem. Over 46,000 watched the 2–3 Rangers play Bud Selig's Milwaukee Brewers, last-place finishers in the AL East in 1993, due to a 69–93 record that placed them 26 games back of Toronto. The starting pitchers were Kenny Rogers and the Brewers' right-hander, Jaime Navarro, following up on an 11–12 campaign. The Brewers, who never trailed in the contest, prevailed, 4–3, with catcher Dave Nilsson pounding his second homer of the year.[10]

The first week of the new major league season also featured a no-hitter by an Atlanta Braves pitcher but not by one of the usual suspects. Starting pitchers Greg Maddux, Tom Glavine, John Smoltz, and Steve Avery collectively possessed three Cy Young awards, five 20-win seasons, and nine All-Star selections. However, it was left-hander Kent Mercker, who had a 15–13 lifetime record and had never pitched beyond the sixth inning in a big-league contest, who threw the first no-hitter of 1994 on April 8 while striking out 10 Dodgers, including the hitting maestro, catcher Mike Piazza, three times. Fans attending that game also witnessed the first Korean to play in the major leagues, 20-year-old Chan Ho Park, greeting him with a standing ovation.

◆　◆　◆

Notwithstanding complaints regarding yet another alteration of MLB traditions, the advent of wild card teams for the postseason promised to add excitement for the array of teams who had been unable to reach the top of their respective divisions. The previous year, the San Francisco Giants, led by Barry Bonds's stellar first year with the ballclub and his third MVP, won 103 games, the second-best mark in the majors and only a game behind the front-running Atlanta Braves. That brilliant record, however, left the Giants on the sidelines when the National League Championship Series was played. A repeat performance from the previous year could easily put San Francisco at the top of the new Western Division. Over in the American League, the New York Yankees finished seven games behind the Toronto Blue Jays, but their 88–74 record was the third-best in their circuit, and a similar showing could put them into the playoffs for the first time since 1981, albeit as a wild card team, again with three other AL squads. The Yankees' non-playoff stretch was longer even than that of the post-glory days when Ford, Mantle, and Maris faded.

Ira Berkow, one of the nation's top sportswriters, discussed the seeming ending of pennant races, with the "supposed purity, sanctity, ennobling essence of two or three teams battling and perspiring for what used to be called the gonfalon." Instead, only days into the 1994 major league season, Berkow wrote, "Baseball, now, is bursting with pennant, or, division races." Rather than two pennant scrambles as in days of yore or even the more recent version of four races, there now might exist as many as half-a-dozen.[11]

During the past few years, Berkow noted, Organized Baseball's efforts to maintain an "exciting and salable" sport had not hurt it, "as disgusting as they were." He listed "artificial turf, designated hitter, domed stadiums, late-late-night playoff and World Series games, moronic mascots." These followed earlier "gimmicks" like using a livelier ball, bringing in the fences, reducing the height of the pitcher's mound, and having uniforms with numbers displayed on the backs. As always, Berkow wrote, "the game will live and die on its merits, on the individual games and performers, and not on wild-card teams."[12]

◆ ◆ ◆

As the new season began, MLB still lacked a permanent commissioner. Talk continued about whom team owners might select, with the name of Democratic senator George Mitchell of Maine again floated. The highly regarded politician had declared his intention not to run for reelection in the fall. He had also recently conveyed to President Clinton an unwillingness to fill a seat on the U.S. Supreme Court. As for the possibility of serving as baseball's top administrator, Mitchell said, "If the position is offered to me, I will consider it at that time." Speaking at a press conference, the senator stated that he had only spoken to a single baseball person during the past several months. The inference was that the individual was Bud Selig, who acknowledged, "We've developed a very good relationship … and I have the highest regard for his ability. He's also a splendid human being." Another baseball official commented on Mitchell's possible selection: "It would give us a man of stature."[13]

◆ ◆ ◆

The lack of a permanent commissioner, controversies about wild-card teams, and the failure to agree to a new collective bargaining agreement were not the only issues confronting major league baseball. Throughout the history of the National and American Leagues, players, including some of the finest, were forced to wrestle with various afflictions and addictions. The founder of the NL, William Hulburt, prohibited gambling and alcohol from baseball contests. Nevertheless, many players drank heavily, including King Kelly, one of the game's early stars but one inclined to imbibe during games. Baseball writers appeared all too fond of the drinking antics of Rabbit Maranville. Three-time batting champ Paul Waner also was noted for his consumption of alcohol. Hall of Fame sluggers Hack Wilson and Jimmie Foxx both curtailed their playing prowess because of a fondness for alcoholic substances. Babe Ruth was another big hitter known to drink profusely, which may have exacerbated the medical problems that curtailed his 1925 season, his poorest until the very end of his career. Managers were not immune, with John McGraw arrested for participating in a drunken brawl in the midst of Prohibition and Joe McCarthy's alcoholic consumption costing his job with the Red Sox.[14]

During the 1950s and 1960s, two of the best teams—the Milwaukee Braves and the New York Yankees—were among the most notorious for heavy drinkers. The Braves' contingent revolved around two-time home run king Eddie Mathews and starting pitchers Bob Buhl, Lew Burdette, and Warren Spahn. The Yankees' drinking buddies included star southpaw Whitey Ford; second baseman Billy Martin; and Mickey Mantle, who had replaced Joe DiMaggio in center field. Because of New York City's standing as the nation's leading metropolitan area and the Yankees' status as major league baseball's premier team, the attention paid to the Yankees' antics was both larger and surprisingly subdued, in keeping with a long-standing determination to whitewash improprieties and indelicacies associated with sports figures.

The reality was that the two players considered most likely to break Babe Ruth's single-season home run record (60) and his lifetime total (714) were Mathews and Mantle. Although both had stellar careers, neither came close to accomplishing those feats. Ironically, teammates, not Mathews and Mantle, performed those heroic exploits. In 1974, Henry Aaron became the all-time career home run leader, having belted over 200 more than Mathews did before ending his career as a part-time player with the Detroit Tigers in 1968. That same year, the injury-plagued Mantle also called it a day, falling far short of Ruth's lifetime total. Mantle came close to the single-season record, hitting 52 as a 24-year-old Triple Crown winner in 1956, five more than Mathews's top year, which occurred as a 21-year-old during his second season three years earlier. In 1961, Mantle and fellow Yankee Roger Maris undertook a concerted assault on Ruth's 60-homer season, but injuries left Mantle seven back of the new record-holder. Maris's 61st homer came in the Yankees' 162nd game, which seemingly piqued the question of who really was the all-time home run king because of Commissioner Ford Frick's pronouncement that an asterisk would accompany any breaking of Ruth's record beyond the old 154-game schedule. Due to considerable pushback, Frick never actually instituted the change he threatened regarding the single season HR record.[15]

Other substances on which ballplayers relied—ones more potentially performance-enhancing, including amphetamines—also made their way around clubhouses, particularly following World War II. Some talked about returning veterans, including the Red Sox's inimitable hitter, Ted Williams, bringing back Dexedrine or "greenies," as the small green pills were called. Following the 1960s, greenies could be found throughout major league locker rooms. Some clubhouses had a pair of coffee pots, one containing coffee alone, the other coffee with liquid amphetamines added. This occurred as MLB, in 1971, banned amphetamines. Usage in no way slackened, although discussion of the subject long remained muted with rare exceptions. Two bestselling books, Jim Brosnan's *The Long Season: An Inside Chronicle of the Baseball Year as Seen by Major League Pitcher* (1960) and Jim Bouton's *Ball Four: My Life and Hard Times Throwing the Knuckleball in the Big Leagues* (1970), published respectively at the start of the 1960s and immediately following its close, related tales of players doping. Among those doing so were Henry Aaron, Mickey Mantle, and Willie Mays.[16]

The great Philadelphia Phillies slugger Mike Schmidt, who starred during the 1970s and 1980s, reported that amphetamines had "been around the game forever." In his autobiography of a kind, Schmidt related, "In my day," they "were widely available in major-league clubhouses." Schmidt indicated, "They were obtainable with a prescription, but be under no illusion that the name on the bottle always coincided with the name of the player taking them before game time." As for his own dabbling in amphetamines, Schmidt acknowledged, "A couple of times in my career, I bit on it." He admitted, "There were a few times in my career when I felt I needed help to get in there."[17]

Drug usage threatened to get out of hand at different points, perhaps particularly during the same period Schmidt starred in and wrote about in his memoir. Both amphetamines and cocaine were easily obtainable and did alter the trajectory of various players and teams of the era. The Pittsburgh Pirates, Kansas City Royals, St. Louis Cardinals, and New York Mets were among those squads. Several of their ballplayers, including All-Stars and award-winning figures, got caught up in the swirl of illicit substances. That led to ruined careers and decimated teams, including two that once exhibited dynastic possibilities. By 1985, several players had been convicted or arrested due to drug offenses. First baseman Willie Aikens, center fielder Willie Wilson, outfielder Jerry Martin, and pitcher Vida Blue, all of whom played with the 1983 Royals, served three months behind bars.[18]

The Pirates went from a World Series title in 1979 to winning only 57 games six years later. The Royals were AL pennant winners in 1980 before sliding to a losing record in 1983, then rebounding to take the 1985 World Series. Whitey Herzog, who managed Kansas City in the late 1970s, stated, "I'll always be convinced that cocaine cost us a World Series with the Royals." The Cardinals, now managed by Herzog, won the World Series in 1982, became an average club at best during the next two seasons, took the NL title in 1985, slid badly the next year, and won the pennant again in 1987 before becoming a middling team for an extended period. Referring to the early 1980s, Herzog later charged, "I'd say we had eleven who were heavy users." The Mets triumphed in the 1986 World Series, then crumbled to uninspired performances by 1991. Drugs beset each franchise, crippling two for several years and causing the third also to fall from grace for a spell.[19]

A series of drug trials that took place near the conclusion of the 1985 season brought unwanted attention to this problem, yet another one besetting Organized Baseball. The revelations that were forthcoming failed to prevent various Mets players from engaging in similar exploits. Among those testifying were former MVPs and batting champs Dave Parker and Keith Hernandez. Parker discussed how heavy cocaine use, which he started during the Pirates' World Series championship season in 1979 and continued through 1982, affected his play. "I felt my game was slipping and I feel it played some part in it." Hernandez referred to "the romance years" pairing cocaine and baseball, when almost 250 players might have taken the drug that he referred to as "the devil on this earth."[20]

Several other players were named or admitted to using cocaine. These included both stars and regular players. Among those revealed or purported to have been involved were the Pirates' Willie Stargell, the Expos' Tim Raines, the Royals' Willie

Wilson, the Cardinals' Joaquin Andujar, and the Royals' Vida Blue, all frontline players. A heavy user of cocaine, Raines admitted during the Pittsburgh trials that he slid headfirst into bases to protect a cocaine vial he kept in his pocket. He would "sneak a snort in the clubhouse bathroom between innings." Enos Cabell testified that pitcher J. R. Richard, a brilliant young strikeout phenom, regularly used cocaine through the point when he suffered a career-terminating stroke in the 1980 season. While his name didn't come up during the Pittsburgh trials, Doc Gooden regularly used cocaine during the Mets' World Championship season in 1986.[21]

MLB commissioner Peter Ueberroth's attempt to address the game's drug epidemic proved disastrous. Attempting to skirt past the players' union, he sought to convince them "to participate voluntarily in his drug-testing program," Murray Chass wrote. "Testing is the only way to show our public and the fans that baseball is clean," Ueberroth exclaimed. "The players could take that cloud and just throw it away, remove it." Donald Fehr suggested that the commissioner's tack was "very possibly, if not probably, a violation of law."[22]

◆ ◆ ◆

Earlier that summer, *Sports Illustrated* issued a special report on what it called "the steroid explosion." William Oscar Johnson, in "Steroids: A Problem of Huge Dimension," largely focused on other sports, especially football, where the rampant usage of steroids was readily apparent by the mid–1980s. But the lengthy article opened with the statement, "It is a spreading wildfire that is touching athletes at every level of sport." Pros and amateurs, men and women, were "routinely ingesting or injecting anabolic steroids to increase their strength or improve their all-around sense of athletic and personal self-worth."[23]

In his column for the *Los Angeles Times*, dated August 11, 1987, and titled "At Stake Is the Integrity of Baseball," Jim Murray delivered a warning to MLB's commissioner. He referred to earlier attempts to rein in illicit actions on the playing field, including the spitball and other "artificial aids" employed by pitchers "to scuff up baseballs." Murray referred to the observation by George Will, another syndicated columnist, that "when you cheat at baseball, you are a 'competitor.'" However, Murray noted that baseball was presently "struggling with its image as a hotbed of drug abuse." Cheating occurred in other sports, with track stars employing steroids. By contrast, "baseball's cheating has always seemed more whimsical than criminal. But times, they are a-changing," Murray wrote.[24]

◆ ◆ ◆

Nearly a decade later, as the 1994 season got underway, problems involving alcohol and drugs continued to afflict the national pastime. In the third week of the new baseball campaign, one of its most iconic figures from days past appeared on the cover of *Sports Illustrated*. Displayed was the weathered face of Mickey Mantle, posed with a wry smile on his face, a World Series championship ring visible. So too were the almost startling words, "I was Killing Myself: My Life as an Alcoholic by Mickey Mantle." For many readers, images of the handsome, baby-faced 19-year-old who first graced the outfield of Yankee Stadium alongside Joe DiMaggio 43 summers earlier sprang to mind. Or the powerful swing of the greatest switch-hitter in major league history. Or the stoic figure, bleeding through his uniform, continuing to lead the Yankees to pennant after pennant until his body and those of his teammates began to give way to still more injuries, age, and other misfortunes.[25]

With assistance from sports journalist Jill Lieber and accompanied by revelatory photos, Mantle reminisced about heavy bouts of drinking, including with his good friend and longtime

Mickey Mantle, one of baseball's most gifted players, played his full career with the New York Yankees, leading them to a dozen pennants and seven World Series titles. His career was marred by injuries and his fondness for the alcohol-frenzied nightlife. Ca. 1960 (National Baseball Hall of Fame Library, Cooperstown, NY).

Yankees teammate Billy Martin, both during his playing days and later. The former great ballplayer discussed the depression and anxiety that accompanied retirement, the bad behavior, the long memory lapses, and his determination to talk with young kids and "older guys" alike regarding drug and alcohol abuse.[26]

♦ ♦ ♦

On a triannual basis, *The National Law Journal* selected "the most influential lawyers in America." Among those recently so labeled were Floyd Abrams, a specialist in First Amendment issues, and 76-year-old Lloyd N. Cutler, who served as counsel in Bill Clinton's White House. Also chosen was Donald Fehr, MLBPA's executive director and general counsel.[27]

Talk continued about the possibility of a strike taking place in September, toward the end of the regular season. However, there was also word that the players might move up their timetable to July, perhaps following the All-Star break. Some were concerned that a later "job action" would not leave much time to resolve contractual issues and allow for the playoffs. Should the playoffs not occur, then the labor dispute would carry over into the 1995 season.[28]

Los Angeles Dodgers outfielder Brett Butler declared, "I'm pessimistic. History has shown that it's always been a war." Montreal Expos first baseman Randy Milligan predicted, "I see 90% chance of a strike." Donald Fehr admitted that a strike remained "a real possibility" due to stalled negotiations and concerns regarding owners imposing a salary cap following the season if no agreement were forthcoming. Bud Selig refused to respond to Fehr's statement.[29]

16

May Days

As the second month of the 1994 major league season began, some things were becoming clear. The newly designed NL West was settling for lackluster team performances, according to win-loss records. Only 12–11 San Francisco, led again by Barry Bonds and Matt Williams but with Bonds off to a slow start, had a winning record, a game better than Los Angeles and a game-and-a-half ahead of Colorado; already several games back, San Diego had former batting champion Tony Gwynn but not much else. The AL West was even worse, with 10–13 Seattle, featuring Ken Griffey, Jr., and left-handed strikeout whiz Randy Johnson, and 9–12 Texas vying for the top spot. The NL Central was most competitive in that circuit, with 15–7 division-leading Cincinnati and fourth-place 12–10 Pittsburgh separated by three games. Sandwiched in between were 12–9 St. Louis and 13–10 Houston and its young star first baseman, Jeff Bagwell.[1]

In the NL East, 15–8 Atlanta ,with speedy football star-outfielder Deion Sanders hitting well above .350 and leading the league in steals, appeared strong yet again, two games ahead of 13–10 Montreal, a young, up-and-coming team. Philadelphia, the defending pennant holder but with ace Curt Schilling having lost his first four decisions, was at the bottom of that division. The AL Central was tight, with 13–9 Cleveland, featuring outfielders Kenny Lofton and Albert Belle, 13–9 Milwaukee, and 13–10 Chicago, which had defending MVP Frank Thomas, leading the pack. Three games back, 9–11 Kansas City did have right-hander David Cone. The AL East was clearly the majors' best, with 17–7 Boston and a resurgent Roger Clemens, 15–8 Baltimore, 15–8 New York, still becoming revitalized with its pitching staff led by Jimmy Key and its lineup including the fiery outfielder Paul O'Neill, and 14–10 Toronto, the two-time defending World Series champ, all appearing competitive.

Two major league batting records had already been set in a season during which batting averages and home runs both appeared to be ascending. Talk of "rabbits" and juiced baseballs abounded. Toronto outfielder Joe Carter, who had belted a walk-off homer to win the 1993 World Series, established a major league mark with 31 RBI in April. Colorado first baseman Andres Galarraga, the defending NL batting champ, drove in one fewer, the best total in the senior circuit's history over the initial month. San Francisco's Matt Williams and Florida's Gary Sheffield had each just cracked home run number 10 in the early season. The hottest pitchers were possibly the White Sox's Jack McDowell and the Cardinals' Bob Tewksbury, both off to 5–0 starts.[2]

The Atlanta Braves and the Montreal Expos, both now in the NL East, promised to remain fierce competitors throughout the 1994 season. After being a league doormat from 1985 to 1990, Atlanta, having added third baseman and MVP Terry Pendleton, had surged to the top of the then NL West in 1991, improving its record by 29 wins. After defeating Barry Bonds's Pirates in the League Championship Series, the Braves fell to the Twins in a seven-game World Series. The next year, the Braves again beat the Pirates in the LCS but lost the World Series to the Blue Jays. The 1993 Braves, after picking up slugging first baseman Fred McGriff, outlasted the Giants, now including Bonds at the heart of their lineup, but dropped the LCS to the Phillies.

Their expectations for 1994 were high once again. Appreciating this, Dave Kindred presented an essay, "Life Is Oh So Good in Atlanta," in *The Sporting News*' May 2 issue. The Braves "fifth-best starter," he noted, had recently tossed a no-hitter. Atlanta lost only one of its initial 14 contests before falling into a mini-slump. Tom Glavine was heard to say, "We're going to lose 50 games." Kindred wrote, "It's the other 112 that matter." Pendleton exemplified what the Braves represented: "a professional outfit that moves with class."[3]

The 1994 version of the Braves included first baseman McGriff, Mark Lemke at second base, Pendleton at third, and hard-hitting rookies Javy Lopez behind the plate and Ryan Klesko in left field. Chipper Jones, viewed as another of the majors' top rookie prospects, had suffered a season-ending knee injury during spring training. The brilliant starting pitchers—Greg Maddux, Glavine, Steve Avery, John Smoltz, and Kent Mercker—were easily the best fivesome in the game. Relievers Greg McMichael and hard-throwing Mark Wohlers had considerable potential. Manager Bobby Cox continued to provide a steady hand.[4]

Quickly, the hard-charging Expos, who had started off 4–9, were right on the heels of the front-running but suddenly slumping Braves. At the batter's box, Montreal could send up 21-year-old first baseman Cliff Floyd, 22-year-old shortstop Wil Cordero, and smooth-hitting outfielders Moisés Alou, Marquis Grissom, and Larry Walker, each only 27 years of age. Coming off his second season in the majors, Alou, possessing a bloodline like Barry Bonds and Ken Griffey, Jr., was the son of former All-Star outfielder and MVP candidate Felipe Alou, one of three brothers who made the majors. Grissom, having completed back-to-back seasons in which he landed in the top 10 voting for NL MVP, had been an All-Star and won a Gold Glove in 1993. The supremely gifted but mercurial Walker, a former All-Star with two Gold Gloves and a fifth-place finish in the 1992 MVP tabulation, had speed, power, and the ability to hit for a high average.

On the mound, Montreal could call on either John Wetteland or Mel Rojas to close out a game. Front-line starters included Ken Hill, Pedro Martinez, Jeff Fassero, Butch Henry, and Kirk Rueter. While not able to equal the Braves' starters, the Expos' pitchers possessed considerable potential, especially Hill, Martinez, and Rueter. The slim—5'11", 170-pound—Martinez, considered too frail by the Dodgers, who questioned his durability and started him only three times, had been viewed as something of a diamond-in-the-rough by the Expos, who placed him in their rotation. He had just achieved his first victory as a starting pitcher, despite igniting a bench-clearing brawl following a brushback pitch. At this early stage of the season, Martinez had walked only eight batters but had hit six. After beating the Padres, he said, "I'm not going to quit pitching inside. I don't care if I hit 1,000 batters."[5]

On May 2, the Expos, the majors' "hottest team" and boasting a "rich farm system," won the 11th game out of their last dozen outings, pounding out 19 hits in a 10–4, comeback victory over the Dodgers, to move within half a game of the Braves. Going three for five, Alou drove in a pair of runs and raised his average to .398, while Ken Hill moved to 5–1, scattering five hits in seven and two-thirds innings.[6]

By contrast, the Braves had gone 2–8 following their torrid 13–1 start. Most recently, they had dropped three straight to the Pirates, with Atlanta's top pitchers, Tom Glavine, Steve Avery, and Greg Maddux, all getting outpitched.[7]

In *USA Today*, Rod Beaton pointed to a seeming sour note amid Montreal's surge in the NL East. Notwithstanding their winning ways, the Expos failed to attract large crowds, a sharp contrast to what was occurring throughout much of major league baseball. Since its inception in 1969, the Montreal franchise had a decidedly mixed appeal for baseball fans in the area. At the original ballpark, Parc Jarry, attendance was generally decent, averaging around 15,000 until the final two years, with 1976 especially disappointing as fewer than 8,000 fans on average turned out for home games. The new Stade Olympique proved more appealing, with Montreal's ticket sales soaring past the two million mark in four of the first seven seasons. Attendance dipped somewhat but remained solid with the exception of the 1991 season, when fewer than one million fans appeared.[8]

It took a full decade before Montreal achieved its first winning season in 1979, jumping to second in the NL East with a 95–65 record, two games back. The next year, the Expos again finished second, this time one game behind, going 90–72. A second-half 30–23 performance in the strike-split 1981 season, fueled by outfielder Andre Dawson, powered Montreal into the playoffs, where they first beat the Phillies in five games before losing to the Dodgers in a heart-wrenching fifth game in the NLCS. Largely a middle-of-the-pack team for the next decade, the youthful Expos came in second in both 1992 and 1993, ending up the latter year at 94–68 after taking 30 of their final 39 games, to wind up three games behind the Phillies.

Beginning on May 6, the Braves hosted the Expos for a three-game set. Greg Maddux went to 5–2, tossing a four-hit shutout while issuing no walks in besting Pedro Martinez, who lasted only five innings. Fred McGriff powered a pair of homers. The Braves' Tom Glavine beat Jeff Fassero, who struck out 11, in the second matchup, 2–1, also giving up only four hits. Ken Hill, now 6–1, nipped John Smoltz, who fell to 2–4, 1–0, although John Wetteland threw the last two innings in relief.

The game was scoreless through seven innings before Smoltz allowed Wil Cordero, on base with a triple, to score on Randy Milligan's sacrifice fly.

◆ ◆ ◆

Also coming off a much-improved 1993 campaign, the New York Yankees, led by manager Buck Showalter, had the best record in baseball as of Friday the 13th. While 22–11 Atlanta was tops in the NL and three and a half games up on Montreal, the Yankees stood at 24–10, albeit only one and a half games better than the Red Sox and two over the Orioles, whose Ben McDonald had just lost his first decision after seven straight victories. The two-time defending World Series champion Blue Jays were foundering, sitting at 17–18, already seven and a half games back. The Yankees were coming off a 10–4, 12-inning affair, capped off by a six-run outburst at the end of the away half. Despite his ninth homer, Paul O'Neill had actually seen his average dip to .459 after going one for five.

The other two AL divisions were decidedly weaker, with the 18–15 White Sox a half-game ahead of the 17–15 Royals in the Central, and the 16–20 Angels and the 14–18 Rangers vying for some version of first place in the West. The White Sox had just lost to the Rangers, 11–7, despite Frank Thomas's 11th homer and a two-for-four outing that lifted his batting average to .336. New Ranger Will Clark also went two for four, raising his average to a robust .390. Four hits, one a triple, led to four RBI for Texas' Juan Gonzalez.

The Braves' Tom Glavine now was at 4–3 after beating the Mets, 7–2, while the Expos' Jeff Fassero went to 3–2 following a 9–1 drubbing of the Cardinals. The 22–12 Reds, frontrunners in the NL Central by four games over the Astros, had just fallen to the 19–16 Giants, a game ahead of the Dodgers in the NL West. Former Giant Kevin Mitchell led the Reds with his 10th homer and .333 average, while Barry Bonds's three-for-four showing, with a double, his ninth homer, a stolen base, and four RBI, suggested he was starting to perform like, well, Barry Bonds. The 18–17 Dodgers beat the woeful Padres, who despite their 10–24 record did display Tony Gwynn, presently batting .407.

O'Neill and Gwynn, both presently above the historic .400 mark, were very different kinds of players on distinct teams. Chosen by Cincinnati in the fourth round of the 1981 amateur draft, O'Neill, born in Columbus, Ohio, in February 1963, made brief appearances with the Reds in both 1985 and 1986 and played somewhat more extensively the next year. By 1988, he was a regular right fielder with the Reds, an important member of the 1990 World Series team, and an All-Star in 1991, when he hit 28 homers and drove in 91 runs. Traded to the Yankees after the 1992 season, O'Neill had his finest season to date in 1993, slugging .504, hitting 20 homers, and batting .311.

With his torrid start in 1994, O'Neill offered the Yankees' "only consistent left-handed power." Considered a good fielder, he possessed "an exceptional arm" in right field. The *New York Times'* George Vecsey predicted O'Neill was going to compel the Yanks to put him the lineup every day, no longer rotating him against left-handers. Pointing to O'Neill's major league-leading .446 batting average, sportswriter Mike Bass said it was "the greatest April of any New York Yankee since the immortal Moose Skowron hit .451 in 1955."[9]

However, his agent, Joe Bick, acknowledged, "Knowing Paul, he's probably thinking disaster is just around the corner." Cognizant of how pessimistic O'Neill was, Bass said the player was "always waiting for the bad streak, constantly focusing on the unsuccessful at-bat." The now 31-year-old O'Neill admitted to appreciating his hot streak and believed he handled adversity better than in the past. Still he continued "small-dunking helmets after outs." Bick declared, "My standard line to him is: You're

Paul O'Neill, the New York Yankees' outfielder, led the American League in batting (.359) during the strike-shortened 1994 season. Ca. 1994 (National Baseball Hall of Fame Library, Cooperstown, NY).

going to have fifteen good years in the majors, and you won't enjoy a minute of it." Following a four-for-five evening with Cincinnati, O'Neill spoke with his agent on his car phone. "You had a pretty good night," Bick said. "I should have been 5 for 5." Soon, O'Neill's average was up to .467 and his on-base percentage was at .569. Then, the two marks were .475, with O'Neill having 56 hits in 118 official plate appearances, and .578, but his name was still not on the All-Star ballot.[10]

Newsday's Mike Lupica wrote about the Yankees' "quiet star," who had only been with team for little more than a season but had exuded "a quiet, old-Yankee grace from the start." Others would, of course, dispute Lupica's analysis, given O'Neill's hyper-intense nature that frequently led to temper tantrums, particularly after flaying at the plate. Coming over from Cincinnati, O'Neill recognized "how Yankees used to behave" and could again. "I've always been intrigued with the history of the game. And just in that sense, Yankee Stadium is the only place to be," O'Neill explained. "I love coming here every day for the games. This is a place and a uniform you don't take for granted. And it's a manager and a group of players you don't take for granted, either. I look forward to coming to the ballpark because of them, too. There's a fraternity here, and you feel it as soon as you walk in the door."[11]

In *The Sporting News*, Lupica expanded his analysis of O'Neill, who insisted on talking about the Yankees' drive for a World Series title rather than his lofty batting average. O'Neill, Lupica pointed out, made "everyone else in the batting order better. That is how it goes when someone hits the ball this way." Presently, O'Neill was "the best hitter on the best team.... He is at the best ballpark, one made for big things. It is that kind of stage."[12]

Already a four-time batting champ, Tony Gwynn had recently hit over .300 for the 11th straight season, a streak second only to Rod Carew over the past three decades. Born in Los Angeles in early May 1960, Gwynn attended San Diego State University, having been recruited as a point guard in basketball. After skipping baseball his first year at SDSU, he eventually became an All-American outfielder before being drafted by the San Diego Clippers of the National Basketball Association in the 10th round in 1981 and by the Padres seven rounds earlier. Batting well over .300 at the A, AA, and AAA levels in the minors, Gwynn joined the major league team for the first team late during the 1982 season, batting .290 in 54 games. After a return to AAA for a few games the next year, Gwynn was back with the Padres for good in 1983, hitting .309 in 86 contests.

Winning his first batting title (.351) and leading the league in hits in 1984, Gwynn was named an All-Star, got his first Silver Slugger Award, and was third in MVP voting as the Padres won the NL pennant, although they dropped the World Series to the Tigers in five games. During the next nine seasons, he led the league in batting average and hits three times and in runs once. He was an All-Star each season but one, received five Gold Gloves awards, and three additional Silver Sluggers. Nineteen ninety-three had been another fine year for Gwynn, who finished runner-up in the batting race with a .358 average, his second-highest yet. He did so for a last-place team with a 61–101 record.

While the Padres, who had sliced their payroll, didn't promise to be any better in 1994, Gwynn remained the game's foremost hitter for average. Or, as one baseball preview indicated, "Tony Gwynn is still Tony Gwynn. 'Nuff said." Gwynn was "a local treasure," read a local newspaper. The Padres' batting savant, Mike Lupica conceded, never received the attention "the game's other great stars" received. "Somehow he is not in there with Barry Bonds and Ken Griffey and Frank Thomas, Juan Gonzalez or Roberto Alomar." Even during down times, with Gwynn having batting practice in an empty stadium, "here is everything still right with baseball. Here is one of the best hitters who has ever lived even if people always seem to be talking about other players, other baseball things." He rapped out two or three hits each game, with virtually no one in attendance.[13]

"I just love to play the game," Gwynn, at the time the holder of a career .329 batting average, offered. "I've learned a lot over the last 12 years. And the biggest thing

I've learned is that you can't let the things going on around you affect you when the game starts. You can't take those things out on the field with you. It would be easy to make excuses. People say, 'They traded [Fred] McGriff on you, they traded [Gary] Sheffield, how can you be hitting better than you ever have?' And I just tell them it's because I love this game more than I ever did." Dallas Green, manager of the New York Mets, said, "I watch Tony Gwynn play this game with quiet class and never get enough credit. He's not showy. He doesn't get caught up in that bravado, macho bull that's so prevalent in our game. He's just a solid professional, in all phases of baseball."[14]

Two other young players, coming off career-best years, were threatening to become a pair of the game's best and most powerful hitters. On that Friday the 13th, one stood at .336 with nine homers while driving in more than a run a game; the other was at .349, also with nine dingers. Born in Boston on the same day as Frank Thomas was in Columbia, Georgia, Jeff Bagwell starred in soccer during high school but got a baseball scholarship to the University of Hartford. There he played under Bill Denehy, an ex-big-league pitcher. He attracted attention through his performance as a third baseman in the Cape Cod League, where both Thomas and Albert Belle played. Chosen by the Red Sox in the 1989 amateur draft's fourth round, Bagwell hit well in the minors, winning a batting title and being named a league MVP but displaying almost no power.

On August 30, 1990, Bagwell was informed that he had been traded to the Astros for 37-year-old Larry Andersen, a reliever Boston hoped would help shore up its lead in the AL East Division. Shortly following the transaction, Peter Gammons, speaking on *Baseball Tonight*, predicted that Boston had just lost a future batting champion. Converted to first base, Bagwell not only made the Astros' roster but also won a position in the starting lineup, playing virtually every game in 1991, hitting .294, driving in 82 runs, and belting 15 homers, despite having the cavernous Astrodome as his home ballpark. He received all but one first-place vote for Rookie of the Year honors. His second season saw most of his power numbers advance—34 doubles, 18 homers, 96 RBI—but he too became a star in 1993. That year, Bagwell posted 37 two-baggers, 20 homers, 88 RBI, a .516 slugging average, a .903 OPS, and a .320 batting average, sixth-best in the league. He accomplished all of that despite missing the final 20 games with a broken hand suffered at the plate.[15]

Favored to win the weak NL Central, the Astros, led by manager Terry Collins, featured Bagwell, who was said to be "moving from young star to established superstar," and second baseman Craig Biggio. With the Astros having finished 85–77, 19 behind the Braves in the NL West, Bagwell was eager for the season to start. The Astros' late-season surge led Bagwell to say, "This is what it's all about."[16]

By early May, the statistician Bill James was already predicting that Bagwell was bound for the Hall of Fame. But Michael Point, writing in the *Austin American Statesman*, contended that Bagwell, whom he called "one of the game's most productive players," required "an All-Star appearance or two to bring his exploits to the attention of casual baseball fans, the ones who ultimately select the team." Point indicated that "hard-core baseball fans, not to mention fantasy league fanatics," were "very familiar with Bagwell's samurai swing and the numbers it puts on the scoreboard."[17]

Another powerful right-handed hitter, Albert Belle, was born in late August 1966, in Shreveport, Louisiana. All-State in baseball during high school, Belle participated in the Junior Olympics, playing in the outfield and pitching for the silver-medal-winning U.S. team. Receiving a scholarship to Louisiana State University, Belle played under coach Skip Bertman, setting a host of school records in helping the Tigers make the 1986 and 1987 College World Series tournament. Selected in the second round of the 1987 MLB draft, Belle excelled at the minor league level but didn't do well during two brief stints with the Indians in 1989 and 1990.

The 1991 season would be far different, as Belle hit 31 doubles and 28 home runs, while driving in 95 runs and batting .282 in only 123 games. He attained his first MVP vote after the following season, during which he had 34 homers and 112 RBI. Belle became an All-Star in 1993, winning a Silver Slugger Award and finishing seventh in the MVP voting after a 36-double, 38-homer (fourth in the AL) campaign with a league-leading 129 RBI, a .552 slugging average, and an OPS of .922.

Although the Indians had finished a disappointing sixth at 76–86 in the AL East in 1993, they looked forward to playing in their new ballpark. They were led by Kenny Lofton, considered by some "the league's most exciting player, slugging Albert Belle and brilliant rookie Manny Ramirez." They also had Carlos Baerga, who might be ready to top Roberto Alomar as the AL's top second bagger, and they had added free agents Dennis Martinez, Jack Morris, and Eddie Murray. Kenny Lofton, Baerga, and perhaps especially Belle appeared on the cusp of superstardom.[18]

By late May, Belle was in the midst of a hitting streak during which he got on base in all but one of his last 14 at-bats. Still on a tear, his average was at .389 as the month neared a close. Belle, Baerga, Ramirez, and Murray were all on a pace to drive in 100 runs. *The Sporting News* placed Belle on its front cover for the July 4 issue. The article by Bruce Schoenfeld, "The Bellewether," referred to a scorching three-week stretch in May, when Belle hit .479 and became AL Player of the Month. "I've had to work harder to get where I am," Belle said. Unlike Barry Bonds or Ken Griffey, Jr., "I pretty much came out of nowhere and probably had to work three times as hard to get my name on the scene."[19]

◆　◆　◆

Meanwhile, Donald Fehr and Bud Selig maintained their indelicate dance that would determine the fate of the 1994 season. Selig continued to bemoan the financial state of several franchises, naming "Pittsburgh, Seattle, San Diego, Milwaukee, Minnesota, Houston, Montreal" before declaring, "You can't move them all." He asked, "Isn't that, then, a manifestation that something is wrong with the system? This is [in] no one's best interests to let this go unattended, players or owners." Fehr again broached the "real possibility" of an in-season strike. Responding to a declaration regarding financial problems besetting small market teams, he said, "We're still going over the data. Remember, they had two years." But Selig insisted, "Baseball can't continue the way it is. I know owners have cried about things for years, but this is different. This is serious trouble."[20]

"I'm not sure enough people understand what's happening," Fehr warned. "Not the players or the owners. The owners are like OPEC. The object is to eliminate competition for players because that drives up salary. They also want to artificially control what they sell, whether it's TV or franchises, to drive up prices." Only 121 of 800 major league players, Fehr worried, had contracts guaranteeing a paycheck for 1995 and beyond.[21]

"There will be a strike this year, and it will be a very long one," predicted Henry Aaron, major league baseball's all-time home run king. "Baseball has reached a point where everyone is reaching out for that last peanut, and the fans are the ones who are going to be hurt. Owners and players are going to have to realize that as much as they take away from baseball, they will have to give something back."[22]

On the last day of May, David Teel, sportswriter for the *Daily Press* of Newport News, Virginia, wrote, "This summer should save baseball. This summer should energize a sport that is burdened by tedious games, senseless fights and boneheaded owners. This summer should enthrall a nation as Paul O'Neill, Frank Thomas and Ken Griffey Jr. pursue venerable records that are decades old." Teel then predicted, "It's not going to happen," stating that O'Neill would not have a shot at hitting .400, while the two sluggers would not be allowed to go after Roger Maris's home run record. Instead, "baseball is going out on strike."[23]

17

A June Swoon?

HEADING INTO THE THIRD MONTH OF THE SEASON, only half of the six new divisions had authentic frontrunners with winning percentages above .600. One had two teams tied at a respectable .569 level, another was led by a .538 ballclub, and the final division had no team even close to .500. Although the 33–15 Yankees had cooled a bit, they still led the 30–19 Red Sox by three and a half games with the 27–21 Orioles six back in the AL East. The AL Central had the 29–19 White Sox two and a half games up on the 26–21 Indians. The 23–26 Rangers led the 23–29 Angels by one and a half games in the AL West. The NL East had the 31–18 Braves three and a half games ahead of the 28–22 Expos. The NL Central saw both the Astros and Reds with 29–22 records, two games ahead of the 26–23 Cards. The West Division was also the NL's weakest, with the 28–24 Dodgers three games ahead of the 25–27 Giants and another game in front of the 23–27 Rockies.

After going hitless in five at-bats in a 10–1 shellacking of the White Sox, Paul O'Neill was down to a .428 batting average. His teammate, third baseman Wade Boggs, a five-time batting champ, had just gotten a pair of hits in four times at the plate to raise his to .342. Chicago's Frank Thomas, one for three against New York, was at .372. Cleveland's powerful hitter, Albert Belle, was batting three points higher than the White Sox's star. Seattle's Ken Griffey, Jr., had a .325 average. Over in the National League, San Diego's Tony Gwynn was sitting on a .393 mark. Houston's Jeff Bagwell was at .330. San Francisco's Barry Bonds was up to .298.

The June 5 cover of *Sports Illustrated* displayed Griffey Jr. staring at another ball he had walloped over the fence. To his right, "BIG NUMBERS" rang out, along with the descriptor, "Ken Griffey Jr. and other stars are chasing baseball's most hallowed records." Below that could be seen, "61 Home Runs." Inside the magazine, Tom Verducci's article, "Shooting Stars," was paired with pictures of Rogers Hornsby and his .424 single-season average and Paul O'Neill's current .456, Hack Wilson and his 190 RBIs and Joe Carter's present 56, Babe Ruth and his 177 runs scored and Frank Thomas and his current 58, and Earl Webb and his 67 doubles and Larry Walker and his 24.[1]

Verducci mentioned other recent moments when thoughts of a .400 average occurred, including for Rod Carew in both 1977 and 1983, Lenny Dykstra in 1990, and John Olerud the previous season. Or of 62 homers, triggered by early-season performances by Reggie Jackson in 1969, Eric Davis in 1987, and Kevin Mitchell in 1989. All of those ultimately fizzled, although Carew still hit .388 in 1977. George Brett, in an injury-shortened campaign three years later, topped Carew by two points, ending up only five hits shy of .400. But as several records now appeared in jeopardy, Verducci indicated that none seemed more vulnerable than Roger Maris's home run total of 61 set in 1961. Now, "the holy grail of hardball—the single-season home run record—seemed within Griffey's reach."[2]

To Verducci and other baseball analysts, "the marks in question" were "genuine." Moreover, "none of the chases is purer or figures to be more thrilling than Griffey's run," he wrote. The Elias Sports Bureau's Steve Hirdt agreed. "That record can't be gerrymandered very easily." By 1994, Maris's record had stood for 32 seasons, just one fewer than Ruth's previous mark, set in a 154-game season. The fact that no one had come close to matching Maris, Hirdt contended, allowed for something of a "surrogate record" as a player neared 50 homers. The media pressure that would accompany a real drive to break the home run record would likely be relentless, as it already had been with Griffey's smashing of Mickey Mantle's total of 20 homers through the month of May. Presently, Griffey was on a pace to smack 74 homers and amass 470 total bases, which would break yet another record, Ruth's 457 in 1921.[3]

Imperiling Griffey's drive for baseball immortality was the very real possibility of a strike. Toronto's Paul Molitor pondered, "What are we supposed to do, forego a strike because Junior's got 50 home runs on September 1?"[4]

Frank Thomas of the Chicago White Sox was also on a pace to better Maris's record. The Big Hurt, as Thomas was known, declared, "I know [this] is an incredible pace, I'm just going to keep riding it as long as I can." Referring to Griffey, Thomas said, "He needs to be in another league now. He's having fun, that's why they call him 'The Kid.'" Colorado's first baseman, Andres Galarraga, was on a pace to break Hack Wilson's National League record of 56 homers, set in 1930, and to add 156 RBI.[5]

One discordant note emerged as Griffey continued his home run march. Now said to be "maybe the game's best player," The Kid blurted out, "I hate to lose. I love the city of Seattle. I'm building a home there, and I love the people. But losing is killing me…. I can't see staying." Claiming his teammates lacked "enough heart to win the division," Griffey indicated he wanted to be traded, even as his Mariners were only one and a half games out of first place in the weak AL West.[6]

◆　◆　◆

Following eight scoreless innings in a 1–0 shutout of the Giants, the Braves' Greg Maddux's record was 9–2, and his ERA was down to 1.34 by the end of May. That set him on a pace to win 29, a total only bettered by Denny McLain's 31 in 1968 during the past 60 years. After a no-decision, eight-inning, two-run outing against the Padres on June 6, Maddux threw a complete game, scattering 11 hits, in beating the Astros, 3–1, six days later. The next outing again resulted in no decision for

Maddux, who went seven and one-thirds innings, relinquishing three runs, against the Reds. On June 22, Maddux fell to the Mets, going the full nine innings and giving up five runs, three earned. He lost again the next time, with five earned runs in six and two-thirds innings charged against him in a 7–2 loss to the Expos, raising his ERA to 1.88 and dropping him to 10–4. Outpitching Maddux, Ken Hill became the first NL pitcher to win 11 games during the 1994 season. Montreal moved within one and a half games of Atlanta.

Maddux's expectations of better performances on the mound—Tom Glavine was also slumping—and for his Atlanta Braves remained in place. Having completed his first season with the Atlanta Braves, right-hander Maddux received his second straight Cy Young Award in the wake of the 1993 season. Born on April 14, 1966, in

San Angelo, Texas, where his father was then stationed, Maddux experienced repeated moves by his family, which included three-year stints in Riverside, California, and Madrid. A multi-sport participant, Maddux was on a state-winning team during his junior year in high school in Las Vegas. Although ready to play ball at the University of Arizona, which had one of the nation's top programs under Jerry Kindall, Maddux received word that the Cubs had drafted him in the second round in 1984. Called up to the major two years later, he struggled in six outings, including five starts, but entered the regular rotation the next season.

Following a terrible rookie year, Maddux became one of the NL's best pitchers and an All-Star in 1988, posting an 18–8 record with a 3.18 ERA; he landed on the cover of the September issue of *Baseball Digest*. The next season, he went 19–12 with a 2.95 ERA, coming in third in the Cy Young Award chase. Nineteen ninety and 1991 saw Maddux win 15 games each year and capture his first two in a succession

Greg Maddux, the Atlanta Braves' right-hander, posted microscopic ERAs during the 1994 and 1995 seasons. He received the National League Cy Young Award in four consecutive years. Ca. 1994 (National Baseball Hall of Fame Library, Cooperstown, NY).

of Gold Glove awards. An All-Star again in 1992, he had a 20–11 record with a 2.18 ERA and a league-best 166 ERA+ (adjusted ERA according to the pitcher's ballpark and the pitcher's league ERA, with 100 average) and 2.58 FIP (measures an ERA according to what it would be with a major-league average defensive team), and won the Cy Young Award. He also compiled a 9.4 WAR, bettering Barry Bonds, the NL runner-up. Having signed with the Braves as a free agent, Maddux won 20 games and the Cy Young Award for the second straight year in 1993, led the league with a 2.36 ERA, a 170 ERA+, a 2.85 FIP, and a 1.049 WHIP (walks plus hits per inning pitched).[7]

Off to another stellar start, Maddux was a different kind of pitcher from strikeout leaders like Seattle's Randy Johnson or Boston's Roger Clemens. As the *Houston Chronicle*'s Jerry Wizig noted, Maddux demonstrated "that a pitcher needn't possess overpowering velocity to dominate batters."[8]

The day after Maddux lost to the Expos, the Royals' David Cone moved his record to 11–4, giving up two earned runs in six and two-thirds innings, leaving his ERA at 2.76. The victory kept Kansas City within striking distance—four and a half games—in the AL Central. Cone had been named his league pitcher of the month for May, after going 5–1, including three straight shutouts, with a 1.94 ERA.

Maddux's conqueror in the final game he pitched during June, Ken Hill, was also competing against him for the title of the NL's best during the 1994 season. Born in Lynn, Massachusetts, during mid–December 1965, Hill grew up in a large African American family close to Boston. His father, a well-regarded baseball coach, imbued his six boys with a love of the sport. While Ken also played basketball and soccer, baseball was his favorite and led him to Division III North Adams State College in Western Massachusetts, where he first was slotted for the infield before being switched to the pitcher's mound. After helping his team to the NCAA tournament, Hill signed a contract with the Detroit Tigers as an undrafted free agent. Soon traded to the St. Louis Cardinals, Hill foundered, going back and forth between starting and relieving, before excelling in the 1987 Florida Instructional League.[9]

Despite struggling again in the minors, a late-season flourish led to his promotion to the Cardinals for a brief stint at the end of the 1988 season. Struggling mightily the next year, Hill led the league in both losses (15) and walks (99), while winning only seven times. His ERA mushroomed the next season but settled down in 1991, and he went 16–9 with a 2.68 ERA in 1992 and a solid 9–7 with a 3.23 ERA in 1993.

The Expos' second game of the 1994 season saw Hill hold the Astros to a single run over six innings, as he outpitched Doug Drabek to notch a 5–1 victory. He won his 11th on June 27, in beating the Braves and their ace, 7–2, before a packed crowd of 45,291. "I feel I can pitch with anybody," indicated Hill. "Maddux is a great pitcher, but I just felt if I pitch my game, I can keep my team in there, like he does."[10]

Born in Kansas City at the beginning of 1963, Cone, whose high school lacked a baseball team, was chosen by his hometown Royals in the third round of the 1981 free agent draft. After a promising start in the minors, he suffered an ACL injury to his left knee, then experienced control issues when he moved to AA and AAA ball.

Finding the strike zone yet again, Cone bounced back, getting a brief callup to the Royals in 1986. He thrived during winter ball, helping Ponce win the Puerto Rican pennant and then the Caguas Criollos capture the Caribbean World Series.[11]

Traded to the Mets during the off-season, Cone landed on the World Champions' roster and did decently in 1987, going 5–6 with a 3.71 ERA in just under 100 innings. The next year, he led the NL in winning percentage (.870) and matched his 20–3 record with a 2.22 ERA; he split a pair of decisions in a losing LCS against the Dodgers. The ensuing three seasons saw Cone perform well, with solid ERAs and winning percentages, and high strikeout totals, the latter resulting in two league titles. During the final game of the 1991 season, with accusations of rape swirling around him, Cone struck out 19 batters, tying a league record held by Tom Seaver and Steve Carlton. More controversies, including an allegation of public masturbation, beset Cone the next season, but he was having another good year on the mound before being traded to the Blue Jays. After helping Toronto win the World Series, Cone returned to Kansas City, with a three-year, $18 million contract that made him the game's best-paid pitcher. Despite a solid 3.33 ERA and 191 strikeouts, the lack of run support doomed Cone to a 11–14 record.[12]

Following that tough first season with the Royals, right-hander Cone was striving for a comeback year. His career to this point had been more than solid, including a 20-win season, a pair of strikeout titles, two All-Star selections, and a third-place Cy Young Award finish. As a late addition to the Blue Jays' roster, he had also helped Toronto win the 1992 World Series. That resulted in Cone's appearing on the April 5, 1993, cover of *Sports Illustrated* as it hawked its "Baseball '93" issue.[13]

However, a fast start made him an early contender for the AL Cy Young Award in 1994. Convinced to rely less on strikeouts, Cone called on his "infinite array of pitches and arm angles" in a May shutout of the Twins. The pitcher explained, "I have to concentrate on getting outs instead of trying to get strikeouts and embarrass people.... With our defense, there's no excuse to walk anybody." After Cone's third career one-hitter against the Angels, Kansas City manager Hal McRae stated, "I know pitching is not easy, but he's making it look easy. There were no threats for nine innings. It made for a very relaxing afternoon to watch a ballgame."[14]

Mark Newman, in *The Sporting News*, agreed that there was a different kind of Cone pitching in 1994. While he had whiffed 10 or more batters in a single contest on 34 occasions, his pitching coach, Bruce Kison, had convinced him of the wisdom to aspire toward "more low-pitch innings" to enable him to pitch deeper into games. Manager Hal McRae recognized, "He's pitching fast and throwing strikes and we know we're going to get a good effort every time he takes the mound."[15]

Looking likely as Cone's top competitor for the AL's best pitcher of the year was the Yankees' left-hander, Jimmy Key. On June 27, he scattered six hits over eight innings in beating the Red Sox before 33,204 fans at Fenway Park, running his record to a major league best 12–1. Right fielder Paul O'Neill went hitless in four at-bats, dropping his average to .380.

Born in Huntsville, Alabama, in April 1961, Key attended Clemson University for three years before being selecting in the third round of the amateur draft in 1982 by the Toronto Blue Jays. After two generally successful seasons in the minors, where he moved up rapidly from the Rookie League to AAA, Key made the Blue Jays' roster as a reliever in 1984. Switched to the starting rotation the next year, he quickly became a dependable addition, making the All-Star team. In 1987, he went 17–6, leading the American League with a 2.76 ERA, and finished second in the Cy Young Award race. He made the All-Star squad a second time in 1991, then led the Blue Jays to the World Series title the next year, twice beating Atlanta and holding the Braves to one run in nine innings of work. But he jumped to the Yankees during the off-season, going on to complete an 18–6 record, despite relievers blowing six potential wins, with a 3.00 ERA and another All-Star selection in 1993.

He began the new season in typical fashion, winning his fifth Opening Day game without a loss in defeating the Rangers, 5–3, at Yankee Stadium on April 4. Nearly two months later, *USA Today*'s Mel Antonen was referring to Key as one of the top two southpaw pitchers in the American League. "Key has command of four pitches," wrote Antonen. "He relies on deception and location. He never throws the same pitch at [the] same speed twice…. Key looks like he throws 90." At this point, Key was 20–4 with a 2.64 ERA at Yankee Stadium, which he loved and why he had agreed to terms with the Yankees. After beating Boston near the end of June, Key was riding an 11-game winning streak. Red Sox manager Butch Hobson asked, "How does he dominate everybody so much? He just moves that ball around so much. Gives you different looks, different angles."[16]

◆　◆　◆

Early in the month, Murray Chass warned that MLB had "reached a critical stage" for the 1994 season as team owners agreed to a salary cap. Acting commissioner Bud Selig indicated that the vote in favor had been unanimous. Declaring that the agreement "reflects the decade and the era we live in," Selig said it was "designed to enhance the game of baseball by providing a fair and equitable allocation of revenues generated by baseball between the clubs and the players." It was supposedly intended to create a "closer sense of unity" among teams and ballplayers.[17]

In his autobiography, Selig admitted, "I knew we were in for the fight of our lives. I'd been telling owners that we had to be prepared to lose the season if the union went out on strike." Selig and his colleagues didn't favor a lockout now, and he considered the possibility of using replacement player at this stage a "horrible" idea.[18]

Deeming the owners' decision "ominous" and "extraordinarily negative," MLBPA chief Donald Fehr warned, "That is an act of people preparing for war," but it would not impact the players' approach. Denouncing the owners' "saber rattling," union counsel Gene Orza declared, "It's perfectly consistent with people who aren't happy with America's system of employee compensation to be unhappy with

America's majority ruling." Orza added, "I think the owners want a strike." Fehr was soon referring to a more dire possibility. "We've heard rumors that some owners want to shut down the industry for a year and a half or more."[19]

In the June 13 issue of *The Sporting News*, Dave Kindred pointed to the possibility of a strike during the ongoing season. He wrote, "If the players say so, yes. And more power to them." For over a century, "the rich folks who owned major league baseball," Kindred contended, "owned more than bats and balls; they also owned the human beings who played." It took until 1976 to gain "the limited freedom" baseball players now had. "Slavery for 107 years. Freedom, sort of, for 18 years," said Kindred. Thus, it made sense for the players to strike, as they had "another 89 years to get even." Moreover, "they may need that long," suggested Kindred. Team owners had been called "men whose fingers tightened automatically over a dollar, and who check their receipts secretly and put on a poor mouth to the players. That was in 1880." Back in that era, as at present, owners, warning about approached bankruptcy, demanded a salary cap.[20]

That had led John Montgomery Ward to pose the question "Is the Base-Ball Player a Chattel?" and to answer "with righteous fury" in the affirmative. Kindred saw contemporary owners repeating the errors of eras past. "Not only do these fools seize every opportunity to belittle the players in their hire, they do everything possible to persuade customers that theirs is a dying business." Wrapping up his essay, Kindred quoted from Red Smith: "Baseball owners have moral scruples against taking any man's dollar when there is a chance to take a dollar and a quarter."[21]

In that same issue, senior writer Steve Marantz discussed the man most recently talked about as MLB's next commissioner: Senator George Mitchell. Marantz's subject declined to explore substantial baseball issues: "the antitrust exemption, expansion, collective bargaining, cable copyright law." He did affirm, "I've been a lifelong baseball fan" but refused to answer the question, "Is baseball in trouble?"[22]

Mitchell's senatorial colleague, Howard Metzenbaum, said, "A baseball players' strike or lockout would ruin the season for fans." The Senate Judiciary Committee readied to vote on a bill that would take away the antitrust exemption MLB had long held. Such an action, Donald Fehr hoped, could prevent a strike. Bud Selig refuted that notion. "The proposed legislation will not change the collective bargaining process nor will it guarantee there won't be a players' strike. The issue must still be resolved between the clubs and the players' union."[23]

Displaying no sympathy for either the owners or players, the Senate Judiciary Committee turned thumbs down on Senator Metzenbaum's proposal to remove MLB's antitrust protection. Prior to the vote, Metzenbaum indicated, "I don't have any sympathies over privileged owners nor do I have any special sympathies for the overpaid players." Judiciary Committee chair Joe Biden of Delaware charged that team owners did not seem "particularly concerned about anything except their self-interests, and the players are right up there with them." He feared that Congress was damned if it did, damned if it didn't. "If we pass the Metzenbaum [bill] and there is a strike, the owners will say we caused it. If we don't pass it and there is a strike, the players will say we caused it."[24]

Expressing pleasure at the 10–7 bipartisan vote, Selig said, "It will allow the collective bargaining process to continue unimpeded." Senator Metzenbaum thought otherwise. "This vote is a terrible loss for fans. Now there is a much greater likelihood that there will be a strike. The owners used unprecedented tactics against this bill." Fehr seemingly agreed: "Unfortunately, this vote will make the current negotiations with the owners even more difficult than they already are."[25]

18

July Was the Hottest Month

UNDER THE LONG-RUNNING 154-GAME SEASONS, standard fare until the early 1960s, the last contests in June would have been the midyear mark. The Yankees and the Braves still remained at the top of their respective leagues, although New York had cooled off a bit to a 47–28 record in the AL East, still four and a half games ahead of the 43–33 Orioles. The Red Sox were now a .500 team. In the Central, the 44–30 Indians were one and a half games up on the 43–32 White Sox. In the woeful AL West, the 35–41 Rangers were two and a half games better than the Mariners, and another game ahead of both the Angels and the A's. In the NL East, the Braves were one and a half games above the Expos. In the Central, the 44–33 Reds were one and a half games ahead of the Astros. In the West, the 41–37 Dodgers were five and a half games better than the Rockies, while the Giants had dropped eight and a half games back.

In their last June game, the Yankees had fallen to the Red Sox 6–5. Paul O'Neill went 0 for 2, his batting average slipping to .365. In a 3–2 win over the Royals, the White Sox's Frank Thomas hit his 29th homer, going one for three for a .371 average. In a 4–2 Indians win over the Orioles, Albert Belle went two for three, enabling him to tie Thomas in the batting race. Teammate Kenny Lofton's one for four left him at .363. The Twins beat the Rangers, 6–4, but Texas' Will Clark went three for four to move to .352.

In a 5–3 win over the Cubs, the Astros' Jeff Bagwell's two-for-four performance also found him at .352. The Mets dropped the Padres, 3–1, although San Diego's Tony Gwynn's two-for-four showing the day before positioned him at .391. From July 1, 1993, through July 1, 1994, Gwynn batted .400.

Near the end of June, the Giants' third baseman, Matt Williams, first tied, then broke, Willie Stargell's NL record for homers before July, belting his 28th and 29th dingers, the latter his sixth in the past eight games. Having starred in three of the previous four seasons, Williams batted cleanup, protecting Barry Bonds in the Giants' lineup. Born in Bishop, California, in late November 1956, Williams was a high school quarterback who received a baseball scholarship to attend the University of Nevada, Las Vegas, where he became a first-team All-American.

Selected third overall in the 1986 draft, he made the Giants' roster within a year, playing both shortstop and third base. Williams struggled at the plate, although he managed 18 homers and a lowly .202 BA in only 292 at-bats with the Giants in 1989. His first full year, 1990, resulted in a 33-homer, league-leading 122-RBI, .277-average, and 301-total base performance, along with an All-Star selection, a Silver Slugger Award, and sixth place in MVP voting. The next season he swatted 34 homers, drove in 98 runs, and won his first Gold Glove for his defense at third base. A down year followed, but in 1993 he rebounded with 38 homers, 105 runs scored, 110 RBI, a .294 average, a .561 slugging percentage, and 325 total bases. He again finished sixth in the MVP balloting, won his second Gold Glove and Silver Slugger awards, and was named to the AP Major League All-Star squad.

In January 1994, Williams inked a new five-year contract with the Giants worth almost $31 million. Regarding his past accomplishments, he told Greg Bortolin of the *Las Vegas Review-Journal,* "First and foremost, I just want to keep it coming. I just strive to be consistent." Bortolin's article, titled "The Humble Home Run Hitter," conveyed Williams's appreciation to the Giants for making him feel like he was an integral part of their organization.[1]

As the 1994 season unfolded, Williams was one of several ballplayers on a pace to equal or better the single-season home run record. In early June, when informed that Roger Maris had hair fall out as he undertook an assault on Babe Ruth's mark, the virtually bald Williams responded, "I won't have that problem." Having hit more homers before July than any National Leaguer ever, he smacked number 30, drove in five runs, and went four for five to help the Giants beat the Expos, 14–7, on July 1.[2]

Los Angeles Times columnist Jim Murray waxed on about the number of homers being belted in major league parks. "Babe Ruth is having a terrible year. So is Roger Maris, Hack Wilson must need a drink somewhere today. Jimmy Foxx and Hank Greenberg must be groaning." All of these ballplayers from days past, with the exception of Ruth,

Matt Williams, the San Francisco Giants' third baseman, appeared poised to break Hack Wilson's NL single-season record of 56 homers before the remainder of the 1994 was cancelled. Ca. 1994 (National Baseball Hall of Fame Library, Cooperstown, NY).

who established the mark, had targeted "the most unattainable record in the books." Even Maris's belting of 61 in 1961 was viewed as a fluke, for he had never smashed more than 39 in a single season and 33 was the highest total he later belted.[3]

Now, however, "home runs are flying out of ball parks like popcorn," Murray wrote. When Ruth smacked 60 in 1927, he had 25 when June came to an end. During the 1994 season, four players were at or above the Bambino's pace, and another six were within striking distance. Among "the biggest threats to the Babe—and Maris," indicated Murray, was Matt Williams, who had 30 homers among his 77 hits, while batting .249. Williams was still more likely to undertake a successful run at Wilson's 64-year-old record of 56 homers; Ruth, after all, had belted 17 homers in September during his record-setting 1927 season. As for Ruth and Maris, Williams also had to contend with Frank Thomas, who was just one behind him, and Ken Griffey, Jr., who already had "an eye-popping 32."[4]

As Murray noted, George Foster was the last National Leaguer to deliver more than 50 homers in a season, belting 52 in 1977, while 1947 was the last time a pair of NL players, Ralph Kiner and Johnny Mize, did so. The last American Leaguer? The Tigers' Cecil Fielder, just two years before. Maris and Mickey Mantle hit 61 and 54, respectively, in 1961.[5]

On July 8, Williams caught up with Griffey, delivering his 32nd and 33rd homers in a 3–2 win over the Phillies. Two days later, the *Minneapolis Star Tribune* suggested that Williams, who tended to warm up as the season progressed, might have a better shot at breaking the home run record than either Griffey or Frank Thomas. But John McGrath of the *Tacoma News Tribune* worried that events might move beyond the control of Williams, Griffey, or Thomas. "It would be a shame," he wrote, "if a work stoppage prevented one of the game's dynamic superstars from challenging the homer record."[6]

William, Griffey, and Thomas all had 35 homers as of July 21. However, talk of a possible strike continued to loom large. All of this was disturbing to baseball fans and historians alike, including Bill James, who likened the present season to "1961, one of the best … ever played." As James indicated, "In 1961 they had something new—expansion. Now it's the three division split. Then, we had Maris chasing Ruth's record. Now we have several people chasing Maris's record."[7]

Williams's greater prominence resulted in a major article in *Sports Illustrated*, "The Strong, Silent Type." Author Rom Fimrite termed Ken Griffey, Jr., and Frank Thomas "the glamour-pusses of this year's big home run parade." By contrast, Williams, "another formidable … power hitter," seemed "mostly ignored." In the field, Williams was even better than Mike Schmidt, the great former Philadelphia Phillies third baseman, or so Giants manager Dusty Baker contended.[8]

By the end of July, sportswriter Mike Klis suggested that Williams and Jeff Bagwell had more to lose than any individual players if a strike occurred. Presently on a pace to hit 59 home runs, Williams, he noted, was "chasing arguably the most-revered record in baseball—Roger Maris's 61 home runs." Attempting to becoming the first Triple Crown winner in the National League since Joe Medwick in 1937, Bagwell was second in both batting average (.366) and homers (35) and led in RBI (104). His teammate, outfielder Mike Felder, declared, "I thought I'd seen in all with Junior last year in Seattle, but Baggie's topped that. He has got to be the best right-handed hitter I've ever seen." The two also appeared to be the leading MVP candidates in the National League.[9]

Some considered Frank Thomas, not Barry Bonds or Ken Griffey, Jr., the best hitter in the game. At times playing first base, Thomas often served as the White Sox's designated hitter, so he was hardly the all-around player the other two were. Raised in Columbia, Georgia, where he was born on May 27, 1968, Thomas played baseball, basketball, and football growing up, and he received a scholarship to play tight end at Auburn University. After one season on the gridiron, he stuck to baseball, becoming an All-American, before being selected seventh overall by the White Sox in 1989. He was promoted to the majors after 181 minor league games.

In his initial 60-game callup, Thomas displayed power with 21 extra-base hits, a discerning eye at the plate, collecting 44 bases on balls, and hit .330 with a .983 OPS and a 177 OPS+. The next three seasons placed him firmly in the upper echelon of the finest hitters in the game. In 1991, he led the AL in walks (138), OBP (.453), OPS (1.006), and OPS+ (180), coming in third in the MVP race and winning the Silver Slugger Award. The next year, he was the league leader in doubles (46), walks (122), OBP (.439), and OPS+ (.975), finishing eighth in the MVP voting. His best year to date was 1993, as he hit 41 homers (third in the AL), drove in 128 runs (second), walked 112 times, hit .317, slugged .607 (third), had a 1.033 OPS (second) and a 177 OPS+ (second), and collected 333 total bases. Voted to the All-Star team for the first team, he won his second Silver Slugger Award and the AL MVP, receiving all the first-place votes, almost doubling the totals of the next two finishers, Toronto's Paul Molitor and John Olerud.

Early during the 1994 season, Chuck Johnson, writing in *USA Today*, pointed to Thomas, Ken Griffey, Jr., and Juan Gonzalez as standing "a powerful cut among most of today's emerging young stars." Johnson said that no such group had emerged since Henry Aaron, Harmon Killebrew, Mickey Mantle, and Frank Robinson did during the 1950s. Thomas acknowledged, "We could be that next generation." Already, he was only the fifth MLB player to hit over .300, knock 20 homers, and deliver 100 RBI, runs scored, and walks three straight years. That put him in elite company: Jimmie Foxx, Lou Gehrig, Babe Ruth, and Ted Williams. "I'm still young and learning … another two seasons away from my prime," said Thomas. Referring to Barry Bonds, Thomas declared, "Barry's the king now, but a lot of young guys are gaining fast. With all this talent coming up, there's going to be some exciting baseball in the next five years of so. They could be talking about us forty years from now."[10]

But as Thomas was among the players striving for baseball immortality, he, like the others, faced the fact that labor strife could end what promised to be a historic season. "There's going to be a strike," Thomas declared. "Players are going to do what they have to do. Owners are going to do what they have to do." That was unfortunate for Thomas personally, because as Murray Chass indicated, he, even more than Griffey, exemplified the surge of offensive output characterizing MLB's first half. Batting .380 with 31 homers and 73 RBI, Thomas had already put up numbers that would amount to "a terrific season for many players. An Exceptional Season." This year he was one of several performing in a stratospheric fashion. *USA Today*'s Rod Beaton pointed to Thomas and Houston's Jeff Bagwell as having an opportunity at a Triple Crown, "an undeniable achievement of greatness."[11]

The two biggest AL stars, Thomas and Griffey, put on a show during the home run contest amid All-Star competition in Pittsburgh's Three Rivers Stadium in early July. The pair were said to have "put on a seat-shattering show … hitting a succession of long-distance upper deck drives that sent the fans scurrying for balls and fellow players searching for adjectives." David Cone remarked, "I watch that, and I don't even know why we pitchers are here." Both Thomas and Griffey swatted balls over 500 feet, leading Barry Bonds, the former Pirate, to ask Pittsburgh's Rich Donnelly, who served as batting practice pitcher, "Dude, did you ever see one hit up there before? Never. They make this stadium look like it didn't exist. It was awesome."[12]

Comiskey Park's large dimensions, baseball historian John Holway noted, worked against Thomas's quest for a home run record. The White Sox's home ballpark required Thomas to send a ball considerably farther than Griffey had to at the Kingdome. The difference was greater still when one considered the inviting right field fence for both Ruth and Maris at Yankee Stadium. The large number of walks—100 before the end of July—Thomas received also worked against him. But that stat, along with his Triple Crown totals and other league-leading indicators, made the White Sox slugger the frontrunner for another MVP Award.[13]

Despite their impressive performance by the end of July, major league baseball's two most gifted stars were probably not likely recipients of that honor for the 1994 season, although that remained subject to change. Both 24-year-old Ken Griffey, Jr., and the recently turned 30-year-old Barry Bonds were now seasoned veterans who were still thrilling fans with their performances at the plate, in the field, and on the bases. From early April, Griffey had been on a home run tear, generally well above the pace set by Babe Ruth and Roger Maris during their record-setting drives. By contrast, Bonds had exploded only during the past few weeks, having been hindered by a series of injuries. Columnist Peter Gammons credited Bonds with playing through those ailments. "If you doubted Barry Bonds's toughness, he continues to play every day with a dislocated shoulder and chips in his elbow that doctors want to cut out."[14]

One record Griffey set was the receipt of more votes—over six million—in All-Star balloting than any player before, surpassing the number Rod Carew received in 1977 by nearly 1.8 million. That suggested Griffey had become the game's most popular ballplayer. During a recent game in California, the hometown fans booed after the Seattle slugger was intentionally walked. When he set a record for homers hit before July 1, "they all stood up and cheered," he recalled.[15]

As Griffey continued his assault on the home run record, sportswriters, his own manager, and fellow ballplayers waxed on about his athletic brilliance. In the *Dayton Daily News*, Ritter Collett referred to Griffey as "the most exciting comet to flash across the baseball skies since the young Willie Mays of the 1950s." His manager, Lou Piniella, remarked, "What's amazing to me, and heartening too, is that this kid is being cheered in other parks." Noting that Griffey didn't place pressure on himself, Piniella said, "He's having fun playing this game. He's as pure a power hitter I've ever seen." Barry Bonds acknowledged, "Griffey is the best player I've ever seen. Most of us have to work on our strength. But he's just a naturally strong kid. He's an awesome, raw talent."[16]

But amid all the accolades, Buck Showalter, manager of the front-running New York Yankees, felt compelled to take digs at both Griffey and Bonds. "I shouldn't say this publicly, but a guy like Ken Griffey Jr, the game's boring to him. He comes on the field, and his hat's on backward, and his shirttail's hanging out. I go to the All-Star game a couple of years ago, and Barry Bonds is there for three days, and the only time he tucked his shirt in was for the game. To me, that's a lack of respect for the game."[17]

Pushing back, Griffey explained his seemingly easy-going manner. "I've always worn my hat backwards," he declared. "Since I was a little kid I wore my hat like that. I have pictures about that at home. I've never worn my jersey out. You can ask anybody in this locker room. If that's the only two things you have to worry about my game then I'm doing all right." Griffey asked rhetorically, "I don't take the game seriously? If you look back at the last five years, at the numbers, that's not serious. I'm one of the most exciting players in the game. No one could say I'm not. I smile. I run in. I show emotion. If I was a free agent now, New York would probably be one of the first places to call me."[18]

Never accused of being mellow, Barry Bonds had followed up his record-tying third MVP campaign with an injury-plagued season that also saw his San Francisco Giants struggle in their divisional race. But more recently, both Bonds and the Giants were heating up, giving hope to the slugger and his ballclub that 1994 wasn't altogether lost and might even become remarkable. After struggling in June, he went on a tear the following month. That particularly happened following the All-Star break, when Bonds discussed the incredible performances of other players. "I'm just letting these other guys have their year, but I'll be back next year and the year after that and the year after that. I'm not done yet. Have those other guys won three MVPs?"[19]

Bonds wasn't just allowing other ballplayers to "have their year," Ross Newhan of the *Los Angeles Times* wrote. "He's always part put-on and larger parts ego and arrogance, but he's also one of baseball's premier talents. This year, however, a dislocated shoulder and elbow spurs that prevent him from extending consistently on pitches he should drive … and which will require surgery when the season ends, have inhibited his ability to re-establish his MVP form." Bonds himself offered, "Look. I'm playing and not making excuses. I'd have to be in the hospital not to play.... I love to play and I'm still a threat."

Right after the All-Star break, the Giants swept four games from the Expos. In the third game, Bonds swatted a pair of homers—the 23rd time of his career with two in the same contest—added a single, and drove in three runs in a 4–2 win. That pushed him up to 27 homers for the season, 10 belted in the previous 20 games, only six behind his league-leading teammate Matt Williams. On July 18, the Giants, having added Darryl Strawberry to their lineup, won their ninth straight game in beating the Phillies 7–5, with Bonds getting his fifth homer in four games; it was also the 250th of his career. He had 12 hits in his last 23 at-bats, with nine RBI. "It's like having Will Clark back, only better," declared Bonds, who was batting third, in front of Williams and Strawberry. Pitchers "may be able to pitch around me and Matt, but they can't get past him." Philadelphia manager Jim Fregosi acknowledged, "I'd walk Barry Bonds every time if I could. When he hit fifth, we were able to eliminate him from the lineup. It's going to be more challenging to do that now."[20]

Two days later, the Giants again beat the Phillies, their 10th win in 11 games, with Williams hitting his 35th home run and Bonds getting his 29th, his sixth in seven games. During those seven road games, Bonds was hitting .451 with 11 RBI. *USA Today*'s Hal Bodley indicated that the Giants possessed "the best talent in the" NL West, and Bonds had "finally gotten a wakeup call," aided by other members of "the fearsome threesome," Williams and Strawberry. The Giants fell to Strawberry's former team, the New York Mets, on July 22, 6–3, although Bonds whacked a double and his 30th homer, certainly moving him into the home run chase. The Giants bounced back the next day, nipping the Mets, 4–2, on Williams's major league-leading 36th homer and Bonds's 31st and eighth in nine games.[21]

Bonds's latest performances on the baseball diamond induced Murray Chass to suggest that Bonds, "a sleeping Giant for much of the season," was positioning himself to make a run for "an unprecedented third consecutive National League most valuable player award and fourth in five years." His "six-game onslaught" prior to the series with the Mets demonstrated that Bonds, despite an injured elbow, could drive his team to the title it had "just missed last season."[22]

Jerry Crasnick of the *Denver Post* agreed with Chass's assessment. Bonds, having hit .386, including eight homers, and driven in 18 runs during the initial 14 games of Darryl Strawberry's addition to the Giants' roster, was "back in his ultra-productive mode," Crasnick wrote. In the process, the Giants had sliced eight games off the Dodgers' once seemingly insurmountable nine-and-a-half-game lead in the NL West. Both Montreal manager Felipe Alou and Philadelphia skipper Jim Fregosi considered Bonds more effective in the third spot in the lineup because it was "tougher to pitch around him." His own manager, Dusty Baker, thought Bonds was enjoying the game more once again. "Darryl has brought some life and laughter to Barry. If you don't hear Barry laughing, you know something is wrong."[23]

The July 26 edition of the *Chicago Tribune* went farther, contending that Thomas and Bonds, rather than Griffey and Williams, were in the running to break the home run record. That same day, Bonds, in a 12–5 beat-down of the Dodgers, grabbed the 300th career stolen base, making him only the sixth player to accomplish that feat along with hitting 250 homers.[24]

By the end of the month, the Giants were only a game behind the Dodgers, after beating the Rockies, 9–4, on July 31. Williams hit a pair of homers, giving him 40 for the season, as he went three for five with five RBI. The 40 homers set a NL record for homers through July; the major league mark of 41 was held by Babe Ruth (1928) and Jimmie Foxx (1932). Bonds hit his 32nd and was two for four at the plate, lifting his average to .307. *The Sporting News* also began talking about Bonds's "belated bid for an unprecedented third consecutive MVP award." It mentioned how the Giants' star, who had "been incendiary with Strawberry's protection in the lineup," could "barely ... contain his glee in actually seeing strikes, even with men in scoring position."[25]

◆　◆　◆

But the likelihood of the season ending abruptly mounted throughout the month, with scribes, players, and management all talking about an impending strike, slated for August 12. Not helping matters was the antagonistic relationship between MLBPA executive director Donald Fehr and MLB's negotiator, Richard Ravitch. Then there was Bud Selig, said by one of his colleagues to be afflicted with "commissioneritis." His "once warm" dealings with Ravitch had "cooled rapidly" after Selig's support for revenue sharing dipped to gain support with other team owners.[26]

Ultimately, it was the acrimony regarding a salary cap that imperiled continuation of the 1994 major league season. By July 9, Minnesota star outfielder Kirby Puckett, in no way a hardliner, expressed his belief that a strike was "inevitable." His teammate, Dave Winfield, didn't understand why anyone could believe players would relinquish hard-won rights. Their boss, Minnesota owner Carl Pohlad, declared, "There is no way the Twins can make it" without a salary cap. Such a cap, Donald Fehr insisted, "would completely destroy free agency." Acknowledging that a gap differential separated major league teams, Fehr charged, "The large markets have said [to the small markets] 'Screw you, unless you help us bust the players first.'" He also warned, "I have the feeling sometimes that I'm playing out a previously written script, that nothing we can do will have the slightest effect."[27]

Following the All-Star Game, played at Pittsburgh's Three Rivers Stadium and won by the Braves' Fred McGriff's two-run homer in the bottom of the ninth inning, Selig spoke to the press. "There's an irony behind this being here. This city has had a franchise all these years and it's now fighting for its baseball life. It's a microcosm of what's going on in this game. There are a lot of franchises like this."[28]

After the union turned down a proposal based on revenue sharing and a salary cap, Selig requested that the players rethink their stance. "We can go on playing these games forever," he said. "But the bottom line is that we need a new system of economics for baseball…. Too many clubs are losing money." Fehr urged MLB to examine other means to bring about revenue sharing. Likening the latest salary cap proposals to those made in 1985 and 1990, Fehr remarked, "The players feel [the] plan would destroy free agency and harm competitive balance."[29]

On July 28, the MLBPA confirmed August 12 as the strike date. Fehr declared, "The purpose of setting a strike date earlier rather than later in the season is to focus on the negotiations and see if we can get the job done." Ravitch grumbled, "I don't think the union had the same kind of regard for the fans as the owners did. We could have locked out the players. We didn't do so because it would not have been good for the game or the fans."[30]

◆ ◆ ◆

Three days later, the national pastime received something of a shot in the arm thanks to induction ceremonies in Cooperstown, New York, the setting for baseball's Hall of Fame. The new inductees included Steve Carlton, Phil Rizzuto, and the late Leo Durocher. Carlton said, "For twenty-four years I did something I loved and got paid for it." His own selection, Rizzuto acknowledged, was largely because Yankees owner "Steinbrenner and my family and friends over the years have put a lot of pressure on the Hall of Fame." Speaking on behalf of his mother, the actress Laraine Day, Durocher's third wife, Chris Day declared, "His last years were spent hoping he would get a call from the Hall of Fame. At first, I thought what a shame it was that he could not have lived to receive it himself. But now I know, as I stand here, that my father stands with us here today. I guess he got time off for good behavior."[31]

19

August Showers

Heading into August with the season on the brink, the major league divisional races remained tight with one exception. The 64–38 New York Yankees, vying with the 65–38 Montreal Expos for the best record overall, led the Baltimore Orioles by eight games in the AL East. The Central had the 62–42 Chicago White Sox, the 59–43 Cleveland Indians, and the 58–47 Kansas City Royals bunched within four and a half games. In the West, the 50–55 Texas Rangers were two games ahead of the 47–56 Oakland Athletics. The Expos led the NL East, three and a half games in front of the 62–42 Atlanta Braves. The 61–43 Cincinnati Reds were atop the Central, two and a half games better than the Houston Astros. In the West, the 52–52 Dodgers were one game ahead of the still surging, 52–54 San Francisco Giants.

On June 1, Orioles shortstop Cal Ripken played in his 2,000th straight contest, leaving him 130 behind the legendary Yankees slugger Lou Gehrig. That same day, Michael Jordan hit his first home run as a minor leaguer, going two for four, lifting his batting average to .193. After the Expos defeated his Cardinals, 3–2, in 10 innings, St. Louis manager Joe Torre praised Montreal as the best team in baseball "because of their speed and their defense." The Giants' Matt Williams slammed his 41st homer, while the Astros' Jeff Bagwell's 39th enabled him to pass both Ken Griffey, Jr., and Frank Thomas.[1]

News of major league baseball financial records leaked, with the Dodgers and White Sox, viewed as two of the "most stable and successful franchises," included in a list of 19 supposedly beleaguered teams. A lawyer involved with collective bargaining declared, "That just shows how phony the list is." Richard Ravitch had delivered the data to Donald Fehr earlier that summer, but the union leader was bound to secrecy by a confidentiality agreement. While refusing to name specific ballclubs, Bud Selig stated, "I actually think another one or two could lose money this year."[2]

Despite his Giants falling to the Reds, 9–7, on August 2, Barry Bonds slugged three homers in a single game for the first time in his career and drove in four runs. "Every day's a big day for Barry Bonds," say Cincinnati shortstop Barry Larkin, who belted two of his own along with a double.[3]

Union-management relations soured further as team owners failed to deliver a scheduled $7.8 million pension payment. The MLBPA's Eugene Orza, second behind Fehr, termed that "the dastardly deed," while some players talked about striking earlier than previously planned. The Dodgers' player representative, Brett Butler, said, "All bets are off. Right now, there is hostility on our side. My sense is that the players are frustrated."[4]

Speaking at a White House press conference, President Bill Clinton declared, "I think it would be heartbreaking for the American people if our national pastime didn't get through this whole season." He referred to the decades-old records that stood in jeopardy of being broken.[5]

The *Philadelphia Inquirer*'s Michael Bamberger spoke with three well-regarded students of major league baseball's labor history—Andrew Zimbalist, John Helyar, and Lee Lowenfish—about the financial state of the game, posing the question, "Is salary cap talk just an owners' ploy?" Bamberger began his piece: "For weeks now, all we've heard from the owners is salary cap. Salary cap, salary cap, salary cap, major-league baseball will perish without a salary cap."[6]

Possibly four or five ballclubs dropped money each year but generally turned a profit the next year, indicated Zimbalist. For over a century, team owners had contended that rising player salaries endangered Organized Baseball, but that was always false, declared Helyar. The demands for a salary cap amounted to a smoke-screen, Lowenfish said. In reality, he offered, owners were concerned about arbitration and free agency.[7]

Frank Thomas and Ken Griffey, Jr., appeared on the August 8 cover of *Sports Illustrated*, with the headline "Top Guns," their names, and the statement, "Two powerful reasons to keep playing ball." In "The Big Heart," Rick Reilly wrote about the 6'5", 275-pound White Sox behemoth who appeared ready, absent a lengthy strike, to shatter Babe Ruth's "records for runs, walks and extra-base hits in a single season." Thomas was also striving to do what no player since Ted Williams had achieved: an on-base percentage at .500 or better and a slugging percentage greater than .700. He appeared primed to become the first since Babe Ruth in 1920 with a .350 batting average, 50 homers, and 150 walks in the same season. There were the possibilities of both a Triple Crown and a new home run mark.[8]

According to Reilly, Thomas was "the unthinkable amalgam of Williams's eyes, Frank Howard's arms, Willie McCovey's legs, Rod Carew's hands and Ernie Banks's smile." Toronto Blue Jay Paul Molitor said, "He's doing things I've never seen in 17 years in the major leagues," while Thomas's teammate, Julio Franco, declared, "Playing with Frank is like being part of history."[9]

"Junior Comes of Age," by Alan Shipnuck, contained a remarkable quote by Reggie Jackson, the famed Mr. October of World Series past. "We love Ken Griffey Jr. because he is everything we would like to be. He's young, he's good-looking, he's got the best smile in the world, and he's a heroic athlete. He is a shot in the arm for baseball. He is what the game needs right now. He is creating excitement and making headlines just by his presence. There hasn't been anyone like that since…. Reggie Jackson." Frank Thomas offered, "The thing about Junior, he has that golden smile. He is like a kid on the sandlot." Jackson agreed, declaring, "Ken Griffey is loved everywhere he goes. Kids love him, the other players love him, everybody loves him. The reason why is, he seems approachable."[10]

On August 8, Bud Selig lowered his estimate of the number of financially foundering teams from 19. "You can debate the numbers," Selig admitted, then said, "But you can't debate a minimum of 12 to 14. And we just can't ignore that anymore." *Financial World* magazine disputed those figures, indicating that a mere handful of teams—Kansas City, Milwaukee, Pittsburgh, San Diego, and Seattle—"would have difficulty competing in a completely free market." Writers Brooke Grabarek and Michael K. Ozanian said, "The baseball strike is completely unnecessary. It revolves around an issue that turns out to be bogus, if you do the arithmetic." The financially distraught teams, Grabarek and Ozanian asserted, should be afforded the opportunity to relocate "to cities that are swelling with support such as St. Petersburgh [*sic*], Fla., where they could thrive."[11]

After cracking his major league-leading 43rd homer in a 5–2 win over the Cubs at Wrigley Field on August 10, Matt Williams insisted yet again, "I am not chasing any record. I have no desire to go after any record. I just play the game." "That may be," wrote the *Chicago Tribune*'s Bill Jauss, who indicated that some fans considered Williams the player with the most to lose should a strike take place. Although Ken Griffey, Jr., and Frank Thomas had received more play, Williams had been the major league home run leader for weeks. Conveying support for the MLBPA, Williams declared, "The union says a salary cap will destroy the game."[12]

Columnist C. R. Roberts, writing for the *Tacoma News Tribune*, indicated that his friend Frank, who resided in Seattle, believed there was only one means to prevent the strike and to keep baseball alive. The president, Frank argued, "should nationalize the game," for baseball was the national pastime and "in the national interest." Thus, present circumstances amounted to "a national emergency." Perhaps Frank was right, Roberts said. But "maybe it's dead already. Dead—stolen by the greed of major league players and owners alike. Dead—lost to agents, advertisers, attorneys, artificial turf and indoor stadiums." At some point, baseball turned into a commercial enterprise, as "something, someone, robbed America of its favorite game. Where once that game revered heroes, now it bows before the dollar almighty." Roberts concluded, "Let them strike, let it die. That way, one day, we might just get it back."[13]

The day before the strike began, Richard Ravitch and Donald Fehr appeared on *Today*, although they evidently did not exchange words before they both spoke on the television program. By all accounts, Ravitch, the top negotiator for baseball owners, and Fehr, the MLBPA executive director, didn't talk to one another later in the day. "The players are resigned and resentful," Fehr indicated. "They are resigned that this has to be and resentful that they are forced to this in an industry that has enjoyed tremendous growth in recent years. They are forced to do this because the owners can't get their house in order." Terming the strike and the disruption of the 1994 season "a tragedy for millions of fans," Ravitch blamed the union for refusing to accept a salary cap. Ravitch clearly had some divisions within his ranks, with Yankees owner George Steinbrenner declaring, "It's very difficult ... to argue competitive balance, per se, when Montreal, with the second-lowest payroll, has baseball's best record."[14]

Fittingly, as matters turned out, Ken Griffey, Jr.—called "the fans' favorite player"—slammed a grand slam, his second of the season and his 40th homer, as Seattle defeated Oakland, 8–1, on August 11. Randy Johnson pushed his record to 13–6 while striking out 15, raising his major league-leading total to 204.[15]

◆   ◆   ◆

The long-anticipated, much-feared strike, major league baseball's eighth work stoppage in 23 years, began on August 12. It came in the wake of Greg Maddux tossing his third shutout to improve his record to 16–6 and lower his ERA to 1.56, more than a run better than the AL's best, 2.65 by Ontiveros of the Oakland Athletics. Maddux's 16 wins tied for second best in the majors with Ken Hill, David Cone, and Mike Mussina of the Baltimore Orioles, one behind Jimmy Key. Both Roger Clemens and Bret Saberhagen had rebounded, each having the second-best ERA in his league. David Cone was having a big comeback year of his own, with a 16–5 record and a 2.94 ERA, third-lowest in the American League. Maddux's low ERA was historically so, a bit higher than Doc Gooden's 1985 season. At that point, Bob Gibson's astonishing 1.12 ERA in 1968, a year of plummeted batting averages, remained the only one lower than Maddux's during the live-ball era.

Tony Gwynn had raised his batting average to .394; second-place Jeff Bagwell was hitting .368. AL leader Paul O'Neill was at .359, two points better than Albert Belle and six ahead of recently slumping Frank Thomas, who already had 106 runs scored and 109 walks. Bagwell, who had just suffered a broken bone in his left hand, hit by a pitch thrown

Tony Gwynn, the San Diego Padres' eight-time batting champ, threatened the .400 mark as Bud Selig called an end to the 1994 major league season. Ca. 1994 (National Baseball Hall of Fame Library, Cooperstown, NY).

by the Padres' Andy Benes, had 116 RBI, four more than AL pacesetter Kirby Puckett. Matt Williams led the home run chase with 43, three more than Ken Griffey, Jr., four ahead of Bagwell, five more than Thomas, six in front of Barry Bonds, and seven more than Belle. Three hitters—Bagwell, Thomas, and Belle—had slugging percentages above .700. An astonishing total of nine players had an OPS higher than 1.000: Thomas, Bagwell, Belle, the Reds' Kevin Mitchell, Griffey, Bonds, O'Neill, Gwynn, and McGriff. In easy striking distance were several more: Moisés Alou, the Royals' Bob Hamelin, the Red Sox's Mo Vaughn, and Larry Walker.

For whatever reasons—a livelier ball, recent expansion, muscled-up ballplayers, poorer pitching—the shortened 1994 season concluded with a series of major league team batting records or near-records. On a day-by-day basis, ballclubs averaged 4.92 runs, a .270 BA, 1.03 homers, a .424 slugging percentage, and a .763 OPS. The run total was the highest since 1938, the batting average tops since a year later, the home run mark the second-highest ever (just behind 1987), the slugging percentage just behind the inflated total in 1930, and the OPS figure surpassed only in 1929 and 1930.[16]

The 70–43 Yankees stood aloft the AL East, six and a half games ahead of the Orioles, with the 55–60 Blue Jays 16 games back. The divisional race in the AL Central remained close, featuring the 67–46 White Sox, the 66–47 Indians, and the 64–51 Royals, who had completed a 14-game winning streak in early August. The West was still more tightly bunched, riddled with mediocrities: the 52–62 Rangers stood a game in front of the Athletics, two ahead of the Mariners, and five and a half better than the Angels.

The 1994 version of the Expos appeared to be the winning ballclub Montreal had long sought. A 74–40 record put them six games ahead of the Braves in the NL East. The 66–48 Reds and the 66–49 Astros were separated by a mere half game. The West had the 58–56 Dodgers three and a half games in front of the Giants, who had recently undergone a losing patch.

Those statistics, which are always such an integral part of major league baseball, were not about to change, although that was not certain at the time. The divisional races were over. So too were the individual assaults on historic records. Greg Maddux would not get to add to his brilliant season. Tony Gwynn would not hit .400. Matt Williams and Barry Bonds would not break Roger Maris's home run record or even approach Hack Wilson's NL mark. Ken Griffey, Jr., and Frank Thomas would not come close to Maris or Babe Ruth.

MLB later announced that Frank Thomas easily beat out Ken Griffey, Jr., Albert Belle and Kenny Lofton for the MVP Award in the American League. Jeff Bagwell was a unanimous winner in the National League, with Matt Williams, Moisés Alou, and Barry Bonds finishing behind him. In a close race, David Cone came out ahead of Jimmy Key in the AL Cy Young Award balloting. Greg Maddux was a unanimous winner in the NL, easily besting Ken Hill and Bret Saberhagen.

The Yankees would not vie for their first pennant in 13 years. The Expos would not win their first title ever. And most unfortunately of all, no World Series would be held for the first time in 90 years.

◆ ◆ ◆

The *New York Times'* astute baseball analysts, Murray Chass and Claire Smith, offered their takes on the strike. Without a shift in the owners' stance, Chass warned in a front-page article, the last seven-and-a-half weeks of the regular season would be wiped out, along with the playoffs and the World Series. Bud Selig was quoted as saying, "There is no doubt in my mind the players are united, as always, and the owners are united this time for a significant series of reasons. But having said that, now we have to figure a way to solve this thing."[17]

Smith emphasized the solidarity of the players, current and former, in refusing to relinquish what they had gained in previous labor skirmishes. Rusty Staub, a longtime Mets player and present broadcaster for the NL team, said, "To just give it back, in the form of a salary cap, I just don't think it's going to happen."[18]

The August 15 edition of *The Sporting News* presented a small child, wearing a baseball cap and uniform, with the headline reading "The Game Goes on." Columnist Mike Lupica slammed team owners, who were "supposed to have more of a love for baseball. It is time for them to stop acting like shakedown artists and prove it." Like Donald Fehr, Lupica thought "there still are too many owners who want this strike." Rather than appearing as the Lords of Baseball, "they looked like the Louts of Baseball."[19]

The Sporting News' next cover displayed an obviously disconsolate player holding a bat and glove as he walked away from an empty stadium. In magnified print, the headline blared, "They're OUT." Lupica's anger had intensified, as he wrote, "The owners got what they wanted last week. They got Closing Day in baseball, way too soon." Now, Bud Selig and Richard Ravitch weren't pinpointing the number of financially strapped teams. They had shifted to talking about "industry-wide losses." Accusing them of "some kind of fancy double-speak code," Lupica worried that "the season could be lost." If that happened, he charged, "it will be the worst scandal in baseball since the Black Sox. This time, it will look as if [the owners] dumped the whole sport."[20]

On the evening of August 23, the *Washington Post* obtained a copy of a 65-page report on the economic state of major league baseball by Professor Roger G. Noll, who taught economics at Stanford and had delivered financial analyses for the MLBPA in 1985. The report was based on financial data delivered to the union by the Player Relations Committee, run by team owners, for the period 1991–1993 plus projections regarding a full 1994 season. The baseball tycoons drew on the same financial information in devising their plan for revenue sharing.[21]

According to Noll, the owners had underestimated anticipated revenues by $50 to $140 million for 1994 alone. They also had possibly bumped up purported front office administrative costs by $100 million annually. "The prophecy of impending doom is far more implausible in 1994 than it was nine years ago," charged Noll. Baseball, he declared, was "financially healthy—healthier than it was in the mid–1980s, when detailed financial data were last made available," notwithstanding a drop in national broadcasting payments. Noll's conclusion? "The issue is simply a fight between owners and players for the last few million dollars of revenue per team in a circumstance in which almost everyone is doing very well financially." The report, along with Donald Fehr's cover letter, was handed to each major league owner. Fehr indicated, "In the MLBPA's view Noll's report should be a valuable contribution to our continuing dialogue about the future of the industry."[22]

Negotiations resumed on August 31, with federal mediators participating. Eight days later, the MLBPA delivered a counterproposal, calling for the 16 teams with the highest payrolls to be taxed, that money to be apportioned among the others, and all squads to share gate receipts. Those ideas went nowhere.[23]

Two weeks later, 34 days into the strike, the Commissioner's Office delivered a resolution terminating the 1994 major league season. Called off were the 669 games still on the books, along with the newly configured playoffs and the World Series. Twenty-six teams, with Baltimore and Cincinnati failing to sign on board, agreed with the one-page document. It read, "In order to protect the integrity of the Championship Season, the Division Series, the League Championship Series and the World Series, the 28 Clubs have concluded with enormous regret that the remainder of the 1994 season … must be canceled and that the Clubs will explore all avenues to achieve a meaningful, structural reform of Baseball's player compensation system in an effort to ensure that the 1995 and future Championship Seasons can occur as scheduled and uninterrupted."[24]

Bud Selig, who had initially set September 9 as the drop-dead point, declared, "Like a lot of things in life, you anticipate something, fear it coming and hope that it doesn't, and when the day is here, there is an incredible amount of sadness. Lest anybody not understand, there can't be joy on any side. One can only hope now that we can constructively move forward to solve our problems." Donald Fehr asked, "What do you expect from a cartel?"[25]

Two days before Selig announced the cancellation of the rest of the current season, the *New York Times*' George Vecsey delivered a blistering condemnation of baseball owners.

> This is failure … sheer, flagrant, blatant failure. When the baseball owners pull the plug on the season in the next day or two, they will be confirming one of the great public miscalculations ever committed in this part of the world. They will be forever redefining a sport, a business, a way of life, a national pastime, as it used to be called but can never be again. They bought into a century of baseball the way nouveau-riche gangsters and junk-mail specialists buy into historic estates. Now they are preparing to cheapen that heritage by closing it down for this season, for the foreseeable future. They must live with the consequences, these Reinsdorfs and Seligs.

The owners, Vecsey wrote, would be remembered as "'the men who killed baseball.' What a way to go down in history. What a failure."[26]

Claire Smith of the *New York Times* presented her early post-mortem on September 14: "The 1994 baseball season is all but hooked up to a suicide machine." The next day, she pointed to the loss of the regular season's last 52 games per team, pennant races, and the World Series, "the biggest tragedy and travesty of all." All of this "because the silly, self-destructive kind of bickering that marred the game at the turn of the century is going strong 90 years later."[27]

Eddie Taubensee, a catcher on the Cincinnati Reds, blasted the new acting commissioner.

> Selig cut the thread between your child and your grandfather, between yesterday and tomorrow. He blew the bridge from then to when…. Selig always will be known as the Man Who Killed Baseball. This is a grim burden, but let us not forget that he was not just a volunteer, he drove the getaway car. Selig wants us to know how unbearable this has been for him, how sad he is to have to do it, how sorry he is, how sorry they all are. It is not for him to say it is sad any more than for the assassin to attend the funeral.[28]

Writing in the *San Diego Union-Tribune*, Wayne Lockwood argued that Selig, like "Shoeless Joe Jackson, Fred Merkle, Johnny Pesky, Ralph Branca, Ralph Terry, Bill Buckner, Mitch Williams and other unfortunates … will forever be remembered for one glaring mistake rather than the sum of otherwise productive careers." Selig would find a place in the "Hall of Shame" for having canceled the 1994 World Series.[29]

A Canadian sportswriter, Steve Milton, began his commentary, "And so Bud and the gang have done what the Black Sox, the Depression, the earthquake and Hitler could not. They've killed the World Series. Murdered it, really. Gunned it down in cold blood and plain daylight. Then mourned its passing with crocodile tears. Held the smoking gun in one hand and pointed fingers with the other."[30]

On the front page of the *San Francisco Chronicle*, columnist Bruce Jenkins damned Selig roundly, ticking off his actions in bringing about the death of the 1994 season. The Milwaukee Brewers owner had orchestrated the campaign to get rid of Fay Vincent. While beginning negotiations in December 1992, he didn't tender the "salary-cap proposal until this June." Selig steered his colleagues in withholding that $7.8 million pension plan payment. He convinced the players to go ahead with this year's All-Star Game to allow a new television deal to begin. It was Selig who reported that 19 teams were financially foundering, then sharply reduced the number. Jenkins charged, "He told so many lies over the past two weeks, it became impossible to take him seriously." In his opinion piece, "Day Dark Out—Our Pastime in Ruins," Jenkins charged, "It wasn't Hitler, the Depression or a major earthquake that killed the national pastime. It was Bud Selig."[31]

Mitch Albom, sports columnist for the *Detroit Free Press*, derided both Selig and Fehr, calling the former "a puppet" and the latter "the mouthpiece for the players," while bemoaning the departure of "your old friend baseball." Asking who were these men with their "navy blue suits and maroon ties and pasty skins," Albom wondered, "What right do they have to control something that was once such a part of the American quilt, a dream that sewed together children from Spokane to Providence on a single summer night, sitting by the radio, marking their blue-lined scorecards, listening to announcers bellow, 'It's a long fly ball, deep to left...'?"[32]

Waxing on, Albom wrote, "When there was nothing else to bring joy to the masses, there was baseball. When there was nothing else to unite father and son, there was baseball. When there nothing for an old man or woman to fill the lonely night, there was baseball. It was, above all else, a metronome of American life, an unbroken ritual from April to October. This has always been what makes it important." The distressed sportswriter wrapped up his ode to the sport he so clearly loved. "Baseball was a heartbeat, and a heartbeat will forgive you, it will let you speed it up, even skip it for a moment, it will keep on going, and be there when you catch up, always, forever, unless you stop the heart. Today they have smashed the heart of the sport. And in so doing, they set a precedent for all the money-grubbers that might own it in the future: If all else fails, it's all right to cancel seasons. It has been done before."[33]

The *Dayton Daily News*' sports columnist, Gary Nuhn, delivered his own commentary on the terminating of the 1994 major league season. He began: "They killed baseball Wednesday. Just got a gun and shot it like a lame horse. Now we know who's on first in the Abbot [sic] and Costello routine. It's the Grim Reaper with Greed on second and Intransigence on third. Beelzebub is in the owners' box. Mighty Casey has struck out, along with Ken Griffey Jr., Tony Gwynn and Common Sense." The sport of "baseball, riddled at every level with haughtiness and dishonesty, has committed suicide after 20 years of constant trying." After blasting "these present baseball outlaws" who had "broken the trust," Nuhn insisted "they cannot break the connection." They had produced "The Death of a Season," but "the game will survive," he wrote, "because it's the perfect game, both conceptually and in practice."[34]

In an opinion piece titled "It will never be the same," *The Sporting News*' contributing writer, Dave Kindred, bemoaned the "serious and lasting damage" major league baseball had inflicted on itself. There were the World Series contests that ended so late that "a generation of children missed moments that make up the mythic memory of the game." There were the embittered labor battles in which "the men who made the game great—the players and only the players" came to be depicted by team owners "not as uniquely talented athletes to be honored with respect but as greedy, spoiled brats." The idea of calling off the World Series demonstrated that MLB's leaders cared not a whit "about the game's traditions, history and emotional connection to the men, women and children who," over a century and longer, had "embraced baseball with a passion so profound as to be instinctive."[35]

Because of all this, Kindred wondered why the public should be concerned about the game's leaders, those who ended a season prematurely and dumped the World Series. "These are men," he wrote, "doing what Hitler couldn't do. Baseball's poor, poor, poor owners would kill a World Series." While declaring that players helped set "this lost summer of baseball" in motion, the owners, Kindred asserted, "deserve the far greater blame."[36]

Displaying a baseball repleted with stars and stitching, the September 26 cover of *The Sporting News* offered a quote by the late Bart Giamatti: "THE PEOPLE OF AMERICA CARE ABOUT BASEBALL, NOT ABOUT YOUR SQUALID LITTLE SQUABBLES. REASSUME YOUR DIGNITY AND REMEMBER THAT YOU ARE CUSTODIAMS OF AN ENDURING PUBLIC TRUST." In a column titled "This one's for you, Bud," Kindred charged that the owners shut down major league baseball "for the macho glee of [it]. They did [it] to show they could strut as cockily as any kid wearing his cap backward. They did to prove again who lives in the big house." Condemning "Bud and His Nightmare Boys," Kindred wrote that the enduring sorrow involved how they had "made the game smaller, if not in reality, certainly in spirit." They had removed "the feeling of awe" many felt on entered a big league ballpark. Moreover "in the mad tradition of burning the village to save it, the owners have torched the World Series," justifying doing so on the "patently absurd" notion that baseball was soon to become financially insolvent.[37]

The *New York Times'* J. Anthony Lukas compared the recent decision to call off the World Series with the preemptive decision, during the summer of 1904, by New York Giants owner John T. Brush and manager John McGraw to refuse to compete against any American League team in the postseason. Lukas referred to the statement by Bowie Kuhn, the former commissioner, warning not to view baseball's entrepreneurial titans as "uniformly evil and stupid." Agreeing that the owners were not evil, Lukas believed that "even a charitable man might conclude" that they were "stupid."[38]

20

Discord Continues

PREMATURELY ENDING THE 1994 REGULAR SEASON, cancelling the playoffs, and failing to hold the World Series for the first time in nine decades evidently wasn't enough for some of the actors involved in the embittered labor strife. Talk of using replacement players the next year could already be heard, leading to a typically caustic analysis by Marvin Miller, former MLBPA executive director. He worried that owners might seek to "decertify" the union, which would require a majority of ballplayers to declare a determination to end their membership. Absent that, the owners could release their entire rosters and "start over." Miller foresaw the owners signing up "scabs to start the season." But he didn't believe that would ultimately prove successful.[1]

Donald Fehr expressed concerns about the status of the next baseball campaign. "Clearly, spring training is now in jeopardy, and if it's going to be saved, something has got to be done over the next several weeks," he declared on September 21 after meeting with a group of players from 20 teams. Speaking the next day before the House Subcommittee on Economic and Commercial Law, Bud Selig, expressing optimism that a deal would be reached with the MLBPA, defended major league baseball's exemption from antitrust law. Disagreeing, Fehr said, "Unlike Mr. Selig, I am not even remotely optimistic there will be agreement in the short term. Spring training is in imminent peril."[2]

As the possibility of resolving the impasse remained remote, Fehr fretted about another area of concern: the seeming readiness of owners to impose a salary cap. That would ensure, he indicated, that big league players would be absent from spring training camps. Bargaining would continue, declared John Harrington, president of the Boston Red Sox and a key negotiator for the owners, even if a salary cap were put into place.[3]

On October 13, the two sides accepted Secretary of Labor Robert Reich's suggestion for a federal mediator, William J. Usery. With little progress taking place, Fehr charged on November 8 that the owners were "hell-bent on imposing [the salary cap]." They "used Usery's presence to shut off negotiations," Fehr declared. The owners also took out a full-page ad in *USA Today* and delivered a press release quoting a "White Paper" in which Selig discussed "some fine tuning" of baseball necessities, thought to mean a salary cap.[4] At the end of November, Usery convinced owners to delay implementation of a cap. On December 5, Richard Ravitch resigned as head of the owners' Player Relations Committee; for the past few months, John Harrington had been acting as the owners' top negotiator. The next day, special meditator Usery fired off a message to the owners. "For my process, implementation would be very, very unfortunate, and I've told the owners that and everyone concerned."

Nevertheless, on December 22, owners, having twice postponed their self-proclaimed deadline for establishing the cap, asserted that bargaining had come to a standstill. They announced their decision to impose a salary cap. In the process, they terminated salary arbitration, created 63 restricted free agents, and discarded many gains made by the MLBPA through collective bargaining over the past quarter of a century. Terming the salary cap imposition "preordained," Donald Fehr declared, "This is certainly a sad day. It's regrettable. I think the owners will come to regret it—sooner than they think."[5]

With spring training only six weeks away, team owners prepared to resort to replacement players. Gene Michael, the Yankees' general manager, stated, "It may not be pretty at the beginning. I'm not comfortable doing it, but I know we're going to have to do something to get baseball back onto the sports page." Bill Giles, the Phillies owner, said, "I think that's probably the direction we're headed."[6]

In his column for *The Sporting News*, Mike Lupica quoted Seymour Siwoff of the Elias Sport Bureau: "Sports is air." As Lupica saw it, "Sometimes it feels as if air is all we have left. But last season, they even tried to take that. They stole the pennant races, and they stole the World Series. In a few months, the owners are willing to ruin spring training." Lupica viewed the owners as "the greediest group than has ever been in any sport." He agreed with Donald Fehr's assessment that they made up "a cartel."[7]

Almost as a sidenote to the labor machinations, longtime Philadelphia Phillies slugger Mike Schmidt, a three-time NL MVP and eight-time home run champion, with four RBI titles, six Silver Slugger awards, and 10 Gold Gloves, became the latest player voted into Cooperstown by the Baseball Writers' Association of America, receiving 96.5 percent of the vote. The 1995 Hall of Fame class would include four others, selected by the Veterans Committee: Negro Leagues pitcher Leon Day; National League founder William Hulbert; old-time pitcher Vic Willis; and outfielder Richie Ashburn, two-time NL batting champion and six-time All-Star, who spent the bulk of his career with the Phillies beginning shortly after World War II.

As the end of January approached, President Clinton directed federal mediator W.J. Usery to get the ballplayers and team owners negotiating again, establishing a February 6 deadline to make strides toward terminating the strike. If that didn't occur, he threatened, the government would probably "propose a solution." Both Selig and Fehr appreciated the president's pronouncement, or so they said. In fact, Clinton lacked the authority to compel a resolution of the labor conflict.[8]

Pressure by the National Labor Relations Board convinced team owners, on February 3, to toss aside their salary cap. They replaced it with a luxury-tax proposal.

Despite the uncertainty caused by the latest actions, the MLBPA considered the possibility that "the old system—with salary arbitration and no restricted free agency" might be "back in place." The owners, for their part, remained antagonistic to that very system.[9]

On February 5, mediator Usery declared that an impasse prevented a settlement. President Clinton responding by insisting the two sides attempt to resolve matters once again. Instead, they began tossing literal and rhetorical salvoes at one another. As the MLBPA ended a month-and-a-half-long signing freeze it had placed on its members, the owners precluded teams from cutting deals with players. "To throw this kind of a bomb into the negotiations suggest pretty clearly that the intent is to have the bomb explode," Donald Fehr complained. He deemed the owners' move "perhaps the most provocative step they could take in a desperate attempt to break off negotiations."[10]

When his deadline came and went with no progress having been made, Clinton indicated that he would request that Congress issue a binding arbitration order. However, both Democratic and Republican members quickly questioned their ability to act in the manner the president wanted. Conveying his opposition, Bud Selig declared, "Binding arbitration is not the solution to this dispute and we reject the idea." Referring to both the players and the owners, federal mediator Usery commented, "I guess it shows how hard they're locked in."[11]

Fehr soon suggested that ballplayers would call off their strike if Congress agreed to a partial removal of baseball's antitrust exemption. The measure, proposed by Republican senator Orrin Hatch of Utah and his Democratic colleague, Daniel Patrick Moynihan of New York, would apply antitrust legislation to baseball and enable players to bring court challenges about changes unilaterally instituted by owners. However, Congress refused to act expeditiously, while individual members took swipes at owners and players. They also condemned both Selig and Fehr for their seeming intransigence.[12]

In the meantime, spring training camps opened but only to replacement players and minor leaguers. The Associated Press' Chris Sheridan's article on spring training effectively asked, "Who's on First? Who Knows? Who Cares?" Fehr declared, "Players not on the 40-man roster, of course, have a legal right to play in replacement games." He continued, "Major-league players, however, have the corresponding right to regard any individuals who play in such games as scabs." They also could urge a boycott of the contests.[13]

In an interview conducted for *The Sporting News*, Bob Costas, who had provided the play-by-play for NBC's *Game of the Week* throughout most of the previous decade, reflected on the state of the game. "Baseball is an interesting game," he said. "It's fun to sit in the sun, fun to talk about something you have in common. And it's a link between generations. Those are significant virtues to get out of something that's just a game. Plus, since you play it every day, your interest in it is renewed day to day, and from season to season." While acknowledging that one could easily romanticize about the sport, Costas stated, "The truth is, there's a lot to appreciate. Baseball is a great game. It has a great history, a textured history, with grand, dramatic events, clowns, characters, buffoons, quirky incidents."[14]

This past season, however, had left Costas angry. He was "angry at what he deems the weak and short-sighted stewardship of the owners; angry at the self-righteous and narrow self-interest of the players." He chastised "the owners for losing a 'feel' for what distinguishes baseball from other sports." He castigated "the players for slavish devotion to one guiding principle—maximization of immediate market value—above institutional concerns." Costas feared that "baseball doesn't know itself, it has completely lost a sense of itself." Largely, this had happened because of "the owners' ineptitude, their continual losses at the negotiating table, which led to economic desperation." The players' association was not blameless, seeking to whip the owners and maximize earning power, while exuding self-righteousness.[15]

During early March, Donald Fehr expressed a readiness to compromise about the luxury tax. The union conveyed its willingness to accept a revenue-sharing plan and exhibited some flexibility about the payroll level when such a tax would take place. The MLBPA refused to budge on arbitration or free agency, both of which management wanted to end or alter. In the middle of the month, the striking players declared their refusal to agree to a settlement that counted replacement games or strikebreakers' statistics among baseball's official records. The major league players did soon consider ending the strike to pressure the owners to negotiate more reasonably or order a lockout.[16]

On March 26, the NLRB cast a vote, 3–2, to obtain an injunction against major league owners. That same day, with the regular season a mere week away, players and owners determined to restart the bargaining process. While Fehr indicated "today's a good day," White Sox owner Jerry Reinsdorf declared there were "certain similarities" between the union chief and Jim Jones, whose followers had engaged in mass suicide in Guyana. "The players are blinding [sic] following Fehr," Reinsdorf exclaimed. Fehr dismissed Reinsdorf's comments. "I assume Jerry's bored. This is second-grade stuff. It doesn't bother me one way or another."[17]

The owners did begin to give way as U.S. District Judge Sonia Sotomayor slated a hearing that might end the strike. Baseball's mandarins now offered to maintain the present salary arbitration system and free agency or toss aside arbitration and reduce from six to four years the time players had to accrue for unrestricted free agency. On March 28, the players agreed to end the strike if Judge Sotomayor ordered an injunction to maintain salary arbitration and free agency.[18]

Sotomayor issued her ruling on March 31, ordering baseball owners to reestablish bidding for free agents, salary arbitration, and the last CBA's anti-collusion provisions. In the 2nd U.S. Circuit Court of Appeals, Judge Roger J. Miner turned down the owners' request for an immediate stay. "Absent a lockout by the clubs, we can get real baseball on the field in a short period of time," Donald Fehr declared. "We could put together a quick spring training, and Opening Day would be delayed a lit-tle bit. We'd hope that the players would play the maximum number of games pos-sible." Bud Selig deemed the judge's decision "disappointing" and possibly "a step backward in our negotiations for a meaningful agreement." He continued to insist, "Major-league baseball still needs a long-term solution to the serious economic problems confronting the game today."[19]

With threats of a lockout circulating, team owners and players tentatively agreed on April 1 to start spring training the following week, with the regular season to begin on April 26. This would end pro sports' longest strike to date. Several teams appeared to vote against a lockout, with Baltimore owner Peter Angelos declaring he would do so "with relish." On April 2, the owners unanimously decided to accept the players' offer to begin the season without an agreement. The 1995 regular season would have 144 games for each team, 18 fewer than the norm.[20]

Acting Commissioner Selig declared, "The clubs hope that the 1995 season—including the postseason—will be played without interruption." He added, "Any-one who has gone through this eight-month experience will let it serve as a poignant reminder that we have a responsibility to make sure it will never happen again, cer-tainly in our lifetime." Referring to the agreement, Selig asserted, "I don't regard it as a surrender. The players were on strike, they made an unconditional offer to come back, and we accepted that offer." Colorado owner Jerry McMorris offered, "We still got to have a deal. The best one is a negotiated deal." Union head Fehr stated, "I think it's clearly a step in the right direction. If they had voted for a lockout, it would have been a clear indication they didn't want peace—at any price."[21]

Bill Dwyre, sports editor of the *Los Angeles Times*, delivered his analysis, "Boys of Summer Take Over from Buffoons of Winter." Similar to Michael Jordan's reac-tion on recently returning to the NBA, commentators could now assert, "They're Back!" With a touch of smirk, Dwyre wrote, "Call it a few days and few dollars short, but call it real baseball. Call it games to be played by players who belong in pinstripes and not in softball knee-socks and jerseys that read Joe's Bar and Grill." Notwith-standing what both sides did "to screw it up—baseball is bigger than the boys who play it and the buffoons who run it."[22]

The costs of the strike? The owners' revenue was short $800 million, while the players' salary hit was $350 million. Also, attendance dropped noticeably in 1995, falling from 31,256 per game to 25,008. "There's a lot of hurt, there's a lot of economic damage that has to be repaired," said Bud Selig. And nothing was really resolved, with owners still capable of imposing a salary cap and the players still able to strike in the midst of the season. "I know there's still a lot of uncertainty out there," indi-cated the MLBPA's Eugene Orza. "I hope with players returning to the field and get-ting absorbed in the game again, it actually will in a strange sort of way invigorate the collective bargaining process and lead to the end of the dispute."[23]

"The game is run by people unworthy of it, from Bud Selig and Donald Fehr on down," opined Mike Lupica as the shortened preseason proceeded apace. During the eight-month-long strike, baseball, Lupica wrote, "was embarrassed on almost a daily basis as the national pastime became a national joke." With the strike concluded, "the embarrassment continues." Montreal—the best team during the abbreviated 1994 season—was engaged in a fire sale of its top players, including Ken Hill, John Wetteland, and Marquis Grissom within the span of three days. This occurred after Larry Walker departed as a free agent. Kansas City shipped off David Cone, the AL Cy Young recipient, to Toronto.[24]

At present, major league baseball lacked a commissioner, a collective-bargaining agreement, and a promise that another strike or lockout wouldn't take place. But the sport, Lupica wrote, "was hard to kill. A hate-filled business is still a wonderful game." He sang the praises of a Triple-A game in the Eastern League which the Reading Phillies played in New Haven, Connecticut, at Yale Field.[25]

"The rich get richer, the fans get dizzier" rang out the headline of Bob Nightengale's latest article in *The Sporting News*. It referred to the Yankees' theft of Wetteland, an All-Star closer, and the Braves' grabbing of Grissom, an All-Star center fielder. The Royals had dumped their ace, Cone, and indicated a readiness to unload many of their remaining top players. To Nightengale, all the frenzied activity underscored as "never before … such a disparity between the big-revenue and small-revenue clubs." Montreal GM Kevin Malone warned, "You have the best team in baseball, and then to have to disassemble it, is discouraging. Every now and then, a small market can make a run, but it's hard to keep everything together."[26]

◆　◆　◆

During the shortened 1995 major league season, the 86–58 Red Sox finished seven games ahead of the 79–65 Yankees, although both made the playoffs out of the AL East. The Mariners, with Ken Griffey, Jr., and Randy Johnson, won the West with a 79–66 record, a game better than the Angels. But the AL and the Central's best were the 100–44 Indians, 30 games in front of the depleted Royals. In the NL East, the 90–54 Braves were 21 wins to the good of both the Mets and the Phillies. The Expos crashed to 66–78, 24 games back. The Central had the 85–69 Reds nine ahead of the Astros. In the West, the 78–66 Dodgers beat out the Rockies by a single game, with both landing in the playoffs, while the Giants, still packing Barry Bonds and Matt Williams, fell to the bottom of the division.

No single-season marks were threatened, mainly because of the shortened season. The batting leaders were Seattle's Edgar Martinez (.356) and Tony Gwynn (.368), the home run champs Albert Belle (50) and Colorado's Dante Bichette (40). Mike Mussina and Greg Maddux each had 19 wins, while Randy Johnson (2.48) and Maddux (1.63) won the ERA titles. The latter two pitchers had remarkable years, with Johnson going 18–2 and striking out 294 batters. Maddox had his finest season, with a 19–2 record and a second straight microscopic ERA.

In the League Divisional Series, Cleveland swept Boston, while Seattle bested New York in five games. Cincinnati swept Los Angeles, and Atlanta knocked out

Colorado in four games. The Indians took the AL pennant in a six-game series against the Mariners, while the Braves won four straight from the Reds. The Braves then captured their first World Series championship since 1957, beating the Indians in six games.

The off-season saw Boston's Mo Vaughn win the AL MVP Award, barely beating out Belle, and Cincinnati's Barry Larkin, coming out ahead of Bichette and Maddux, received the NL Award. The two Cy Young winners were Johnson and Maddux, the Atlanta star's fourth straight.

As for Ken Griffey, Jr., and Barry Bonds, their seasons had been somewhat disappointing, according to their standards. Injuries limited The Kid to half of Seattle's games, and his numbers—17 homers, 42 RBI, a .258 BA—reflected that fact, although he again was named an All-Star and Gold Glover. Bonds, who batted .294, played in all 144 San Francisco games, tying for the league lead, while scoring 109 runs (second in the NL), batting in 104 (sixth), stealing 31 bases (11th), hitting 33 homers (fourth), slugging at a .577 (fifth) clip, having 292 total bases (fifth), and compiling an OPS+ of 170 (second). He led the league in walks (120), intentional walks (22), OBP (.431), and OPS (1.0009). His 7.5 WAR was second-best, behind Maddux, and tops for position players. Expectations were high but resulted in only 12th place in MVP voting. After five straight seasons of winning both the Gold Glove and Silver Slugger awards, Bonds received neither but was named an All-Star for the sixth year in a row.

◆ ◆ ◆

On September 18, as the 1995 regular season neared an end, major league team owners announced that Randy Levine would serve as their top negotiator. Eleven days later, the U.S. Appeals Court for the Second Circuit sustained Judge Sonia Sotomayor's earlier ruling allowing for an injunction, which had been issued by the National Labor Relations Board, against unfair labor practices.

During mid–November, owners presented a proposal, setting a luxury tax as high as 50 percent on payrolls surpassing $44 million as well as a limit on team salaries, enabling them to amount only to 50 percent of revenues. In early February 1996, the players countered, calling for a 2.5 percent tax on player salaries for three years with a luxury tax to be instituted in 1999. The money collected would be handed out to the least affluent teams. The two sides went back-and-forth for several months, with Donald Fehr and Bud Selig engaged in a verbal tussle during the 1995 World Series.

Nearing the conclusion of a four-year battle that had led to dismayed fans, enraged ballplayers, and furious proprietors, team owners agreed to terms on November 26, 1996, which the players soon ratified. With the owners abruptly reversing course from just three weeks before, plans were made for interleague play, a luxury tax, and revenue sharing. The vote in favor was 26–4, with opposition presented by the Chicago White Sox, Cleveland Indians, Kansas City Royals, and Oakland Athletics.[27]

The plan would remain effective through 2000, with the players possessing an option to extend it one year longer. Teams from each league would compete against one another starting in the 1997 season. A luxury tax would be set at 35 percent for 1997 and 1998, 34 percent for 1999, with no tax in the first and final two years of the contract. Revenue sharing would provide assistance for the 13 teams with the lowest revenues, with players paying a 2.5 percent tax in 1996 and 1997. Other provisions included awarding of service time credit for time missed during the strike, allowing free agency twice within a five-year period, and the setting up of three-person arbitration panels.[28]

"It's a landmark day," hailed Acting Commissioner Bud Selig, who convinced enough of his colleagues that this was the best deal they could cut. "The difficult times are now behind us." Chicago White Sox owner Jerry Reinsdorf crowed, "It's good for the White Sox because it dooms the small-market teams. There will be less for us to compete against." In fact, the actions of two opponents of the pact helped sway many other owners. Reinsdorf had recently signed Albert Belle to a "record five-year, $55-million contract," and Wayne Huizenga, owner of the Florida Marlins, handed Bobby Bonilla "a four-year, $23.3-million" deal. His colleagues, including Selig, felt particularly "betrayed" by Reinsdorf's action. As *Sports Illustrated* soon pointed out, Reinsdorf didn't simply alter major league baseball's pay structure, "he destroyed it," with Belle getting $2.5 million more annually than Ken Griffey, Jr., the game's next highest-salaried player.[29]

Bob Padecky of the *Santa Rosa Press Democrat* indicated that baseball still had yet to "heal all the wounds left from the canceling of 1994 World Series." Searingly, he wrote, "Get Rid of That Puppet, Find a Real Man. Bud Selig has had the most shameful conduct of any man holding the commissioner's job." Padecky charged, "It was Selig and…. Reinsdorf who created this mess in the first place." Baseball required "a real commissioner as much as it needed a labor agreement," Padecky insisted, while delivering other admonitions. "Please, Whatever You Do, No More Thumb-Sucking in Public…. Shut Up About the Money Already…. Do Not Dump on the Fans…. An Autograph Should Come from the Heart, Not from the Pocketbook…. Let's Read 'Em and Let's See If We Weep…. Hear No Evil, Feel No Evil." These referred to major league baseball acquiring a reputation as "a very expensive nursery school," the greed that saturated the game, the need to freeze ticket prices, the bilking of fans at card shows, the failure of owners to engage in financial disclosure, and the bitching by "certain leftfielders in the game."[30]

Dave Kindred turned to Marvin Miller for his perspective on the latest deal between players and management. "If the owners truly believed small-market teams would fail, they'd act in their own self-interest to share revenue in a meaningful way. Their refusal to do that is proof that no such catastrophe looms," reasoned Miller. The real enemy of the owners, Kindred wrote, "is themselves." They attacked both the players needed to sell the game and each other.[31]

The disharmony that had long afflicted baseball was likely to continue. One source of continuing contention was the commissioner's post. "Hiring a more independent chief executive officer" than Selig "would be a peace offering to Fehr and the players," the *Washington Post*'s Mark Maske suggested. But then he wrote, "No one [among the owners] cares what he [Fehr] thinks."[32]

The formal acceptance of the new CBA didn't occur until March 14, 1997. It instituted revenue sharing and placed a luxury tax on the handful of teams with the highest payrolls for both the upcoming season and the one following that.[33]

On July 9, 1998, during a season when attendance was up as a new home run chase was waged by St. Louis Cardinals first baseman Mark McGwire and Chicago Cubs outfielder Sammy Sosa, major league owners voted 30–0 to hand Selig the title of permanent commissioner. "I'm a fan," said Selig. "There is no one who can love the game more than I do. Its history and tradition and above all its decency." He admitted, "We've had eight work stoppages [so] we have to ensure the next generation doesn't have to endure any more." Selig, who was receiving a five-year contract with a $3 million annual salary, said, "I'm a baseball man. I've been a baseball man all my adult life."[34]

Anticipating the expected news, Donald Fehr said, "I don't think him being named commissioner will change the way we have conducted business the last couple of years." Referring to dealings with Paul Beeston, the ex-Toronto Blue Jays executive now serving as MLB's chief executive officer, Fehr indicated, "We now have an office to deal with on a daily basis. That's why we don't treat this as an item of significant change." Selig expressed belief that he could work with Fehr. "Human events tore us apart at times," Selig admitted. "But we've gotten along for the most part. We've reduced the acrimony."[35]

On October 27, President Clinton signed the Curt Flood Act of 1998, which Congress had passed earlier in the month. The measure rescinded portions of the 76-year-old Supreme Court ruling that provided an exemption for Organized Baseball from antitrust legislation. The new law did not apply to issues regarding relocation, expansion, or the minors.[36]

The White House issued a statement by the president regarding the Curt Flood Act. The nation's chief executive officer affirmed, "It is especially fitting that this legislation honors a courageous baseball player and individual, the late Curt Flood, whose enormous talents on the baseball diamond were matched by his courage off the field."[37]

21

Labor Woes
and the National Pastime

BASEBALL'S LABOR WARS NEITHER BEGAN NOR ENDED with the strike during the 1994 major league season that led to cancellation of more than 900 regular season games, the scheduled expanded rounds of playoffs, and that year's World Series. In fact, for well over a century, relations between players and management had proved contentious. That produced blacklisting, walkouts, lockouts, strikes, and the creation of new leagues, only one of which proved long-lasting. Players, even stars like Home Run Baker, who sat out the 1915 season due to a contractual dispute, occasionally refused to play for a time or walked away from the game altogether.

For decades, the disputes were generally over the same issues: the determination of team owners to cap salaries and their insistence on retaining legal control over players. Baseball proprietors, striving to monopolize the professional version of their sport, wanted to stave off having to compete for the services of players. They worried about rival leagues or even their own inclination to pay top dollar to afford their teams the chance to compete for pennants and World Series championships.

Relying on the reserve clause they had created as early as 1879, owners also desired to lock in their players once they initially signed them, enabling teams to retain, trade, or simply shed them at will. They sought to maintain a tight rein on team balance sheets, financially rewarding players if they chose to or playing hardball at the bargaining table. Not allowed to have representatives with them during such negotiations until the 1970s, players were often forced into a take-it-or-leave-it proposition.

Even baseball's very finest ballplayers had little to call on amid such talks, as the brilliant Yankees center fielder Joe DiMaggio quickly encountered during his first years in the majors. Teams could draw on their own public relations networks, which generally included backing from sportswriters beholden to them. During a contractual clash before the start of DiMaggio's third season with the Yankees, the team owner, Colonel Jacob Ruppert, declared, "I've forgotten all about him. Presidents go into eclipse, kings have their thrones moved from under them, business leaders go into retirement, great ballplayers pass on, but still, everything moves in its accustomed stride." That statement followed DiMaggio's sophomore year, when he led the majors with 46 homers and 418 total bases, drove in 167 runs, and batted .346, while helping lead the Yankees to their second straight World Series title.[1]

Players fought back in various manners, including by establishing labor organizations or moving over to other leagues, one of which they literally created. One of the game's early stars, the New York Giants' John Montgomery Ward, battled for players' rights, helping to establish the Brotherhood of Professional Baseball Players. Although initially insisting he was not attacking the reserve clause, Ward, drawing on legal training, proceeded to do precisely that, using both the written word and his organizing abilities. In 1890, that helped to bring about formation of the Players' League, in many ways a successful but short-lived venture as it went after the National League's reserve clause and salary cap.

Two subsequent endeavors, the Protective Association of Professional Baseball Players, or the Players Protective Association, and the Baseball Players Fraternity, founded in 1900 and 1912, respectively, adopted different approaches regarding the supposedly sacrosanct reserve clause. The PPA challenged the clause, receiving support from the fledgling American League before it reached an accord with the more established NL. The Fraternity insisted it was not calling into question the reserve clause, seeking instead, as had both the Brotherhood and the PPA, to improve working conditions for professional baseball players. The PPA faded away after the AL and NL reached an accord, while the Fraternity waned along with the Federal League amid unrelenting hostility from major league owners.

In 1922, the National Baseball Players Association of the United States appeared and then vanished, largely to be forgotten. Its call for the condition of players to be bettered again produced invectives and angry responses by major league baseball magnates. That same year, the U.S. Supreme Court unanimously ruled, notwithstanding all evidence to the contrary, that professional baseball did not amount to interstate trade or commerce; hence, it was not subject to antitrust legislation.

Nearly a quarter of a century passed before the next labor drive took hold in big league ranks, when, just following World War II, attorney Robert Murphy set up the American Baseball Guild. Yet again confronting implacable opposition from the powers that be, the Guild nevertheless bequeathed some genuine benefits for major leaguers. Those also undoubtedly resulted because of legal challenges to the reserve clause and the threat posed, for a time, by the rival Mexican League, which grabbed some players, including both current and future stars. Team owners eventually agreed to establish a minimum player salary, spring training per diem money, and a pension fund.

With legal and political pressure mounting in the courts, Congress, and sports columns, owners also faced growing resentment by players regarding working conditions, the minimum salary, the pension fund, and surging receipts from television and radio broadcasts, particularly for the All-Star Game and the World Series. The refusal to allow players or their representatives to sit at bargaining tables regarding the media was yet another factor in convincing the players of the need to establish the Major League Baseball Players Association, which appeared during the mid–1950s.

During its first years of existence, Bob Feller and Ralph Kiner, nearing the ends of their distinguished big-league careers, struggled to make the MLBPA a viable entity, often in the face of antagonism from team owners and indifference from many players. After the retirements of Feller and Kiner, Robin Roberts, Harvey Kuenn, Jim Bunning, and Bob Friend took the lead in seeking more money for the pension fund and a higher minimum salary, in particular. Lacking much in the way of skillful administrative assistance, they determined in 1966 to hire a full-time executive director for the MLBPA.

Ultimately, the players chose a union economist, Marvin Miller, who would lead the Association for the next decade and a half. Very quickly, Miller transformed the virtually impotent MLBPA into a force to be reckoned with, obtaining in less than two years the first collective bargaining agreement in professional sports, a sizable increase in the minimum salary, improved pension funding, and arbitration rights regarding player-team contractual disputes. He also lent support to veteran ballplayer and several-time All-Star Curt Flood in his legal battle against the reserve clause. While the Supreme Court ruled against Flood, the case and other actions by the MLBPA helped to pave the way for free agency by the mid–1970s, thanks to successful arbitration decisions involving star pitchers Catfish Hunter, Andy Messersmith, and Dave McNally.

The union and its executive director, first Miller and then his successor, Donald Fehr, became embroiled in a series of contentious collective bargaining battles. A dispute regarding the pension plan led to a 13-day strike in 1972, the first in major league history. The owners conducted a 17-day lockout the following year, thereby delaying the start of spring training. Another nearly two-and-a-half-week lockout took place three years later. The 1976 season began with no CBA in place, but an agreement mid-year cemented free agency. A week-long strike at the end of spring training in 1980 concluded with a promise to continue discussions and, ultimately, a new CBA. With owners demanding compensation for free agency the next year, the players carried out a 50-day-long strike two months into the season, causing it to be split in half with an expanded round of playoff games. A one-day strike took place in early August 1985 over the pension plan and the owners' insistence on a cap for player salary arbitration earnings. A five-week lockout began in mid–February 1990, when owners became enraged about arbitrator rulings against them for colluding not to bid on free agents and to keep salaries in check. Commissioner Fay Vincent urged an end to the lockout provided the union agreed not to strike. His action upset many team owners, who, led by Bud Selig and Jerry Reinsdorf, orchestrated Vincent's removal.

The determination of owners to institute a salary cap and to devise a system of revenue sharing produced an impasse that ultimately led to a players' strike on August 12, 1994. Just over a month later, Acting Commissioner Selig called off the remainder of the season, the playoffs, and—for just the second time since the World Series began in 1903—the meeting between pennant winners to determine Organized Baseball's champion.

The labor acrimony that had long beset major league baseball thus produced that ultimate indignity for lovers of the sport. In the midst of a potentially historic season when well-established records threatened to be shattered, the MLBPA, led by Donald Fehr, and team owners, spearheaded by Acting Commissioner and Milwaukee Brewers owner Selig, proved incapable of resolving their dispute. Home run-thumping Matt Williams, the injured Jeff Bagwell, Triple Crown aspirants Frank Thomas and Albert Belle, and pitching wizard Greg Maddux were left on the sideline. So too were the game's best all-around players, Ken Griffey, Jr., who was one of several sluggers seeking to set a new home run mark, and Barry Bonds, whose month-long surge suggested he might be capable of putting together yet another MVP season.

In one sense, Fehr and Selig were simply performing the roles they had been selected to handle. Like his predecessor, Marvin Miller, Fehr was the players' advocate as no one had been before them. In many regards, he was acting from a defensive posture, attempting to hold onto gains the union had achieved over a nearly three-decade span, including free agency and ever-mounting player salaries. In the process, the MLBPA had become perhaps the world's most powerful labor union.

Selig, encouraged by Chicago White Sox owner Reinsdorf and other owners, insisted on the necessity of restricting team expenses. Having lost fight after fight against the players and their union, the owners, again led by Selig, drew a line in the sand, insisting on revenue sharing, which they adamantly asserted was necessary for the financial well-being of several teams and major league baseball in general. Having dawdled on agreeing to revenue sharing, which was within their power to determine, the owners demanded what amounted to give-backs from the players regarding both free agency and salaries. As they had during earlier labor struggles, the owners believed they "needed a win" over the players. Repeating a belief held earlier by some in their ranks, team owners appeared ready to lose large portions of a major league season, at a minimum.

Ultimately, notwithstanding team owners' and, in particular, his own professed love of the game, Selig and his fellow "Lords of the Realm" proved willing to toss aside a bevy of games, playoff rounds, and—most significant of all—the 1994 World Series. In the end, they prevented the Fall Classic from being played for only the second time in its 92-year history. That was equivalent to the Super Bowl, the NBA championship final, the Stanley Cup finals, horse racing's Triple Crown, or the entire Grand Slam series in tennis and golf being called off.

But in many ways, it was more than any of that because the World Series retained an aura unlike any other sporting event for fans of the game. Much like Walt Whitman, Mark Twain, and Jacques Barzan earlier, along with Stephen Gould and Bart Giamatti more recently, numerous Americans continued to view baseball as the National Pastime. They included in their midst a disproportionate number of writers and other intellectuals, drawn to the sport's romantic allure. However, the seemingly cavalier refusal to let the World Series be played during the summer of

1994 proved dispiriting, disheartening, and infuriating to countless followers of the game.

If what had already been wrought wasn't bad enough, the clash between the MLBPA and team owners carried over into spring training of the following year, imperiling the 1995 season too. The potentiality of another array of games—in this case, possibly every one for each major league roster—being canceled was only thwarted by an injunction from the National Labor Relations Board and a federal judge's ruling. Judge Sonia Sotomayor effectively compelled owners to pursue free agents, accept salary arbitration, and agree not to engage in collusion regarding free agents. The actual new CBA wasn't formally completed until mid–March 1997.

Shortly afterward, the *Los Angeles Times* suggested that if one was unable to attend Opening Day at Dodger Stadium or couldn't catch ESPN's triple-header, there were always peanuts; Cracker Jack; and Ken Burns's nine-part documentary, *Baseball*. Best of all, "it's that time of the year when you go to the ballpark and feel the excitement, see the green grass, smell the peanuts and hear the parking lot attendant say, '$8, please.'"[2]

In an article titled "Passe Pastime?" the *Christian Science Monitor* declared, "The national game is struggling to hold onto its shrinking place in the American sports fan's heart." The paper pointed to declining interest from African Americans kids, while noting that "top-notch talent" was appearing in the Caribbean and portions of Southeast Asia. It considered it "inconceivable that this most venerable of American big-time sports" wouldn't retain the allegiance of its fans. "Baseball, after all, is life in miniature, with its lulls, dramatic bursts, and indeterminate contest lengths. It's also laden with history."[3]

Unfortunately, that history was laden with not only genuine heroics but also the antics of John McGraw, John Brush, Bud Selig, and Donald Fehr in bringing about a refusal to hold the World Series. Team owner Brush's 1904 New York Giants, led by manager McGraw, had twin 30-game winners—Joe McGinnity and Christy Mathewson—in dropping only 47 out of 158 (including five ties) games. They seemingly matched up well against the defending champion Boston Americans, featuring Cy Young, but what would have been the second World Series never occurred. Ninety years later, the Montreal Expos might have met the New York Yankees in the World Series, which would have been the first such appearance for the Canadian team and the 34th for the boys from the Bronx. It also would have been the initial time Montreal's Moisés Alou, Larry Walker, and Pedro Martinez were in the World Series—likewise for New York's veteran captain, Don Mattingly. Neither of those Series, of course, actually took place, leaving never-to-be filled voids in baseball's historical record.

◆ ◆ ◆

Nearly 30 years after the 1994–1995 strike, another labor battle threatened the 2022 major league baseball season. While the leading figures involved were different, similar issues rose to the fore: arbitration, free agency, the minimum salary, a luxury tax, and the ability of less well-heeled teams to compete with the richest ballclubs or even those in the middle of the-pack, financially speaking. Once again, baseball moguls, virtually all billionaires, aspired to whip and break the still largely never bested MLBPA. Fans and pundits expressed dismay about the possible demise of the game's era of relative labor peace and warned, as they had in the past, that the sport would be irreparably damaged. Ultimately, the owner-directed lockout ended, with Opening Day postponed a mere week and no games canceled.

During the years between MLB's latest labor fights, many of the key actors in the 1994–1995 strike had passed from the scene, some literally, or acquired baseball immortality. Ken Griffey, Jr., Frank Thomas, Tony Gwynn, Greg Maddux, Bud Selig, and Marvin Miller had been inducted into the Hall of Fame. Notwithstanding his prominent role in calling off the remainder of the 1994 season, the playoffs, and the World Series, Selig easily gained entrance.

In fact, all, except labor chieftain Miller, had done so readily, on the first ballot. Notwithstanding his obvious importance to the game, Miller repeatedly was turned down for admission, being selected only after he had demanded, following numerous rejections, that his name be removed from consideration. Still more unfortunately, he wasn't elected until seven years following his death in 2012. Players who had already been admitted considered it outrageous that Miller hadn't received the nod. Tom Seaver deemed it a "national disgrace." Henry Aaron declared, "Miller should be in the Hall of Fame if the players have to break down the door to get him in." Brooks Robinson recalled, "Marvin Miller taught us all to stand up for ourselves. It's time we took the responsibility and stood up for him."[4]

Miller eventually received the honor he so richly deserved. So did Jeff Bagwell, although rumors of performance-enhancing drug use kept him from being selected until the seventh year he was eligible. Not so Bobby Cox, Tony La Russa, and Joe Torre, all World Series–winning, award-winning managers readily welcomed to the Hall of Fame, notwithstanding their association with players rumored to be involved with PEDs. The vote tabulation for Cox, La Russa, and Torre was unanimous, while Miller got only half the ballots necessary at that point, six years before he was selected.

The story was far bleaker for some of the greatest players of the modern era, indeed in the history of the sport. Those included Barry Bonds and Roger Clemens, each of whom became seven-time recipients of MLB's top awards—in Bonds's case, the MVP Award, and in Clemens's case, the Cy Young Award, along with an MVP Award of his own. Evidently spurred by Mark McGwire's smashing of the single-season home run mark and the acclaim McGwire and Sosa received in challenging Ruth and Maris during the 1998 season, Bonds topped them all with 73 homers in 2001. Bonds, along with several others, might well have broken the record earlier, during that shortened 1994 campaign. He also went on to best Ruth's and Aaron's lifetime totals, hitting 762 homers before being effectively blackballed before he could break more records and leaving him just shy of the still-vaunted 3,000-hit total. Clemens ended up with 355 wins and seven ERA titles; he might have won another, given that he was second in the American League when the 1994 season abruptly ended. That would have placed him closer to Lefty Grove's record of nine such crowns.

Many, however, viewed the statistics compiled by Bonds and Clemens during the latter portion of their careers with suspicion. They believed the game's greatest hitter and pitcher in the post Mays-Mantle-Aaron-Koufax era had padded their numbers by relying on illicit substances of various kinds, no matter that players had long done precisely that. Hence, baseball writers refused to vote either Bonds or Clemens into the Hall of Fame, leaving their fate in the hands of the Veterans Committee as of late 2022; that committee summarily rejected them.

Also, yet to be added to the Hall is another key figure from the labor wars that led up to the 1994 strike and cancellation of the World Series for only the second time in major league history: Curt Flood. At the 50th anniversary of the absurd Supreme Court ruling that went against him, the now long-deceased, seven-time Gold Glove recipient, who hit over .300 in six seasons and ended with a .293 lifetime batting average, remains on the outside looking in, rhetorically speaking. Despite being one of the key players on three pennant teams, two of which won the World Series, Flood continues to be ignored or forgotten for his most noteworthy contributions to major league baseball, as Marvin Miller was for so long. And as Negro Leagues veterans were, until recently.[5]

Curt Flood's widow, the Black actress Judy Pace-Flood, asserts, "I think it's disgusting and delusional that he's not in the Baseball Hall of Fame." Refuting the notion that he "was a pretty good player," she counters, "There's no person of African descent who played baseball in the '50s and '60s that were pretty good players. There was no such thing as a pretty good Black player sitting on the bench. You had to be outstanding." Recalling that such ballplayers had to contend with Jim Crow edicts, racial epithets, and too many beer cans, Pace-Flood argues, "The hardest place to be as an African American player at that time was a center fielder."[6]

Agreeing with Pace-Flood, USA Today's Bob Nightengale notes that baseball pioneers Jackie Robinson and Larry Doby; Negro Leagues stalwart and celebrant Buck O'Neil; and Miller, the owners' adversary, have all entered the Hall. So too should Flood, Nightengale insists, writing, "The man changed baseball, and all of sports, forever. He sacrificed his life to make a greater place for every professional athlete who put on a uniform, with Time magazine calling him, 'One of the 10 most influential athletes of the century.'" Simply but emphatically, Pace-Flood declares about her late husband, "He's part of American history. He should be in the Hall of Fame."[7] The fact that he's not, like the persistent, mean-spirited refusal to admit Marvin Miller, demonstrates that baseball's labor wars, including those from the long ago and more recent past, have hardly receded from the memory of many of the game's most influential representatives.

Chapter Notes

Preface

1. John Drebinger, "Sports of the Times: The Home-Run Whirligig," *New York Times*, July 30, 1961, p. S2; Arthur Daley, "Sports of the Times: Second Thoughts," *New York Times*, September 18, 1961, p. 38; "No * Will Mar Homer Records, Says Frick With †† for Critics," *New York Times*, September 22, 1961, p. 38; James Reston, "Chapel Hill, N.C.: The Asterisk That Shook the Baseball World," *New York Times*, October 1, 1961, p. E8; John Drebinger, "Record of Maris Has No Asterisk," *New York Times*, December 23, 1961, p. 18; Arthur Daley, "Sports of the Times: Without an Asterisk—," *New York Times*, February 25, 1962, p. S2.

2. Weston Ulbrich, "Mark Twain, the Hartford Baseball Crank," Greater Hartford Twilight Baseball League, April 15, 2021, https://www.ghtbl.org/twain; John Thorn, "Whitman, Melville, and Baseball," June 15, 2012, https://ourgame.mlblogs.com/whitman-melville-and-baseball-662f5ef3583d; Matthew Trueblood, "Jacques Barzun and Baseball in America," *Banished to the Pen*, October 26, 2012, http://www.banishedtothepen.com/jacques-barzun-and-baseball-in-america/.

3. Stephen Jay Gould, "The Streak of Streaks," *New York Review of Books* 35 (August 18, 1988): 8–12; A. Bartlett Giamatti, *Take Time for Paradise: Americans and Their Games* (London: Bloomsbury, 2011).

Chapter 1

1. The Boston Americans became the Boston Red Sox on December 19, 1907, according to an article, "To Be Known as 'Red Sox,'" published on that date in the *Boston Globe*. See Tommy McArdle, "Why Boston's Baseball Team Is Called the Red Sox," Boston.com, May 2, 2019, https://www.boston.com/sports/boston-red-sox/2019/05/02/how-did-the-red-sox-get-their-name/.

2. Bob Ryan, *When Boston Won the World Series: A Chronicle of Boston's Remarkable Victory in the First Modern World Series of 1903* (Philadelphia: Running Press, 2003); Roger Abrams, *The First World Series and the Baseball Fanatics of 1903* (Boston: Northeastern University Press,

2003); Louis P. Masur, *Autumn Glory: Baseball's First World Series* (New York: Hill and Wang, 1903); Andy Dabilis and Nick Tsiotos, *The 1903 World Series: The Boston Americans, the Pittsburgh Pirates, and the "First Championship of the United States"* (Jefferson, NC: McFarland, 2004). The AL Boston squad won 5 of the first 15 World Series and might have taken a sixth.

3. While devised by Henry Chadwick during the 19th century, the Earned Run Average (ERA) wasn't generally recorded until the National League began officially compiling that pitching statistic in 1912. Retroactively, baseball statisticians have tabulated ERAs for pitchers throughout early major league history.

4. "Baseball Notes," *Washington Post*, July 6, 1904, 8; Charles C. Alexander, *John McGraw* (Lincoln: University of Nebraska Press, 1995), 108–109. A New York journalist, Jim Price, initially called the Highlanders the Yanks in 1904. See "Yankees Will Start Home from South Today," *New York Evening Journal*, April 7, 1904; Bryan Hoch, "How They Came to Be Called the Yankees," *MLB.com*, December 1, 2021, https://www.mlb.com/news/new-york-yankees-team-name-origin. The Highlanders began to be referred to as the Yankees in the *New York Times* at the start of the 1906 season. But both nicknames continued to be used for a time, including in the same headline. "15,000 See Yankees Take First Game," *New York Times*, April 15, 1906, 10; "Yankees Beat Cleveland: Athletics Win and Lose, and Highlanders Are Now Only Five Points Behind the Leaders," *New York Times*, July 19, 1906, 8. The official name change occurred in 1913.

5. John P. Rossi, *The National Game: Baseball and American Culture* (Chicago: Ivan R. Dee, 2000), 68–69.

6. "Scores M'Graw and Brush," *Washington Post*, August 1, 1904, 8.

7. Mark Mancini, "The Team That Boycotted the World Series," October 22, 2016, https://www.mentalfloss.com/article/65374/team-boycotted-world-series.

8. Lyle Spatz and Steve Steinberg, *1921: The Yankees, the Giants, and the Battle for Baseball Supremacy in New York* (Lincoln: University of Nebraska Press, 2010), 3; Charles Alexander, *Our*

Game: An American Baseball History (New York: Henry Holt, 1991).

9. Statement by John Brush, *Sporting Life*, October 1, 1904, 5.

10. "Views of the Message," *Sporting Life*, October 1, 1904, 5.

11. Statement by John McGraw, *Sporting Life*, October 15, 1904, 6; "McGraw Assumes Responsibility," *Sporting Life*, October 15, 1904, 6–7.

12. "McGraw Assumes Responsibility," 7; "Doing in the World of Sports," *San Francisco Chronicle*, October 16, 1904, 37.

13. Abrams, *The First World Series*, 176.

14. "Brush Consents to Game," *Washington Post*, October 18, 1904, 8; Tim Murnane, "Brush Sees His Mistake," *Boston Globe*, October 30, 1904, S3.

15. "World's Series Possible," *Sporting Life*, October 22, 1904, 4; "Timely Topics," *Sporting Life*, October 22, 1904, 4.

16. Steven A. King, "The Strangest Month in the Career of Rube Waddell," in *The National Pastime: From Swampoodle to South Philly* (Philadelphia: SABR, 2013).

17. "National League Moguls Ready for Early Series," *Los Angeles Times*, August 3, 1918, 15; "Baseball Season Will Close Sept. 1," *New York Times*, August 3, 1918, 6.

18. "Flat Series Sum Protects Players," *Washington Post*, September 1, 1918, 12.

19. Randy Roberts and Johnny Smith, *War Fever: Boston, Baseball, and America in the Shadow of the Great War* (New York: Basic Books, 2020), 198–200.

20. "Players in World Series Uneasy Over Meagre Receipts," *New York Times*, September 9, 1918, 8.

21. "Players Start Strike Then Call It Off," *San Francisco Chronicle*, September 11, 1918, 10; Robert W. Creamer, *Babe: The Legend Comes to Life* (New York: Fireside, 1992), 181.

22. "Boston World's Champions by Defeat of Chicago, 2–1," *Washington Post*, September 12, 1918, 8; Kerry Keene, Raymond Sinibaldi, and David Hickey, *The Babe in Red Stockings: An In-Depth Chronicle of Babe Ruth with the Boston Red Sox, 1914–1919* (Champaign, IL: Sagamore, 1997), 216–217; "Players Divide Spoils," *New York Times*, September 13, 1918, 12.

23. J.V. Fitz Gerald, "Action of Players Blow to Baseball," *Washington Post*, September 13, 1918, 8.

24. Kenesaw M. Landis to Mr. President, January 14, 1942, National Baseball Hall of Fame Library.

25. Franklin D. Roosevelt to My dear Judge, January 15, 1942, National Baseball Hall of Fame Library.

26. *Ibid.*

27. Murray Chass, "Owners Terminate Season Without the World Series," *New York Times*, September 15, 1994, B14.

28. Jon Pessah, *The Game: Inside the Secret World of Major League Power Brokers* (Boston: Little, Brown, 2015), 112.

29. Robert Lipsyte, "In Memoriam," *New York Times*, September 15, 1994, 1.

30. Mark Maske, "Baseball Players Offer to End Strike," *Washington Post*, April 1, 1995.

31. *Ibid.*

32. Ross Newhan, "Baseball Players End Strike; Owners on Deck: Sport: Decision follows a judge's ruling in their favor and could pave the way for an end to the 232-day walkout. But owners may vote on a lockout," *Los Angeles Times*, April 2, 1995; Ronald Blum, "Both Sides Lost Big in Dispute," *The Record*, April 3, 1995, C1.

33. Mark Maske, "Baseball Strike Ends," *Washington Post*, April 3, 1995.

Chapter 2

1. Robert F. Burk, *Never Just a Game: Players, Owners, and American Baseball to 1920* (Chapel Hill: University of North Carolina Press, 1994), 50–80; Richard Hershberger, "The First Baseball War: The American Association and the National League," *Baseball Research Journal* 49 (January 2021).

2. Burk, *Never Just a Game*, 81–115; Tim Keefe, "The Brotherhood and Its Work," *Players' National League Guide* (Chicago: W.J. Jefferson, 1890), 7; Robert A. McCormick, "Baseball's Third Strike: The Triumph of Collective Bargaining in Professional Baseball," *Vanderbilt Law Review* 35 (October 1982): 1142; Lee Lowenfish, *The Imperfect Diamond: A History of Baseball's Labor Wars* (New York: Da Capo Press, 1991), 30; Robert Elias and Peter Dreier, *Major League Rebels: Baseball Battles over Workers' Rights and American Empire* (Lanham, MD: Rowman & Littlefield, 2022), 3–41.

3. Brian Blickenstaff, "Baseball's Forgotten Brotherhood, The First Athlete Union in American Pro Sports," *Vice Sports*, October 20, 2016; John Montgomery Ward, "Is the Base-Ball Player a Chattel?" *Lippincott's Monthly Magazine* (August 1887); David Pietrusza, *Major Leagues: The Formation, Sometimes Absorption and Mostly Inevitable Demise of 18 Professional Baseball Organizations, 1871 to Present* (Jefferson, NC: McFarland, 1991); James Hawking, *Strikeout: Baseball, Broadway and the Brotherhood in the 19th Century* (Santa Fe: Sunstone Press, 1999); David Stevens, *Baseball's Radical for All Seasons: A Biography of John Montgomery Ward* (Lanham, MD: Scarecrow Press, 1998); Bryan Di Salvatore, *A Clever Base-Ballist: The Life and Times of John Montgomery Ward* (Baltimore: Johns Hopkins University Press, 1999).

4. Ward, "Is the Base-Ball Player a Chattel?"

5. "Ward Talks," *Sporting Life*, November 16, 1887, 1.

6. "Brotherhood's Triumph," *Sporting Life*, November 23, 1887, 2; "Baseball Matters: Interviews with Presidents Ward and Stearns," *New York Times*, November 13, 1887, 6; "The Men Make Their Point," *New York Times*, November 18, 1887, 2.

7. "The Brotherhood of Ball Players," *San Francisco Chronicle*, November 22, 1887, 1; "They Are

All Satisfied: The Recognition of the Baseball Brotherhood Is Generally Approved," *Washington Post*, November 22, 1887, 1; "Brotherhood's Triumph," 2.

8. John Montgomery Ward, "Our National Game," *The Cosmopolitan* V (October 1888): 443–455.

9. *Ibid.*, 445, 448.

10. Blickenstaff, "Baseball's Forgotten Brotherhood"; McCormick, "Baseball's Third Strike," 1142; Lowenfish, *The Imperfect Diamond*, 33–34; "Mr. Spalding's Scheme: For the Classification of Players in the Minor Leagues," *Washington Post*, July 14, 1889, 3.

11. "The League Strike," *The Sporting News*, September 14, 1889, 1; "The Ball Players' Revolt," *New York Times*, 2, September 23, 1889; "The Die Is Cast," *The Sporting News*, November 9, 1889, 3; McCormick, "Baseball's Third Strike," 1142; Emma Baccellieri, "Solidarity and Betrayal: The Rise and Fall of the Players' League," *Sports Illustrated*, January 5, 2022; Robert P. Gelzheiser, *Labor and Capital in 19th Century Baseball* (Jefferson, NC: McFarland, 2006); Ed Koszarek, *The Players League: History Clubs, Ballplayers and Statistics* (Jefferson, NC: McFarland, 2006); Charles C. Alexander, *Turbulent Seasons: Baseball in 1890–1891* (Dallas: Southern Methodist University Press, 2011); Scott D. Peterson, *Reporting Baseball's Sensational Season of 1890: The Brotherhood War and the Rise of Modern Sports Journalism* (Jefferson, NC: McFarland, 2015); Robert B. Ross, *The Great Baseball Revolt: The Rise and Fall of the 1890 Players League* (Lincoln: University of Nebraska Press, 2016); Leonard Koppett, "During the Brotherhood Revolt the Mood in Baseball Wasn't Fraternal," *Sports Illustrated*, June 1, 1981.

12. *Manifesto of the Brotherhood of Professional Baseball Players*, November 6, 1889; Lowenfish, *The Imperfect Diamond*, 36.

13. "Late News: Alleged Details of the Players' League," *Sporting Life*, November 6, 1889, 1.

14. "The Players' Aims," *Sporting Life*, November 27, 1889, 5.

15. "The Brotherhood," *The Sporting News*, September 21, 1889, 1.

16. *Ibid.*

17. "The Brotherhood Bugaboo," *The Sporting News*, November 16, 1889, 4; editorial beginning "The League harpies," *The Sporting News*, December 7, 1889, 4.

18. *Ibid.*

19. *Ibid.*

20. "Professional Baseball," *New York Times*, November 4, 1889, 4.

21. "The Issue of the Day: The Brotherhood's Movement," *Sporting Life*, November 13, 1889, 3.

22. *Ibid.*

23. "The Brotherhood's Secession—Its Status and Effects," *Sporting Life*, November 13, 1889, 4.

24. *Ibid.*

25. "The New Players' League Considered," *Sporting Life*, December 25, 1889, 4.

26. "The League's Address," *New York Times*, November 22, 1889, 2.

27. *Ibid.*

28. Lowenfish, *The Imperfect Diamond*, 40.

29. "1890 Players League Team Statistics," *baseball-reference.com*, https://www.baseball-reference.com/leagues/PL/1890.shtml; Ethan M. Lewis, "'A Structure to Last Forever': The Players' League and the Brotherhood War of 1890," 2001, https://www.ethanlewis.org/pl/ch1.html; "The Players' League this year," *The Sporting News*, March 8, 1890, 4; "Both Confident: The Ball League and the Brotherhood, *San Francisco Chronicle*, March 24, 1890, 1.

30. "The League and the Brotherhood," *The Sporting News*, March 22, 1890, 4; "Spalding's Extreme Views," *Sporting Life*, May 10, 1890, 1; Benjamin G. Rader, *Baseball: A History of America's Game* (Urbana: University of Illinois Press, 2008), 67.

31. "A Compromise, Never: The Players' League Must Surrender, Says Spalding," *New York Times*, August 9, 1890, 3.

32. Ross quoted in Baccellieri, "Solidarity and Betrayal."

33. "The Reasons for It," *The Sporting News*, November 8, 1890, 4.

34. Reddy, "Better Be Careful," *The Sporting News*, November 15, 1890, 1.

35. "The Players' League," *The Sporting News*, November 29, 1890, 4; "Al Johnson's Scheme: A Secret Movement Looking to the Revival of the Players' League," *Washington Post*, December 15, 1890, 2.

36. "A League Victory: The Players' Brotherhood Agrees to Dissolve," *Los Angeles Times*, January 17, 1891, 5.

Chapter 3

1. Marc Normandin, "The History of Baseball Unionization: The Players Protective Association," https://www.marcnormandin.com/2020/03/04/the-history-of-baseball-unionization-the-players-protective-association/; David Q. Voigt, "Serfs versus Magnates: A Century of Labor Strife in Major League Baseball," in *The Business of Professional Sports*, eds. Paul D. Staudohar and J. A. Mangan (Urbana: University of Illinois Press, 1991), 105; Lowenfish, *The Imperfect Diamond*, 61; "Radical Baseball Changes," *New York Times*, October 14, 1900, 9; David Q. Voigt, "The Owner-Player Conflict," *Baseball Research Journal* (1973); Michael J. Haupert, "The Economic History of Major League Baseball," EH.net, http://eh.net/encyclopedia/the-economic-history-of-major-league-baseball/; "Union of Ball Tossers: Mr. Gompers Advises Forming Labor Organization," *Washington Post*, April 3, 1900, 8.

2. "Union Bides Its Time: Ball Players' Organization Is Still an Infant," *Washington Post*, June 16, 1900, 8; "Ball Players' Union: All Organization

Effected at a Meeting in New York," *Washington Post*, July 30, 1900, 8.

3. "Ball Players' Union," 8.

4. "Radical Baseball Changes: Proposed by the Protective Association to the National League," *New York Times*, October 14, 1900, 9.

5. Charles Zuber, "The Reserve Rule," *Sporting Life*, November 3, 1900, 2.

6. "Taffy for Players," *Sporting Life*, November 10, 1900, 4.

7. "The National League players," *The Sporting News*, November 3, 1900, 4.

8. "The National League committee," *The Sporting News*, November 10, 1900, 4.

9. Zimmer and The Players Protective Association," *Baseball History Daily*, https://baseballhistorydaily.com/2012/12/21/zimmer-and-the-players-protective-association/; "Ball Players Defied: National League Rejects All Their Claims and Demands," *New York Times*, December 15, 1900, 11; Frank Patterson, "They Side-Stepped," *The Sporting News*, December 22, 1900, 1; J. L. Sweeney, "Player-Magnate Trouble," *The Sporting News*, December 22, 1900, 1.

10. "Players Humiliated," *Sporting Life*, December 22, 1900, 2; "Players Next Move," *Sporting Life*, December 22, 1900, 2; "A Sop to Players," *Sporting Life*, December 29, 1900; "Players' Slogan," *Sporting Life*, December 29, 1900, 1; "Players Issue a Statement," *New York Times*, March 10, 1901, 8.

11. "Radical Baseball Changes," *New York Times*, October 14, 1900, 9; Normandin, "The History of Baseball Unionization"; "Zimmer and The Players Protective Association"; "Ball Players Defied," *New York Times*, December 15, 1900, 11; "Baseball Badly Mixed," *New York Times*, December 16, 1900, 9.

12. Francis C. Richter, "Compromise Sure," *Sporting Life*, February 16, 1901, 3; "Brooklyn Willing," *Sporting Life*, February 16, 1901, 3.

13. Francis C. Richter, "The Sky Clearing: Accord between Players and Magnates Assured," *Sporting Life*, February 23, 1901, 3; "Will Be Expelled," *Sporting Life*, February 23, 1901, 3; "Will Hear Ball Players: National League Committee to Confer with Charles Zimmer," *New York Times*, February 26, 1901, 10; "Presto Change!" *Sporting Life*, March 2, 1901, 3; "The Legislation," *Sporting Life*, March 9, 1901, 2.

14. "Players Issue a Statement: Baseball Protective Association Explains President Zimmer's Action," *New York Times*, March 10, 1901, 8; Francis C. Richter, "Taylor's Tips," *Sporting Life*, March 23, 1901, 1.

15. "Will Hear Ball Players," *New York Times*, February 26, 1901, 10; "Baseball Rules Changed," *New York Times*, February 28, 1901, 7; "Players Issue a Statement," *New York Times*, March 10, 1901, 8; "Zimmer Will Not Play Baseball," *New York Times*, March 21, 1901, 7.

16. Normandin, "The History of Baseball Unionization."

17. "Ball Players Incorporate: Protective Association to Be Known as National and American Fraternity," *Washington Post*, September 6, 1912, 8; "Players Organize for Protection," *Los Angeles Times*, September 7, 1912, 118; "What the Baseball Fraternity Really Is," *New York Times*, September 8, 1912, 2; "Baseball Fraternity Elects Its New Officers," *San Francisco Chronicle*, October 29, 1912, 11.

18. "Not Opposed to Union," *Washington Post*, September 8, 1912, S1.

19. Ernest J. Lanigan, "Players in Politics," *The Sporting News*, September 19, 1912, 4; "Late News: Ask Rule Against Rowdies," *The Sporting News*, October 24, 1912; "Has Method to Stop Rowdyism," *Washington Post*, December 15, 1912, S3.

20. Michael Schiavone, *Sports and Labor in the United States* (Albany: State University of New York, 2015), 12; Adam Dorhauer, "The Unionization of Baseball," *The Hardball Times*, December 3, 2015.

21. "Baseball Players Tied Hand and Foot," *New York Times*, April 25, 1913, 9.

22. "Fogel Proclaims Neutrality!" *Sporting Life*, September 13, 1913, 1; "Does Not Seek War," *New York Times*, September 7, 1913, 5.

23. "Fogel Proclaims Neutrality!" 1.

24. "Neutral, Not Loyal!" *Sporting Life*, September 13, 1913, 4.

25. Lowenfish, *The Imperfect Diamond*, 80, 95.

26. Joe Vila, "Base Ball War Talk!" *Sporting Life*, September 13, 1913, 1.

27. "Players Make Demands on National Commission: White Slaves," *Los Angeles Times*, September 26, 1913, III3.

28. "Players Have Grievances," *New York Times*, October 21, 1913, 7; "Ball Players in Big Revolt," *Los Angeles Times*, October 24, 1913, III4.

29. "Will Not Deal with Fultz," *New York Times*, October 29, 1913, 9; "To Restrict Players," *New York Times*, October 30, 1913, 10; "To Ignore Ball Players: American League Will Not Take Up So-Called Grievances," *New York Times*, November 6, 1913, 12.

30. "Former Stars as Outlaw Managers," *New York Times*, April 15, 1913, 9; untitled article, "In the impending clash," *New York Times*, November 2, 1913, Article 4, 1; "Federal Wants Fultz," *New York Times*, November 9, 1913, 1; "Fultz to Lead Federal League," *New York Times*, December 2, 1916, 9; "Ward May Lead Federal League," *New York Times*, December 20, 1913, 11.

31. "Deeds, Not Words," *Sporting Life*, January 3, 1914, 4; "Raising Modern Demons," *Sporting Life*, January 3, 1914, 4.

32. "What Federals Must Accomplish," *The Sporting News*, January 15, 1914, 4; Stuart Banner, *The Baseball Trust: A History of Baseball's Antitrust Exemption* (New York: Oxford University Press, 2013), 27; Emil H. Rothe, "Was the Federal League a Major League?" SABR Research Journals Archives, http://research.sabr.org/journals/federal-league-a-major-league#:~:text=All%0in%20all%2C%20101%20men,their%20careers%20as%20major%20

leaguers; "Tinker and Miner Brown Jump to Federal League," *The Sporting News*, January 1, 1914, 1; "Base Ball War Fury," *Sporting Life*, January 24, 1914, 1; "Base Ball War News," *Sporting Life*, January 31, 1914, 1; "The Plans of Battle," *Sporting Life*, February 14, 1914, 1; "Progress of the War," *Sporting Life*, February 28, 1914; "War Passions Rise!" *Sporting Life*, March 7, 1914; "Law and Base Ball," *Sporting Life*, March 21, 1914; "War Spirit Is Strong," *Sporting Life*, April 11, 1914, 1; "Base Ball War News," *Sporting Life*, April 25, 1914, 1; "The Base Ball Issues," *Sporting Life*, May 23, 1914, 1; "On Verge of Big Raid?" *Sporting Life*, May 30 1914, 1; "Federal War Moves!" *Sporting Life*, June 20, 1914, 1; "Base Ball War News," *Sporting Life*, August 8, 1914, 1; "More Base Ball War Moves," *Sporting Life*, December 12, 1914, 1; "Acute War Greets New Year," *Sporting Life*, January 2, 1915, 1; Marc Okkonen, *The Federal League of 1914–1915* (Garrett Park, MD: SABR, 1989): Robert Peyton Wiggins, *The Federal League of Base Ball Clubs* (Jefferson, NC: McFarland, 2009); Daniel R. Levitt, *The Outlaw League and the Battle That Forged Modern Baseball* (Lanham, MD: Ivan R. Dee, 2012); Bob Ruzzo, "Fate and the Federal League: Were the Federals Incompetent, Outmaneuvered, or Just Unlucky?" *Baseball Research Journal* (Fall 2013); Craig Calcaterra, "Today in Baseball History: The Federal League Begins Play," April 13, 2020, *MLB/NBC Sports*, https://mlb.nbcsports.com/2020/04/13/today-in-baseball-history-the-federal-league-begins-play/. Emil H. Rothe contends that 172 players with former National League or American League service played in the Federal League, a far higher figure than most chroniclers estimate.

33. Levitt, *The Outlaw League and the Battle That Forge Modern Baseball*, x, 68–75, 145.

34. "Chicago Federals to Build New Park," *The Sporting News*, January 1, 1914, 1.

35. F.C. Lane, "The Famous Federal Suit," *Baseball Magazine* 14 (March 1915): 65; "Editorials," *Baseball Magazine* 15 (September 1915): 17–18; Ruzzo, "Fate and the Federal League"; Banner, *The Baseball Trust*, 58; Robert C. Cottrell, *Blackball, the Black Sox and the Babe: Baseball's Crucial 1920 Season* (Jefferson, NC: McFarland, 2002), 17–20.

36. Federal Base Ball Club of Baltimore, Inc. *v.* National League of Professional Base Ball Clubs, 259 U.S. 200 (1922); Nathaniel Grow, *Baseball on Trial: The Origin of Baseball's Antitrust Exemption* (Urbana: University of Illinois Press, 2014).

37. "Baseball Players' Union Progressing," *New York Times*, August 17, 1922, 17; "Ball Players Seek to Secure Reforms," *New York Times*, October 12, 1922, 30; Robert F. Burk, *Much More Than a Game: Players, Owners, & American Baseball Since 1921* (Chapel Hill: University of North Carolina Press, 2001), 5–6.

38. "Whose 'Condition' Concerns Most?" *The Sporting News*, August 24, 1922, 4.

39. "Unnecessary, Says Heydler," *New York Times*, August 17, 1922, 17.

40. "Ball Players Seeks to Secure Reforms."

41. "Ball Players to Form Union Is Latest Report," *San Francisco Chronicle*, October 12, 1922, 27.

42. "Says Frank Frisch Is Union Nominee," *New York Times*, December 16, 1922, 20; "Burns Withdraws from Union Race," *New York Times*, December 23, 1922, 14; "Landis Is Non-Committal," *New York Times*, October 12, 1922, 30.

43. "Ball Players Seek to Secure Reforms," *New York Times*, October 12, 1922, 30; "Outlines Purposes of Players' Union," *New York Times*, December 25, 1922, 20.

44. "Nothing to Lose but Their Chains," *New York Times*, December 26, 1922, 11.

45. Association of Professional Ball Players of America, "Ballplayers Helping Ballplayers," https://apbpa.org/; Association of Professional Baseball Players of America, Hoboken Historical Museum, https://hoboken.pastperfectonline.com/bysearchterm?keyword=Association%20of%20Professional%20Baseball%20Players%20of%20America; Burk, *Much More Than a Game*, 7–8.

Chapter 4

1. Elias and Dreier, *Major League Rebels*, 80–84; Hy Hurwitz, "Players' Guild Formed Here to Bargain with Ball Clubs,' *Boston Globe*, April 18, 1946, reprinted as "American Baseball Guild Formed," in *Middle Innings: A Documentary History of Baseball, 1900–1948*, ed. Dean A. Sullivan (Lincoln: University of Nebraska Press, 1998): 208; "Seeks to Organize Baseball Players," *New York Times*, April 18, 1946, 32; Robert Weintraub, "Failed Baseball Union Helped Pave Way for Success," *New York Times*, December 1, 2012; Mickey Gallagher, "From the Red Side of the Field: The American Baseball Guild," July 16, 2019, https://seattledsa.org/2019/07/from-the-red-side-of-the-field-the-american-baseball-guild/; Marc Normandin, "The History of Baseball Unionization: Where Murphy Money Came From," October 9, 2020, https://www.marcnormandin.com/2020/10/09/the-history-of-baseball-unionization-where-murphy-money-came-from/; Wallace Green, "Company Union! Murphy Shouts at Player-Owner Meeting," *The Harvard Crimson*, August 2, 1946; Dorhauer, "The Unionization of Baseball."

2. "Seeks to Organize Baseball Players," 32. The points from the Guild's program are contained in that article. That precise verbiage is repeated here.

3. *Ibid.*

4. "Newest Jump by Owen Fails to Jar Rickey," *The Sporting News*, April 18, 1946, 4; "Jumpers in Mexico Make Pathetic Picture," *The Sporting News*, April 25, 1946, 12; John Virtue, *South of the Color Barrier: How Jorge Pasquel and the Mexican League Pushed Baseball toward Racial Integration* (Jefferson, NC: McFarland, 2007); G. Richard McKelvey, *Mexican Raiders in the Major Leagues: The Pasquel*

Brothers vs. Organized Baseball, 1946 (Jefferson, NC: McFarland, 2006); Dan Joseph, *Baseball's Greatest What If: The Story & Tragedy of the Brooklyn Dodgers' Pete Reiser* (Mechanicsburg, PA: Sunbury Press, 2021), 143–144; Elias and Dreier, *Major League Rebels*, 45–54.

5. Jose Hanes, "Player Raids Bare Bush-League Mexican Setup," *The Sporting News*, April 18, 1946, 9; Alfonso Flores, "'Send Chandler Here,' Pasquel's Reply to Purported Peace Inquiry by U.S.," *The Sporting News*, April 18, 1946, 9.

6. "Sees It Doomed to Fail," *New York Times*, April 18, 1946, 32.

7. "Union Would Knock Game Flat on Back, Says Griff," *The Sporting News*, April 25, 1946, 3.

8. "Guild to Investigate Reports of Baseball 'Intimidation,'" *Washington Post*, April 19, 1946, 12; "Baseball Guild Will Investigate Reports of Player 'Intimidation,'" *New York Times*, April 19, 1946, 22.

9. "CIO and AFL Approve," *New York Times*, April 19, 1946, 22; "No Comment by Owners," *New York Times*, April 19, 1946, 22.

10. Shirley Povich, "This Morning," *Washington Post*, April 19, 1946, 12.

11. Ed Rumill, "Guild Head Quizzed on Objectives," *The Sporting News*, April 25, 1946, 1.

12. *Ibid.*, 1, 3.

13. "Ruth May Head Mex Loop," *The Sporting News*, May 2, 1946, 1; Dan Daniel, "Ruth Reveals His Grievance Against Yankees," *The Sporting News*, June 12, 1946, 1–2.

14. "Guild Head Quizzed on Objectives," 3.

15. "Baseball Guild Reveals Charges Against Griffith and Senators," *New York Times*, April 30, 1946, 25: "Charges Filed by Baseball Guild Against Nat's Griffith," *Washington Post*, April 30, 1946, 1; Jack Malaney, "Guild Charges Washington Club with 'Unfair Labor Practices,'" *The Sporting News*, May 2, 1946, 4.

16. Shirley Povich, "This Morning," *Washington Post*, May 1, 1946, 12; Shirley Povich, "The Old Fox Charges of Intimidation 'Ridiculous,'" *The Sporting News*, May 2, 1946, 4.

17. "Minimum of $7,500 in Majors Sought," *New York Times*, May 3, 1946, L16.

18. Dan Daniel, "MacPhail Jolts Mexican Hayride in New York: Court Order to Restrain Raids Asked," *The Sporting News*, May 9, 1946, 1, 4; "Text of Decision Granting Yankees Temporary Injunction against Raids," *The Sporting News*, May 23, 1946, 2.

19. Harold C. Burr, "Reiser Snubs 100 Grand Bid from Mexico," *The Sporting News*, May 9, 1946, 2; Joseph, *Baseball's Greatest What If*, 145–146.

20. Harold Burr, "Dodgers File Action against Mexican League in St. Louis," *The Sporting News*, May 9, 1946, 4.

21. Alphonso Flores, "Pasquels to Toss Bigger, Better Bait at Musial: Refuse to Give Up after Stan Snubs $130,000 Bid," *The Sporting News*, June 19, 1946, 2; "Stan Musial Says: 'Mexican Matter Over—for Present,'" *The Sporting News*, June 19, 1946, 2.

22. Dick Hyland, "Why Williams Nixed Mex 70 G's," *Baseball Digest* 5 (August 1946): 29–30.

23. Edgar G. Brands, "Game in Court First Time Since '31," *The Sporting News*, May 23, 1946, 3.

24. "Ninety Per Cent of Pirates in Union," *The Sporting News*, May 23, 1946. 10.

25. "Ty Cobb Regards Individual Traits as Obstacle to Player Unionization," *The Sporting News*, June 12, 1946, 12.

26. "Bucs Threaten Game Strike Tomorrow: Union Pact Demanded by Players," *Los Angeles Times*, June 6, 1946, A7; "Action Taken Just Before Game Is Blow at New Guild," *Washington Post*, June 8, 1946; Oscar Ruhl, "Strike Averted, but Guild Stays Active: Regard for Benswanger Shaped Course—Handley," *The Sporting News*, June 19, 1946, 3.

27. Ruhl, "Strike Averted," 3–4.

28. "Murphy Runs into Obstacles in Seeking Labor Board Test," *The Sporting News*, June 19, 1946.

29. "Concessions to Players Foreseen by Scriveners: Minimum Pay Wins Favor of Many Writers," *The Sporting News*, June 19, 1946, 5–6.

30. "Setback for Guild but Problems Remain," *The Sporting News*, June 19, 1946, 12; William Marshall, *Baseball's Pivotal Era, 1945–1951* (Lexington: University Press of Kentucky), 449.

31. "$5000 Minimum Salary, Share of Own Sale Sought by Players," *Washington Post*, July 20, 1946, 8; "Revival of Player's Fraternity on Way," *The Sporting News*, July 31, 1946, 12; "Baseball's Magna Charta Is Drawn Up," *The Sporting News*, August 7, 1946, 10.

32. "American Baseball Guild Dies," *The Sporting News*, August 28, 1946, 10; Dan Daniel, "MacPhail Blue Print Charts Game's Course: Points Out Policy Path for Majors," *The Sporting News*, September 4, 1946, 1, 3; Lowenfish, *The Imperfect Diamond*, 149; "MLBPA Report on Salaries," in *Late Innings: A Documentary History of Baseball, 1945–1972*, ed. Dean A. Sullivan (Lincoln: University of Nebraska Press, 2002), 132.

33. "$5000 Minimum Salary Share of Own Sale Sought by Players," 8.

34. "Change in Advisory Council First Since 1921," *The Sporting News*, September 4, 1946, 3.

35. "168-Game Season Longest in History of Major Loops," *The Sporting News*, September 4, 1946, 3; Dan Daniel, "Players Win New Concessions from Majors: Magnates Okay Requests on Waivers and Arc Ball," *The Sporting News*, December 11, 1946, 1–2.

36. J.G. Taylor Spink, "Deep Pay Cuts Facing Some Prewar Stars: Free Hand for Slashes until 1948," *The Sporting News*, January 8, 1947, 1.

37. Elias and Dreier, *Major League Rebels*, 49.

38. "Stephens Jumps to Mexican Loop," *Los Angeles Times*, March 6, 1946, 6; "Stephens Leaves Mexico, Rejoins Browns," *Los Angeles Times*, April 6, 1946, p. 6; Bob French, "Meet Don Jorge Pasquel," *Baseball Digest* 5 (May 1946): 27–29.

39. Elias and Dreier, *Major League Rebels*, 62–74; "Gardella Suit Threatens Baseball's Reserve

Clause," *Los Angeles Times*, February 10, 1949, C1; Shirley Povich, "Court Ruling May Affect Baseball: This Morning," *Washington Post*, February 10, 1949, 1; Thomas S. Mulligan, "He Helped Blaze Free Agents' Trail," *Los Angeles Times*, October 22, 1994, C1; David Mandell, "Danny Gardella and the Reserve Clause," *The National Pastime* 26 (2006), https://sabr.org/journal/article/danny-gardella-and-the-reserve-clause/.

40. Milton Richman, "Former Giant Thinks He Is Helping 'To End Evil,'" *Washington Post*, February 11, 1946, B4.

41. Elizabeth Muratore, "Gardella's Lawsuit Pushed Baseball's Labor Boundaries," National Baseball Hall of Fame, https://baseballhall.org/discover/going-deep/gardellas-lawsuit-pushed-baseballs-labor-boundaries; Richard Goldstein, "Danny Gardella, 85, Dies; Challenged Reserve Clause," *New York Times*, March 13, 2005, 46; Ron Briley, "Danny Gardella and Baseball's Reserve Clause: A Working-Class Stiff Blacklisted in Cold War America," *Nine* 19 (Fall 2010): 52+; Dan Daniel, "Gardella Case May Ditch Radio, Video: New Ruling in Suit Stirs Club Owners," *The Sporting News*, February 16, 1949, 1; J.G. Taylor Spink, "Game Faces Biggest Legal Test Since '22: Raises Question Whether Radio and TV Put O.B. into Interstate Commerce," *The Sporting News*, February 16, 1949, 3.

42. "Suspended Ball Players Reinstated by Chandler," *Los Angeles Times*, June 6, 1949, C1; Shirley Povich, "Owen's Plea Was Big Factor in Commissioner's Action," *The Sporting News*, June 15, 1949, 11.

43. Dan Daniel, "'Bulwark Reserve Clause—Johnson: U.S. Senator Urges Action to Avert Peril," *The Sporting News*, May 2, 1951, 1–2.

44. Jack Walsh, "Ex-Star Calls Game Great Moral Force," *Washington Post*, July 31, 1951, 13; Lowenfish, *The Imperfect Diamond*, 176; J. Gordon Hylton, "Why Baseball's Antitrust Exemption Still Survives," *Marquette Sports Law Review* 9 (Spring 1999): 396–402; Richard Beverage, *The Los Angeles Angels of the Pacific Coast League: A History, 1903–1947* (Jefferson, NC: McFarland, 2011), 156.

45. *Toolson v. New York Yankees*, 346 U.S. 356 (1953); "Baseball Wins Court's Ruling," *Los Angeles Times*, November 10, 1953, C1; Hy Turkin, "Path Now Clear for Progress—Frick: Court Ruling Called Signal for Advances," *The Sporting News*, November 18, 1953, 1.

Chapter 5

1. John Helyar, *Lords of the Realm: The Real History of Baseball* (New York: Ballantine, 1994), 13; Lowenfish, *The Imperfect Diamond*, 183–185; Charles P. Korr, *The End of Baseball as We Knew It: The Players Union, 1960–81* (Urbana: University of Illinois Press, 2002), 17; Shirley Povich, "Owners Bow to Players' Rights," *Baseball Digest* 13 (September 1954): 91–92.

2. "Ball Players' Attorney Reports 'Definite Progress' on Proposals," *New York Times*, September 1, 1953, 26.

3. Peter Seidel, "June 4, 1953: Pirates Trade Ralph Kiner to Cubs Just before Game Time," SABR, https://sabr.org/gamesproj/game/june-4-1953-pirates-trade-ralph-kiner-to-cubs-just-before-game-time/; Matt Schudel, "Ralph Kiner, Hall of Fame Baseball Slugger for Pirates and Broadcaster for Mets, Dies at 91," *Washington Post*, February 6, 2014; https://www.washingtonpost.com/sports/ralph-kiner-hall-of-fame-baseball-slugger-for-pirates-and-broadcaster-for-mets-dies-at-91/2014/02/06/51455fb8-8f6e-11e3-b46a-5a3d0d2130da_story.html.

4. "Chandler Hits Owners Over Pension Fund," *Los Angeles Times*, January 20, 1954, C2.

5. Shirley Povich, "Owners Bow to Players' Rights," *Baseball Digest* 13 (September 1954): 90–91.

6. *Ibid.*, 92; "Frick Announces Pension Balance," *Washington Post*, January 22, 1954, 30.

7. "New Plan Would Drop Ford Frick," *Washington Post*, February 17, 1954, 10.

8. Lowenfish, *The Imperfect Diamond*, 187–188; Mark Armour and Dan Levitt, "A History of the MLBPA's Collective Bargaining Agreement: Part 1," *The Hardball Times*, November 7, 2016, https://tht.fangraphs.com/a-history-of-the-mlbpa-collective-bargaining-agreement-part-1/; "Players Organize and Retain Lewis," *New York Times*, July 13, 1954, 26; "Major League Baseball Players' Association Constitution, Bylaws, and Articles of Association," in *Late Innings*, 82–84; John Sickels, *Bob Feller: Ace of the Greatest Generation* (Washington, D.C.: Brassey's, 2004), 248.

9. "MLBPA Report on Salaries," 132; Lowenfish, *The Imperfect Diamond*, 189; John Drebinger, "Majors' Players Meet Here Today: Spokesmen Likely Will Renew Demands Barred by Owners," *New York Times*, December 18, 1954, 19.

10. Joseph M. Sheehan, "Baseball Players Protest Owners' Rejection of Demands: TV Pact, Salaries of Chief Concern," *New York Times*, December 15, 1955, 55.

11. Oscar K. Ruhl, "Players' Pension Plan Now 'Finest Anywhere,'" *The Sporting News*, February 13, 1957, 7.

12. Ruhl, "Players' Pension Plan Now 'Finest Anywhere'"; Oscar Kahan, "Athletes' Pitch for Increase to $7,500 Denied," *The Sporting News*, February 13, 1957, 7; Ed McAuley, "Battle of '53 Helps Explain Feller Attitude," *The Sporting News*, July 17, 1957, 12.

13. "New Incentives for Careers in Game," *The Sporting News*, February 13, 1957, 12; Jimmy Powers, "The Powerhouse," *The Sporting News*, February 13, 1957, 12; "'Raise Your Boy to Play Ball'—Frisch: 'Pay, Pension, Way of Life Can't Be Beat,' Says Flash," *The Sporting News*, February 20, 1957, 1–2.

14. *Radovich v. National Football League*, 352 U.S. 445 (1957); Lowenfish, *The Imperfect Diamond*, 190.

15. Russell D. Buhite, *The Continental League: A Personal History* (Lincoln: University of Nebraska Press, 2014); Chris Blake, "Rickey Shaped Baseball's Future Via Continental League," National Baseball Hall of Fame, https://baseballhall.org/discover/inside-pitch/rickey-reshaped-baseballs-future-via-continental-league; Michael Shapiro, *Bottom of the Ninth: Branch Rickey, Casey Stengel and Daring Scheme to Save Baseball from Itself* (New York: Times Books, 2009); "Press Release Issued by William A. Shea, July 27, 1959, in *Late Innings*, 141–144.

16. "MLBPA Report on Salaries," 132; "Baseball Players Fire Attorney," *Washington Post*, March 25, 1959, C5; Marilyn Green, "History of Labor Struggles in MLB: The MLBPA and Marvin Miller," *The Cardinal Nation*, January 22, 2022, https://thecardinalnation.com/history-of-labor-struggles-in-mlb-the-mlbpa-and-marvin-miller/; Brian McKenna, "Robert Cannon," SABR, https://sabr.org/bioproj/person/robert-cannon/; Korr, *The End of Baseball as We Knew It*, 20–22.

17. McKenna, "Robert Cannon"; Korr, *The End of Baseball as We Knew It*, 22–32.

18. Lowenfish, *The Imperfect Diamond*, 191.

19. Korr, *The End of Baseball as We Knew It*, 25, 29, 34; Green, "History of Labor Struggles in MLB"; McKenna, "Robert Cannon"; Lowenfish, *The Imperfect Diamond*, 196; Marvin Miller, *A Whole Different Ball Game: The Inside Story of the Baseball Revolution* (Chicago: Ivan R. Dee, 2004), 8.

20. Miller, *A Whole Different Ball Game*, 4–6; Shirley Povich, "This Morning…," *Washington Post*, April 3, 1966, C1.

21. Miller, *A Whole Different Ball Game*, 3–10.

22. Robert Burk, *Marvin Miller: Baseball Revolutionary* (Urbana: University of Illinois Press, 2015), 102; Miller, *A Whole Different Ball Game*, 10, 33.

23. "Baseball Players Name Cannon Administrator," *Washington Post*, January 28, 1966, D2; "Judge Cannon Quits as Player Representative," *Washington Post*, February 5, 1966, D1; Leonard Koppett, "Players to Name Baseball Adviser," *New York Times*, March 5, 1966, 41; Green, "History of Labor Struggles in MLB"; McKenna, "Robert Cannon"; Lowenfish, *The Imperfect Diamond*, 197.

24. Miller, *A Whole Different Ball Game*, 34.

25. The great sportscaster Red Barber stated, "Marvin Miller, along with Babe Ruth and Jackie Robinson, is one of the two or three more important men in baseball history." See George Castle, *Baseball's Game Changers: Icons, Record Breakers, Scandals, Sensational Series, and More* (Guilford, CT: Lyons Press, 2016), 8; Stevens, *Baseball's Radical for All Seasons;* Di Salvatore, *A Clever Base-Ballist*; Robert C. Cottrell, *The Best Pitcher in Baseball: The Life of Rube Foster, Negro League Giant* (New York: New York University Press, 2010); Robert C. Cottrell, *Two Pioneers: How Hank Greenberg and Jackie Robinson Transformed Baseball—and America* (Washington, D.C.: Potomac Books, 2012).

26. "Players Pick Union Leader," *Washington Post*, March 6, 1966, C2; David R. Jones, "Creative labor man to Go to Bat for Ballplayers," *Washington Post*, March 7, 1966, 32; McKenna, "Robert Cannon"; Korr, *The End of Baseball as We Knew It*, 35–36.

27. Burk, *Marvin Miller*, 103–106.

28. "Seraph Questions Motives of Roberts in Nomination," *The Sporting News*, March 26, 1966, 27.

29. Dick Kaegel, "Miller Confident Despite Players' Noisy Opposition," *The Sporting News*, March 26, 1966, 27; Miller, *A Whole Different Ball Game*, 38.

30. Miller, *A Whole Different Ball Game*, 44; Kaegel, "Miller Confident Despite Players' Noisy Opposition."

31. Marc Normandin, "50 Years Ago, Marvin Miller and the MLBPA Changed Sports Forever," *SBNATION*, June 11, 2018, https://www.sbnation.com/mlb/2018/6/11/17437624/mlb-mlbpa-cba-marvin-miller-robert-cannon.

32. Korr, *The End of Baseball as We Knew It*, 38.

33. Miller, *A Whole Different Ball Game*, 45.

34. *Ibid.*

35. *Ibid.*, 46.

36. *Ibid.*, 47.

37. Michael Leahy, *The Last Innocents: The Collision of the Turbulent Sixties and the Los Angeles Dodgers* (New York: Harper, 2016), 173–175, 342–350.

38. Bill Shaikin, "Fifty Years Ago, Dodgers' Sandy Koufax and Don Drysdale Engaged in a Salary Holdout That Would Help Change Baseball Forever," *Los Angeles Times*, March 28, 2016, https://www.latimes.com/sports/dodgers/la-sp-koufax-drysdale-holdout-20160329-story.html#:~:text=In%201965%2C%20Koufax%20won%2026,most%2Dvaluable%2Dplayer%20award.&text=The%20Dodgers%20paid%20Koufax%20%2485%2C000,who%20won%2023%2-0games%2C%20batted%20; Howard Cole, "Sandy Koufax, Don Drysdale 1966 Million-Dollar Contract Holdout," https://www.si.com/mlb/dodgers/news/book-excerpt-1966-sandy-koufax-don-drysdale-contract-holdout; Buzzie Bavasi, "The Great Holdout," *Sports Illustrated*, May 15, 1967, 79.

39. Murray Robinson, "Fans Getting Fed Up with Players' Greed," *The Sporting News*, April 2, 1966, 14.

40. Jack Mann, "The $1,000,000 Holdout," *Sports Illustrated*, April 4, 1966, 26–29.

41. *Ibid.*, 28–29.

42. Paul Cox, "Feller Forecasting Giants Will Trip Champion Dodgers," *The Sporting News*, April 9, 1966, 28.

Chapter 6

1. Frederick Klein, "No Nonsense and Fact-Packed—That's Miller: Players' New Director

Expert as a Negotiator," *The Sporting News*, May 28, 1966, 7.

2. Miller, *A Whole Different Ball Game*, 65–69, 91; "Major Leagues Reject Request of $150,000 for Players' Office," *Washington Post*, May 4, 1966, D1; Bob Addie, "Baseball Tug-of-War," *Washington Post*, May 4, 1966, D1.

3. "Players Go Ahead with Office Plans," *Washington Post*, May 6, 1966, E2; Leonard Koppett, "Baseball Labor Dispute Still a Battle of Words," *New York Times*, June 7, 1966, 58; Miller, *A Whole Different Ball Game*, 69, 74–75, 91.

4. Miller, *A Whole Different Ball Game*, 76–78.

5. *Ibid.*, 80–84, 91; Klein, "No Nonsense and Fact-Packed—That's Miller"; Lowenfish, *The Imperfect Diamond*, 201.

6. "Baseball Owners Accused of Greed," *Los Angeles Times*, August 27. 1966, A1.

7. Miller, *A Whole Different Ball Game*, 91–92; Lowenfish, *The Imperfect Diamond*, 201; Korr, *The End of Baseball as We Knew It*, 55; Bob Addie, "Players Win Improved Pensions," *Washington Post*, December 2, 1966, E3; Joseph Durso, "Major League Players Seeking Annual Minimum of $10,000," *New York Times*, December 1, 1966, 79.

8. David R. Jones, "New Era Looms in Baseball Player-Club Relations," *New York Times*, February 12, 1967, 183.

9. Red Smith, "Baseball's Slaves Ask Emancipation," *Washington Post*, February 14, 1967, 55.

10. "Big Leagues Name Labor Negotiator," *Washington Post*, August 11, 1967, D2; Robert D. McFadden, "John Gaherin, 85, Negotiator for Newspapers and Baseball," *New York Times*, January 31, 2000, 23; Korr, *The End of Baseball as We Knew It*, 60–61.

11. Korr, *The End of Baseball as We Knew It*, 65.

12. Heyler, *Lords of the Realm*, 29, 85.

13. Leonard Koppett, "Sports of the Times: Storm Warnings," *New York Times*, August 2, 1967, 28.

14. Robert Lipsyte, "Sports of the Times: The Specter Afield," *New York Times*, January 18, 1968, 31.

15. *Ibid.*

16. "Owners' Concession Approved by Players," *Los Angeles Times*, January 27, 1968, A5; "MLBPA, Owners Sign First Basic Agreement," in *Late Innings*, 222–225; "Cot's Baseball Contracts: A Clearinghouse for MLB Salary and Payroll Details," https://legacy.baseballprospectus.com/compensation/cots/league-info/cba-history/; Miller, *A Whole Different Ball Game*, 97.

17. "Cot's Baseball Contracts"; Miller, *A Whole Different Ball Game*, 105.

18. Normandin, "50 Years Ago, Marvin Miller and the MLBPA Changed Sports Forever."

19. "Top Stars Back Threatened Baseball Strike," *Los Angeles Times*, December 5, 1968, A14; "Baseball Strike Threat Increases,' *Washington Post*, January 18, 1969, C1; Harry Bernstein, "Miller Claims Owners Worried," *Los Angeles Times*, January 31, 1969, E1; "Baseball Strikes Moves Nearer,"

Washington Post, February 4, 1969, B1; Shirley Povich, "This Morning," *Washington Post*, February 10, 1969, C1; "Pension Fuss Unsettled as Sitout Nears: Chisox Open Camp Chisox Given an 'Out,'" *Washington Post*, February 14, 1969, C1; "Owners, Players Refuse to Budge," *Washington Post*, February 19, 1969, C1; "Pension Fund Compromise Ends Baseball Strike Threat," *Washington Post*, February 26, 1969, D1.

20. Leonard Koppett, "Stormy Future Likely for Reserve Clause," *New York Times*, March 19, 1969, 53; Bob Addie "Players Divided," *Washington Post*, November 16, 1969, 44.

21. Korr, *The End of Baseball as We Knew It*, 8.

22. Curt Flood, *The Way It Is* (New York: Trident Press, 1971); Brad Snyder, *A Well-Paid Slave: Curt Flood's Fight for Free Agency in Professional Sports* (New York: Plume, 2007); Robert M. Goldman, *One Man Out: Curt Flood versus Baseball* (Lawrence: University Press of Kansas, 2008); *The Curious Case of Curt Flood*, HBO documentary (2011); Peter Dreier and Robert Elias, *Baseball Rebels: The Players, People, and Social Movements That Shook Up the Game and Change America* (Lincoln: University of Nebraska Press, 2022), 117–125.

23. Allen Barra, "How Curt Flood Changed Baseball and Killed His Career in the Process," *The Atlantic* (July 12, 2011), https://www.theatlantic.com/entertainment/archive/2011/07/how-curt-flood-changed-baseball-and-killed-his-career-in-the-process/241783/.

24. Mike Elk, "How Clemente Got the Players' Union Behind Curt Flood," September 15, 2021, *Payday Report*, https://paydayreport.com/how-clemente-got-the-players-union-behind-curt-flood/; Red Smith, "Reserve Clause Hit by Super Team," *Washington Post*, January 2, 1970, D6; Miller, *A Whole Different Ball Game*, 180–181; Krister Swanson, *Baseball's Power Shift: How the Players Union, the Fans, and the Media Changed American Sports Culture* (Lincoln: University of Nebraska Press), 162.

25. Leonard Koppett, "Hot Issue Now on Bargaining Table," *The Sporting News*, July 8, 1972, 6.

26. Curt Flood to Bowie Kuhn, December 24, 1969; Jemele Hill, "Curt Flood Belongs in the Hall of Fame," *The Atlantic*, February 10, 2021, https://www.theatlantic.com/ideas/archive/2021/02/curt-floods-fight-was-about-so-much-more-than-baseball/617931/; "Flood Set to Sue Baseball, Challenging Reserve Clause," *Washington Post*, December 30, 1969, D1.

27. "Flood Set to Sue Baseball, Challenging Reserve Clause," *Washington Post*, December 30, 1969, D1; "Flood, Fellow Players Agree: Fight to Finish," *Washington Post*, January 3, 1970, 54.

28. "Flood Says he Does Not Expect to Play Anymore," *Los Angeles Times*, March 6, 1970, E1; Mike Bathet, "Reserve Clause Robs Players of Dignity, Argues Attorney," *Los Angeles Times*, March 15, 1970, C5.

29. Red Smith, "Flood Likely to Open Gates," *Washington Post*, May 6, 1970, D3; Red Smith,

"Athletes Stand Up for Their Rights," *Washington Post*, April 22, 1970, D3.

30. Charles Maher, "Baseball Life Term," *Los Angeles Times*, May 30, 1970, C2.

31. Koppett, "Hot Issue Now on Bargaining Table."

32. *Ibid.*

33. "Flood Suit Against Baseball Opens in New York Tuesday," *Washington Post*, May 17, 1970, C10; Leonard Koppett, "Ex-Stars Back Reserve Clause Change," *New York Times*, May 22, 1970, 20; Leonard Koppett, "Hall of Famers Go to Bat for Flood," *The Sporting News*, June 6, 1970, 5.

34. Koppett, "Ex-Stars Back Reserve Clause Change"; Koppett, "Hall of Famers Go to Bat for Flood." Also speaking on behalf of Flood were Jim Bouton, former star pitcher and author of the recently released *Ball Four*, a rollicking look at big league players beyond the baseball diamond, and former team owner Bill Veeck, another maverick.

35. Koppett, "Ex-Stars Back Reserve Clause Change"; Koppett, "Hall of Famers Go to Bat for Flood."

36. Leonard Koppett, "Baseball's Arguments Are Pathetic," *The Sporting News*, June 20, 1970, 4.

37. *Ibid.*

38. "Federal Judge Rules against Flood on Reserve Clause," *Washington Post*, August 13, 1970, H1.

39. *Curt Flood v. Bowie Kuhn, et al.*, 407 U.S. 258.

40. *Ibid.*

41. Merrell Whittlesey, "Did High Court Err? Everybody Has Opinion," *The Sporting News*, July 8, 1972, 5.

42. Ralph Ray, "Catalyst for Bargaining, Says Miller of Decision," *The Sporting News*, July 8, 1972, 5, 8.

43. Bara, "How Curt Flood Changed Baseball and Killed His Career in the Process"; Joseph Durso, "Curt Flood Is Dead at 59; Outfielder Defied Baseball," *New York Times*, January 21, 1997, D23.

44. "Players Gaining $4 Million," *Washington Post*, May 26, 1970, D1.

45. "Players Sue Over TV Contract," *Washington Post*, July 6, 1971, D2.

46. Red Smith, "Owners Refuse to Own Up," *Washington Post*, July 9, 1971, D3.

47. "No Agreement! Baseball Players Strike Today," *Los Angeles Times*, April 1, 1972, B1; "Players Vote Baseball Strike: It's Strike One Called against Major Leagues," *Washington Post*, April 1, 1972, A1; "Owners Spurn Strike Compromise," *Washington Post*, April 4, 1972, D1.

48. "Owners Spurn Strike Compromise," D1.

49. Cover, *Sports Illustrated*, April 10, 1972; William Leggett, "Digging in at Crooked Creek," *Sports Illustrated*, April 10, 1972, 44–46; Cot's Baseball Contracts, https://legacy.baseballprospectus.com/compensation/cots/league-info/cba-history/.

50. "13-Day Baseball Strike Ends," *Washington Post*, April 14, 1972, A1.

51. Ron Rapoport, "Labor Expert: Owners' Error Forced Strike," *Los Angeles Times*, April 13, 1972, G1.

52. Ross Newhan, "Miller Warns Owners Another Dead End Possible in '73," *Los Angeles Times*, May 3, 1972, H1.

53. Christopher D. Chavis, "October 3, 1972: Fenway faithful are left wondering 'what if' as Tigers win AL East by a half-game," SABR, https://sabr.org/gamesproj/game/october-3-1972-the-fenway-faithful-are-left-wondering-what-if-we-had-one-more-game/.

54. "Baseball Owners, Players in Standoff," *Washington Post*, February 18, 1973, C10; "Pact Opens Baseball Camps," *Washington Post*, February 26, 1973, D1, D3; "Cot's Baseball Contracts," https://legacy.baseballprospectus.com/compensation/cots/league-info/cba-history/.

55. Dave Brady, "Curt Flood's Fight Was Not in Vain," *Washington Post*, February 28, 1973, D1.

Chapter 7

1. Malcolm Gladwell, "Talent Grab," *The New Yorker* (October 1, 2010), https://www.newyorker.com/magazine/2010/10/11/talent-grab.

2. "Catfish's Happy New Year: $3.7 Million," *Los Angeles Times*, January 1, 1975, F1; Mike Lupica, "47 Years Ago, Catfish Became 1st Free Agent," *MLB.com*, December 30, 2021, https://www.mlb.com/news/catfish-hunter-first-free-agent-baseball; Matt Kelly, "Catfish Hunter Signs Free Agent Contract with New York Yankees," National Baseball Hall of Fame, https://baseballhall.org/discover/inside-pitch/catfish-hunter-signs-with-yankees; Miller, *A Whole Different Ball Game*, 116; "Hunter Complaint Admitted by Miller," *Washington Post*, October 12, 1974, C5.

3. Ralph Ray, "Owners Rush to Court on Seitz Ruling," *The Sporting News*, January 10, 1976, 26; Miller, *A Whole Different Ball Game*, 114; "Freedom Asked for 2 Pitchers," *Washington Post*, October 16, 1975, B1.

4. "Arbitrator Rules 2 Pitchers 'Free,'" *Washington Post*, December 24, 1975, C1; Ray, "Owners Rush to Court on Seitz Ruling."

5. Ray, "Owners Rush to Court on Seitz Ruling."

6. *Ibid.*

7. *Ibid.*

8. "Judge Upholds Arbitrator Ruling for Baseball Players," *Washington Post*, February 5, 1976, F1; "Baseball Owners Lose Appeal," *Spartanburg Herald*, March 10, 1976, B2; Ross Newhan, "It's Official: Messersmith Is Open for Bids," *Los Angeles Times*, March 16, 1976, D1; David Hill, "MLB History: Andy Messersmith, Dave McNally Become Free Agents," *Call to the Pen*, https://calltothepen.com/2016/12/23/mlb-history-andy-messersmith-dave-mcnally-become-free-agents/; Eric Stephen, "40 Years Ago Today, Andy Messersmith Becomes a Free Agent," SBNation,

December 23, 2015, https://www.truebluela.com/2015/12/23/7526915/andy-messersmith-arbitration-decision-free-agency-dodgers-1975; Ralph Ray, "Owners Rush to Court on Seitz Ruling," *The Sporting News*, January 10, 1976, 26.

9. "Miller Says Players May Hold Own Season," *Washington Post*, March 7, 1976, D6.

10. Douglas S. Looney, "At Last, Spring Is Sprung," *Sports Illustrated*, March 29, 1976, 20–22.

11. Jerome Holtzman, "Owners Okay New Labor Contract after Delay," *The Sporting News*, July 31, 1976, 7; Ralph Ray, "Complex Labor Pact Called 'Experimental,'" *The Sporting News*, August 7, 1976, 9; "Cot's Baseball Contracts," https://legacy.baseballprospectus.com/compensation/cots/league-info/cba-history/; "Majors Settle with Players," *Washington Post*, July 13, 1976, D1, D3; Ross Newhan, "Baseball's Golden Era," *Los Angeles Times*, December 6, 1976, E1.

12. "Major Settle with Players," D3; Holtzman, "Owners Okay New Labor Contract after Delay."

13. Ray, "Complex Labor Pact Called 'Experimental'"; Jerome Holtzman, "Tracing Free Agency's Beginnings," December 8, 2004, *MLB.com*, http://mlb.mlb.com/content/printer_friendly/mlb/y2004/m12/d08/c919874.jsp/.

14. "Baseball Players Board Authorizes a Strike," *Washington Post*, March 5, 1980, D1-D2.

15. Ralph Ray, "Owners Call Federal Mediator at 11th Hour," *The Sporting News*, April 12, 1980, 17.

16. *Ibid.*

17. Dave Kindred, "Season to Open on April 9 as Scheduled," *Washington Post*, April 2, 1980, D1, D3; "Autry: Cancel Season," *Washington Post*, April 4, 1980, D3.

18. Shirley Povich, "What Miller Wants Is Usually What Players Get," *Washington Post*, April 13, 1980, N1.

19. Jane Leavy and Peter Mehlman, "Witching Hour for Baseball Is Just Days Away," *Washington Post*, May 18, 1980, F1, F6.

20. *Ibid.*, F6; Mike Littwin, "He's a Tough Out," *Los Angeles Times*, May 21, 1980, E1, E13.

21. Littwin, "He's a Tough Out," E13.

22. Peter Gammons, "Batter Up! Baseball Strike Averted," *Boston Globe*, May 23, 1980, 1; Murray Chass, "A Breather for Baseball," *The Sporting News*, June 7, 1980, 9, 44; "Cot's Baseball Contracts," https://legacy.baseballprospectus.com/compensation/cots/league-info/cba-history/; Robert Levey, "Baseball Agreement Revealed in Detail," *Boston Globe*, June 27, 1980, 1.

23. Ralph Ray, "Miller Assails Owner Claims," *The Sporting News*, June 14, 1980, 5.

24. Jerome Holtzman, "Owners Flash Hard-Line Signal to Players," *The Sporting News*, June 21, 1980, 36.

25. Ross Newhan, "Baseball Closes In on a Strike Again," *Los Angeles Times*, February 7, 1981, C1, C8.

26. Fred Rothenberg, "Marvin Miller Prefers Retirement," *Los Angeles Times*, May 27, 1981, 6.

27. Jane Leavy, "Baseball Players Begin Strike after Last-Minute Talks Fail," *Washington Post*, June 13, 1981, A1; Chris Bumbaca, "Explaining the 1981 MLB Season: How Baseball Survived Shortened Year," *USA Today*, March 15, 2020, https://www.usatoday.com/story/sports/mlb/2020/03/15/1981-mlb-season-coronavirus-delay-baseball/5054780002/; "1981: No Ball, One Strike," The Yearly Reader, https://thisgreatgame.com/1981-baseball-history/; Cover, *Sports Illustrated*, June 22, 1981; Jeff Katz, *Split Season: 1981: Fernandomania, the Bronx Zoo, and the Strike That Saved Baseball* (New York: Thomas Dunne Books, 2015).

28. Jerry Kirshenbaum, "Scoreboard," *Sports Illustrated*, June 22, 1981, 17.

29. Jim Kaplan, "No Games Today," *Sports Illustrated*, June 22, 1981, 18–21.

30. *Ibid.*, 21.

31. Jane Leavy, "Talks Set to Resume Today," *Washington Post*, July 1, 1981, D1, D4; Jane Leavy, "Hope Fades for Season; No Talks Scheduled," *Washington Post*, July 13, 1981, D1; "Ball Season Fading, Miller Says," *Globe and Mail*, July 24, 1981, 45.

32. "Baseball History: The MLB Strike of 1981," *Call to the Pen*, https://calltothepen.com/2011/11/09/baseball-history-the-mlb-strike-of-1981/; Tom Verducci, "Inside the Chaos of 1981—MLB's Last Severely Shortened Season," *Sports Illustrated*, May 29, 2020, https://www.si.com/mlb/2020/05/29/pete-rose-1981-baseball-strike; Ryan Fagan, "Baseball Strikes and Lockouts: A History of MLB Work Stoppages," *The Sporting News*, May 2, 2018, https://www.sportingnews.com/au/baseball/news/mlb-free-agents-labor-dispute-history-1994-1981-strike-1990-lockout-marvin-miller-mlbpa/1xfjbtlblmanp1gq65rsrt6dke; Doug Pappas, "A Contentious History: Baseball's Labor Fights," ESPN Baseball, http://static.espn.go.com/mlb/columns/bp/1427632.html.

33. "Baseball Strike Settled," *Los Angeles Times*, July 31, 1981, 1; Murray Chass, "Strike Over, Baseball Resumes Aug. 9," *New York Times*, August 1, 1981, 1.

34. Jane Gross, "Strike Losses Heavy and Widespread," *New York Times*, August 1, 1981, 17.

35. Al Harvin, "Mixed Reaction by Fans," *New York Times*, August 1, 1981, 19.

36. "Cot's Baseball Contracts," https://legacy.baseballprospectus.com/compensation/cots/league-info/cba-history/; Pappas, "A Contentious History."

37. Jim Kaplan, "Let the Games Begin," *Sports Illustrated*, August 10, 1981, 21.

38. Lowenfish, *The Imperfect Diamond*, 227.

39. Gladwell, "Talent Grab."

40. *Ibid.*

Chapter 8

1. Murray Chass, "'It's Time for Labor Peace,' Says Moffett," *The Sporting News*, January 3, 1983, 39.

2. Harrison Smith, "Ken Moffett, Low-Key Mediator in High-Profile Labor Disputes, Dies at 90," *Washington Post*, November 30, 2021, https://www.washingtonpost.com/obituaries/2021/11/30/ken-moffett-dead/; Richard Sandomir, "Ken Moffett, Top Federal Mediator and Union Official, Dies at 90," *New York Times*, December 5, 2021, A24.

3. Gordon Edes, "Marvin Miller Is Back in His Old Role," *Los Angeles Times*, November 24, 1983, D2; "Fehr Elected by Players," *New York Times*, December 9, 1983, B5.

4. Miller, *A Whole Different Ball Game*, 327–328; "Cot's Baseball Contracts," https://legacy.baseballprospectus.com/compensation/cots/league-info/cba-history/.

5. "Cot's Baseball Contracts," https://legacy.baseballprospectus.com/compensation/cots/league-info/cba-history/.

6. *Ibid.*

7. Ross Newhan, "Owners Seek a Salary Cap for Baseball," *Los Angeles Times*, May 21, 1985, D1; Murray Chass, "Peace Be with Baseball," *The Sporting News*, August 19, 1985, 2–3; Murray Chass, "The Main Event of '81 Is Dropped in New Pact," *The Sporting News*, August 19, 1985, 2.

8. Marc Normandin, "The Past, Present, and Future of MLB Collusion," SBNation, January 10, 2018, https://www.sbnation.com/mlb/2018/1/10/16863052/mlb-collusion-history-bud-selig-free-agency; Jeff Barto, "1985 Winter Meetings: Free-Agent Freezeout: Collusion I," *Baseball's Business: The Winter Meetings: 1958–2016*, Volume 2 (SABR, 2017), https://sabr.org/journals/winter-meetings-v2-1958-2016/.

9. Lowenfish, *The Imperfect Diamond*, 264.

10. Abrams, *Legal Bases*, 143–144.

11. Ross Newhan, "Why Are Owners Going Slowly on Free Agents?" *Los Angeles Times*, November 26, 1985, C2; Ross Newhan, "Closing Their Ranks, Owners Have Stopped Free-Agent Movement," *Los Angeles Times*, January 10, 1986, OCB1, B10; Ross Newhan, "Baseball Union Turns in Grievance on Free Agency," *Los Angeles Times*, February 5, 1986, C1, C6.

12. Miller, *A Whole Different Ball Game*, 346; Roger Abrams, *Legal Bases: Baseball and the Law* (Philadelphia: Temple University Press, 1998), 138–139.

13. Fred Mitchell, "Union Boss Frets Over 'Bad Blood,'" *Chicago Tribune*, January 11, 1987, 2; Les Bowen and Paul Hagen, "Owners Strike Out in Landmark Decision," *Philadelphia Daily News*, September 22, 1987, 78; Marty Noble, "Now It's Players 2, Owners 0," *Newsday*, September 1, 1988, 173; Steve Beitler, "The Empire Strikes Out: Collusion in Baseball in the 1980s," *Baseball Research Journal* (2007), https://sabr.org/journal/article/the-empire-strikes-out-collusion-in-baseball-in-the-1980/; Murray Chass, "7 in Baseball Collusion Case Win Free Agency," *New York Times*, January 23, 1988, , 48; Abrams, *Legal Bases*, 144; Murray Chass, "Gibson, Six Others Are Free-Look Free Agents," *The Sporting News*, February 1, 1988, 32.

14. Chass, "Gibson, Six Others, Are Free-Look Free Agents," 32.

15. Houston Mitchell, "Greatest Moment in Dodger History No 1: Kirk Gibson's World Series Home Run," April 30, 2021, https://www.latimes.com/sports/newsletter/2021-04-30/kirk-gibson-home-run-dodgers-dugout.

16. Dave Nightingale, "'Iron Fist' Going Back in the Glove," *The Sporting News*, January 5, 1987, 54.

17. Daniel Okrent, "On the Money," *Sports Illustrated*, April 10, 1989, 43.

18. *Ibid.*, 43–44, 46, 48.

19. "Cot's Baseball Contracts," https://legacy.baseballprospectus.com/compensation/cots/league-info/cba-history/.

20. Richard Justice, "For the Boys of Summer, It Looks Like Silent Spring," *Washington Post*, February 4, 1990, B1; Alan Solomon, "Players Doing the Limbo," *Chicago Tribune*, February 10, 1990, 3; "Baseball Put on Hold," *Telegram & Gazette*, February 10, 1993, 13; "Fehr, Players Stress Solidarity," *St. Petersburg Times*, February 28, 1900, 5C; Murray Chass, "In a Word, Owners Vote for Lockout," *The Sporting News*, February 19, 1990, 34.

21. Craig Neff, "Scorecard," *Sports Illustrated*, February 18, 1990, 9.

22. "Silent Spring," *Sports Illustrated*, March 19, 1990, 72–75.

23. Manny Topol, "Baseball Lockout It's All Over," *Newsday*, March 19, 1990, 82; Murray Chass, "Ah, Spring: 4-Year Pact Opens Camps," *The Sporting News*, March 26, 1990, 30.

24. Chass, "Ah, Spring," 30.

25. *Ibid.*; James Reston, *Collision at Home Plate: The Lives of Pete Rose and Bart Giamatti* (New York: HarperCollins, 1991).

26. Manny Topol, "Another $102.5 Million Added to Collusion Ledger," *Evening Sun*, September 18, 1990, D2; Murray Chass, "Players Get $102.5 Million in Collusion Case," *New York Times*, September 18, 1990, D25.

27. "Owners, Players Settle 5-Year Collusion Dispute," *Austin American Statesman*, December 6, 1990, C2; Murray Chass, "Collusion Is Resolved; Minors Still an Issue," *New York Times*, December 6, 1990, D24.

28. Chass, "Collusion Is Resolved," D25-D26.

29. Tim Kurkjian, "What Price Success?" *Sports Illustrated*, December 17, 1990, 48.

30. *Ibid.*, 50.

31. Peter Schmuck, "Fehr Says Strike Funds Already Being Collected," *Baltimore Sun*, March 5, 1991, 5D; "Baseball Union Builds Strike Fund," *New York Times*, March 11, 1991, C2; "Dividing Up, Looking Back," *New York Times*, March 11, 1991, C2; Claire Smith, "Too Much Money Is Never Enough," *New York Times*, May 22, 1991, B11; "Negative Collusion Numbers," *New York Times*, September 27, 1991, B11.

32. James Edward Miller, "Labor's Last Heavy Hitter," *New York Times Book Review*, July 14, 1991, 12.

33. *Ibid.*

34. Richard Sandomir, "Players Association Priority: Taking Care of Business," *New York Times*, August 11, 1991, S6.

35. Murray Chass, "Prepare for Lockout in Spring of '93, Fehr Is Warning Players," *New York Times*, March 31, 1992, B14.

36. *Ibid.*

Chapter 9

1. "Baseball Back at Milwaukee but It's Only Exhibition," *New York Times*, April 9, 1967, S208; "10 Milwaukee Games Slated by White Sox," *New York Times*, October 31, 1967, 54.

2. "Milwaukee Bids for a Ball Club," *New York Times*, November 7, 1967, 58.

3. Ross Newhan, "Analysis: Lockout: Plenty of Blame Shared," *Los Angeles Times*, March 11, 1990.

4. Murray Chase, "Baseball's Labor Dispute Settled with Compromise on Arbitration," *New York Times*, March 19, 1990, 1, C8; Richard Justice, "Gates Open for Baseball," *Washington Post*, March 20, 1990.

5. Chase, "Baseball's Labor Dispute Settled with Compromise on Arbitration"; Justice, "Gates Open for Baseball."

6. Justice, "Gates Open for Baseball."

7. Memorandum from Francis T. Vincent Jr., Commissioner, Major League Baseball, 1991.

8. Glen Macnow, "Owners Get Their Shot at Vincent and Result Will Be a War," *Philadelphia Inquirer*, September 2, 1992, F1; Fay Vincent, *The Last Commissioner: A Baseball Valentine* (New York: Simon & Schuster, 2002), 277–287.

9. Dave Sell, "18 Owners Tell Vincent to Quit," *Washington Post*, September 4, 1992; Claire Smith, "Vincent Will Not Go Without a Struggle," *New York Times*, September 4, 1992, B9.

10. Murray Chass, "Players Union Has Link to Commissioner's Situation, Too," *New York Times*, September 6, 1992, L5.

11. Dave Kindred, "A Burden Too Heavy to Carry," *The Sporting News*, September 7, 1992, 6.

12. *Ibid.*

13. Dave Sell, "Baseball's Vincent Resigns," *Washington Post*, September 8, 1992.

14. *Ibid.*; Larry Whiteside, "Vincent Quits as Baseball Chief," *Boston Globe*, September 8, 1992, 1.

15. Ira Berkow, "No Matter What's Said, Reinsdorf Can Be Found in Eye of Storm," *New York Times*, September 6, 1992, 3.

16. Murray Chass, "On the Way Out, Vincent Finally Gets a Consensus," *New York Times*, September 8, 1992, B12.

17. "Players Feeling Uncertain," *New York Times*, September 9, 1992, B10.

18. Claire Smith, "Winners and Losers Emerge in Vincent's Wake," *New York Times*, September 8, 1992, B11-B12.

19. Murray Chass, "Selig Goes in for Vincent at First," *New York Times*, September 10, 1992, 11.

20. Claire Smith, "Whatever His Title, Selig's in the Hot Seat," *New York Times*, September 10, 1992, 13.

21. Murray Chass, "Baseball Owners Lean Toward Lockout," *New York Times*, September 11, 1992, 11; Claire Smith, "Fehr Awaits 2 Words: Delay Ball," *New York Times*, September 11, 1992, B11.

22. Chass, "Baseball Owners Lean Toward Lockout."

23. Smith, "Fehr Await 2 Words."

24. *Ibid.*

25. *Ibid.*

26. Marty Noble, "Analysis Unified Owners Ready for War," *Newsday*, September 13, 1992, 9; Craig Daniels, "Was Vincent Ousted to Prepare for an All-Out War?" *Financial Post*, September 14, 1992, 50; Mark Maske, "Fehr Expresses Fear Owners Want Lockout," *Washington Post*, September 20, 1992, D13.

27. Josh Getlin, "The Season of Discontent: Soured by Soaring Salaries and Teams That Don't Care About Their Fans, Many in the Bleachers Are Ready to Turn Out the Lights and Go Home," *Los Angeles Times*, September 23, 1992, 1.

28. Duncan Brantley, "Fehr and Loathing in Baseball," *Sports Illustrated*, September 21, 1992, 8.

29. "Brown Not Interested," *New York Times*, September 11, 1992, B11.

30. Ira Berkow, "Welcome to the Major Leagues, Bud Selig Presiding," *New York Times*, September 27, 1992, 1.

31. *Ibid.*

32. Dave Anderson, "You'll Never Guess What's Finally Here," *New York Times*, October 4, 1992, 1.

33. Murray Chass, "For Baseball, the Worst of Times May Come After the Best of Seven," *New York Times*, October 19, 1992, 1, C8; "A Distant Second," *New York Times*, October 19, 1992, 1.

34. Glen Macnow, "The Forecast for Major-League Baseball: A Nasty Winter: The Game Already Is Beset by Troubles. Now Things Could Get Worse. Would You Believe No 1993 Season?" *Philadelphia Inquirer*, October 27, 1992, D1.

35. Murray Chass, "Thud! Economic Report Lands on Baseball's Desk," *New York Times*, December 7, 1992, C2.

36. Marty Noble, "Share the Wealth," *The Sporting News*, December 21, 1992, 26.

37. *Ibid.*

38. *Ibid.*

39. Murray Chass, "Baseball Owners Vote to Reopen Labor Talks," *New York Times*, December 8, 1992, B17, B19.

40. Claire Smith, "At Capitol Hill, It's Batters Up," *New York Times*, December 10, 1992, B19.

41. Claire Smith, "Baseball Executives Are Taken to Task," *New York Times*, December 11, 1992, B9; Russell Schneider, "Senate Looks at Baseball's Government," *Cleveland Plain Dealer*, November 29, 1992, 7C.

42. Smith, "Baseball Executives Are Taken to Task," B9.

Chapter 10

1. Sen Timothy E. Wirth, "Crisis Might Require Government Intervention," *The Sporting News*, January 4, 1993, 7.

2. Tim Kurkjian, "Dark Days for Baseball," *Sports Illustrated*, December 21, 1992, 44.

3. *Ibid.*

4. Bob Verdi, "'Baseball Is Like Fingernails on a Chalkboard,'" *The Sporting News*, December 28, 1992, 7.

5. *Ibid.*

6. *Ibid.*

7. Marty Noble, "The Money Pit," *The Sporting News*, January 18, 1993, 22–23.

8. *Ibid.*, 23.

9. *Ibid.*

10. Murray Chass, "Baseball; Owners' Labor Agent Doesn't Favor Lockout," *New York Times*, January 14, 1993, B13; Marty Noble, "Ravitch Says He Will Not Seek Lockout," *Newsday*, January 14, 1993, 140.

11. Chass, "Baseball; Owners' Labor Agent Doesn't Favor Lockout," B13.

12. Murray Chass, "Owners Link Salaries to Revenue Sharing," *New York Times*, February 18, 1993, B17.

13. *Ibid.*

14. E.M. Swift, "The Perfect Square," *Sports Illustrated*, March 8, 1993, 32.

15. *Ibid.*, 33–34.

16. Richard Ford, "Stop Blaming Baseball," *New York Times Magazine* (April 4, 1993): 37+.

17. *Ibid.*

18. Murray Chass, "Buy the Crackerjacks While It Lasts," *New York Times*, April 20, 1993, B12.

19. Tom Verducci, "Sign of the Times," *Sports Illustrated*, May 3, 1993, 14–16.

20. *Ibid.*, 16, 18–20; Cover, *Sports Illustrated*, May 24, 1993.

21. Tom Verducci, "Have You Seen This Man?," *Sports Illustrated*, July 5, 1993, 38.

22. *Ibid.*, 38, 40.

23. Dave Van Dyck, "For Baseball Owners, More Profit Comes Before Tradition," *Baseball Digest* (June 1993): 29–30.

24. Ross Newhan, "September Strike Hinted by Players," *Los Angeles Times*, July 14, 1993, OCC13; Mike Penner, "Baseball May Come Up Short," *Los Angeles Times*, July 16, 1993, OCC1; Murray Chass, "Fehr Raises Possibility of Late Work Stoppage," *New York Times*, July 24, 1993, L31.

25. Murray Chass, "No Lockout, but a War of the Words," *New York Times*, August 14, 1993, L27; Ronald Blum, "Strike Possibility Diminishes after Owners Rule Out Lockout," *Phoenix Gazette*, August 13, 1993, D2; Mark Maske, "'93 Strike Unlikely; Pledge Soothes Baseball Players," *Washington Post*, August 14, 1993, F1.

26. George Vecsey, "The Players Should Copy the Matador," *New York Times*, August 8, 1993, L1.

27. *Ibid.*

28. John Rawlings, "The Players' Choice," *The Sporting News*, September 6, 1993, 9.

29. *Ibid.*

30. *Ibid.*

31. *Ibid.*

32. Peter Pascarelli, "Relax, Realignment Will Not Hurt Baseball," *The Sporting News*, September 20, 1993, 12.

33. Murray Chass, "Call It Baseball or Call It Business, It's Still Booming," *New York Times*, August 8, 1993, E2.

34. Tim Kurkjian, "New Power Supply," *Sports Illustrated*, July 26, 1993, 18, 20–22.

35. *Ibid.*, p. 18, 20.

36. Peter Gammons, "At Long Last, Game's the Thing," *Boston Globe*, September 10, 1993, 75.

37. Mark Newman, "A Fitting Finish," *The Sporting News*, October 4, 1993, 12–15.

38. Steve Rushin, "Home Sweet Homer," *Sports Illustrated*, November 1, 1993, 18–26.

39. George Vesey, "Joe Carter Puts an End to the World Series," *New York Times*, October 25, 1993, 31.

40. *Ibid.*

Chapter 11

1. John Thorn, "Stop Me If You've Heard This One Before," *The Sporting News*, October 18, 1993, 9.

2. *Ibid.*

3. *Ibid.*

4. *Ibid.*

5. John Rawlings, "A Healthy Game in a Difficult Era," *The Sporting News*, October 25, 1993, 9.

6. *Ibid.*

7. WAR Formula for Position Players: Fan Graphs (fWAR): WAR = (Batting Runs + Base Running Runs + Fielding Runs + Positional Adjustment +League Adjustment + Replacement Runs)/ (Runs Per Win); Baseball-Reference (bWAR): WAR = (Player Runs-Average Player Runs) + (Average Runs—Replacement Level Runs).

WAR Formula for Pitchers: Fan Graphs (fWAR): War = [[([(League "FIP"—"FIP") / Pitcher Specific Runs Per Win] + Replacement Level) * (IP/9)] * Leverage Multiplier for Relievers] + League Correction; Baseball-Reference (bWAR): WAR = Replacement Level + Wins Above Average + (Wins Above Average) * (1.00 + Leverage Multiplier)/2).

8. Mark Newman, "An Age-Old Occurrence," *The Sporting News*, February 21, 1994, 18–19.

9. Michael Knisley, "Monument to Greatness," *The Sporting News*, October 11, 1993, 31–42.

10. Tony DeMarco, "Buyer Beware," *The Sporting News*, November 15, 1993, 37–39.

11. Peter Pascarelli, "Another Awful Offseason," *The Sporting News*, December 6, 1993, 34–35.

12. *Ibid.*, 34.

13. *Ibid.*

14. *Ibid.*, 34–35.

15. Murray Chass, "Players Still Waiting for Owners' First Pitch," *New York Times*, December 9, 1993, B31.

16. Peter Pascarelli, "Baseball's Hits Are Buried by Its Many Strikeouts," *The Sporting News*, January 3, 1994, 26.

17. *Ibid.*

18. Peter Pascarelli, "Baseball in Jeopardy? And the Answer is…," *The Sporting News*, January 10, 1994, 35.

19. *Ibid.*

20. *Ibid.*

21. *Ibid.*

22. Barry Cooper, "Bonds, Thomas Voted Best Players Choice Awards Go to NL, AL MVPs at Disney Event," *Orlando Sentinel*, January 9, 1994, C15.

23. Mark Newman, "One More Chance," *The Sporting News*, January 10, 1994, 33–34.

24. *Ibid.*

25. Claire Smith, "Carlton Will Enter Hall Alone," *New York Times*, January 13, 1994, B9, B11.

26. *Ibid.*, B9.

27. William C. Rhoden, "Keep the Vote Between the Lines," *The Sporting News*, January 31, 1994, 7.

28. *Ibid.*

29. Robert McG. Thomas Jr., "At Long Last, Rizzuto Makes Hall of Fame," *New York Times*, February 26, 1994, 29, 36.

30. Jim Hodges, "Rizzuto, Durocher Join Hall: Baseball: One Ex-Yankee Shortstop Overjoyed, but Mystery Surrounds Whether 'the Lip' Will Be Represented at Induction," *Los Angeles Times*, February 26, 1994.

31. "Hall of Famers," *The Sporting News*, March 7, 1994, 23.

32. Dave Kindred, "Dare Jordan," *The Sporting News*, January 17, 1994, 7.

33. *Ibid.*

34. *Ibid.*

35. Bob Greene, "For Michael Jordan, spring is no Chicago White Sox fantasy camp," *Chicago Tribune*, January 13, 1994.

36. *Ibid.*

37. *Ibid.*

38. Murray Chass, "Our Irrational Pastime: Division Setup Still Not Set Up," *The Sporting News*, January 11, 1994, B10.

39. Claire Smith, "Perhaps a New Era, but Note the Asterisk," *New York Times*, January 19, 1994, B14.

40. Claire Smith, "Central Divisions Are Added to Baseball's Lineup," *New York Times*, January 20, 1994, B9, B15.

41. Peter Pascarelli, "Next Question," *The Sporting News*, January 31, 1994, 33–34.

42. *Ibid.*, 33.

43. Murray Chass, "Labor Talks to Start. Labor Talks to Start," *New York Times*, February 17, 1994, B16.

44. Claire Smith, "Players' Labor Motto: Expect the Worst," *New York Times*, March 3, 1994, B14.

45. Murray Chass, "Baseball; Owners Promise to Open the Books," *New York Times*, March 8, 1994, B16.

46. Mark Maske, "Labor Negotiations Are Sputtering," *Washington Post*, March 20, 1994, D4.

47. Larry Whiteside, "Selig, Metzenbaum Play Hardball during Hearing," *Boston Globe*, March 22, 1994, 66.

48. *Ibid.*

49. *Ibid.*; Michael Bamberger, "For Selig, A Grilling on Baseball's Future," *Philadelphia Inquirer*, March 22, 1994, E1.

50. Ronald Blum, "Strike Cloud Casts Shadow over Openers," *Houston Chronicle*, April 3, 1994, 1.

Chapter 12

1. Josh Leventhal, *Take Me Out to the Ballpark: An Illustrated Tour of Baseball Parks Past and Present* (New York: Black Dog & Leventhal, 2000); Philip J. Lowry, *Green Cathedrals: The Ultimate Celebration of Major League and Negro League Ballparks* (New York: Walker & Company, 2006); Eric Enders, *Ballparks Then and Now* (San Diego: Thunder Bay Press, 2002).

2. *Ballparks: Yesterday & Today* (Lincolnwood, IL: Publications International, 2015).

3. Trent Frayne, "SkyDome Remains Unknown Ballpark," *The Globe and Mail*, February 24, 1989, A19; "Sky's the Limit," *Windsor Star*, April 8, 1989, E1; Dave Perkins, "Jay's New Home a Monument to People with Money to Burn," *Toronto Star*, June 6, 1989, F1; Ken Picking, "SkyDome Is a Hit with Toronto Fans," *USA Today*, June 6, 1989, C6.

4. Philip Bess, *City Baseball Magic: Plain Talk and Uncommon Sense about Cities and Ballparks* (Saint Paul: Knothole Press, 1999); Tommy Craggs, "Why Your Stadium Sucks: U.S. Cellular Field," *Deadspin*, July 31, 2009, https://deadspin.com/why-your-stadium-sucks-u-s-cellular-field-5327239.

5. Toni Ginnetti, "New Sox Logo Debuts with Birth of Ballpark," *Chicago Sun-Times*, February 3, 1991, 10; Andrew Bagnato, "Final Touches Being Put on Comiskey II," *Chicago Tribune*, February 7, 1991, 1; "Comiskey Nearly Done," *Chicago Sun-Times*, February 9, 1991, 87; Jerome Holtzman, "'New Tradition' Just Too Costly," *Chicago Tribune*, 1; "Changing Baltimore's Skyline," *Baltimore*, January 1, 1994, A14; "Special Attention to Downtown," *Baltimore*, January 30, 1992, A6.

6. John Rosin, "Did Babe Ruth Grow Up on 2nd Base?" *Hidden Baltimore*, October 16, 2012, https://hiddenbaltimore.wordpress.com/2012/10/16/the-ruth-family-saloon/; "Fans Privy to Ruthian Find," *The Globe and Mail*, February 11, 1992, D10.

7. Bill Koch, "Cleveland's Field of Dreams," *Cincinnati Post*, March 30, 1994, 1A; Leventhal, *Take Me Out to the Ballpark*.

8. David Sartin, "Jacobs Pays $10 Million to Put Name on Ballpark," *Plain Dealer*, February 24, 1994, 3B; Leventhal, *Take Me Out to the Ballpark*.

9. Ken Herman, "Field of Dreams—Or Foul Ball?" *Houston Post*, March 31, 1994, A1. Leventhal, *Take Me Out to the Ballpark*.

10. Leventhal, *Take Me Out to the Ballpark*.

11. Lewis H. Diuguid, "Play Ball! Spring Training in Florida and Arizona," *Washington Post*, February 13, 1994.

12. *Ibid.*

13. *Ibid.*

14. *Ibid.*

15. Steve Marantz, "Training Arrives and It's Not a Moment Too Soon," *Los Angeles Times*, February 27, 1994.

16. *Ibid.*

17. *Ibid.*

18. *Ibid.*

19. Mark Ruda, "Scouting Michael Jordan: Can His Airness Make It in Baseball?" *Baseball America* (March 1994).

20. *Ibid.*

21. *Ibid.*

22. *Ibid.*

23. *Ibid.*

24. *Ibid.*

25. Tim Kurkjian, "Reading the Signs," *Sports Illustrated*, February 28, 1994, 64–65.

26. Steve Wulf, "Err Jordan—Try as He Might, Michael Jordan Has Found Baseball Beyond His Grasp," *Sports Illustrated*, March 14, 1994.

27. Murray Chase, "Vincent, Bowing to Owners' Will, Resigns as Baseball Commissioner," *New York Times*, September 8, 1992.

28. Bud Selig, "One of Baseball's Enduring Myths," *The Sporting News*, March 14, 1994, 8.

29. *Ibid.*

30. *Ibid.*

31. *Ibid.*

32. *Ibid.*

33. "So Good … So Young," *Sports Illustrated*, April 4, 1994, cover; Tom Verducci, "Kids: A Proliferation of Exciting Young Stars Has Put a Fresh Face on the Game," *Sports Illustrated*, April 4, 1994, 52.

34. *Ibid.*, 53.

35. *Ibid.*, 54.

36. *Ibid.*; "Scouting Reports," *Sports Illustrated*, April 4, 1994, 93.

37. Verducci, "Kids," 54.

38. *Ibid.*, 54–55.

39. Aaron Skirboll, *The Pittsburgh Cocaine Seven: How a Ragtag Group of Fans Took the Fall for Major League Baseball* (Chicago: Chicago Review Press, 2010); Douglas M. Branson, *Major League Turbulence: Baseball in the Era of Drug Use, Labor Strife and Black Power, 1968–1988* (Jefferson, NC: McFarland, 2021).

40. Verducci, "Kids," 55–56.

41. *Ibid.*, 58.

42. *Ibid.*

43. *Ibid.*

44. *Ibid.*, 58–59.

45. *Ibid.*, 60.

46. *Ibid.*

47. Tim Kurkjian, "No Worries for a Winner," *Sports Illustrated*, April 4, 1994, 94; Steve Wulf, "Refurbished and Realigned," *Sports Illustrated*, April 4, 1994, 100; Tom Verducci, "The Shape of Things to Come," *Sports Illustrated*, April 4, 1994, 106.

48. Tim Kurkjian, "Handling the Investment," *Sports Illustrated*, April 4, 1994, 112; Steve Wulf, "New Division, Same Result," *Sports Illustrated*, April 4, 1994, 122; Tom Verducci, "A Cleared Path to the Top," *Sports Illustrated*, April 4, 1994, 128.

49. Cover, "Baseball 94," *The Sporting News*, April 4, 1994, 1; Cover, "The Sun Also Rises," *The Sporting News*, April 4, 1994, 1; Verdi, "No Baseball News Will Be Good News in 1994," *The Sporting News*, April 4, 1994, 8.

Chapter 13

1. Ron Fimrite, "Getting It All Together," *Sports Illustrated*, April 8, 1974.

2. Pat Sullivan, "Bonds as Prep: Signs of a Superstar," *San Francisco Chronicle*, July 7, 1993, C1.

3. Craig Calcaterra, "Today in Baseball History: When Mantle and Mays Were Banned from Baseball," *MLB/NBC Sports*, March 18, 1920.

4. Hank Hersch, "30/30 Vision: Pittsburgh's Barry Bonds Sees Those Numbers Coming," *Sports Illustrated*, June 25, 1990.

5. "A list of amateur players selected," *Santa Cruz Sentinel*, June 4, 1985, B2.

6. "Transactions," *Santa Cruz Sentinel*, June 6, 1985, B3; "Transactions," *Santa Cruz Sentinel*, June 9, 1985, C6.

7. "Transactions," *Desert Sun*, May 26, 1986, B5; "Transactions," *Desert Sun*, May 27, 1986, C4; "Good bat, good legs, no arm," *San Bernardino Sun*, June 26, 1986, C2.

8. Tom Barnidge, "Paradoxical Bonds Reaches the Pinnacle," *The Sporting News*, October 29, 1990.

9. Jeff Pearlman, *Love Me, Hate Me: Barry Bonds and the Making of an Antihero* (New York: HarperCollins, 2006), 91.

10. "Baseball Forms Economic Group," *Santa Cruz Sentinel*, December 16, 1990, 4; "The Pirates expect," *Santa Cruz Sentinel*, January 9, 1991, B3; "Fernando, Others, Get Hefty Raises," *Santa Cruz Sentinel*, February 1, 1991, B3; "Pirates Win Again; Bonds Loses Case," *Santa Cruz Sentinel*, February 18, 1991, B3; "Bonds and Leyland Feuding," *Santa Cruz Sentinel*, March 5, 1991, B3; Bruce Jenkins, "Catch Phrase: 'I'm Underpaid,'" *Santa Cruz Sentinel*, March 6, 1991, B1.

11. Peter Gammons, "Pirates' Bonds Shakes off Other Players' Criticism," *Boston Globe*, August 30, 1991, 47.

12. Cover, "Bonds Away," *Sports Illustrated*, May 4, 1992.

13. Murray Chass, "Bonds Now 2 for 3 in M.V.P. Titles for the 90's," *New York Times*, November 19, 1992, B11, B13; "Associated Press Names Bonds Player of the Year," *Washington Post*, E7A.

14. Murray Chass, "Giants Make Investment: $43 Million in Bonds," *New York Times*, December

6, 1992,Sect. 8, pp. 1, 6; "Giants' New Owner Keeps Busy," *Santa Cruz Sentinel*, December 7, 1992, B4; Mark Maske, "Giants Post $43 Million for Bonds," *Washington Post*, December 6, 1992, D1.

15. Dave Anderson, "If Only Barry Bonds Were Too Expensive," *New York Times*, December 7, 1992, C3.

16. Craig Marine, "Is Bonds a Jerk? Sure, But He's Still an Artist," *St. Louis Post-Dispatch*, May 16, 1993, F6.

17. Cover, *Sports Illustrated*, May 24, 1994; Richard Hoffer, "The Importance of Being Barry," *Sports Illustrated*, May 24, 1993, 12–21.

18. *Ibid.*, 14.

19. *Ibid.*, 15.

20. *Ibid.*, 16–17.

21. Thomas Boswell, "The Best Player in Baseball," *Washington Post*, June 6, 1993, D1, D9.

22. "HOW DO YOU PITCH THIS GUY?" *The Sporting News*, June 14, 1993, 1; Bruce Schoenfeld, "Barry at the Bat," *The Sporting News*, June 14, 1993, 10–12.

23. Schoenfeld, "Barry at the Bat," 11–12.

24. Ken Rosenthal, "In Baseball's Showcase Game, Count on Bonds to Steal the Show," *Baltimore Sun*, July 12, 1993, C6.

25. Brian Schmitz, "Yield on Majors' Bonds Becoming Jordanesque," *Orlando Sentinel*, July 13, 1993, D1.

26. Cover, "Barry Bonds: Best All-Around Player in Majors?" *Baseball Digest*, August 1993.

27. Mike Downey, "With Places Still to Go, Bonds Not Ready to Slow Down," *Los Angeles Times*, October 3, 1993, OCC11.

28. Ross Newhan, "Bonds Add to MVP Collection," *Los Angeles Times*, November 10, 1993, OCC2; "Bonds Retains Title as Baseball's Best," *Springfield* (IL) *State Journal Register*, November 2, 1993, 19.

29. Larry Stone, "A League of His Own," *The Sporting News*, March 7, 1994, 22.

30. *Ibid.*

31. *Ibid.*

32. *Ibid.*

33. *Ibid.*

Chapter 14

1. Rick Cassano, "The Moeller Years: Coach Reflects on Griffey Jr., in High School," *Dayton Daily News*, January 6, 2016.

2. Todd Miles, "From the Beginning, It Was Easy to See Ken Griffey Jr. Was the Real Thing," *Bellingham Herald*, July 19, 2016; Matt Kelly, "10 Scouting Reports that Saw Greatness Coming," *MLB.com*, May 24, 2020, https://www.mlb.com/news/mlb-draft-scouting-reports-that-saw-the-future; Ross Newhan, "Mariners Are Expected to Make Ken Griffey Jr. No. 1 Draft Pick," *Los Angeles Times*, May 31, 1987, C4; Mark Whicker, "Ken Griffey Jr.'s Hall of Fame Career Got a Boost from Scout Bob Harrison," *Los Angeles Daily News*, January 5, 2016, https://www.dailynews.com/2016/01/05/whicker-ken-griffey-jrs-hall-of-fame-career-got-a-boost-from-scout-bob-harrison/.

3. Steve Vrablik, Scouting Report on Ken Griffey Jr., June 1987, https://bleacherreport.com/articles/1633315-full-scouting-reports-for-the-10-greatest-mlb-players-of-this-generation.

4. Bob Finnigan, "Young Cry for Help—At 17, Griffey Jr. Attempted Suicide; Now He Warns Others," *Seattle Times*, March 15, 1992.

5. *Ibid.*; David Hill, "Seattle Mariners: Ken Griffey Jr. Details Quiet Struggles," *Call to the Pen*, May 12, 2021, https://calltothepen.com/2021/05/12/seattle-mariners-ken-griffey-jr-details-quiet-struggles/.

6. Marty York, "Griffey Jr. Destined for Stardom, Scouts Contend," *The Globe and Mail*, January 3, 1989, A20.

7. Peter King "Man-Child Ken Griffey Jr. Is Mariners' Teen Sensation," *Newsday*, March 20, 1989, 91; Rod Beaton, "The Phenoms of '89; Not Many Get Star Billing Right Off Bat," *USA Today*, March 22, 1989, C1.

8. "Like Father, Like Son," *The Sporting News*, April 10, 1989; Jim Street, "Clock Strikes Griffey Time," *The Sporting News*, April 10, 1989, 12, 14; "As Griffey Jr. Starts Out in Seattle, Griffey Sr. Hangs on in Cincinnati," *Los Angeles Times*, March 31, 1989, B1; Tim Pearrell, "Additions May Push Kansas City to Top," *Richmond Times-Dispatch*, April 6, 1990, A6.

9. Cover, "Ken Griffey, Jr. Follows in His Dad's Footsteps," *Baseball Digest*, March 1990.

10. Cover, "The Natural," *Sports Illustrated*, May 7, 1990; E.M. Swift, "Bringing Up Junior," *Sports Illustrated*, May 7, 1990, 38–42.

11. Swift, "Bringing Up Junior," 39.

12. *Ibid.*

13. Bob Sudyk, "Griffey Jr., a Natural at Being Baseball's New Star Attraction," *Los Angeles Times*, May 11, 1990, OCP11.

14. "Stardom Easy for Griffey Jr.," *Windsor Star*, May 15, 1990, B2; Paul Carbray, "A Chip Off the Old Block; Junior's 'Good Genes' Make Griffey Sr., a Proud Papa," *Colorado Springs Gazette*, June 2, 1990, G1.

15. "M's Play a Real Father-Son Game," *The Sporting News*, September 10, 1990, 20; Sports People, "Father-Son Night," *New York Times*, September 2, 1990, 10.

16. Jim Donaghy, "Alomars Are All-Star Starters," *Austin American Statesman*, July 4, 1991, E1; Thomas Boswell, "And the Winners Are...," *Washington Post*, October 4, 1991, D1; Bob Sherwin, "Griffey and Mays—A New Legend Catches on," *Seattle Times*, July 7, 1991, C1.

17. Jeff Lenihan, "Here Are Stars That Should Shine in San Diego," *Star Tribune*, July 5, 1992, C13.

18. Thomas Boswell, "In the Season Past, Baseball Finds Future," *Washington Post*, October 5, 1993, B1.

19. Jim Thomas, "Kid's Stuff Griffey Jr. Makes Greatness Look Easy," *St. Louis Post-Dispatch*, August 12, 1993, D1.

20. *Ibid.*

21. Bob Sherwin, "The Kid Is All Right," *Calgary Herald*, July 13, 1993, D4.

22. Mark Maske, "Griffey Making a Tough Transition," *Los Angeles Times*, August 29, 1993, 850; Milton Kent, "Griffey Continues to Amaze," *Houston Chronicle*, September 9, 1993, 7.

23. "Griffey Must Settle for a Piece of Eight," *Los Angeles Times*, July 30, 1993, C1; "Junior Hits Another Milestone," *Toronto Star*, September 15, 1993, C3; "Mariners' Griffey Jr. Piles Up Records at Tender Age of 23," *Vancouver Sun*, September 15, 1993, D11.

24. Alan Solomon, "Sox Should Roll to Central Flag," *Chicago Tribune*, March 29, 1994, 8; Dwight Jaynes, "A Title Year for Mariners?" *The Oregonian*, March 28, 1994, D1; Bob Finnigan and Bob Sherwin, "Center Field of Dreams," *Seattle Times*, March 31, 1994, 10.

25. Steve Marantz, "The Family Man," *The Sporting News*, April 4, 1994, S4.

26. *Ibid.*, S4, S7.

Chapter 15

1. Bruce Levine, "Cubs Classics: Tuffy Rhodes' Historic Opening Day," Marquee Sports Network, 2020, https://www.marqueesportsnetwork.com/cubs-classics-kerry-woods-20k-game/; Paul Hofmann, "April 4, 1922: Cubs' Tuffy Rhodes Goes Deep Three Times on Opening Day," SABR, https://sabr.org/gamesproj/game/april-4-1994-cubs-tuffy-rhodes-goes-deep-three-times-on-opening-day/; Paul Mirengoff, "Hillary Rodham Clinton at the Old Ball Game," Powerline, March 29, 2020, https://www.powerlineblog.com/archives/2020/03/hillary-rodham-clinton-at-the-old-ball-game.php.

2. Adrienne Goehler, "Reliving the 1994 MLB Strike 28 Years Later," *FanNation*, February 21, 2022, https://www.si.com/mlb/indians/opinion/reliving-the-1994-mlb-strike-as-2022-labor-negotiations-continue; Joseph Wancho, "April 4, 1994: Indians Open Jacobs Field in Style with Extra-Inning Win," SABR, https://sabr.org/gamesproj/game/april-4-1994-indians-open-jacobs-field-in-style-with-extra-inning-win/; Tom Verducci, "Grand Opening," *Sports Illustrated*, April 11, 1994, 42–44, 48; Mark Newman and John Rawlings, "A Tale of Two Cities," *The Sporting News*, April 11, 1994, 14–16.

3. Verducci, "Grand Opening," 43. "Lemon Takes 20th for Indians, 6 to 0," *New York Times*, September 20, 1956, p. 39.

4. *Ibid.*, 44, 48.

5. "Value on the Diamond Continues to Increase," *Fort Lauderdale Sun Sentinel*, April 10, 1994, C14.

6. *Ibid.*, 48; Newman and Rawlings, "A Tale of Two Cities," 14–15.

7. Matthew Postins, "Rangers History Today: The Dawn of The Ballpark in Arlington," April 11, 2021, *FanNation*, https://www.si.com/mlb/rangers/news/today-in-texas-rangers-history-april-11-1994#:~:text=The%20game%20was%20on%20April,%2D1993)%20the%20previous%20season; Bill Sullivan, "Ballpark Applauded by Ryan," *Houston Chronicle*, April 2, 1994, 3; Tim Kurkjian, "A Major Step Up," *Sports Illustrated*, April 11, 1994, 8.

8. Ross Newhan, "Wild About the West," *The Sporting News*, April 11, 1994, 17–18.

9. *Ibid.*

10. Postins, "Rangers History Today: The Dawn of the Ballpark in Arlington."

11. Ira Berkow, "Wild Thing That's Called Wild Card," *New York Times*, April 7, 1994, B9.

12. *Ibid.*

13. Murray Chass, "Mitchell Moves into Position for Top Baseball Job," *New York Times*, April 13, 1994, B13, B15.

14. Zev Chafets, *Cooperstown Confidential: Heroes, and the Inside Story of the Baseball Hall of Fame* (New York: Bloomsbury, 2009), 61–62.

15. Eddie Mathews, *Eddie Mathews and the National Pastime* (Milwaukee: Douglas American Sports Publications, 1994); John Klima, *Bushville Wins! The Wild Saga of the 1957 Milwaukee Braves and the Screwballs, Sluggers, and Beer Swiggers Who Canned the New York Yankees and Changed Baseball* (New York: St. Martin's Griffin, 2015); Randy Roberts and Johnny Smith, *A Season in the Sun: The Rise of Mickey Mantle* (New York: Basic Books, 2018). Shirley Povich, "Mantle Has Rare Chance to Beat Ruth's 60," *Washington Post*, July 25, 1961, p. A14; Shirley Povich, "This Morning…," *Washington Post*, September 15, 1961, p. D1; Jim Murray, "Failure at 58?" *Los Angeles Times*, September 20, 1961, p. C1; "Maris' 60 Is 162-Game Mark, Says Ford Frick," *Los Angeles Times*, September 27, 1961, p. C6; Shirley Povich, "This Morning…," *Washington Post*, September 29, 1961, p. D1; Jim Murray, "New York Parade," *Los Angeles Times*, October 4, 1961, p. C1; Paul Zimmerman, "Baseball Game of Statistics," *Los Angeles Times*, September 9, 1962, p. 12.

16. Jim Brosnan, *The Long Season: An Inside Chronicle of the Baseball Year as Seen by Major League Pitcher* (New York: Harper & Row, 1960); Jim Bouton, *Ball Four: My Life and Hard Times Throwing the Knuckleball in the Big Leagues* (New York: World Publishing Company, 1970); Rachel Sasser, "Remember When Everyone in the MLB Was Using Greenies?" August 10, 2018, https://www.razorgator.com/blog/remember-when-everyone-in-the-mlb-was-using-greenies/; Emily Bell, "Drunk in the Dugout: A History of Beer and Baseball," VinePair, July 20, 2016, https://vinepair.com/articles/were-not-the-only-ones-drinking-during-a-baseball-game/; Will Carroll, "Under the Knife: Amphetamines and Baseball," Baseball Prospectus, February 2, 2006, https://www.baseballprospectus.com/news/

article/4740/under-the-knife-amphetamines-and-baseball/; Bryan Zarpentine, "Is Lost Era of Post-WWII Drug Culture What Baseball is Missing?" The Versed, May 11, 2017, https://www.theversed.com/10586/is-lost-era-of-post-wwii-drug-culture-what-baseball-is-missing/#.C12ajEE7DC.

17. "Steroids, Spitballs, and Greenies: A Baseball Hypocrisy," Sportales, https://sportales.com/blogging/steroids-spitballs-and-greenies-a-baseball-hypocrisy/; Mike Schmidt, *Clearing the Bases: Juiced Players, Monster Salaries, Sham Records, and a Hall of Famer's Search for the Soul of Baseball* (New York: Harper, 2006); Murray Chass, "Schmidt an Open Book on Greenies," *New York Times*, February 28, 2006, D1.

18. Skirboll, *The Pittsburgh Cocaine Seven*; Jeff Pearlman, *The Bad Guys Won: A Season of Brawling, Boozing, Bimbo Chasing and Championship Baseball with Straw, Doc, Mookie, Nails, the Kid, and the Rest of the 1986 Mets, the Rowdiest Team to Ever Put on a New York Uniform—and Maybe the Best* (New York: Harper Perennial, 2011); Tim Weiner, "Indictments of Suspected Dealers May Come This Week in Pittsburgh," *Philadelphia Inquirer*, May 12, 1985, E1.

19. Bradford Lee, "Baseball's Cocaine Blues, Part Two" SBNation, May 19, 2021, https://www.royalsreview.com/2021/5/19/22417790/baseballs-cocaine-blues-part-two; Thomas Boswell, "Herzog: 11 Cardinals in Early '80s Used Cocaine Heavily," *Washington Post*, September 28, 1985.

20. Michael Goodwin, "Parker Admits to Cocaine Use," *New York Times*, September 12, 1985, D35; "Pittsburgh Cocaine Trial: Baseball's 2nd Biggest Scandal: One Year Later," *Los Angeles Times*, September 21, 1986; Murray Chass, "Focal Point on Players in Baseball Drug Trial," *The Sporting News*, September 16, 1985, 4, 59.

21. Tim Raines, *Rock Solid: My Life in Baseball's Fast Lane* (New York: Triumph Books, 2017); Mark Asher, "Cabell Implicates Richard as Cocaine-Use Partner," *Washington Post*, September 10, 1985; Robert Silverman, "The Hell-Raising, Cocaine-Snorting '86 Mets: Craziest Team in Major League Baseball History," *Daily Beast*, April 13, 2017, https://www.thedailybeast.com/the-hell-raising-cocaine-snorting-86-mets-craziest-team-in-major-league-baseball-history?ref=scroll.

22. Murray Chass, "Players on Tests: Deal with Union," *The Sporting News*, October 7, 1985, 34.

23. William Oscar Johnson, "Steroids: A Problem of Huge Dimensions," *Sports Illustrated*, May 13, 1985, 38–42, 44, 49–50, 52, 54, 56, 61.

24. Jim Murray, "At Stake Is the Integrity of Baseball," *Los Angeles Times*, August 11, 1987, D1.

25. Cover, "I Was Killing Myself: My Life as an Alcoholic by Mickey Mantle," *Sports Illustrated*, April 18, 1994.

26. Mickey Mantle, "Time in a Bottle," *Sports Illustrated*, April 18, 1994, 66–72, 74, 76–77.

27. "A Few Dozen People of Power," *New York Times*, April 1, 1994, B8.

28. Peter Pascarelli, "Labor Update," *The Sporting News*, April 25, 1994, 14.

29. "Union Takes One Step Closer to Baseball Strike," *Cincinnati Post*, April 20, 1994, D3; "Talking Strike," *Colorado Springs Gazette*, April 20, 1994, D5; "Baseball Players Might Meet Here," *Pittsburgh Post-Gazette*, April 20, 1994, D2.

Chapter 16

1. Randy Franz and Larry Rocca, "They Might Be Giants around the Majors," *Orange County Register*, May 1, 1994, C10.

2. Jake Curtis, "Year of the Homer," *Houston Chronicle*, May 1, 1994, 4; "A Tale of Two Aces," *Journal Star*, May 1994, C3.

3. Dave Kindred, "Life Is Oh So Good in Atlanta," *The Sporting News*, May 2, 1994, 7.

4. Charles Odum, "Braves Lose Jones After a Knee Injury," *Orlando Sentinel*, March 20, 1994, C14.

5. "National League Roundup," *Los Angeles Times*, May 1, 1994, 7.

6. "Red-Hot Expos Turning Up Heat," *Edmonton Journal*, May 3, 1994, F3.

7. "Pirates Sweep Braves, Trump Atlanta's Aces," *Washington Post*, May 2, 1994, C6.

8. Rod Beaton, "Expos' 12–2 Streak Fails to Draw Fans," *USA Today*, May 5, 1994, C6.

9. Jack O'Connell, "Baseball Preview Yankees Tuning Out a Thirtysomething Rerun," *Hartford Courant*, April 1, 1994, C1; Jim Henneman, "AL Preview Orioles '94," *Baltimore Sun*, April 1, 1994, E12; George Vecsey, "Here Comes Big Monday Once Again," *New York Times*, April 1, 1994, B11; Mike Bass, "O'Neill at .446 and Waiting for New York Sky to Fall," *St. Louis Post-Dispatch*, May 7, 1994, C4.

10. Bass, "O'Neill at .446 and Waiting for New York Sky to Fall"; Jon Heyman, "Ten Reasons Why the Yankees Have Won Ten in a Row," *Newsday*, May 17, 1994, A58; Buster Olney, "Paul O'Neill, Yankees," *San Diego Union-Tribune*, May 23, 1994, D7.

11. Mike Lupica, "Walk Silently; Carry a Big Bat," *Newsday*, May 26, 1994, A106.

12. Mike Lupica, "Lining Up on Broadway," *The Sporting News*, June 6, 1994, 9.

13. "Baseball '94," *Pittsburgh Post-Gazette*, April 3, 1994, D11; Wayne Lockwood, "Padres' Stock Low on Baseball Exchange, but They Aren't Like Laughingstocks of '93," *San Diego Union-Tribune*, April 4, 1994, D2; Mike Lupica, "Gwynn Soars above Rubble," *Newsday*, April 28, 1994, A87.

14. Lupica, "Gwynn Soars above Rubble."

15. Luis Torres, "Trade Retrospective Special: Red Sox Send Jeff Bagwell to the Astros for Larry Andersen," SBNation, August 1, 2017, https://www.beyondtheboxscore.com/2017/8/1/16066426/jeff-bagwell-astros-red-sox-hall-of-fame-larry-andersen-trade; Dave Fleming, "Bagwell-for

Andersen," Bill James Online, January 29, 2017, https://www.billjamesonline.com/bagwell-for-andersen/; Greg Bortolin and Kevin Iole, "For Astros' Bagwell, Season Can't Start Soon Enough," *Las Vegas Review-Journal*, April 3, 1994, E8.

16. Tim Pearrell, "Astros Get Nod in a Weak Division," *Richmond Times-Dispatch*, April 2, 1994, E10; Michael Point, "How They Handle Adversity Will Mold Rangers, Astros," *Austin American Statesman*, April 3, 1994, E14; Mike Zizzo, "Braves Taught Bagwell Lesson," *Orlando Sentinel*, April 3, 1994, C6.

17. Neil Hohlfeld, "Statistician James Sees Bagwell in Hall of Fame," *Houston Chronicle*, May 10, 1994, 6; Bill James, *The Politics of Glory* (New York: Macmillan, 1994); Michael Point, "Busy Throwing Away the Game," *Austin American Statesman*, May 22, 1994, E6.

18. Steve Milton, "Baseball '94 American League," *The Spectator*, April 2, 1994, C9; Marc Topkin, "American League Preview," *St. Petersburg Times*, April 3, 1994, C10.

19. Cover, "Cleveland Heights," *The Sporting News*, July 4, 1994; Bruce Schoenfeld, "The Bellewether," *The Sporting News*, July 4, 1994, 10–12.

20. Dave van Dyck, "Selig Says Owners, Players Must Deal with Problems," *Chicago Sun-Times*, May 1, 1994, 17; Ronald Blum, "Players, Owners Schedule Meeting," *Pittsburgh Post-Gazette*, May 13, 1994, C4; Mike Eisenbath, "Striking Out? Baseball Hits 'Serious Trouble' Series," *St. Louis Post-Dispatch*, May 15, 1994, F1.

21. Larry Whiteside, "They're Not Playing Ball," *Boston Globe*, May 16, 1994, 38.

22. Mike Eisenbath, "Money Matters Baseball Picture Is Dominated by Green," *St. Louis Post-Dispatch*, May 16, 1994, D1.

23. David Teel, "Baseball about to Ruin One of Finest Summers," *Newport News Daily Press*, May 31, 1994, D1.

Chapter 17

1. Cover, "BIG NUMBERS," "61 Home Runs," *Sports Illustrated*, June 5, 1994; Tom Verducci, "Shooting Stars," *Sports Illustrated*, June 5, 1994, 18–22.

2. Verducci, "Shooting Stars," 19, 21.

3. *Ibid.*, 21.

4. *Ibid.*, 22.

5. Mike Dodd, "Race for Records Heats Up," *USA Today*, June 3, 1994, A1.

6. Sam Carchidi, "A Young Mariner, Tired of Losing, Is Aging Fast in Seattle," *Philadelphia Inquirer*, June 5, 1994, D7.

7. Cover, "New Stars on the Rise," *Baseball Digest*, September 1988.

8. Jerry Wizig, "Maddux Quietly Gets Outs," *Houston Chronicle*, June 12, 1994, 5.

9. Gregory H. Wolf, "Ken Hill," SABR, https://sabr.org/bioproj/person/ken-hill/.

10. "Memorable Night for Expos," *Kitchener-Waterloo Record*, June 28, 1994, D1.

11. Tara Krieger, "David Cone," SABR, https://sabr.org/bioproj/person/david-cone/.

12. https://sabr.org/bioproj/person/david-cone/.

13. Cover, "Nothing but Heat," *Sports Illustrated*, April 5, 1993.

14. Jim Souhan, "Cone's New Approach Beats Twins," *Minneapolis Star Tribune*, May 12, 1994, C1.

15. Mark Newman, "The New David Cone," *The Sporting News*, June 20, 1994, 20.

16. "Home Sweet Home in American League," *The Spectator*, April 5, 1994, B2; Mel Antonen, "Top Lefties Alvarez, Key Match Pitches Wednesday," *USA Today*, May 31, 1994, C8; Nick Cafarado, "Key Handcuffs Red Sox," *Boston Globe*, June 28, 1994, 61.

17. Murray Chass, "Baseball; Owners Pass Cap Plan to Present to the Players," *New York Times*, June 9, 1994, B15.

18. Bud Selig, *For the Good of the Game: The Inside Story of the Surprising and Dramatic Transformation of Major League Baseball* (New York: William Morrow, 2019), 157–158.

19. Larry Whiteside, "Owners OK Plan, but Fehr Blasts It," *Boston Globe*, June 9, 1994, 73; Jerome Holtzman, "Union Cries Foul after Owners Pass Strike Amendment," *Chicago Tribune*, June 9, 1994, 3; Richard Justice, "Baseball Faces Strike, Again," *Washington Post*, June 12, 1994, A1.

20. Dave Kindred, "Living in the Strike Zone," *The Sporting News*, June 13, 1994, 6.

21. *Ibid.*

22. Steve Marantz, "The Maine Man," *The Sporting News*, June 13, 1994, 12–15.

23. "Bill Might Help Avert Ball Strike," *Colorado Springs Gazette*, June 23, 1994, F5.

24. Robert Naylor, "Senate Committee Rejects Exemption Removal," *Austin American Statesman*, June 24, 1994, C5.

25. Steve Zipay, "Metzenbaum Bill Defeated," *Newsday*, June 24, 1994, A94; John Helyar, "Baseball-Players Union Strikes Out with Senate Panel," *Wall Street Journal*, June 24, 1994, B8.

Chapter 18

1. Greg Bortolin, "The Humble Home Run Hitter," *Las Vegas Review-Journal*, January 28, 1994, E1.

2. Rick Hummel, "Clark for Whiten," *St. Louis Post-Dispatch*, June 12, 1994, F9.

3. Jim Murray, "All or Nothing for This Williams," *Los Angeles Times*, July 3, 1994, C1.

4. *Ibid.*

5. *Ibid.*

6. "Williams Pulls Even with Griffey as Giants Beat Phillies," *The Oregonian*, July 9, 1994, B1; "Baseball Insider," *Minneapolis Star Tribune*, July 10, 1994, C14; John McGrath, "Maris' Record—and

Controversy—Lasts On and On," *Jefferson City News Tribune*, July 14, 1994, C1.

7. "Thomas Make It Three-Way Race by Belting 35th Home of Season," *The Oregonian*, July 22, 1994, B1; "Strike Would Wipe Out Season's Special Achievements," *St. Louis Post-Dispatch*, July 29, 1994, B4.

8. Ron Fimrite, "The Strong, Silent Type," *Sports Illustrated*, July 25, 1994, 30–32, 37.

9. Mike Klis, "Williams, Bagwell Have the Most to Lose from a Season-Ending Strike," *Colorado Springs Gazette-Telegraph*, July 31, 1994, C3; Randy Franz and Lawrence Rocca, "Then There Were Two around the Majors," *Orange County Register*, July 31, 1994, C10.

10. Chuck Johnson, "Young Sluggers Step to the Fore," *USA Today*, May 2, 1994, C3.

11. Murray Chass, "Baseball: Notebook; Behind Heavy Hitters, Offense Is Soaring Up, Up and Away," *New York Times*, July 10, 1994, A5; Rod Beaton, "Best Bets for Triple Crown Have Others Hot at Heels," *USA Today*, July 14, 1994, C3.

12. "Griffey, Thomas Put on Homer Show," *The Globe and Mail*, July 12, 1994, C5.

13. John B. Holway, "Homing in on the Comiskey Factor," *Chicago Tribune*, July 27, 1994, 21; Ed Spaulding, "Team-by-Team Notes," *Houston Chronicle*, July 27, 1994, 6; Bob Hertzel, "Being Best Isn't Enough Griffey Short on MVP Credentials," *The Record*, July 31, 1994, S8.

14. Peter Gammons, "Divide and Conquer? Harrington Hopes So," *Boston Globe*, July 3, 1994, 46.

15. "Record-Chasing Griffey Is Top Dog in All-Star Voting," *The Spectator*, July 4, 1994, C3; "Griffey's Star Shines Bright," *St. Petersburg Times*, July 4, 1994, C1.

16. Ritter Collett, "Popular Griffey Playing with Mays-Like Fervor," *Dayton Daily News*, July 8, 1994, D3; Ross Newhan, "Baseball All-Star Report: Bonds Is Struggling a Bit This Season," *Los Angeles Times*, July 13, 1994, 10.

17. Pete Godwin, "Names: Showalter Rips Griffey, Bonds," *Boston Globe*, July 10, 1994, 49.

18. Nick Cafarado, "Griffey Upset by Showalter Comments," *Boston Globe*, July 11, 1994, 39.

19. Newhan, "Baseball All-Star Report: Bonds Is Struggling a Bit This Season," 10.

20. Don Bostrom, "Straw Is Really Stirring Things Up in San Francisco," *Morning Call*, July 19, 1994, C5.

21. Hal Bodley, "Great Season for Bad Pitches, Errors, Too," *USA Today*, July 20, 1994, C3.

22. Murray Chass, "Baseball: Notebook," *New York Times*, July 24, 1994, A5.

23. Jerry Crasnick, "Bonds Back in MVP Form for Surging Giants," *Denver Post*, July 25, 1994.

24. "The Buzz's Inside Look at the Major Leagues," *Chicago Tribune*, July 26, 1994, 9; Wendy E. Lane, "Williams Pops No. 38 as Giants Jolt L.A.," *Austin American Statesman*, July 27, 1994, C5.

25. "What We Might Be Missing," *The Sporting News*, August 8, 1994, 18.

26. Alan Truex, "Personality Clashes Cloud Labor Talks," *Houston Chronicle*, July 3, 1994, 7.

27. Dennis Brackin, "Worlds Apart: Players-Owners Acrimony over Cap Makes Strike Likely," *Minneapolis Star Tribune*, July 10, 1994, C10.

28. Ben Walker, "Game's Over, Season Now in Jeopardy," *Las Vegas Review-Journal*," July 14, 1994, E1.

29. Larry Whiteside, "Two Sides Laboring Through," *Boston Globe*, July 20, 1994, 74.

30. Jerome Holtzman, "Players Hope Strike Date Speeds Talks," *Chicago Tribune*, July 29, 1994, 1.

31. Jerome Holtzman, "Fame Day a Real Rush for 'Lefty' Carlton, Rizzuto, Durocher Enter Baseball's Hall," *Chicago Tribune*, August 1, 1994, 1.

Chapter 19

1. Rick Hummel, "Torre: Speed, Defense Make Expos Dangerous," *St. Louis Post-Dispatch*, August 2, 1994, C5; "Williams Hammers 41st Homer; Bagwell Passes Thomas, Griffey," *The Oregonian*, August 2, 1994, D1.

2. Ross Newhan, "Owners' List of Clubs Losing Money Decried Baseball," *Los Angeles Times*, August 3, 1994, 1.

3. "National League Roundup: Bonds' Three Home Runs Not Enough for Giants," *Los Angeles Times*, August 3, 1993, 5.

4. Ronald Blum, "Players May Strike Earlier," *Las Vegas Review-Journal*, August 4, 1994, D1.

5. *Ibid.*

6. Michael Bamberger, "Is Salary Cap Talk Just an Owners' Ploy?" *Salt Lake Tribune*, August 7, 1994, C2.

7. *Ibid.*

8. Cover, "Top Guns," *Sports Illustrated*, August 8, 1994; Rick Reilly, "The Big Heart," *Sports Illustrated*, August 8, 1994, 17–22.

9. Reilly, "The Big Heart," 18–19.

10. Alan Shipnuck, "Junior Comes of Age," *Sports Illustrated*, August 8, 1994, 24–30.

11. "A Walk Through the Parks," *The Globe and Mail*, August 9, 1994, C7.

12. Bill Jauss, "Williams Downplays 'The Chase,'" *Chicago Tribune*, August 11, 1994, 5.

13. C. R. Roberts, "Death of Baseball Would Permit Its Resurrection as a Game," *Jefferson City News Tribune*, August 9, 1994, B1.

14. "They're Outta Here," *Austin American Statesman*, August 12, 1994, D1.

15. "A Fitting End: Griffey's Slam Ushers in Strike," *Chicago Tribune*, August 12, 1994, 10.

16. "Major League Batting Year-by-Year Averages," *baseball-reference.com*, https://www.baseball-reference.com/leagues/majors/bat.shtml.

17. Murray Chass, "Baseball; No Runs, No Hits, No Errors: Baseball Goes on Strike," *New York Times*, August 12, 1994, A1.

18. Claire Smith, "Some Wonder if This Is When Cheering Stops," *New York Times*, August 12, 1994, B9.

19. Cover, "The Games Goes On," *The Sporting News*, August 15, 1994, 1; Mike Lupica, "New Owners, Same Old Story," *The Sporting News*, August 15, 1994, 7.

20. Cover, "They're OUT," *The Sporting News*, August 22, 1994, 1; Mike Lupica, "Throwing the Last Pitch," *The Sporting News*, August 22, 1994, 7.

21. Mark Maske and Tracee Hamilton, "Players' Study Finds Owners Underestimated Profits," *Washington Post*, August 24, 1994, C1.

22. *Ibid.*

23. Goehler, "Reliving the 1994 MLB Strike 28 Years Later."

24. Peter Schmuck, "Called Out on Strikes," *Austin American Statesman*, September 15, 1995, C1.

25. *Ibid.*; Mitch Albom, "Greed Has Turned a Beloved Friend into a Stranger," *Austin American Statesman*, September 15, 1994, C1.

26. George Vecsey, "Baseball: Sports of the Time; Owners Strike Out in Betrayal of History," *New York Times*, September 12, 1994, C2.

27. Claire Smith, "'94 Season: May It Rest in Disarray," *New York Times*, September 14, 1994, B11; Claire Smith, "Take 700 Players and 28 Owners and It Winds Up to 0 Solution," *New York Times*, September 15, 1994, B13.

28. Allan Ryan, "Baseball Parting Words: What Some Experts Say," *Toronto Star*, September 16, 1994, F3.

29. Wayne Lockwood, "Hall of Shame Awaits If Selig Calls," *San Diego Union-Tribune*, September 13, 1994, D1.

30. Steve Milton, "Mission Accomplished," *The Spectator*, September 15, 1994, D1.

31. Bruce Jenkins, "Dark Day—Our Pastime in Ruins," *San Francisco Chronicle*, September 15, 1994, A1.

32. Albom, "Greed Has Turned a Beloved Friend into a Stranger."

33. *Ibid.*

34. Gary Nuhn, "Baseball Outlasts Fools Who Run It," *Dayton Daily News*, September 15, 1994, D2.

35. Dave Kindred, "It Will Never Be the Same," *The Sporting News*, September 19, 1994, 7.

36. *Ibid.*

37. Cover, "THE PEOPLE OF AMERICA," *The Sporting News*, September 26, 1994, 1.

38. J. Anthony Lukas, "The Year the World Series Was Canceled," *New York Times*, October 23, 1994, E15.

Chapter 20

1. Steve Marantz, "Will They Break?" *The Sporting News*, September 26, 1994, 14–16.

2. "Fehr: Next Victim May Be Camps," *Chicago Tribune*, September 22, 1994, 10.

3. "Will Congress Play Ball?" *Kingston Whig-Standard*, September 23, 1994, 19.

4. Ross Newhan, "Mediator Usery to Enter Baseball Negotiations," *Los Angeles Times*, October 14, 1994, C1, C5; Ross Newhan, "Baseball Talks Center on Truth in Advertising," *Los Angeles Times*, November 9, 1994, 5; Murray Chass, "As Talks Near, An Ad Stirs Unrest," *New York Times*, November 9, 1994, B23.

5. Ross Newhan, "Owners Delay Implementation," *Los Angeles Times*, December 1, 1994, C5; Mark Maske, "To Little Fanfare, Ravitch Resigns Baseball Post," *Washington Post*, December 6, 1994, B1; "Ravitch Gives up on Talks," *Windsor Star*, December 6, 1994, B4; "Mediator: Don't Impose Cap Now," *Newsday*, December 7, 1994, A65; "Owners, Playing Hardball, Impose Cap," *Austin American Statesman*, December 23, 1994, C1.

6. "Briefly: Baseball Teams Gear Up to Hire Replacement Players," *Vancouver Sun*, January 4, 1995, C8; Mark Maske, "Owners Begin Setting Replacement Procedures," *Washington Post*, January 5, 1995, D1.

7. Mike Lupica, "The Air Up There," *The Sporting News*, January 9, 1995, 7.

8. Douglas Jehl, "Strike Brings Clinton Up to Plate," *New York Times*, January 27, 1995, N1.

9. Ross Newhan, "Pressured Owners Drop Salary Cap," *Los Angeles Times*, February 4, 1995, C1; Mark Maske, "Owners Withdraw Salary Cap," *Washington Post*, February 4, 1995, H1; Murray Chass, "Salary Vanishes; Problems Don't," *New York Times*, February 5, 1995, S1.

10. Ronald Blum, "Angry President Plays Hardball," *Las Vegas Review-Journal*, February 6, 1995, E1.

11. Mark Maske, "Clinton Tosses Baseball to Congress," *The Gazette*, February 8, 1995, A1; Ronald Blum, "Baseball No Hit in Congress," *Las Vegas Review-Journal*, February 9, 1995, D1.

12. "Repeal of Antitrust Exemption Could End Strike, Fehr Says," *The Record*, February 11, 1995, E3; "Senators Scold Selig, Fehr," *Springfield* (IL) *State Journal Register*, February 16, 1995, 27.

13. Chris Sheridan, "Replacements Take Field," *Las Vegas Review-Journal*, February 17, 1995, A1; Chris Sheridan, "Who's on First? Who Knows? Who Cares?" *The Oregonian*, February 17, 1995, A1; "Major-Leaguers Ask Boycott of Spring Exhibition Games," *Houston Chronicle*, February 23, 1995, 9.

14. Steve Marantz, "Voice of Reason," *The Sporting News*, February 13, 1995, 18–20.

15. *Ibid.*

16. Ross Newhan, "Strike Talks Take a Turn for the Better," *Los Angeles Times*, March 4, 1995, C1; Ross Newhan, "Players Draw the Line Against Replacement Games, Records," *Los Angeles Times*, March 16, 1995, C3; Mark Maske, "Players May End Ball Strike to Force Owners' Hand," *Edmonton Journal*, March 22, 1995, D1.

17. "Ray of Hope?" *Newsday*, March 27, 1995, A46.

18. Ronald Blum, "Owners Make New Offer," *Dayton Daily News*, March 28, 1995, D1; Ronald

Blum, "Players Vote: End Baseball Strike, If...," *San Francisco Chronicle*, March 29, 1995, A1.

19. "Baseball Owners Get Next Move," *Orlando Sentinel*, April 1, 1995, A1.

20. Mark Maske, "Angelos Says He Would Vote Against Lockout 'With Relish,'" *Washington Post*, H3.

21. "Baseball Comes Back, Better Late than Never," *Austin American Statesman*, April 3, 1995, C1.

22. Bill Dwyre, "Boys of Summer Take Over from Buffoons of Winter," *Los Angeles Times*, April 3, 1995, C1.

23. Blum, "Both Sides Lost Big in Dispute," C1.

24. Mike Lupica, "A Hate-Filled Business Is Still a Great, Great Game," *The Sporting News*, April 17, 1995, 8.

25. *Ibid.*

26. Bob Nightengale, "The Rich Get Richer, the Fans Get Dizzier," *The Sporting News*, April 17, 1995, 14.

27. Murray Chass, "Reluctant Baseball Owners Approve Pact with Players," *New York Times*, November 27, 1996, 1.

28. *Ibid.*, B13.

29. Philip Hersh, "Baseball Toasts an Armistice Day of Its Own but Can Labor Deal Heal Wounds?" *Chicago Tribune*, November 27, 1996, 1; Bob Nightengale, "Peace at Last," *Los Angeles Times*, November 27, 1996, 1; Bob Nightengale, "Reinsdorf Has Reason to Smile—On Both His Faces," *The Sporting News*, December 2, 1996, 24; Gerry Callahan, "Double Play," December 2, 1996, *Sports Illustrated*, 32.

30. Bob Padecky, "Next Step for Baseball: Stop Acting Like Children," *Santa Rosa Press Democrat*, December 1, 1996, C1.

31. Dave Kindred, "The Jerry-mandering Is Over," *The Sporting News*, December 9, 1996, 8.

32. Mark Maske, "On the Heels of Labor Harmony, Some Commissioner's Shoes to Fill," *Washington Post*, January 11, 1997, F1.

33. "Labor," *Washington Post*, March 14, 1997, C3.

34. Jon Heyman, "Bud's A Good Move, But," *Newsday*, July 10, 1998, A81; Larry Whiteside, "Selig Makes It Official—He's the Commissioner," *Boston Globe*, July 10, 1998, C5.

35. I.J. Rosenberg, "Selig Becomes Commish Today," *Atlanta Constitution*, July 9, 1998, C5.

36. "Antitrust Exemption Is Partly Revoked," *New York Times*, October 28, 1998, 7.

37. "Clinton Statement on Curt Flood Act of 1998." *U.S. Newswire*, October 27, 1998, 1.

Chapter 21

1. David Halberstam, *Summer of '49* (New York: William Morrow, 1989), 52.

2. "Caption Only," *Los Angeles Times*, April 1, 1997, 1; "Laugh Line," *Los Angeles Times*, April 1, 1997, 3.

3. "Passe Pastime?" *The Christian Science Monitor*, April 3, 1997, 20.

4. Emma Baccellieri, "Marvin Miller: The Late, Reluctant Hall of Fame Inductee," *Sports Illustrated*, September 8, 2021, https://www.si.com/mlb/2021/09/08/marvin-miller-hall-of-fame-induction-reluctant.

5. Peter Dreier, "As Lockout Begins, Baseball's Hall of Fame Blacklists Curt Flood—Again," *TPM*, December 4, 2021, https://talkingpointsmemo.com/cafe/as-lockout-begins-baseballs-hall-of-fame-blacklists-curt-flood-again.

6. Bob Nightengale, "Hall Push Renews for Trailblazer Flood," *USA Today*, June 20, 2022, C1.

7. *Ibid.*

Bibliography

Books

Abrams, Roger. *The First World Series and the Baseball Fanatics of 1903*. Boston: Northeastern University Press, 2003.

_____. *Legal Bases: Baseball and the Law*. Philadelphia: Temple University Press, 1998.

Alexander, Charles C. *John McGraw*. Lincoln: University of Nebraska Press, 1995.

_____. *Our Game: An American Baseball History*. New York: Henry Holt, 1991.

_____. *Turbulent Seasons: Baseball in 1890–1891*. Dallas: Southern Methodist University Press, 2011.

Banner, Stuart. *The Baseball Trust: A History of Baseball's Antitrust Exemption*. New York: Oxford University Press, 2013.

Bess, Philip. *City Baseball Magic: Plain Talk and Uncommon Sense About Cities and Ballparks*. Saint Paul: Knothole Press, 1999.

Beverage, Richard. *The Los Angeles Angels of the Pacific Coast League: A History, 1903–1947*. Jefferson, NC: McFarland, 2011.

Bouton, Jim. *Ball Four: My Life and Hard Times Throwing the Knuckleball in the Big Leagues*. New York: World, 1970.

Branson, Douglas M. *Major League Turbulence: Baseball in the Era of Drug Use, Labor Strife and Black Power, 1968–1988*. Jefferson, NC: McFarland, 2021.

Brosnan, Jim. *The Long Season: An Inside Chronicle of the Baseball Year as Seen by Major League Pitcher*. New York: Harper & Brothers, 1960.

Buhite, Russell D. *The Continental League: A Personal History*. Lincoln: University of Nebraska Press, 2014.

Burk, Robert F. *Marvin Miller, Baseball Revolutionary*. Urbana: University of Illinois Press, 2015.

_____. *Much More Than a Game: Players, Owners, and American Baseball Since 1921*. Chapel Hill: University of North Carolina Press, 2001.

_____. *Never Just a Game: Players, Owners, and American Baseball to 1920*. Chapel Hill: University of North Carolina Press, 1994.

The Business of Professional Sports. Eds. Paul D. Staudohar and J. A. Mangan. Urbana: University of Illinois Press, 1991.

Castle, George. *Baseball's Game Changers: Icons, Record Breakers, Scandals, Sensational Series, and More*. Guilford, CT: Lyons, 2016.

Chafets, Zev. *Cooperstown Confidential: Heroes, and the Inside Story of the Baseball Hall of Fame*. New York: Bloomsbury, 2009.

Cottrell, Robert C. *The Best Pitcher in Baseball: The Life of Rube Foster, Negro League Giant*. New York: New York University Press, 2001.

_____. *Blackball, the Black Sox and the Babe: Baseball's Crucial 1920 Season*. Jefferson, NC: McFarland, 2002.

_____. *Two Pioneers: How Hank Greenberg and Jackie Robinson Transformed Baseball—And America*. Washington, D.C.: Potomac, 2012.

Creamer, Robert W. *Babe: The Legend Comes to Life*. New York: Fireside, 1992.

Dabilis, Andy, and Nick Tsiotos. *The 1903 World Series: The Boston Americans, the Pittsburgh Pirates, and the "First Championship of the United States."* Jefferson, NC: McFarland, 2004.

Di Salvatore, Bryan. *A Clever Base-Ballist: The Life and Times of John Montgomery Ward*. Baltimore: Johns Hopkins University Press, 1999.

Dreier, Peter, and Robert Elias. *Baseball Rebels: The Players, People, and Social Movements That Shook Up the Game and Changed America*. Lincoln: University of Nebraska Press, 2022.

Elias, Robert, and Peter Dreier. *Major League Rebels: Baseball Battles Over Workers' Rights and American Empire*. Lanham, MD: Rowman & Littlefield, 2022.

Enders, Eric. *Ballparks Then and Now*. San Diego: Thunder Bay, 2002.

Flood, Curt. *The Way It Is*. New York: Trident, 1971.

Gelzheiser, Robert P. *Labor and Capital in 19th Century Baseball*. Jefferson, NC: McFarland, 2006.

Giamatti, A. Bartlett. *Take Time for Paradise: Americans and Their Games*. London: Bloomsbury, 2011.

Goldman, Robert M. *One Man Out: Curt Flood Versus Baseball*. Lawrence: University Press of Kansas, 2008.

Grow, Nathaniel. *Baseball on Trial: The Origin of Baseball's Antitrust Exemption*. Urbana: University of Illinois Press, 2014.

Halberstam, David. *Summer of '49.* New York: William Morrow, 1989.

Hawking, James. *Strikeout: Baseball, Broadway and the Brotherhood in the 19th Century.* Santa Fe: Sunstone, 1999.

Helyar, John. *Lords of the Realm: The Real History of Baseball.* New York: Ballantine, 1994.

James, Bill. *The Politics of Glory.* New York: Macmillan, 1994.

Joseph, Dan. *Baseball's Greatest What If: The Story & Tragedy of the Brooklyn Dodgers' Pete Reiser.* Mechanicsburg, PA: Sunbury, 2021.

Katz, Jeff. *Split Season: Fernandomania, the Bronx Zoo, and the Strike That Saved Baseball.* New York: Thomas Dunne, 2015.

Kerry, Keene, Raymond Sinibaldi, and David Hickey. *The Babe in Red Stockings: An In-Depth Chronicle of Babe Ruth with the Boston Red Sox, 1914–1919.* Champaign, IL: Sagamore, 1997.

Klima, John. *Bushville Wins! The Wild Saga of the 1957 Milwaukee Braves and the Screwballs, Sluggers, and Beer Swiggers Who Canned the New York Yankees and Changed Baseball.* New York: St. Martin's Griffin, 2015.

Korr, Charles P. *The End of Baseball as We Knew It: The Players Union, 1960–81.* Urbana: University of Illinois Press, 2002.

Koszarek, Ed. *The Players League: History Clubs, Ballplayers and Statistics.* Jefferson, NC: McFarland, 2006.

League Pitcher. New York: Harper & Row, 1960.

Leahy, Michael. *The Last Innocents: The Collision of the Turbulent Sixties and the Los Angeles Dodgers.* New York: Harper, 2016.

Leventhal, Josh. *Take Me Out to the Ballpark: An Illustrated Tour of Baseball Parks Past and Present.* New York: Black Dog & Leventhal, 2000.

Levin, Morris, ed. *National Pastime: From Swampoodle to South Philly—Baseball in Philadelphia and the Delaware Valley.* Phoenix: SABR, 2013.

Levitt, Daniel R. *The Outlaw League and the Battle That Forged Modern Baseball.* Lanham, MD: Ivan R. Dee, 2012.

Lowenfish, Lee. *The Imperfect Diamond: A History of Baseball's Labor Wars.* New York: Da Capo, 1991.

Lowry, Philip J. *Green Cathedrals: The Ultimate Celebration of Major League and Negro League Ballparks.* New York: Walker, 2006.

Marshall, William. *Baseball's Pivotal Era, 1945–1951.* Lexington: University Press of Kentucky, 1999.

Masur, Louis P. *Autumn Glory: Baseball's First World Series.* New York: Hill and Wang, 1903.

Mathews, Eddie. *Eddie Mathews and the National Pastime.* Milwaukee: Douglas American Sports, 1994.

McKelvey, Richard. *Mexican Raiders in the Major Leagues: The Pasquel Brothers vs. Organized Baseball, 1946.* Jefferson, NC: McFarland, 2006.

Miller, Marvin. *A Whole Different Ball Game: The Inside Story of the Baseball Revolution.* Chicago: Ivan R. Dee, 2004.

Okkonen, Marc. *The Federal League of 1914–1915.* Garrett Park, MD: SABR, 1989.

Pearlman, Jeff. *The Bad Guys Won: A Season of Brawling, Boozing, Bimbo Chasing and Championship Baseball with Straw, Doc, Mookie, Nails, the Kid, and the Rest of the 1986 Mets, the Rowdiest Team to Ever Put on a New York Uniform—and Maybe the Best.* New York: Harper Perennial, 2011.

_____. *Love Me, Hate Me: Barry Bonds and the Making of an Antihero.* New York: HarperCollins, 2006.

Pessah, Jon. *The Game: Inside the Secret World of Major League Power Brokers.* Boston: Little, Brown, 2015.

Petersen, Scott D. *Reporting Baseball's Sensational Season of 1890: The Brotherhood War and the Rise of Modern Sports Journalism.* Jefferson, NC: McFarland, 2015.

Pietrusza, David. *Major Leagues: The Formation, Sometimes Absorption and Mostly Inevitable Demise of 18 Professional Baseball Organizations, 1871 to Present.* Jefferson, NC: McFarland, 1991.

Rader, Benjamin G. *Baseball: A History of America's Game.* Urbana: University of Illinois Press, 2008.

Raines, Tim. *Rock Solid: My Life in Baseball's Fast Lane.* New York: Triumph, 2017.

Reston, James. *Collision at Home Plate: The Lives of Pete Rose and Bart Giamatti.* New York: HarperCollins, 1991.

Roberts, Randy, and Johnny Smith. *A Season in the Sun: The Rise of Mickey Mantle.* New York: Basic, 2018.

_____. *War Fever: Boston, Baseball, and America in the Shadow of the Great War.* New York: Basic, 2020.

Rossi, John P. *The National Game: Baseball and American Culture.* Chicago: Ivan R. Dee, 2000.

Ryan, Bob. *When Boston Won the World Series: A Chronicle of Boston's Remarkable Victory in the First Modern World Series of 1903.* Philadelphia: Running Press, 2003.

Schiavone, Michael. *Sports and Labor in the United States.* Albany: State University of New York, 2015.

Schmidt, Mike. *Clearing the Bases: Juiced Players, Monster Salaries, Sham Records, and a Hall of Famer's Search for the Soul of Baseball.* New York: Harper, 2006.

Selig, Bud. *For the Good of the Game: The Inside Story of the Surprising and Dramatic Transformation of Major League Baseball.* New York: William Morrow, 2019.

Shapiro, Michael. *Bottom of the Ninth: Branch Rickey, Casey Stengel and Daring Scheme to Save Baseball from Itself.* New York: Times, 2009.

Sickels, John. *Bob Feller: Ace of the Greatest Generation.* Washington, D.C.: Brassey's, 2004.

Skirboll, Aaron. *The Pittsburgh Cocaine Seven: How a Ragtag Group of Fans Took the Fall for Major League Baseball.* Chicago: Chicago Review Press, 2010.

Snyder, Brad. *A Well-Paid Slave: Curt Flood's Fight for Free Agency in Professional Sports.* New York: Plume, 2007.

Spatz, Lyle, and Steve Steinberg. *1921: The Yankees, the Giants, and the Battle for Baseball Supremacy in New York.* Lincoln: University of Nebraska Press, 2010.

Stevens, David. *Baseball's Radical for All Seasons: A Biography of John Montgomery Ward.* Lanham, MD: Scarecrow, 1998.

Sullivan, Dean A. *Late Innings: A Documentary History of Baseball, 1945–1972.* Lincoln: University of Nebraska Press, 2002.

_____. *Middle Innings: A Documentary History of Baseball, 1900–1948.* Lincoln: University of Nebraska Press, 1998.

Swanson, Krister. *Baseball's Power Shift: How the Players Union, the Fans, and the Media Changed American Sports Culture.* Lincoln: University of Nebraska Press.

Vincent, Fay. *The Last Commissioner: A Baseball Valentine.* New York: Simon & Schuster, 2002.

Virtue, John. *South of the Color Barrier: How Jorge Pasquel and the Mexican League Pushed Baseball Toward Racial Integration.* Jefferson, NC: McFarland, 2007.

Weingarten, Steve, and Bill Nowlin, eds. *Baseball's Business: The Winter Meetings: 1958–2016.* Volume 2. Phoenix: SABR, 2017.

Wiggins, Robert Peyton. *The Federal League of Base Ball Clubs.* Jefferson, NC: McFarland, 2009.

Newspapers, Magazines, Web Sites

Atlanta Constitution
The Atlantic
Austin American-Statesman
Baltimore Sun
Banished to the Pen (baseball blog tied to *Effectively Wild* podcast)
Baseball Almanac
Baseball America
Baseball Digest
Baseball History Daily (web site)
Baseball Magazine
Baseball Prospectus
Baseball-Reference.com
Baseball Research Journal
Baseball Weekly
Bellingham (WA) Herald
Bill James Online
Boston Globe
Calgary Herald
Call to the Pen (fansided.com)
Chicago Sun-Times
Chicago Tribune
Christian Science Monitor
Cincinnati Post
Colorado Springs Gazette-Telegraph
Cosmopolitan
Daily Beast
Daily Press (Newport News, VA)
Dayton Daily News
Deadspin
Denver Post
Desert Sun (Palm Springs, CA)
Edmonton Journal
Evening Sun (Hanover, PA)
FanNation
Financial Post
Gazette (Colorado Springs, CO)
Globe and Mail (Toronto, Ontario)
Hardball Times
Hartford Courant
Harvard Crimson
Houston Chronicle
Journal Star (Lincoln, NE)
Kingston Whig-Standard (Kingston, Ontario)
Kitchener-Waterloo Record (Waterloo Region, Ontario)
Las Vegas Review-Journal
Lippincott's Monthly Magazine
Los Angeles Times
Marquette Sports Law Review
MLB/NBC Sports
MLB.com
Morning Call (Lehigh Valley and Allentown, PA)
National Baseball Hall of Fame
New York Evening Journal
New York Review of Books
New York Times
New York Times Book Review
New York Tribune
New Yorker
News Tribune (Jefferson City, MO)
Newsday
Nine
Orange County Register (Orange County, CA)
The Oregonian (Portland, OR)
Orlando Sentinel
Payday Report (Pittsburgh, PA)
Philadelphia Inquirer
Phoenix Gazette
Pittsburgh Post-Gazette
Plain Dealer (Cleveland, OH)
Press Democrat (Santa Rosa, CA)
The Record (Bergen County, NJ)
Richmond Times-Dispatch
SABR Research Journals Archives
St. Louis Post-Dispatch
St. Petersburg (FL) Times
Salt Lake Tribune
San Bernardino Sun
San Diego Union-Tribune
San Francisco Chronicle
Santa Cruz Sentinel
SBNation
Seattle Times
Society for American Baseball Research (SABR)
The Spectator
Sport
Sporting Life
The Sporting News
Sports Illustrated
Star Tribune (Minneapolis, MN)

State Journal Register (Springfield, IL)
Sun Sentinel (Fort Lauderdale, FL)
Toronto Star
TPM
U.S. Newswire
USA Today

Vancouver Sun
Vanderbilt Law Review
Wall Street Journal
Washington Post
Windsor Star (Windsor, Ontario)

Index

Numbers in **bold italics** indicate pages with illustrations

251

254

Index